IRISH ANGLICANISM, 1969–2019

Irish Anglicanism, 1969–2019

*Essays to Mark the
150th Anniversary of the
Disestablishment of the Church of Ireland*

KENNETH MILNE & PAUL HARRON

editors

FOUR COURTS PRESS

Set in 10.5 pt on 12.5 pt Ehrhardt MT for
FOUR COURTS PRESS LTD
7 Malpas Street, Dublin 8, Ireland
www.fourcourtspress.ie
and in North America for
FOUR COURTS PRESS
c/o IPG, 814 N Franklin St, Chicago, IL 60622

A catalogue record for this title is available
from the British Library.

ISBN 978-1-84682-819-5

Printed in England by
CPI Antony Rowe, Chippenham, Wilts.

Contents

Abbreviations

ACC	Anglican Consultative Council
ACRE	Advisory Committee on Religious Education
AMICUM	Anglican–Methodist International Commission for Unity in Mission
APB	*Alternative Prayer Book* (1984)
APCK	Association for Promoting Christian Knowledge
ARCIC	Anglican–Roman Catholic International Commission
BCC	British Council of Churches
BCP	*Book of Common Prayer*
CAB	Chaplaincy Accreditation Board
CACTM	Central Advisory Council on Training for the Ministry
CCBI	Council of Churches for Britain and Ireland (now Churches Together in Britain and Ireland – CTBI)
CCEE	Consilium Conferentiarum Episcoporum Europae
CCI	Conference of Churches in Ireland
CCMS	Council for Catholic Maintained Schools
CCR	Church of Ireland dioceses of Cork, Cloyne and Ross
CEC	Conference of European Churches
CIC	Church of Ireland Centre (DCU Institute of Education)
CICE	Church of Ireland College of Education
CICU	Church of Ireland Choral Union
CIP	Church of Ireland Publishing
CITC	Church of Ireland Theological College
CMS	Church Mission Society
COMECE	Commission of the Bishops' Conferences of the European Community
CPE	clinical pastoral education
CSCWC	Conference of Secretaries of Christian World Communion
CSSC	Controlled Schools Support Council
D&D	Church of Ireland dioceses of Down and Dromore

D&R	Church of Ireland dioceses of Derry and Raphoe
DCIF	Dublin City Interfaith Forum
DCU	Dublin City University
ECTS	European Credit Transfer System
ECUSA	Episcopal Church of the USA
EKD	Evangelische Kirche Deutschland
ELLC	English Language Liturgical Consultation
FSMs	free school meals
GAFCON	Global Anglican Future Conference
GDPR	General Data Protection Regulation
GS	General Synod
HE	higher education
HOB	House of Bishops
IALC	International Anglican Liturgical Consultations
ICC	Irish Council of Churches
IICM	Irish Inter-Church Meeting
IMC	Irish Manuscripts Commission
ISE	Irish School of Ecumenics
JCCMI	Joint Committee for Church Music
JGS	*Journal of the General Synod*
KPS	Kildare Place Society
LEC	local education council
LWF	Lutheran World Federation
NCCA	National Council of Curriculum and Assessment
NIFCON	Network for Inter Faith Concerns
NIFENAC	Network for Inter Faith European North American Concerns
NSM	non-stipendiary ministry
OLM	ordaincd local ministry
PROCMURA	Programme for Christian–Muslim Relations in Africa
PROI	Public Record Office of Ireland
QUB	Queen's University Belfast
RB	Representative Body (of the Church of Ireland)

RCB	Representative Church Body
RE	religious education
ROCC	Role of the Church Committee
RSCM	Royal School of Church Music
RSUA	Royal Society of Ulster Architects
RSV	Revised Standard Version
SEC	Secondary Education Committee
SPG	Society for the Propagation of the Gospel
TCD	Trinity College Dublin
TRC	Transferor Represenatatives' Council
VEC	Vocational Education Committee
WCC	World Council of Churches

Illustrations

Acknowledgments

The editors thank the archbishop of Armagh, the Most Revd Dr Richard Clarke, and all the authors for their ready acceptance of our invitation to contribute and for the time and thought that they have given to the writing of their individual essays.

Mr Peter Cheney of the Church of Ireland Press Office helped considerably with various aspects of the project, for which we are most grateful, while Dr Catherine Smith of the General Synod Office, Mr Trevor Stacey of the Representative Church Body's Property Department and Ms Sarah Dunne of its Investments Department all deserve thanks for their generous assistance with the essay on General Synod and RCB developments. As ever, the RCB librarian and archivist, Dr Susan Hood, and her colleagues in the library were unfailingly supportive of our endeavours.

Our best thanks are due to the Standing Committee of the General Synod, the Central Communications Board and its Literature Committee for their support, and in particular to the honorary secretary of the Literature Committee, Dr Raymond Refaussé, for his support at all stages of the work.

Four Courts Press has, as always, been extremely helpful in bringing about the publication of this book, the latest of many volumes pertaining to the Church of Ireland that the press has so professionally published over the years. In particular, we wish to acknowledge with many thanks the invaluable contribution that Mr Sam Tranum has made to bringing this present project to fruition.

We would also like to express to the dean, chapter, board and staff of Christ Church Cathedral, Dublin and St Anne's Cathedral, Belfast our appreciation of their generosity and helpfulness in making available to us their splendid facilities to launch the book.

Foreword

*Richard Clarke, archbishop of Armagh and
primate of all Ireland*

I am truly delighted that this volume has seen the light of day, and I am more than grateful to all those who have brought it to fruition. Over the past couple of years I have nursed the hope that the year 2019 might provide the opportunity for the Church of Ireland to consider how both its context and also much of its self-understanding have changed since the church celebrated the centenary of its disestablishment in 1969. This has not been, I wish to suggest, with either narcissistic or triumphalist intent, but rather because I believe that it is only when we are honest enough to look carefully at how we have changed over the years that we can then face into the future with a cold-eyed realism coupled with a warm Christian conviction and faith.

The fifty years that have elapsed since 1969 are not precisely coterminous with my own sojourn within the ordained ministry. I was, however, accepted for ordination training by the Church of Ireland late in 1967, and may therefore reasonably suggest that I have had more than a passing interest in the life of the Church of Ireland over the past half-century. What now follows in this extended foreword is, however, neither *faux* autobiography nor a protracted exercise in nostalgia; I will certainly attempt to keep personal reminiscence at bay so far as this is possible. Clearly a number of the matters mentioned in this foreword are covered in greater detail and with proper objectivity in later chapters. These are instead a few comments on some of those facets of the life of the Church of Ireland (and many others might have been considered in this foreword) that appear to have changed radically over the past fifty years, as seen from the perspective of a single individual who has worked very contentedly in five dioceses in both ecclesiastical provinces (and in both of the island's political jurisdictions) as – variously – deacon, priest, bishop, archbishop, curate, country rector, city cathedral dean, university chaplain and hospital chaplain.

The Church of Ireland made a modest occasion of the centenary of its disestablishment in 1969, as was probably in keeping with its character at that time. There were a couple of books produced, and note should be taken in particular of a delightful series of essays edited by Fr Michael Hurley SJ giving an ecumenical perspective on how the Church of Ireland was perceived from outside its ranks.[1] There were also, no doubt, a number of celebratory services although I do not recall attending any of these. But little else marked the year as particularly momentous for the church. Events in Northern Irish society were beginning to escalate

---

1 Michael Hurley SJ, *Irish Anglicanism, 1869–1969* (Dublin, 1970).

into violence, and this would quickly demand much of the Church of Ireland, particularly – in the first instance – at local and parochial level. In the world beyond
the Church of Ireland (and Ireland as a whole) relatively little occurred that might
be considered as of historical and global note other than the continuing carnage of
the Vietnam War, although a significant first was achieved on 20 July of that year
when the space mission Apollo 11 landed two men on the moon. This was all in
some contrast to 1968, a year of student revolt in a number of European countries,
the suppression by the USSR of the 'Prague Spring' in Czechoslovakia, major
race riots in Chicago and the tragic assassinations of Martin Luther King Jnr and
Robert Kennedy, all of which serve to keep that year rather more vividly in the
mind's eye for those of us who were then of an age to take an interest in world
events. But there was perhaps some degree of 'after-burn' of the 1968 student
protest movement within the Church of Ireland of 1969, and I seem to recall a
decorous waving of placards by divinity students (as they were then termed) at the
General Synod of that year, protesting at the utter disconnection of the Church of
Ireland from the reality of the outside world. Reflecting on the past half-century
probably the most radical changes in the life of the Church of Ireland from its
outward appearance in 1969 (which are also matters that have affected the life of
almost every parish on the island) have been the ordination of women to the three
orders of ministry, and the massive transformation in liturgical forms and practice.
They are unconnected and so – reasonably enough – they will each be considered
in turn before moving to other features of change within the Church of Ireland.

By the late 1960s, the nursery slopes of modern liturgical revision were being
cautiously explored by the Church of Ireland. There was a soft-covered 'red
book' produced at that time continuing a very conservative revision of Morning
and Evening Prayer in modern language, and also a more radical revision of
the Baptismal Office. By 1973, there was a 'grey book' which contained a new
experimental Eucharistic rite, not dissimilar from the first of the Rite II Holy
Communion liturgies today. Then came the 1984 *Alternative Prayer Book* and,
twenty years later, a *Book of Common Prayer* containing liturgies from the 'old'
Book of Common Prayer in addition to liturgies in more vernacular language. This
all sounds very straightforward, but one should not underestimate either the massive amount of careful work this required from the Liturgical Advisory Committee
(in addition to great patience from the membership of General Synod, as each
clause and comma in the new liturgies had to be carefully considered and accepted
by two-thirds of both clergy and laity). There was also the considerable difficulty
in persuading many Church of Ireland congregations that liturgical change was in
fact a good idea. New baptismal rites proved generally acceptable fairly quickly,
but the new services of Holy Communion were an entirely different matter, where
doctrinal niceties were given very detailed scrutiny both inside and outside the
walls of synod. It is, however, probably fair to say that although there are certainly
parishes were the 'modern' liturgies (now not so modern) are rarely if ever used,
it would seem that there is widespread usage of the services which have arrived

over the past fifty years. A concern felt by many that the traditional services would disappear completely has been obviated to a great degree by their presence in the 2004 *Book of Common Prayer*. The modern liturgies also encourage a role for members of the congregation in the leading of sections of public worship (which was virtually impossible with the older Prayer Book) and this, it seems, is now virtually universal throughout the Church of Ireland and fully accepted – indeed, a welcome development, particularly as it instils a fuller understanding that worship is indeed communal.

The developments in liturgy have, naturally enough, had other effects. As has been noted in the Anglican Communion worldwide, the absence of a single 'definitive' liturgy, whether in individual provinces or through the whole Communion, has undoubtedly had a disunifying effect on the psyche of Anglicanism. Although most modern Anglican liturgies display a visible relationship to a central liturgical core, the variations are such as to dilute the sense of a single worshipping community. The other obvious effect is that permission to use variations within liturgy has, in some places (including within the Church of Ireland), led to any resemblance to Anglican liturgy, or to a set liturgy of any kind, being entirely coincidental. This has also at times encouraged the absence of liturgical robes entirely in a few parishes, although this remains canonically illegal. For many (and not the elderly alone) this all represents a highly unfortunate by-product of a desirable greater flexibility in worship. It is scarcely being priggish or pedantic to suggest that one of the characteristic glories of Anglicanism is indeed its liturgical foundation, which, at its best, encourages a distinctive spirituality among its members that is of both depth and breadth.

From the vantage point of fifty years' distance, it seems extraordinary to recall that a Church of Ireland service in 1969 would have been conducted by a male who would equally certainly have been 'full-time', as non-stipendiary ordained ministry had not yet been approved. There would have been an outside chance that a male lay-reader – there were no female lay-readers until the early 1970s – would have assisted at this 1969 service in some way, and in rare circumstances might have led the entire service in case of unavoidable absence of a cleric.

A pivotal moment in change was of course the opening of ordination to women. The Church of Ireland approved the ordination of women to the diaconate (about which there was little enough controversy) in the late 1980s, followed by approval of ordination to priesthood and episcopate in 1990. This latter engendered more controversy than had ordination to the diaconate, but the Church of Ireland for the most part took the matter calmly enough, and in its stride. Certainly very few people believed that they could no longer in conscience remain within the Church of Ireland as a result of the decision. Those who opposed the ordination of women were not ostracized, and those clergy who were opposed to the ordination of women were able to continue in ministry without difficulty or disrespect. It is to its credit that the Church of Ireland did not distinguish in this instance between the appropriateness of ordination to priesthood and episcopate. This was both doctrinally and ecclesiologically sound, and it avoided the immense divisions that the Church of England faced (and continues to face), even if it took the Church of Ireland almost twenty-five years to consecrate a woman as a bishop after it had become legal to do so.

Although this is an issue to be discussed in greater detail elsewhere in this volume, across the Church of Ireland as a whole, there has been – I believe – contented and joyful acceptance of women's ministry. It has been valued highly. Speaking with experience as a bishop in both the Republic of Ireland and Northern Ireland, I have encountered virtually no opposition to the appointment of women clergy to parishes. It may be that there is unvoiced (or very quietly voiced) prejudice against women's ministry in some quarters but, if there is, it has certainly been insufficient to cause instability in the church as a whole. It is, however, disturbing how relatively few women – ordained and lay – have been given major responsibility in the governing structures of the church at this stage. A quota system might be of some value, although whether this would produce the desired results is always open to question.

Non-stipendiary ministry and a large increase in the number of trained lay readers has also had an immense effect on the 'delivery' of worship throughout the church. It is not simply that some places would have been almost certainly deprived of worship and pastoral care as the number of stipendiary clergy declined, but also that the church as a whole has benefitted from the understanding that those called to ministry are not a separate caste. They are indeed of the same cloth as the whole people of God.

A highly significant although more subtle change – certainly from the perspective of the cleric – is the manner in which the nexus of relationships between the priest, the parish and the parishioners has altered radically over the past half-century. This is not to indulge in misty-eyed wistfulness for the past nor is it cynicism about the present, but rather what I hope is cold-eyed realism. In the period immediately following our chosen year of 1969, the relationship between those who identified in some respect as parishioners and the parish itself as a structure was (for the most part) relaxed, undemonstrative and generally uncomplicated. This is not to suggest that there might not have been 'difficult parishioners' (certainly from a rector's perspective) in virtually every parish on the island, but, on the whole, if a rector visited the people of the parish with regularity, cared (in particular) for the sick, housebound or bereaved and did not serve up either heresy or nonsense – or both – in the course of a reasonably well-conducted Sunday service, there was little further expectation that he (and it was 'he' at that stage) could not fulfil with a relative straightforwardness. The existence of parish organizations was a given, and they usually received sufficient support to make them not only viable but valuable. In general, even parishioners who rarely if ever attended church services had some sense of belonging to the community represented by the local parish and were content to receive some pastoral attention from 'the clergy'. This may not have been true of some urban parishes where – even at that stage – a congregation might well have become scattered and unconnected with the church *as community*, but what is suggested above is probably a reasonably accurate picture of much parish life, north and south, other than in places beset by societal violence. Much has happened over the past fifty years to alter a great deal of this picture. My hope is that comments I now make will not be construed as judgmental or cynical. This is not the intention.

There seems little doubt but that a great deal of societal culture has influenced the everyday life of the church, and in many respects. There is an inevitability in this – the church has always been affected by the society in which it exists. This is not secularization per se, but rather what may be the effects of the surrounding societal mindset on much of the Church of Ireland. The first of these factors is a prevailing and growing *individualism*. The sense of community itself has greatly diminished in every facet of Irish life. The core identity of an individual is no longer related as readily to any community. ('On-line communities' are most certainly nothing of the kind.) Greater mobility of every kind has no doubt been a factor in an atomization of Irish life. What seems certain is that the people no longer identify themselves to as great a degree, as once was the case, in terms of their membership of a church community. Coupled with individualism has been a greater emphasis, again in every area of Irish life, on both accountability and consumerism. Is this or that person doing the job in the way that *I* think they should be doing it, and am *I* getting value – monetary value but nor only monetary value – from my engagement with this or that organization?

This has inevitably placed greater pressure on clergy to meet expectations of a very different kind within parish life, and there is no doubt that it has been extremely stressful for numbers of clergy. If this reality is coupled with greater financial demands on parishioners to maintain their local communities and the greater workload that clergy must undertake in a highly litigious environment with responsibility for protocols, form-filling and administrative requirements (and these are by no means all generated by the church), the life of the parish clergy has changed immeasurably. One might add that even the traditionally important and central aspect of parish visiting has become more difficult through two factors, both related to overall societal changes over the decades. The first is that people spend less time in their homes – even at weekends – than would have been the case fifty years ago and are less likely to 'be in' (certainly during the daytime) than would have been the norm a few decades ago. The second is that the idea of *anyone* – clerical or not – simply 'calling in' on a household, other than by prior arrangement and with a specific agenda, is no longer universally accepted as welcome or even appropriate. Few, I believe, could deny that the effects of these different dynamics have made intra-parochial relationships certainly different, and by no means more relaxed, than would have been the case half a century ago.

At this point, it may be worth commenting on the understood need for greater care from clergy when it comes to relationships with individual parishioners, particularly the young. The introduction of strict regulations by the Church of

Ireland in the matter of ministry among children and young people – known as 'Safeguarding Trust' – in the early 1990s has without doubt changed relationships within parishes and in the wider church. There is no doubt that such protocols were necessary, and remain essential for the protection of children from harm. This need for protection from abuse of any kind is now understandably being developed to include adults who may be vulnerable in any respect. This again is unquestionably necessary, but at the same time we should not doubt that clergy in particular are now tempted to protect *themselves* from any possible complaint of misbehaviour. Although necessary as protocols for safeguarding may be, it will continue to have the effect of pastorally distancing the priest from his or her people.

In looking back over the past fifty years, we must also note the quiet but vital work done by clergy in the northern part of the Church of Ireland during the Troubles. Those of us who were ministering principally in the southern part of the island were aware – and indeed in genuine awe – of the example being given by our colleagues during that terrible time. It was certainly given a human face in the media during the latter half of the period of widespread violence by Archbishop Robin Eames, but he was the first to acknowledge the bravery and calm devotion to duty being shown by so many of the clergy in the northern dioceses. As I have learnt since my move to Armagh, the pain of many people has not greatly diminished since the physical violence has diminished, and clergy today are still having to show great pastoral sensitivity and diligence in ministering to the many who suffered trauma and bereavement during the thirty years of violence that began fifty years ago.

Fifty years ago saw post-Vatican II ecumenism flowering in Ireland (particularly in the Republic), albeit perhaps more in the local context than within the central church. There was a feeling of warmth and a general belief – again inevitably to a greater degree in the southern part of the Church of Ireland – that barriers between the different Christian traditions could be removed and that succeeding decades would see major changes being effected. This belief has in some respects taken a strange turn over the decades, in that local ecumenism has probably become more sporadic (and even stale in some ways) whereas relationships between church leaders are for the most part warmer and more relaxed than ever before. The Church of Ireland has also taken its place internationally to an astonishing degree in ecumenical dialogue. In the late 1960s, Archbishop Henry McAdoo was at the forefront, as co-chair of the international commission of dialogue between Anglicans and Roman Catholics. In more recent years, Church of Ireland bishops and archbishops have been heavily involved in international commissions between the Anglican Communion and Methodism, Eastern Orthodox, Oriental Orthodox and Old Catholics, and with fruitful relationships with the Lutheran Porvoo Communion. For a small church within the totality of the world of Anglicanism, this is surely of some note.

Finally an important area in which we have seen massive changes in perspective has been with regard to what would, in 1969, have been termed as the 'overseas mission' of the church. Following my graduation from Trinity College Dublin, but before embarking on a theology degree in London University, I took what would today be called a gap year in the city of Isfahan in Iran with the Church Missionary Society. As I look back I now see that this period – the early 1970s – was very much an interim period between 'traditional' missionary activity abroad (where mission-aries were understood as bringing the Gospel to the unenlightened) and today's understanding of linking with church projects in other countries. In Isfahan (the centre of the Anglican diocese of Iran in those years), there were large numbers of CMS missionaries from Britain and Australia in leadership roles in the diocesan schools and hospitals and in the administration. The bishop of the diocese (Hassan Dehqani-Tafti) was Iranian – he was the first Iranian bishop – and there was no question but that it was he who was spiritually leading the diocese, but there was equally a certainty that the presence of expatriate missionaries in other major lead-ership positions was essential for the smooth running of diocesan institutions and projects. Some of those missionaries who had come to Iran from other countries literally spent a lifetime there. This was no temporary assistance.

Spending a brief time (again under the auspices of CMS) in Zambia within the last couple of years revealed to me, as nothing else could, how the relationship of the Church of Ireland to 'overseas mission' has changed utterly, and positively so. Those who work with local churches in other countries are now operating within those churches very much as servants, bringing particular expertise where this might be of use, but essentially as companions in the faith rather than as purveyors of the faith. This does not diminish our understanding of the work of previous generations of missionaries, who laid foundations for so much that is visible today. It is, however, a reminder – if such were needed – that the days of ecclesiastical colonialism (even if this was a largely subliminal perspective) have gone for ever.

There is much else that might have been discussed in a foreword such as this, but the intention has not been to give a comprehensive overview, or even a sum-mary of what is to follow, but rather to reflect on a number of changes that have affected the life of the Church of Ireland for almost all its committed members, lay and ordained, and in almost every parish on the island. And there is no doubt but that God is calling us to go on changing. Perhaps not entirely appropriately, I conclude with reference to advice from John Henry Newman. He once famously wrote that 'to live is to change and to be perfect is to have changed often'. But we might wish to balance this with other advice from the same source: 'Nothing would be done at all if one waited until one could do it so well that no one could find fault with it.'

I

An historical overview of the period

Kenneth Milne

The Act of Union of 1800 not only combined the kingdoms of Great Britain and Ireland but also joined the established churches of England and Ireland into 'one Protestant episcopal Church, to be called the United Church of England and Ireland, whose 'doctrine, worship, discipline and government shall be, and shall remain in full force for ever'. In effect, 'for ever' proved to be just seventy years, for the Irish Church Act of 1869 'disestablished' (and disendowed) the Irish provinces of that united church, depriving the Church of Ireland of the constitutional role as the state church of the kingdom of Ireland that it had enjoyed since the Reformation and which its leaders cherished and clung to tenaciously, if unsuccessfully.

The history of any conflict, it is sometimes asserted, is written by the victors. Not so, it would appear, where the bitter controversy occasioned by the disestablishment of the Irish church was concerned; what might be deemed the losing side, the Church of Ireland, commemorated, however modestly, the event on its centenary in 1969–70, as the archbishop of Armagh has recalled in his foreword to this present collection of essays. It is now doing so again, fifty years later. Indeed, disestablishment is a prime example of an event that was regarded at the time as little short of a catastrophe for the church but can now be seen as having been its salvation. Many members of the church who endured the trauma of disestablishment were to experience in their lifetimes further, perhaps even greater anxieties as the movement for Irish independence gained momentum, with who knows what implications for the Church of Ireland had it still retained its established status.

The contributors to this present volume, to whom the editors extend their gratitude, were asked to focus on the diversity of the life of the Church of Ireland since 1969, when the centenary of disestablishment was marked, and to reflect on the all-Ireland nature of the church. We hope that taken together these chapters will provide an audit of how the church has conducted its ministry in both political jurisdictions of Ireland and may thus provide some guidance as to how best it might perform in the future.

Archbishop Clarke has alluded to Fr Michael Hurley's splendid gesture in editing a volume of essays 'presented to the Church of Ireland on the occasion of the centenary of its Disestablishment', which was 'an expression of recognition and gratitude'. By definition, therefore, while scholarly, it emphasized the positive rather than the negative. The contributors to this present volume were not, we hope, subject to any such inhibitions. Another centenary publication was a special issue of the monthly review *Theology*, regarded by its distinguished editor, G.R. Dunstan, as 'an offering of filial piety to that Church and of affection for its members', in which Dunstan remarked that at one of the most turbulent periods of communal violence in the North and thanks to 'the disciplined spirituality, deep in the Christianity of the place', 'to visit Ireland is still to visit a courteous society'.[1]

While the contents of that issue of *Theology* treated, as was to be expected, the political and ecclesiastical aspects of the disestablishment process, it was striking that the opening essay was 'On Irish spirituality: the influence of three teachers of prayer in the Church of Ireland', by G.O. Simms, the archbishop of Armagh. The three exemplars cited by Archbishop Simms were John Henry Bernard (archbishop of Dublin, then provost of Trinity), who sought to interpret the voice of the Church of Ireland as 'authentically Anglican, despite its "Irish brogue"'; Robert Malcolm Gwynn (biblical scholar and 'practical mystic'), who was driven by 'his gentle Christian conscience' to espouse the social aspirations of the Irish Citizen Army; and Michael Ferrar (warden of the Divinity Hostel, forerunner of the present Church of Ireland Theological Institute), who 'never ceased to relate prayer to life and to lead others in new ways of living within the limits of a religious minority with graciousness and tolerance'.

A criticism sometimes levelled at those who write about the Church of Ireland and their publishers is the prevalence of an undue preoccupation with the past, and it would certainly seem that more is written about its history than about any other aspect of the church's life. Yet remembering is important, as the *Book of Common Prayer* (2004) acknowledges by the inclusion of a list of persons associated with dioceses of the Church of Ireland over the centuries 'to remind us of the continuing work of the Holy Spirit in the Church in all ages'. Names such as those invoked by Archbishop Simms should remind us that this work is ongoing.

However, a preoccupation with the past can be to the detriment of our responsibility to present and future generations, and the contributors to this volume surely provide us with much thought as to how past performance measures up to what was to be hoped for. It is a pity that the word 'mission' has become rather tired and hackneyed so that it has lost something of its potency, for that is what the church is all about, and the House of Bishops, in putting before the church the following Five Marks of Mission, provide a benchmark against which to measure past performance:

1. To proclaim the Good News of the Kingdom
2. To teach, baptize and nurture new believers
3. To respond to human need by loving service

---

1 *Theology*, 123:599 (May 1970), p. 193.

4.   To transform unjust structures of society, to challenge violence of every kind and pursue peace and reconciliation
5.   To strive to safeguard the integrity of creation, and sustain and renew the life of the earth

No doubt every age sees itself as one of unprecedented change: how could it be otherwise? But what is markedly unprecedented in the case of the past fifty years has been the pace of change. Our planet has seen, on the one hand, huge advances in technology encompassing heretofore unknown phenomena such as social media and artificial intelligence, while at the same time failing miserably where our care of the environment is concerned. Our continent is experiencing great movements of people unparalleled since the end of the Second World War, and who could claim to have foreseen the fall of the Iron Curtain, the disintegration of the Soviet bloc and the adherence of some of its former components to the European Union (if not always to the values of its founders).

If we focus our attention more closely on our own island we find that fifty years ago we were on the brink of a thirty-year conflict, the epicentre of which lay in Northern Ireland, but its roots in the revolutionary period of 1912–22 having considerable political and security implications for the entire island. J.C. Beckett, the distinguished historian of the Queen's University Belfast, had written in 1966:

> Though the settlement [of 1921–2] left a legacy of bitterness, issuing occasionally in local and sporadic disturbances, it inaugurated for Ireland a longer period of general tranquillity than she had known since the first half of the eighteenth century.[2]

But another Irish historian, Ronan Fanning of University College Dublin, commenting in 1994 on what Beckett had written,[3] while conceding that 'few historians would have withheld assent from what Professor Beckett wrote, when he wrote it', suggested that later historians, writing under Beckett's title, 'might instead conclude that the events of 1968–9 inaugurated in Ireland [a] longer period of violence than she had known since the seventeenth century'.

Political developments in Ireland during the past fifty years are outlined in two of the following chapters, indicating the vast changes that have occurred. Few observers would have predicted the power-sharing political structures put in place in Northern Ireland under the Belfast Agreement of 1998, or indeed the dropping by the Republic, following a decisive referendum result, of the contentious

---

2 J.C. Beckett, *The making of modern Ireland, 1603–1923* (London, 1966), p. 461. Beckett contributed an article to the 'disestablishment' issue of *Theology*, entitled 'Disesablishment in the nick of time', which, in revised form, appeared in his *Confrontations: studies in Irish history* (London, 1972), under the more staid title of 'The Church of Ireland: disestablishment and its aftermath'.   3 Ciaran Brady (ed.), *Interpreting Irish history: the debate on historical revisionism* (Dublin, 1994), p. 149.

territorial claims inherent in articles 2 and 3 in the constitution, which had been of great solace to northern nationalists while obnoxious to unionists. Similarly, few if any observers of the Southern scene anticipated the transformation that has overtaken society there. Divorce, the legalizing of the importation and sale of 'artificial means of contraception' (the term used in Free State legislation), statutory provision for civil partnerships (irrespective of gender) followed by marriage (likewise, irrespective of gender), and most recently and perhaps most controversially (and by a two-to-one referendum result), the liberalization of the state's abortion laws. The long-derided interpretation of the law on censorship of publications had gone in 1967, as also, by referendum in 1972 had the 'special place' (whatever that meant) accorded to the Holy Catholic Apostolic and Roman Church in the constitution. What seems not to have occasioned any regret on the part of other churches was the simultaneous removal of the 'recognition' given by that same article 44 of the constitition to, inter alia, the Church of Ireland, whose title had until then been enshrined in the Irish constitution.

As in the response of clergy to changes within the political environments in which they minister, so too have there been important developments in inter-church relationships, greatly encouraged by the stimulus to ecumenical activity provided by the Second Vatican Council. Inter-church and ecumenical activity (not necessarily the same thing) have led to such significant developments as the covenant entered into between the Church of Ireland and the Irish Methodist Church, while the setting up of ARCIC III has renewed hopes of meaningful discussions with the Roman Catholic Church following a period of some stagnation, at higher, if not necessarily at local levels. F.S.L. Lyons (like J.C. Beckett, a committed member of the Church of Ireland) had, in his Ford Lectures in Oxford in 1978,[4] identified at least four 'cultures' that existed and 'clashed' in Ireland: Gaelic, English, Anglo–Irish and Ulster Protestant, the last being most particularly represented by the Presbyterian Church. It is therefore reassuring to know that the Church of Ireland wishes to maintain close relations with that church and other churches through regular conversations[5] and through the clear commitment that it has shown to the two Irish ecumenical instruments, the Irish Council of Churches and the Irish Inter-Church Meeting.

A striking feature of a changing society common to both Northern Ireland and the Republic has been a rapid growth in ethnic diversity, census returns indicating that 10 per cent of the current population of the Republic were born outside Ireland. Such diversity has added urgency to the need for Christians to seek a closer understanding of those other world faiths that are now so regularly encountered in all parts of the country, leading to a more structured approach to achieving such vitally important dialogue.

Education, the subject of two essays in this volume, because the structures of the educational systems diverged widely almost from the setting up of the two political

---

4 F.S.L. Lyons, *Culture and anarchy in Ireland, 1890–1939* (Oxford, 1979).   5 *Journal of the General Synod* (2018), p. 320.

jurisdictions, is an area in which public policy and church interests have frequently led to discord in past generations. In more recent times we find that considerable measures have been introduced in Northern Ireland to accommodate the requirements of the Roman Catholic Church and that changes in the educational system in the Republic have also taken note of minority views in a fast-changing scene that had scarcely been reorganized in its essentials until the second half of the twentieth century. The largely denominational system at both primary and post-primary levels in the Republic suited both the 'majority' and 'minority' communities until fairly recently, and indeed can be said to have eased the impact of curriculum changes that came with independence, especially the emphasis on teaching Irish language and history (the latter for some time regarded as the handmaid of the former). The wishes, indeed the requirements, of a more diverse society, have brought about an increasing demand for more diversity in the control of schools.

Changes in liturgy and ministry have been of enormous consequence. The preface to the 1984 *Alternative Prayer Book* (superseded by the 2004 *Book of Common Prayer*) noted that the Church of Ireland had inherited 'a long tradition of liturgical worship going back to Celtic times', and that since disestablishment it has been accepted that revision is a continuing process. Yet what needs always to be borne in mind is the admonition in the 'preface' to the 2004 *BCP* that

> we must always remind ourselves that words, however memorable, beautiful or useful, are not to be confused with worship itself. The words set out on these pages are but the beginning of worship. They need to be appropriated with care and devotion by the People of God so that, with the aid of the Holy Spirit, men and women may bring glory to the Father and grow in the knowledge and likeness of Jesus Christ.

The ordination of women to the priesthood and the episcopate was the culmination of a long process whereby women were granted admission to all offices in the Church of Ireland.[6] In fact women (or, more accurately, a limited category of women) were granted the parliamentary franchise before they could take seats in the General Synod – they had to wait for fifty years after disestablishment to do so, and it was 1960 before the restriction on the number of women who could sit on a select vestry was lifted. In the event, the arrival on the scene of priests and (at the time of writing) a bishop who are women, while eliciting considerable interest within the Church of Ireland and elsewhere, created scarcely any turbulence. That they were received, even welcomed, owed much to the manner in which they and their male advocates had prepared public opinion for this development.

All such changes in the internal life of the church have made great demands on church administration and it is clear that the central deliberative and administrative

6 See Kenneth Milne, 'Disestablishment and the lay response' in Raymond Gillespie and W.G. Neely (eds), *The laity and the Church of Ireland* (Dublin, 2002), pp 226–49.

organs of the church (and indeed of individual dioceses and parishes) have taken on board the need to keep abreast of the rapid transformation that has come about in the field of communications. It is something of a truism to make the point that the church is primarily in the business of communication, but it is none the less imperative to stress that fact. And both the message and the medium need to keep up with the times.

Writing in 1971, and with the church's nineteenth-century experience in mind, Donald Harman Akenson remarked that thanks to a myriad of commissions and committees, 'the British parliament was as well informed about the operation of the Irish church as it was about any institution in the whole empire'.[7] The disestablished church continues to attract the attention of historians, possibly in some measure thanks to the welcome and freedom of expression that it extends to scholars, and not least because of the research facilities with which it provides them. Its size makes for a convenient case study, while its story touches on many aspects of the history of the country. This being so, the past fifty years have seen a considerable output of publications relating to the Church of Ireland, and among the most notable of these has been *The Church of Ireland and its past: history, interpretation and identity*, an examination of the historiography of the church, and of the various strands that can be detected in the approaches of the many historians who wrote about it over the centuries.[8] David Hayton's 'concluding reflexions', with which that volume ends, tell of a 'profound shift' in the way in which the history of the Church of Ireland has been written, as new aspects of the church's life have been studied, and the distinctive manners to be perceived on the part of those who write from within the church's membership and those from without. He concludes, however, that there will continue to be a place for both.

This chapter began with a reminder that the 1970 issue of *Theology*, marking the centenary of disestablishment, began, rather unexpectedly, with Archbishop Simms' tribute to 'teachers of prayer' who had influenced the Church of Ireland's spirituality in the past. Perhaps it is not only symmetrical but also timely to quote words used by the present archbishop of Armagh, Dr Richard Clarke, addressing the General Synod in May 2018. Having reviewed the salient issues that had claimed the attention of the church in the previous twelve months, he commended to the Church of Ireland an initiative pioneered by the archbishop of Canterbury some years previously: a call to a global wave of prayer from Ascension to Pentecost.

> But, essentially, we must always remember that at every time of the year and in every place, you and I must become better at the business of praying … surely something on which the church must be truly able to rely, if it is to face its future with confidence, with hope, and hence even with joy.

7 Donald Harman Akenson, *The Church of Ireland: ecclesiastical reform and revolution, 1800–1885* (London, 1971), p. 164.   8 Mark Empey, Alan Ford and Miriam Moffitt (eds), *The Church of Ireland and its past* (Dublin, 2017), p. 311.

Many generations have passed since the Church of Ireland had a privileged voice in Dublin Castle but it does now have the opportunity, indeed the obligation, to ensure that its voice is heard in what is often called 'the public square' in Ireland. Furthermore, thanks to developments in inter-church relations that were unimaginable 150 years ago, the Church of Ireland has a voice in the worldwide ecumenical movement. Likewise, through the Republic of Ireland's continued membership of the European Union the church can avail itself of the wider opportunities for contributing to Christian witness on the continent of Europe provided by article 17 of the Lisbon Treaty of 2007, which guarantees that the EU 'shall maintain an open, transparent and regular dialogue' with the churches. As an earnest of its commitment to doing so, the EU has set up structures to secure the implementation of this guarantee so far as it is concerned, and the Irish government has committed itself to establishing a similar structural instrument for state-church liasion. Much will depend on church readiness (and competence) to respond. And what might be distinctive about the Church of Ireland's Anglican voice?

Archbishop McAdoo, writing at the start of the fifty years under review in this volume, maintained that 'there is no specifically Anglican corpus of doctrine' and that there was no writer whose work was an essential part of it either in respect of content or with regard to the form of its self-expression.[9] He did, however, stress that 'the distinctiveness lies in method rather than in content', and it may be that it is this method that the Church of Ireland can contribute to theological discourse at a time when controversy rather than conversation has been the most marked characteristic of debate in this country on issues, particularly those pertaining to human relationships, that call for insights based on scripture, tradition and reason, which are the Anglican *sine qua non*.

9 H.R. McAdoo, *The spirit of Anglicanism* (London, 1965), p. v.

2

Worship in the Church of Ireland

The Rt Revd Harold Miller, bishop of Down and Dromore

In many ways, the development of worship in the Church of Ireland from 1969 up to the present day is the story of my personal adult life. Liturgy has been an almost all-consuming passion for me, and it is a privilege to write this essay for a book to celebrate 150 years of disestablishment in the Church of Ireland.

OUR LITURGICAL ROOTS

The time of disestablishment itself also focused on worship. It was a time of high Tractarianism in England, and the new prayer book, finally launched in 1878, with the canons developed by the church, was to be highly influential in the years up to the 1960s. What was arrived at, after many controversies and debates, in the 1878 *Book of Common Prayer,* was actually a very conservative revision. The post-disestablishment prayer book was almost indistinguishable, to the untrained reader, from its 1662 antecedent. That was also the case after the revisions of 1926, and the addition of new evening services made in the 1930s.

So, in the early 1960s, the Church of Ireland was a church rooted in a prayer book going back to the sixteenth and seventeenth centuries. Indeed, many continued to refer to it (wrongly) as '1662'. In its liturgical practice, though not universally in its teaching, the Church of Ireland had an essentially 'low-church' ethos. No cross was allowed on or near the holy table until the bill proposed by W.S. Milner was passed by General Synod in 1964.[1] There were to be no candles on the Communion table, no coloured stoles, Communion wafers or incense, and the service you would have heard read in each church throughout the island would have been pretty well exactly the same, apart from hymns, occasional prayers and the sermon. The consistency, familiarity and even simplicity of the *Book of Common Prayer* held the church together in its ethos and teaching. The mid-twentieth-century world in which it existed was a world in which people were clear about denominational identity and allegiance, and a world in which a large number of people were regular weekly worshippers. Their faith and life were formed by these liturgies.

---

1 'Billy' Milner was a parishioner in St Nicholas' Carrickfergus. He was not a 'high churchman', but simply couldn't see why the Church of Ireland forbade a cross at such a central place as the communion table.

THE LITURGICAL ADVISORY COMMITTEE

This book tracks some of the changes that have taken place since the centenary of disestablishment. So, we begin in 1969. However, the foundation for the changes that took place over the last fifty years was laid in Ireland in 1964, when the General Synod made the radical decision to appoint a Liturgical Advisory Committee, with the following remit:

(a) To formulate and suggest to the General Synod such liturgical proposals relating to public worship, as may seem to be desirable to the Committee from time to time;

(b) To consider and report on, if requested to do so by the General Synod, such other liturgical proposals relating to public worship as may be brought before the said body from time to time;

(c) To foster the study of the *Book of Common Prayer* and of the public worship of the Church by preparing articles relating to these subjects and offering them for publication;

(d) To report to the General Synod annually.

A wide remit indeed!

The idea of a liturgical committee or commission was not unique to the Church of Ireland. The Lambeth Conferences had been encouraging careful liturgical revision, while preserving also a vital degree of commonality of worship in the Anglican Communion – something which had been a unifying factor over generations.[2]

THE LITURGICAL RENEWAL MOVEMENT

In terms of the worldwide church, the foundations of liturgical revision go back much further. Essentially, they emerged from the 'liturgical renewal' movement, which, although dating back as far as 1832 in France, gathered steam at the beginning of the twentieth century. In the Church of England in the 1930s, this was particularly seen in the introduction of 'parish Communion' ('the Lord's people around the Lord's table on the Lord's day'). The liturgical renewal movement both looked forward and looked back. Much of its impetus came from the discovery of early liturgical texts and documents, such as the *Didaché*, dating from the first century and rediscovered in 1873. These discoveries took the church catholic back to its common roots, and it is hardly surprising to see that there is now much more agreement in liturgical shape and forms, and at times even in common wording, across the denominations.

So, the Church of Ireland entered 1969, the centenary year of disestablishment, cognizant of changes that had been taking place in liturgical thinking worldwide.

2 It is, however, true to say, that there was never simply 'one' version of the *Book of Common Prayer* in the communion. Some provinces inherited liturgy based more in the 1637 Scottish *BCP*, and others inherited liturgy based in 1662.

Much of this liturgical thinking had been incorporated into the Eucharistic rite of the newly united Church of South India in 1962, as it sought to find a truly ecumenical liturgy, based on good biblical and historical research. The Church of Ireland was also aware that changes were under way in the Church of England – and it is important not to forget that the Church of Ireland has historically depended very heavily indeed on the scholarship and work of its much larger 'sibling' across the water, when it comes to liturgical change. The other key factor is that the Roman Catholic Church had also been reviewing, and very radically revising, its liturgy, according to many of the same principles, during the Second Vatican Council (1962–5) under Pope John XXIII.

WORSHIP IN 1969 AND THE YEARS OF BOOKLETS

Snapshot in 1969

If we were to imagine a typical Church of Ireland church in 1969, the congregation would still be used to the (essentially) 1662 *Book of Common Prayer*. Regular worshippers would know it off by heart. It would be a matter of pride to be able to say the Apostles' Creed without looking at the text. In all our worship forms up to this point, God is addressed as 'thee', 'thou', etc.,[3] which carries with it a range of Shakespearian English, not used in everyday life, but normal within the walls of a church. The liturgy is very much fixed, and the minister leading simply needs to read it. Extempore prayer is almost unknown, except for a prayer on occasion before or after a sermon. Psalms and canticles are chanted to Anglican chant, and hymnody is essentially 'four-square',[4] and has been inherited with some additions through from the introduction of regular hymn-singing in the Victorian era – though much of it goes back earlier, emerging from times of renewal in the church, and some is even from the early centuries. Morning and Evening Prayer are the main diet of Sunday public worship. Holy Communion is celebrated monthly at main services, though not always in the evening, with perhaps quieter Eucharistic services early on a Sunday morning or midweek. And, in many places, when Holy Communion is celebrated at a main service, it follows Morning Prayer, and a break is provided so that people who do not wish to communicate may leave.

The first 'booklets'

The first official change in this era of Church of Ireland worship came in 1967, in a draft revised Service of Holy Communion (the 'white book'), which is now

---

3 Interestingly, the later tradition of capitalizing personal pronouns in relation to God seems to be unknown in any of the editions of the *Book of Common Prayer,* and indeed in the Authorised (King James) version of the Bible. It is a later affectation, presumably intended to give particular reverence to God.   **4** In other words, it generally had a particular metre, as can be seen by looking at the index of any traditional hymnal. Much modern Christian music is totally different.

largely forgotten. This was a very mild revision in terms of wording. The English was 'Revised Standard Version' English, with God still addressed as 'thee' and 'thou', but with people addressed as 'you'. However, it was the first time that there was provision for an Old Testament reading and psalm in the actual Communion service (up to then it was simply an Epistle and Gospel); for the first time the sermon (which *shall* be preached) was preached before the Nicene Creed; for the first time a litany form of intercession was provided; the peace is introduced (though in words only with no suggestion of actually sharing it),[5] and the present shape of the thanksgiving prayer begins to emerge. Visually, the first part of the service began to be led from the prayer desk, with the priest moving to the holy table for the ministry of the sacrament.

Then, in 1969, came the 'red booklet', which provided a new version of Morning and Evening Prayer, again in RSV English, a new version of the litany, and a service which, although theologically lacking when tested by the liturgical principles of today, nevertheless has a very important place in history: an order for the baptism of children. This was the first service in the Church of Ireland in which God was addressed throughout as 'you', and it was accepted with great enthusiasm. Perhaps it was the relief of having a service that was more accessible, especially in the days when many parents, often relatively unchurched, presented their children for baptism. But undoubtedly, this is one of the earliest services in a thoroughgoing 'you' form in the entire communion.

From this point onwards, every new Church of Ireland service addressed God as 'you', and even the informal prayers of people which, up to then, had often used the 'language of Zion',[6] began to speak of God in 'you' language. There was clearly some concern in the early days about over-familiarity, without always recognizing that the earlier 'thee' and 'thou' were also familiar personal pronouns.

Next, there came the 'blue booklet' of 1972, with a 'you form' Communion service, which places the Gloria at the beginning for the first time, removes the old Prayer for the Church Militant, adds the New Testament commandments, alongside the abbreviated form of the ten, separates out the peace but still does not suggest even the slightest physical contact, begins to clarify the fourfold action of the Eucharist,[7] and adds more seasonal material for the offertory, proper prefaces and blessing than previously had been available.

---

5 Bishop Colin Buchanan used to compare the 'words only' peace to the smile on the Cheshire cat. The physicality of sharing the peace is actually very important. It highlights that there is a horizontal dimension to worship as well as a vertical one. The peace is the time to ensure that we are 'in love and charity with our neighbours'.   6 The phrase 'language of Zion' was colloquially used to mean that people had learnt, over many years, to pray in King James Version English, using 'thy', 'thou', 'wouldest' etc. It was quite an art!   7 The 'fourfold action' was an insight of Dom Gregory Dix, in his formative book, *The shape of the liturgy* (London, 1945). In Cranmer, we have a sevenfold action: taking the bread, breaking the bread, giving thanks over the bread, taking the wine, giving thanks over the wine, giving the bread, giving the wine. In the more simplified actions of Dix, the key Eucharistic actions are: taking, giving thanks, breaking and giving.

In 1973, that service was incorporated along with services of Morning and Evening Prayer and the litany in 'you form' in the 'grey booklet', which was used in many places until the *Alternative Prayer Book* appeared in hardback in 1984.

The Joint Liturgical Group in Great Britain

A couple of other things that appeared in the 1973 'grey book' should be specifically noted. These had their genesis in the work of the Joint Liturgical Group. The Joint Liturgical Group was a very imaginative idea, gathering together liturgists in Great Britain, from the Methodist Church, the Presbyterian Church, the Congregational Church and the Baptist Church, along with the Church of England, to look at common liturgical interests. Two of the key planks of the 1973 revision come from that source. First of all, the weekday intercessions and thanksgivings, which have been forgotten in most other places in these islands, but still have a very valued place in the *Book of Common Prayer* (2004); and secondly, the revised calendar and thematic lectionary, which have long since been abandoned. Some may remember those days in which each Sunday (beginning with the ninth Sunday before Christmas) had a theme, such as 'The Creation', 'Christ the Healer', 'Those in Authority' and 'Endurance'. After a couple of decades of this calendar and twice-yearly lectionary most had thoroughly tired of it, but it had its place in the history of liturgical revision, and its roots in the Joint Liturgical Group.

Funeral services

The other booklet of this era was the brown 'Funeral services' booklet of 1977, which again proved very popular. It gave briefer and more focused readings, with additional and more specific prayers, and felt more immediately accessible to many people.

Authorizing services in the Church of Ireland.

All the services mentioned in the various booklets – white, red, blue, grey, brown – have something in common, usually expressed on the front inside page. They were approved by the House of Bishops for experimental use, as is allowed by the constitution of the Church of Ireland.[8] This gives the opportunity for the whole church to 'trial' services, to feed back on them to the Liturgical Advisory Committee and eventually to bring them to the General Synod, in a two-year bill, to become formally Church of Ireland services. This process, for anyone who is a member of General Synod, can be extremely tedious, but is nevertheless of great importance. Every 'i' is dotted and 't' crossed. Members of General Synod have

8 Chapter 1, section 26 (3).

the opportunity to bring amendments, and to consider new bills carefully before they become statutes. And all of this is because of the way Anglicans do theology.

The Latin 'tag' that is used for this way of proceeding theologically is '*lex orandi, lex credendi*'. This translates directly as 'the law of prayer, the law of belief', but it might be better expressed like this: what we pray regularly, we come to believe; and what we believe moulds the way in which we pray. So, if you were to ask a Church of Ireland person to say what the church believes, they will probably point you to the *Book of Common Prayer*. Of course, the reason why they would do so is not that the prayer book trumps the scriptures, but that it is entirely suffused with the scriptures, and biblical in its teaching. On another level, they may point you to the historic creeds, but at least two of these are acts of worship as well as statements of faith. They may invite you to read the Articles of Religion, confessing what we believe about central and controversial aspects of our faith; or they may simply invite you to read and learn the prayers, or to join us in worship.

So, the words with which we worship are of great importance, the balance of the different elements of worship are also of great importance, because they tell us what is important, as in the Acts 2:42 agenda for worship (which consists of 'the apostles' teaching, the fellowship, the breaking of bread and the prayers'), and what is to be given priority when the people of God assemble together.

THE ALTERNATIVE PRAYER BOOK (1984) AND ALTERNATIVE OCCASIONAL SERVICES (1993)

Many parts of the Anglican Communion had experimented with new forms of service in the 1970s, often in booklet form. As these developed, and were honed by use and experience, provinces had three possible ways forward. One was to keep producing booklets (but in many places there was a desire for a more 'permanent' book); another was to revise and update the actual prayer book of that province (for some places that may have been a step too far, and for England it was a near impossibility because of the constitutional status of the 1662 *Book of Common Prayer*); and the third way forward (taken by England in 1980, Ireland in 1984 and Canada in 1985) was to produce a parallel book of alternative services. In Ireland, this was entitled the 1984 *Alternative Prayer Book*. It was a book based on the material which had already been gathered and used, which had the inner logic of the contents of an Anglican prayer book but, apart from an order for the baptism of children (still none for adults!), it had none of the occasional offices, and no ordination services. It did, however, contain all the readings for Sundays and key festivals in full, in the New International Version, which would prove popular with some, but not with others. It also included the 'David Frost' Psalter,[9] as in the English

9 This Psalter was originally published as *The Psalms: a new translation for worship*, by Collins in 1977. The author, helped by a team of Hebrew experts, David Frost, was a fellow in English of St John's College, Cambridge.

Alternative Prayer Book, and also David Frost's memorable prayer, 'Father of all, we give you thanks and praise' as a post-Communion prayer in the Eucharistic rite, and a late evening office. The latter was mostly used for small groups and for quiet evening services, but it included a heading unknown in the Church of Ireland up to this point, which says a lot about the new world of Anglican liturgy: 'Open or Silent Prayer'. For the first time, the people of God are being encouraged to bring their own extempore prayers into the context of public worship.

The 1984 *Alternative Prayer Book* was generally, but not universally, well received. Some feared that it might be the harbinger of a 'Romeward trend', and it arrived after fifteen years of the Troubles in Northern Ireland, when many wanted to hold on to the known, fearing change. This meant that some churches, and some parts of the Church of Ireland, welcomed the book more than others, and parishes were inclined to identify as '*BCP* parishes' or '*APB* parishes' in their preferences, so it was not always seen as a source of unity, though greatly appreciated by many who loved it. The *APB* was to continue in use for twenty years. It was not experimental, but 'by authority of the General Synod of the Church of Ireland'.

In England, the 1980 *Alternative service book* was a much fuller prayer book. Right from the beginning, it included services for thanksgiving for the birth of a child and thanksgiving after adoption; for baptism and confirmation (acting with the presupposition that baptism of adults is normative); for marriage, for funerals and various ancillary aspects; and for ordinations to all three orders. The question is: 'Why did it take so long to get these services in Ireland?' Well, they came out gradually. There was possibly an underlying fearfulness in many bishops at the time about revising the marriage service, because of legal requirements to say that the rites and ceremonies of the Church of Ireland had been used; and there was certainly an episcopal fearfulness about revising the ordinal, and removing the imperative 'Take thou authority' in case the new rite might in some way be considered inadequate.

The year 1987 saw three new booklets arrive in the style of the *APB*: 'Confirmation', 'The marriage service' and 'Funeral services'. These provided more creative, imaginative and, in the case of confirmation, a more fulsome liturgy. This was followed by a booklet of services for ministry with the sick, which included the anointing with oil, the laying on of hands and a form, which has proved invaluable, of commendation at the time of death. Then, in 1993, these were gathered, along with ordination services, in the buff-coloured 1993 *Alternative occasional services*.

HYMNS AND SONGS

History of hymnody in church

For centuries, hymn-singing in the Church of Ireland was a rarity. When Thomas Cranmer compiled his reformed ordinal, he attempted writing a version of the *Veni Creator* but his hymn-writing was such that his version of that hymn didn't really last.[10] Of course, there had been hymn-writing in the days of the early church, an example of which is the '*Te Deum*', but the church generally stuck with the Psalms, as part of the divine scriptures, and other biblical hymns, like the '*Benedictus*', the '*Magnificat*' and the '*Nunc dimittis*' – songs from the Gospel according to Luke. Most of the Reformation hymns, including those attributed to Luther and those used in Geneva, were versions or explications of psalms. This developed in the eighteenth century with Isaac Watts, in his 'Christianized' psalms, and hymnody was generally reserved for revival movements, like the Methodists, under John and Charles Wesley. Even (perhaps especially) carols, many of which are a lot older, were not sung in church, apart from 'While shepherds watched their flocks by night', which is a paraphrase from Luke's Gospel. So, if you ever find a *Book of Common Prayer* of the United Church of England and Ireland from the first part of the nineteenth century, it may well include a metrical psalter, which provided some more hearty singing. That was the closest you got to hymns!

In the Church of Ireland, the first collection of hymns, *Hymns for public worship*, was produced in 1856. It had only 180 hymns, and required each individual bishop to give permission for its use. It was very popular, and widely used – so, eight years later, the first official *Church Hymnal* was produced for the Church of Ireland, and it was revised and doubled in size around the time of disestablishment, and issued as an authorized second edition. The Victorian Age was, of course, a period of much hymn-writing, and hymn-singing soon grew in popularity. What is interesting is that, unlike the Church of England, or the other Anglican churches in these islands, the Church of Ireland has, ever since, had an officially authorized *Church Hymnal*.

The fourth edition of the *Church Hymnal* was published in 1960. It was a hymn book of quality. In the fashion of the day, it presumed the passing on of a large number of great hymns from one generation to another. It was also, as in that musical period, relatively classy, with some unpopular and unsingable tunes. For example the tune 'Converse' was removed from 'What a friend we have in Jesus', so that congregations could be taught the more upmarket 'Manor house', but they simply got the old book out and sang it to the popular tune.

A period of creative music

So, we enter 1969 with a stable 'official' collection of hymns at a time where there had been very little new hymn-writing. But all of that was changing. Bishop Michael Baughen[11] had launched the first edition of *Youth praise* in 1966, with a range of old and new, formal and informal hymns and songs, largely for use in

10 To give a flavour: 'Come, holy ghost, eternal god, preceding from above,/ Both from the father and the son, the god of peace and loue:/ Visite our myndes, and into us thy heavily grace inspyre,/ That in all trueth and godliness we maye have true desyre.'   11 Michael Baughen was one of the most prolific hymn-writers of the late twentieth century. One of his most famous hymns is 'Lord, for the years'. He became bishop of Chester.

youth fellowships and youth services. Another volume was to follow. Again in the 1960s, Fr Geoffrey Beaumont[12] was writing new tunes for famous hymns, most of which have long since been forgotten, but his tune 'Hatherop Castle', for 'O Jesus I have promised', is still in use. And then, Charismatic Renewal arrives, with such a plethora of new worship songs that we can hardly remember them all. Some were gathered in the 1970s in volumes like *Sound of living waters* and *Fresh sounds*. Many have dated, but some classics have stood the test of time.[13] Add to that hymn-writers like Timothy Dudley-Smith, Fred Kaan and F. Pratt Green, the emergence of Taizé chant, and Iona songs, and we see such a rich upheaval of music taking place that the church could hardly keep up with it. At times, those in authority emphasized that the Church of Ireland had an authorized hymnal, fearing the new, and a lawless use of new material, but at the end of the day the new hymns and songs proved very popular and refreshing, and it became clear that the provision officially offered by the Church of Ireland had become woefully inadequate.

Irish church praise (1990)

What emerged from this, in 1990, was the supplement *Irish church praise*. In the foreword, Archbishop Robin Eames writes: '[P]assing years have produced different attitudes to the ways in which we express our love for God in worship. This book takes account of such developments, and in it you will find hymns from a wide range of different sources.' So, *Irish church praise* included new worship songs; old popular hymns that were 'official' for the first time, like 'Amazing grace', 'Great is thy faithfulness' and 'How great thou art'; new 'four-square' hymns, like 'Christ triumphant' and 'Forth in the peace of Christ we go'; new forms of canticles, like 'Tell out, my soul' and 'Jubilate everybody', and the popular tunes to hymns like 'What a friend we have in Jesus', 'Take my life and let it be', and 'O for a thousand tongues'. After thirty years of solid but starchy hymnody, *Irish church praise* became very popular indeed, and paved the way for the revision of the *Church Hymnal*, which was launched in its fifth edition ten years later, in the year 2000.

Church Hymnal (5th ed., 2000)

The new edition of the *Church Hymnal*, edited by Bishop Edward Darling, with Dr Donald Davison as music editor, heralded the beginning of the new millennium in the Church of Ireland, and was available for the General Synod of that year, meeting in University College Dublin. It is now, like previous editions, more or less ubiquitous in parish churches throughout this island. The committee set

---

12 Geoffrey Beaumont was an Anglican priest, and a member of the Community of the Resurrection at Mirfield. He founded the '20th Century Church Light Music Group' with Patrick Appleford. He died in 1970.   13 E.g. 'Alleluia, alleluia, Give thanks to the risen Lord', 'He is Lord', 'A new commandment I give unto you'.

up by the General Synod to produce this new volume faced a set of interesting issues and challenges that previous compliers did not have to face. First of all, in the last years of the twentieth century, there was a real concern that the days of books were coming to an end. After all, people use leaflets or screens. Was a small church, the size of the Church of Ireland going to have the ability and the number of purchasers to sustain having its own hymnal? Then there was the question of how many editions to produce. The committee concluded, and the General Synod agreed, that there should be two – full music and melody line. The committee had looked at other publications in melody line editions, like *Rejoice and sing* (the hymnal of the United Reformed Church in England), and liked what we saw. It was also thought that many people now have a facility to read a line of music, and that the melody line would assist in worship. The other major question was what about 'thy', 'thou' forms of hymns? – should they all be put into 'you' form?[14] And what about language that is seen as exclusive of women ('men', 'mankind', etc.)?

In relation to the last of those questions – the question of language – the answer arrived at was that each hymn should be treated in its own right. Generally, the words were only changed in a minimal way in well-known hymns, which were in people's memory. The committee did not, for example, attempt to change 'Thine be the glory' to 'Yours is the glory'! Again, with language that was not inclusive of women, a relatively conservative call was made. Language relating to God using the male pronoun would not be changed, but language relating to people would be changed if it could be done seamlessly. Although one or two of the changes made still grate with some ('I thy true heir' in 'Be thou my vision'; 'Pleased as man with us to dwell' in 'Hark! the herald-angels sing' are the main examples), most have been well accepted and many are not even noticed.

The other controversial aspect of the new hymnal proved to be the weight of the book, as the bible paper which was expected was not available at the time of publication. That was a challenge to some, but was ameliorated when the large-print edition became available in words only, and proved exceptionally popular. It was a best-seller!

It is important to note some key factors about the contents of the book, which give it a particular ethos, and have proved popular. First of all, *Church Hymnal* (5th ed., 2000) was given an essentially creedal structure, based around the grace of God in revelation and the faith by which that is received and lived. So, the main contents of the book are in two sections: 'A. The Love of God' and 'B. The Life of Faith'. This is a nuanced and theological approach to worship. The third 'section' is an addendum to the structure, and is specifically 'liturgical material'. Unlike any previous edition of the *Church Hymnal*, the book gives 'windows' into different styles of material, and almost invites people to explore other examples of those styles beyond the book. So, there are songs from different parts of the world;

---

14 The *Irish Presbyterian hymnbook* of 2004 was much more radical and thoroughgoing in its rewriting of material in 'you' form. It makes the *Church Hymnal* of 2000 look pretty conservative.

simple 'choruses'; rounds; worship songs; Taizé chants; plainsong hymns; Iona material; modern hymns set to old tunes; Christmas carols (previously relegated to the back of the book in a separate section); hymns in Irish; Gospel songs; and the list goes on. Much of the rarely used material from the previous edition has been removed, but the key and core 'historic' hymns have been retained. There are also excellent and helpful thematic and biblical indices.

Thanks & praise

The *Church Hymnal* (5th ed.) was never intended to be a complete end in itself. When the committee that compiled the hymnal completed its work, it was concerned that, in a period where creative Christian music was continuing to be written, congregations would be enabled to continue to widen and enhance their repertoire. That led to the production of another supplement, this time called *Thanks & praise* – resonant words from the preface to the Eucharistic prayer. It is available in full music and words editions. I personally had the privilege of editing *Thanks & praise*, with Dr Peter Thompson as music editor. It was launched in 2015, with 227 new items. Although arranged alphabetically, they are ordered in an index according to the creedal structure of *Church Hymnal* (5th ed., Oxford). Again the material is a very wide range of styles, with extra provision for children, and a good deal of new material coming from Irish sources, including Keith Getty. It also includes an enhanced Liturgical section, which includes two Communion settings. *Thanks & praise* has a range of popular old with popular new, and hymns and songs yet to be discovered widely.

Resources for use with Church Hymnal (5th ed.) and Thanks & praise

The number of resources which are available for use alongside the official books is phenomenal. First of all, there is a Braille edition of both books, completed by the Braille unit in Maghaberry Prison, which also provided the Braille edition of the 2004 *Book of Common Prayer*. Then there is recorded church music of a large number of the hymns and songs, available for churches that do not have live music. These are on CDs. Then there is a superb Companion available to each book. The hymnal companion is by bishop Edward Darling, and the companion to the supplement is by Peter Thompson. And finally, Bishop Edward Darling has completed a great labour of love in the 2015 edition of *Sing to the word*, which suggests appropriate hymns and songs from *Church Hymnal* (5th ed.) and *Thanks & praise* for each Sunday of the Christian year, according to the three-year cycle of *The revised common lectionary*.

Singing the Psalms

Another set of musical books that has been produced under the aegis of the Liturgical Advisory Committee is the three volumes of *Singing the Psalms*, in which

Alison Cadden and Peter Thompson have worked together to produce a set of responsorial psalms. There is a general recognition that many churches are finding singing psalms to Anglican chant increasingly challenging, and *Singing the Psalms* is offered as one resource to enable the words of scripture to be sung in their own right in a fresh way. On occasion some of these have been used very powerfully at the Eucharist during General Synod, and I would commend them.

THE BOOK OF COMMON PRAYER (2004)

The wider background: IALCs

As the 1990s progressed, liturgical thinking had moved apace, in a range of different ways. First of all, there had been several international Anglican liturgical consultations (IALCs), since that body had been set up, rather informally, in 1985. It emerged out of a group of Anglicans meeting after they had been participants at Societas Liturgica in Boston,[15] in that year. The subject matter was around the question of whether baptism was full and complete sacramental initiation into the church, which should lead to children receiving Holy Communion. The first I knew of it was when I was invited to attend the first IALC, again made up largely of liturgical scholars who had attended Societas, in Brixen in the north of Italy, in the summer of 1987. I simply loved it, became a member of Societas, and attended, first informally, and later as an official delegate from the Church of Ireland. I participated in seven or eight of the key meetings. In the 1990s, starting from the particular interest developed in Christian Initiation, the IALCs very productively focused on three key areas of liturgical thinking: baptism, Eucharist and ministry. These areas had given the title to the famous World Council of Churches 'Lima document' of 1982, and they were, of course, critical areas in relation to liturgical texts. In the IALC statements after the three key meetings in these areas of study (Toronto in 1991, Dublin in 1995 and Berkeley in 2001), the question of the key elements and understandings of each liturgy were laid out, and a liturgical structure developed. One of the key understandings with regard to baptism was that 'baptism is baptism is baptism' – in other words, there should be essentially one order of baptism whether for infants, children or adults. There was also a new emphasis on the plentifulness of water, whether in submersion or pouring. In the Eucharist, the fivefold structure we now see as normal, with the Gathering of God's People, Proclaiming and Receiving the Word, the Prayers of the People, Celebrating at the Lord's Table and Going out as God's People, was clarified. In ordination, the sense that the liturgy is recognizing a ministry that God has already given, and the role of the whole people of God in ordaining, as well as the distinctive aspects of the three orders of ministry, were emphasized. All our new liturgies in the *Book of Common Prayer* 2004 were written in the light of these consultations, which provided a means of unifying Anglican thinking and liturgical structures throughout the communion.

15 Societas Liturgica is an international, ecumenical society for the study of liturgy.

The wider background: ELLC

After the texts of some of the canticles in the prayer book are the letters 'ELLC'. In the acknowledgments at the back of the book is a paragraph that says 'The English Language Liturgical Consultation (ELLC) for texts excerpted or adapted from *Praying Together* copyright 1988.' The English Language Liturgical Consultation provided ecumenically agreed texts for the key texts which were used in common. For example; texts for the Apostles' and Nicene creeds, for the *Gloria in excelsis*, the *Sanctus* and *Benedictus qui venit* and the Lord's Prayer. These were the texts in essence used by the Roman Catholic Church and the major Protestant denominations, so that the same words were used wherever you were in the English-speaking world. It is sad that, in recent years, the Roman Catholic Church chose to jettison these agreed texts, and make their translations more literal. It is even sadder that this leads to the very first words of a liturgy being confusing. When the president at worship says, 'The Lord be with you', at an ecumenical service, we now have to think as to whether the answer will be 'and also with you' or 'and with your spirit'. The Liturgical Advisory Committee of the Church of Ireland chose, on principle, to adopt ELLC texts, even where we might have preferred them to be different, for the sake of inter-church harmony. The only place where this was changed by General Synod (in my own view wrongly), was in the contemporary version of Lord's Prayer, where 'save us from the time of trial' (ELLC) was changed by an amendment to 'lead us not into temptation'.[16] The Church of England also made the same call.

The wider background: The revised common lectionary

In the period before the finalizing of material for the 2004 prayer book, it had become increasingly clear that we were in need of a more coherent and fulsome 'table of the Word' in our Sunday worship. the *Joint liturgical group lectionary* was increasingly inadequate, and we began to look towards *The revised common lectionary*, which had been completed in 1992, and was finding a large degree of acceptance across the denominations – even in some that had not regularly used a lectionary. This lectionary had its roots in the Roman *Lectionary for Mass* of 1969, but had been developed by Protestant scholars as the *Common lectionary* in the 1980s. It was a three-year lectionary, with Year A being the year of Matthew, Year B being the year of Mark, and Year C being the year of Luke, so that the synoptic Gospels were read in a semi-continuous way. John's Gospel was distributed to be used on high days and holy days, and to fill in gaps in the year of Mark (being the

16 There are some difficulties translating this part of the Lord's Prayer. The problem with 'lead us not into temptation' is that the Letter of James says 'No one, being tempted, should say, "I am being tempted by God", for God cannot be tempted by evil, and he himself tempts no one' (James 1:13). The word in Greek means both testing/trial and tempting, and here it probably means that we are asking the Father to save us from trials that are too great to endure, especially at the end time.

short Gospel). The lectionary had been revised over the years to provide key linked readings in the parts of the year leading into and out of Christmas and Easter, but to provide semi-continuous reading of Old Testament and New Testament passages other than the Gospels, in the ordinary times of the year.

The revised common lectionary was based on a calendar starting on the first Sunday of Advent, had three readings and a psalm for each service, and two possible 'strands': the semi-continuous, which is different at points to the Roman Catholic lectionary, and the paired option, which is largely the same. This lectionary had been used experimentally in the Church of Ireland in the later 1990s, had gained wide approval, and is incorporated into the 2004 prayer book.

The wider background: the Church of England

The Church of England was also tiring of the 1980 *Alternative service book*, and seeking its own way forward into the future. As I have mentioned earlier, the Church of England could not change the *Book of Common Prayer*, except by an act of Parliament, and decided to move forward in a different way, with a series of books called Common Worship, rather than a revised or alternative prayer book. These provide wonderful resources for daily prayer, pastoral situations and seasonal material, but are not generally in the hands of the ordinary worshipper.

The new Church of Ireland Book of Common Prayer

In the Church of Ireland, there was much discussion about a way forward for worship in the new millennium. At one stage, the Liturgical Advisory Committee contemplated a revised service book which, like the *Alternative Prayer Book* would run parallel to the *Book of Common Prayer*. That idea did not gain traction in the General Synod, where it became clear that the church wanted a unifying book that would include both traditional and contemporary services alongside each other – a brand new prayer book, which people could have in their hands, treasure and use privately as well as in public worship. This would be a book that would not bind people into one style or the other, but respect both. The traditional services would stay as they were, and the contemporary services would be revised in the light of modern liturgical thinking. That book, bringing together the best of every world, appeared in 2004, was launched in Armagh Cathedral by Rowan Williams, the archbishop of Canterbury, and has become greatly loved over the last fifteen years. It is produced in a pew version, a presentation version, a large print version, a desk version, an 'altar' version, a Braille version, an Irish version – and in the year 2018 was reprinted in a new edition that includes a new service of Morning and Evening Prayer for use on Sundays. It is the lynchpin of the theology and worship of the Church of Ireland, even if viewed on PowerPoint, printed on bulletins or used for the more informal style of worship allowed by the *Service of the word* structure.

Enriching the seasons

The 'new' service of Morning and Evening Prayer for use on Sundays became available for the first time in print during December 2018. It is a richer form of worship for use on Sundays in the Church of Ireland, with new 'Jewish-style' benedictions (prayers blessing God for who he is and what he has done), a wider provision for penitence, intercession and thanksgiving, and an enhanced proclamation of the Word, with preparatory versicles and responses and new 'collects of the Word'. One of the key aspects of this service is that the general order, for use in ordinary time, is enhanced by the provision of five other 'orders' for use at the key Christological seasons (Advent, Christmas, Epiphany, Lent and Easter). If we are honest, our *Book of Common Prayer* is very limited in its seasonal material, and we have depended very much on material produced by the Church of England to complement it. There is only really one seasonal service in the *BCP* – for Ash Wednesday. I personally produced *Week of all weeks* to provide some more informal provision for Holy Week services, appropriate to the way in which Holy Week is celebrated in the Church of Ireland. So these services, authorized by the House of Bishops for experimental use, are a new departure, and one very much to be welcomed. It is vital that we, as 'church' learn to both lament and rejoice, to prepare and to tell the story, to value and enter into the different seasons of faith in a wholehearted and life-changing way, as the great story of faith becomes our corporate story, and my personal story too.

THE DIFFERENCE IN FIFTY YEARS …

A chapter of this length only allows us to scrape the surface of the phenomenal amount of work that has been done in relation to the worship of the Church of Ireland over the last fifty years. We began with a much more monochrome worship environment, and have moved to worship that is more inculturated into particular contexts. We find a whole range of liturgical styles, with some of the ritualistic fears of the 1870s – or even the 1970s – abated. Even liturgical 'garb' is no longer monochrome. Music in church fifty years ago was simply organ and choir; church architecture assumed Victoriana; the people were rarely involved in the more 'spiritual things', and behaved more passively. We also began in 1969 with a world in which communication was essentially bookish. Now, electronic communication sits alongside the printed word, and can also serve the needs of the kingdom in the sphere of liturgy.[17]

But the real question is this: is our worship forming us as servants of God and disciples of Jesus Christ? If it is only a 'tramping of the courts', as in Isaiah 1, then no liturgy or prayer book can rescue it; but if it is authentic prayer of the gathered believers loving the Lord with all their heart and soul and mind and strength, then it is surely the gateway to heaven.

17 So, we have the Daily Worship app from the Church of Ireland, which allows people to say the daily office on their phone, tablet or computer. Unimaginable fifty years ago!

3

Music in the Church of Ireland

Kerry Houston

Sing psalms and hymns and spiritual songs with thankfulness in your hearts to God.

–Colossians 3:16

Music has been an integral part of the daily life of the church in Ireland since earliest times. Its value as an evangelical tool has been powerfully harnessed – a strong sense of *Bis orat qui bene cantat* (Who sings well prays twice). St Augustine captures this well: 'Singing is for one who loves.'

The rich monastic foundation of the early Irish church resulted in a strong and vibrant chant tradition. Indeed there is considerable evidence of the transmission of chant from Ireland to Britain and continental Europe when Irish monks travelled there, and conversely many of these brought music from overseas back to Ireland. The strong monastic tradition in Ireland also resulted in a diocesan system becoming fully developed rather later here than in Britain and other parts of Europe. When dioceses were established in Ireland, the monastic roots resulted in a large number of small dioceses compared to other countries. Indeed four archbishoprics were established in Ireland while England had just two.[1] Many of the cathedrals were quite small (some very small). The largest of the Irish cathedrals, St Patrick's in Dublin, is medium-sized by English standards. Charles Villiers Stanford described St Patrick's as 'a picturesque building in the pure early English style much resembling its contemporary at Salisbury, but on a far smaller scale'.[2]

The Reformation and the dissolution of the monasteries in Ireland resulted in considerable disruption to music in the church's liturgies. It required new music to be composed in the English language for the services of the *Book of Common*

---

1 The four archbishoprics in Ireland were Armagh, Dublin, Tuam and Cashel. This was reduced to two in the Church of Ireland under the provisions of the Church Temporalities Act (1833) when Armagh and Tuam were united as were Dublin and Cashel. The Roman Catholic Church in Ireland retains the four ancient archbishoprics. 2 Charles Villiers Stanford, *Pages from an unwritten diary* (London, 1914), p. 36. Stanford was born in Dublin but spent most of his career in England. He is best remembered for his sacred compositions for the Anglican Church but currently there is a revival of interest in his contributions to other musical genres.

Prayer as the Latin repertoire that was being used in cathedrals and monasteries was left largely redundant.

Little is known of the function of music in parish churches in Ireland before the Reformation but it is likely that it had a minimal role. Another disruption to the musical life of the church in Ireland came with the Cromwellian interregnum when the *Book of Common Prayer* and the music associated with it was abandoned. The restoration of Charles II in 1660 re-established the *Book of Common Prayer* in worship in Ireland and marked the beginning of a period of relative stability and security for the Church in Ireland and its musicians. The Union with Ireland Act (1800) united the parliaments and churches of Ireland and England 'for ever'.[3] In the case of the church this just lasted until 1 January 1871, when the Church of Ireland was disestablished via the provisions of the Irish Church Act (1869), which dissolved its union with the Church of England.[4]

DISESTABLISHMENT

The Irish Church Act had far-reaching implications for the church and its musicians. Most of the endowments that had been in place for centuries were removed. Revd Edward Seymour, precentor of Christ Church Cathedral, declared 'this was the darkest period of misfortune the old cathedral has ever seen – this act of the legislature reduced it to a hopeless state of poverty and degradation from which it seemed useless even to attempt to raise it'.[5] Mrs Cecil Frances (Fanny) Alexander, best remembered for hymns such as 'Once in royal David's city', addressed disestablishment in one of her less well known hymns: 'Fallen, fallen, fallen is now our country's crown, *Dimly dawns the New Year on a churchless nation*, Ammon and Amalek tread our borders down.'

The reactions of Fanny Alexander and Edward Seymour proved to be too pessimistic and indeed disestablishment was a catalyst for some imaginative schemes to support music in the newly disestablished church. Two pertinent examples are the Guinness Choir scheme at St Patrick's Cathedral and the Roe endowment at Christ Church Cathedral.[6]

The place of music in worship in the Church of Ireland outside the cathedral foundations was not firmly grounded until the decades immediately before disestablishment. Before that, there is little evidence of systematic musical activities in churches outside the larger urban areas – very few churches had organs until

---

3 The act is available online at www.legislation.gov.uk/apgb/Geo3/39-40/67/contents. 4 The act is available online at www.irishstatutebook.ie/eli/1869/act/42/enacted/en/html. 5 John Skelton Bumpus, 'Irish church composers and the Irish cathedrals', *Proceedings of the Musical Association*, 26 (1899–1900), p. 151. 6 For more information on the Guinness scheme see Kerry Houston, 'Guinness is good for you' in Kerry Houston, Maria McHale and Michael Murphy (eds), *Documents of Irish music history in the long nineteenth century* (Dublin, 2019), pp 224–38. More information on the Roe scheme may be found in Barra Boydell, *A history of music at Christ Church Cathedral, Dublin* (Woodbridge, 2014), pp 173–5.

the late nineteenth century. It is significant to note that the constitution of the Church of Ireland does not address the role of music in the church or of its church musicians.

For the church and its musicians, the first hundred years of disestablishment presented other challenges, including the home rule movement, two world wars and the establishment of the Irish Free State (later the Republic of Ireland). This period saw some retrenchment in the church, with waning influence, falling membership and less financial security. However, pragmatism at many levels ensured that the musical heritage of the church continued and in many cases thrived.

MUSIC IN THE CHURCH OF IRELAND 100 YEARS AFTER DISESTABLISHMENT

The centenary of the disestablishment of the church is a pertinent starting point for discussion here. How did the political, social and religious events in both Northern Ireland and the Republic of Ireland affect music in the church? How will these factors continue to impact on music in the church in the future? These are complex questions as the changes were not uniform throughout the country.

Urban development (especially in Dublin) resulted in many church members moving from city-centre dwellings to the new suburbs. This gave rise to strong growth in congregations in what were to become suburban churches which were originally built for smaller rural congregations. Inner city churches suffered from sharply declining congregations. In many cases churches that had strong choral traditions and were equipped with large good-quality organs saw decline while smaller suburban churches that were not really designed for large-scale musical activity were finding growing congregations.

The pattern in the northern dioceses of the church was a little different, as numbers were stronger and the decline in the traditional parish choir was not as marked. However, contemporary worship-song-style of music and praise bands gained popularity there more quickly than in southern dioceses.

THE CATHEDRAL TRADITION

Thirty Church of Ireland cathedrals remain open in 2019. The bishop of Cashel, Ferns and Ossory has no less than six cathedrals in his united dioceses. There are a few exceptions to the traditional pattern: the diocese of Clogher has two cathedrals dedicated to St Macartan – one in Clogher and one (spelt Macartin) in Enniskillen; Belfast Cathedral is a cathedral for both the united dioceses of Down and Dromore and the diocese of Connor; and St Patrick's Cathedral in Dublin is a national cathedral with representatives on the chapter drawn from every diocese in Ireland. The musical establishments at these cathedrals vary greatly. The largest provide fully professional choirs and organists, while others have a semi-professional foundation and some cathedrals in rural settings operate primarily as parish churches. It is not possible to detail the activity of every cathedral here so a representative selection is presented.

William Sydney Greig was organist of St Patrick's Cathedral, Dublin from 1960 until 1976 and was just the third organist to hold the post in the previous hundred years.[7] Harry Grindle has commented that Greig 'seems to have been content for the most part to maintain the tradition as he inherited it'.[8] Indeed the maintenance of tradition was a hallmark of the Church of Ireland for much of the twentieth century, when it felt somewhat under threat as a small minority church in many parts of the country. St Patrick's was one of many places that jealously guarded its inherited past.

When I was a chorister at St Patrick's in the 1970s, my memories are of great contrasts. We sang matins and evensong every day (but with no evensong on Saturdays), often to an almost empty cathedral – sometimes completely empty apart from the choir and clergy. The cathedral was very cold in winter, with very few lights turned on. We were provided with thick cloaks to put over our robes to keep us warm(ish). I often wondered why we kept this daily routine. Part of the reason was religious devotion, but another part was a determination to cling on to a centuries-old heritage.

In contrast to these somewhat dreary weekday services, there were great state occasions such as the service preceding the inauguration of Erskine Childers as fourth president of Ireland (1973) and, just seventeen months later, his state funeral. These were attended by heads of state from all over the world.[9] Evensong on the eve of the opening of the General Synod and the Christmas Eve carol service were always impressive occasions.

The Christmas Eve carol service is the longest running annual broadcast on Raidió Teilifís Éireann. It followed a pattern similar to carol services in many other parts of the world but there were some items that were peculiar to St Patrick's. First, the Advent season was acknowledged by the singing of the introit 'Drop down ye heavens' to a curious anonymous setting. The '*Magnificat*' was sung at the opening of the service (to a unison chant again of unknown origin) and Charles Wesley's Christmas hymn 'Hark the herald' was paired with the tune *Judas Maccabaeus* despite the difficulty in making Wesley's words fit Handel's tune. An elaborate fanfare for trumpets, timpani and organ precedes the opening verse of the hymn.

Another musical peculiarity at St Patrick's was the inclusion of two anthems at Sunday evensong. The second of these was usually an extended verse anthem.

7 Charles Marchant had been organist of St Patrick's from 1879 to 1920 and he had been succeeded by George Hewson, who held the post from 1920 to 1960. For more information on this see Kerry Houston, 'From Marchant to Greig: a seamless thread through an uncertain terrain' in Kerry Houston and Harry White (eds), *A musical offering: essays in honour of Gerard Gillen* (Dublin, 2018), pp 178–92.   8 W.H. Grindle, *Irish cathedral music* (Belfast, 1989), p. 122.   9 For details of state funerals at St Patrick's see Kerry Houston, 'Two state funerals: windows into Irish religious, political and social life' in Salvador Ryan (ed.), *Death and the Irish: a miscellany* (Dublin, 2016), pp 223–6.

The historic reason for the inclusion of a second anthem was to ensure that the congregation remained to hear the sermon and also to be present for the collection hymn. This elaborate evensong on Sundays resulted in it being referred to colloquially as 'Paddy's opera' – a tradition that continued until the end of the twentieth century.[10]

Sydney Greig expanded the repertoire at St Patrick's somewhat with the introduction of music by composers such as Benjamin Britten and Herbert Howells. More contemporary repertoire was introduced by his successors John Dexter, Peter Barley and Stuart Nicholson.

In addition to maintaining the traditional cathedral choir of boys and men, St Patrick's established a girls' choir, as is the case in many other cathedrals in Ireland. The repertoire of the choir at St Patrick's often includes compositions and arrangements by the musicians working there.

Just a few hundred yards from St Patrick's, Christ Church Cathedral also supports a healthy musical tradition. However, the first few years under discussion here were rather bleak at Christ Church. While St Patrick's had been able to retain its choir school (now the only choir school in Ireland), declining numbers had resulted in the closure of the choir school at Christ Church in 1972.[11] Daily choral matins was sung at Christ Church until 1976 along with its sister cathedral St Patrick's – now St Patrick's is the only cathedral in the world to continue to sing this daily office. After the closure of the choir school, Christ Church boys attended St Patrick's Cathedral school but the writing was on the wall – the boys' choir was in terminal decline. Women were introduced to bolster the treble line. There was just one boy left in choir by the time Peter Sweeney was appointed organist in 1981. Sweeney rebuilt the musical establishment with considerable success on a new model – that of an all-adult choir. He also spearheaded the replacement of the existing but very dilapidated and inappropriately 'improved and enlarged' cathedral organ with a fine new instrument in an imposing new case in 1984. Sweeney's pioneering work has been built upon by his successors, Mark Duley, Judy Martin and Ian Keatley. Various configurations of staffing the choir were tested and now the choir is a combination of vicars choral and choral scholars. There is also a girls' choir and a sub group of the main cathedral choir styled the 'cathedral consort'. Both Christ Church and St Patrick's offer choral scholarship schemes to encourage university students to sing at the liturgies. This is replicated at other cathedrals around the country.

Harry Grindle took the helm as organist at St Anne's Cathedral, Belfast in 1964.[12] His predecessor Charles (Captain) Brennan had held the post for the previous sixty years. Brennan was the first organist of the newly built cathedral so he did not inherit a traditional male-only cathedral choir model. The rather unusual

---

10 For a detailed description of this service see Stanford, *Pages*, pp 36–7.   11 The choir school at Christ Church had been founded in 1480, while that at St Patrick's traces its roots to 1432.   12 St Anne's Cathedral, Belfast has the unusual position of being a cathedral for the diocese of Connor and the united dioceses of Down and Dromore with both bishops holding seats in the cathedral.

make-up of the cathedral choir at St Anne's seems to have been based on Brennan's personal preferences. This resulted in a choir of boy trebles and adult sopranos and contraltos with adult men providing the tenor and bass parts of the choir. It was a large choir (more than fifty voices at some times). This configuration was probably unique in the Anglican Communion. Harry Grindle's tenure at St Anne's encompassed the most challenging times of the Troubles, but he maintained and developed a very strong cathedral tradition and guided the cathedral choir to a model closer to what would be found in most Anglican cathedrals. He established regular BBC broadcasts, including the iconic BBC Radio 3 choral evensong. An imaginative initiative from St Anne's came with the establishment of an ecumenical cross-community choir school. This is a virtual choir school in the sense that it does not have any buildings or physical infrastructure. Singing coaches from the cathedral provide vocal tuition in three schools: Edenbrooke Primary, Sacred Heart Boys' Primary and Cliftonville Integrated School. Some of the students progress to become members of the cathedral choir.

Other northern cathedrals suffered as a result of the Troubles but maintained their choral traditions. The strongest of these were St Columb's Cathedral, Derry and St Patrick's Cathedral, Armagh, which maintain a traditional cathedral choir model. St George's Church, Belfast has preserved a strong musical traditional also.

Another cathedral that has a thriving choral foundation is St Fin Barre's Cathedral, Cork. The boys' choir was re-established by Andrew Padmore, who inherited a very small adult choir when he succeeded Jonathan (Jock) Horne, who had been cathedral organist from 1922 until 1977. This tradition has been continued by his successors Colin Nicholls, Malcolm Wisener and Peter Stobart. There is a flourishing girls' choir also, who participate fully in the cathedral's liturgies. The cathedral now supports an extensive diocesan music outreach project.[13]

DIOCESAN DEVELOPMENTS

In addition to initiatives on a church-wide basis, such as the provision of hymnals and revised liturgies, many dioceses established schemes to suit their local needs. These vary greatly in different parts of the island and include choral festivals, organ teaching schemes and courses for choir directors. (I am greatly indebted to David McConnell for clarifying much of the material below referring to the Joint Committee for Church Music in Ireland and related projects.)

Choral festivals had become a prominent feature in the Church of Ireland from the late nineteenth century. These were normally organized on a diocesan basis, but in larger centres there were also choral unions based around clusters of parishes. Festival booklets were published which contained liturgies with accompanying responses, psalms, canticle settings, hymns and anthems. The first known book was

13 United Dioceses of Cork, Cloyne and Ross, 'Diocesan Church Music Scene', cork.anglican.org/dcms.

published in 1888. The Church of Ireland Choral Union (CICU) was established in 1947 to provide mutual support for choral unions in Ireland and to coordinate the publication of choral-union festival books. A parallel development in the second half of the twentieth century was the affiliation of many parishes in Ireland to the Royal School of Church Music (RSCM).[14] By the mid-1960s the RSCM recognized its growth in membership in Ireland by the appointment of a 'special commissioner' – Donald Leggatt – who was on the staff of the music department of Campbell College, Belfast. The number of churches becoming affiliated to the RSCM continued to increase, reaching 165 by 1984.

As the work of the CICU and the RSCM had many overlaps and intersections, the two bodies agreed to form a type of coalition via the establishment of the Joint Committee for Church Music in Ireland (JCCMI). This was formed in 1976, with eight representatives from each body. The committee had two co-chairmen – one from each body. The first were Bishop Edwin Owen (CICU) and Revd Canon Sterling Mortimer (RSCM) with Mr David McConnell as the honorary secretary. While the CICU was firmly based in the Church of Ireland, the RSCM is not a denominational body, although the strongest representation tended to come from the Church of Ireland. The disparity of the two bodies prevented the coalition from becoming a marriage. The committee reported annually to its two parent bodies. Although the JCCMI was relatively short-lived (it was disbanded in 2000), it acquired considerable traction and gained the support of many younger parish musicians. It filled a lacuna in the provision of basic liturgical and musical information and training for parish musicians. This was largely provided in the form of one-day courses for 'reluctant organists' in rural venues, and supported by annual tours of Ireland by RSCM staff. The committee produced a newsletter three or four times a year. This newsletter was distributed to all Church of Ireland musicians in the greater Dublin area and to musicians nationwide working in churches affiliated to the RSCM.

JCCMI received financial support from diocesan councils and an annual subsidy was negotiated with the RSCM. It also attracted some private donations. Significantly, just as the constitution of the Church of Ireland does not address musical matters, the first report of the Priorities Fund of the Church of Ireland did not consider music either. However, the importance of the work of the JCCMI was recognized via a loan from the Priorities Fund to cover initial cash-flow needs.

The CICU continued its function of publishing choral festival books about once every two years, with active input from the JCCMI as regards the choice of music. These choral festival books were produced up to 1989. However liturgical reform with more flexible, informal and less structured worship made the demand for the type of material being provided by the CICU less

---

14 The Royal School of Church Music was founded in 1927 to support church music in England, but later it expanded to incorporate an international remit. While it was securely based in the Church of England in its early days, it now has a strong ecumenical profile.

relevant in many situations. Modern-language liturgies resulted in some of the music published by CICU becoming somewhat obsolete. The sort of 'half-way house' between full cathedral-style sung liturgies and parish liturgies that was supported by the CICU lost ground and the demand for choral festival books collapsed quite suddenly after 1990. In the early 1960s, as many as 3,500 books were distributed annually. This had reduced to just over 1,000 by the late 1980s. The CICU was effectively without a purpose. General meetings were held annually until November 1995. The final AGM took place in Overseas House (Rathmines, Dublin) on 7 November 1998, which was the catalyst for the disbanding of JCCMI. The JCCMI newsletter had continued, but its publication was increasingly irregular – the final issue was in 1998.[15] The initial energy of the JCCMI had waned and the committee formally wound itself up at a meeting in Dublin in April 2000. Other arrangements for supporting parish music were already being considered and led to the establishment of RSCM Ireland in 2002 and the appointment of a part-time coordinator.

In parallel to the JCCMI, the prominent Belfast-based church musician and hymnologist Dr Donald Davison was pivotal in the setting up of the relatively short-lived Ulster Church Music Centre. Based in St John's Church, Malone Road in Belfast, it provided training for organists and published newsletters.

The JCCMI undertook a nationwide survey in 1985. One of the outcomes of this survey was the publication of a collection of seventy-five simplified accompaniments edited by Dr Edgar (Billy) Boucher. Sadly, most of the stock was destroyed by a flooding incident before the volume was circulated widely. However a new venture in this vein is available on the Church Music Dublin website.[16]

An enquiry from the diocesan councils of Dublin and Glendalough in June 1988 about the shortage of parish-church organists was the catalyst for the JCCMI to compile a very significant and insightful report in 1990: *Silent worship? A report on music in the Church of Ireland, with some recommendations for the future*.[17] This tantalizingly titled report addressed pertinent issues facing church musicians in 1990 and many of these remain very relevant almost thirty years later. The report is both factual and philosophical. It is also very future-orientated and made shrewd and discerning recommendations. Unfortunately, *Silent worship* does not seem to have been circulated widely, which is perhaps part of the reason that its impact was limited.

Key recommendations of *Silent worship* include the establishment of diocesan organ scholarship schemes, the formation of diocesan music committees, with the appointment of full-time professional diocesan music advisers and the

---

15 A full set of newsletters (1976–98) is deposited in the RCB Library. There are also copies (1976–84) at Trinity College Dublin and the National Library of Ireland.   16 Dioceses of Dublin and Glendalough, 'Simple accompaniments', www.churchmusicdublin.org/simple-accompaniments. 17 The cost of producing this report was supported by the Diocesan Councils of Dublin and Glendalough. The text is available at www.churchmusicdublin.org/silent-worship.

establishment of diocesan organ advisory committees. It also recommended that the General Synod Boards of Education should be asked to promote music teaching in all schools in their jurisdiction, including organ teaching.

Regrettably, most of these recommendations have not been implemented or have been implemented only in part. Organ scholarship schemes are mainly centred on the cathedrals and some universities. Outside this, the most developed scheme is that operating in the united dioceses of Dublin and Glendalough, where a combination of diocesan and parish funds are used to support the training of organists for the archbishop's certificate in church music.[18] This training is organized by a diocesan church music committee, which later adopted the title Church Music Dublin. Other dioceses have developed schemes tailored to suit local situations.

The lack of any centralized oversight of the maintenance and refurbishment of organs has been particularly problematic. The Church of Ireland is the custodian of many organs of considerable historic importance but a lack of expert advice on how to address the challenges of this stewardship has resulted in some very inappropriate restorations or refurbishments under the guises of 'improvements' or 'enlargements'. In many other cases, organs of artistic merit have been neglected or abandoned. State support for historic organs, which is available in other countries, is available only in very limited ways in Ireland.[19] Sadly, contracts for work on some of these organs have been awarded to builders with little experience in dealing with historic instruments. This has not been a result of any wilful vandalism by select vestries (or indeed by the organ builders), but a result of lack of expertise in this very specialized area. The appointment of diocesan or even national organ advisor(s) could have alleviated this continuing problem. However, significant historic restorations and installations of major new instruments of a high quality have taken place in churches including St Patrick's Cathedral, Dublin; Christ Church Cathedral, Dublin; St Fin Barre's Cathedral, Cork; Christ Church Cathedral, Waterford; St Canice's Cathedral, Kilkenny; St Bartholomew's Church, Dublin; St Patrick's Cathedral, Armagh; St Columb's Cathedral, Derry; Down Cathedral and St George's Church, Belfast.

Silent worship identifies many of the possible reasons for a shortage of church organists including changes of lifestyle making a regular Sunday commitment unattractive, the poor quality of many church organs and inadequate level of maintenance,[20] lack of proper salary structures, pressure to perform music of poor quality (including hymns and songs of a trivial or superficial nature). *Silent*

---

18 Details of this scheme may be found at www.churchmusicdublin.org. 19 An example of an organ-restoration project that has been sensitively handled is the case of St Fintan's Church in Durrow, Co. Laoise. This church is custodian of the Samuel Greene organ, which had been built for the chapel of Trinity College Dublin in 1798 and moved to Durrow in 1842. A staged restoration has taken place with assistance from the Heritage Council. 20 Many parish-church organs were built in the late nineteenth century and the first part of the twentieth century and are of a very undistinguished quality.

worship's recommendation that these problems be addressed has been heeded only in some churches. This has been uneven and generally confined to larger urban areas. One important initiative was the drawing up of recommended remuneration scales for parish-church musicians, which was spearheaded by Church Music Dublin. Agreed scales are now published regularly in conjunction with the Advisory Committee on Church Music of the Roman Catholic Episcopal Commission for Liturgy.[21]

One of the recommendations with regard to the building up of church choirs was the introduction of choral scholarship schemes and the support of existing junior choirs with the establishment of junior choirs in parishes where they had not existed.[22] This has happened in only very few parishes but where such schemes have been introduced they have proved very successful in attracting younger members to church choirs and providing the basis for many who will make a long term commitment to church music.

HYMNS AND PSALMS (AND SPIRITUAL SONGS)

While the singing of hymns and worship songs is a central part of services in most parish churches today, this is a relatively new development in the larger chronological history of the church. In the immediate post-restoration period, metrical psalms were permitted (in the church), and by the eighteenth century hymns that were not metrical psalms or biblical paraphrases were being added. An important milestone was the publication of a metrical psalter in London in 1696. This was the work of two Irishmen, Nahum Tate (1652–1715) and Nicholas Brady (1659–1726).[23] This book was widely used in churches of the Church of Ireland that had a musical element in their services. Indeed it was often bound together with the *Book of Common Prayer*. However no hymnal or metrical psalter was published as an official Church of Ireland hymnal until the immediate pre-disestablishment period. *Hymns for public worship* was produced by the Association for the Promotion of Christian Knowledge in 1856. This was followed by the first edition of the *Church Hymnal* in 1864, which went through several editions with supplements. A strong representation of cathedral musicians on the editorial boards of these hymnals is notable.[24]

The chief hymnal in use in the Church of Ireland during the last forty years of the twentieth century was the fourth edition of the *Church Hymnal*, which was published in 1960. It contained 164 hymns that had not been present in the previous edition. George Hewson (1881–1972) was the musical editor of this

---

21 Dioceses of Dublin and Glendalough, 'Remuneration', www.churchmusicdublin.org/fee-guidelines. 22 The report emphasises the importance of teaching junior choirs how to read music and not to sing by rote. 23 Nahum Tate provided the libretto for the centenary ode for Trinity College Dublin, 'Great parent, hail!', composed by Henry Purcell (1659–95). 24 The most important of these were Robert Prescott Stewart, Charles Marchant, Charles Kitson and George Hewson.

handsomely produced volume. Hewson's personal tastes may be seen in the book – particularly his choice of relatively high keys for some of the tunes, which made them rather more suited to trained cathedral singers than general church congregations.[25] Indeed Hewson makes reference to the choice of keys in the preface of the hymnal:

> The keys of some hymns have been altered ... It should be borne in mind that lowering the pitch may have a bad effect and ruin the character of a melody. The 'Old Hundredth' and 'Hanover' both lose their life and vibrancy if not sung in the key of A major.[26]

There are instances of the tunes of some hymns in this book soaring to F on the top line of the treble clef and even G – beyond the capability of most congregations. The inclusion of chorales harmonizations of J.S. Bach is perhaps a result of Hewson's professorial role at Trinity College. Bach's harmonizations are highly valued for academic study. Most of these harmonizations are to be found in the section of the book marked 'chiefly for the use of choirs'.

The hymnal contains 688 hymns, with a Christmas carol section at the back containing 31 carols. There is also a small section entitled 'Hymns from ancient Irish sources'.[27] These hymns include texts attributed to St Columba and St Patrick as well as other early Irish writers. The tunes include some by Charles Wood,[28] Revd John Purser Shortt,[29] George Hewson and Thomas R.G. Jozé, together with arrangements of Irish traditional tunes by George Hewson, Leopold Dix, Charles Kitson, Charles Wood and Charles Villiers Stanford.

The carol section has a strong Irish flavour also, with tunes composed by Revd Frederick James Powell[30] and Johnathan (Jock) T. Horne,[31] and arrangements of tunes by Charles Wood, George Hewson, Charles Kitson together with carols whose primary sources are in the libraries of Trinity College, Dublin and St Patrick's Cathedral, Dublin. An interesting feature of the 1960 hymnal is the care

---

25 The hymnal was published just as Hewson was retiring from the post of organist of St Patrick's Cathedral in Dublin, which he had held since 1920. Interestingly, the previous edition of the *Church Hymnal* was published in 1919 under the joint musical editorship of Charles Kitson, who was to resign from the post of organist of Christ Church Cathedral in the following year, and Charles Marchant, who died in office as organist of St Patrick's in the same year.   26 *Church Hymnal* (Dublin, 1960), p. xi.   27 The second edition of the *Church Hymnal* (1915) was the first to include a section with this title – during the First World War and on the eve of the 1916 Rising.   28 Charles Wood was born in 1866 in Armagh, where his father was a lay vicar at the cathedral. He spent his professional career in England and his compositions include a large amount of Anglican church music. An annual church music summer school is held in Armagh – the Charles Wood Summer School.   29 Purser Short was a canon of St Patrick's Cathedral, Dublin from 1933 until his death in 1966.   30 This tune is used for words penned by H.F. Selwood Lindsay, who published a biography of David Wilson (dean of St Patrick's Cathedral, Dublin 1935–50). Wilson was responsible for the introduction of the annual festival of nine lessons and carols in St Patrick's.   31 Horne was organist of St Fin Barre's Cathedral, Cork 1922–77, having been organist of St Canice's Cathedral Kilkenny before that.

that was taken to distinguish between Christmas carols and Christmas hymns. In the Christmas hymn section, two items that had been in the carol section of the previous hymnal were transferred to the hymn section in the 1960 book, while one item from the hymn section of the previous hymnal was now placed in the carol section. More than half of the expanded carol section of the 1960 hymnal is comprised of carols that had not been included in the previous hymnal. Another indication of the care that the editorial board gave to this matter is revealed in the placement of Fanny Alexander's hymn 'Once in royal David's city'. This does not appear in either the Christmas hymn section or with the Christmas carols but in the section 'Hymns for children'. The editors state in the preface that the hymns in this sections are 'intended for the use of young children under the age of ten'.[32] The placement of 'Once in royal David's city' in this section is quite correct as Alexander envisaged this hymn as an evangelical tool and published it as part of her 1848 collection 'Hymns for little children'. This fine 1960 hymnal did not undergo a comprehensive revision until the publication of the fifth edition in 2000.

The latter part of the twentieth century saw a great increase in interest in hymn writing, often referred to as the 'hymn explosion'. Liturgical reforms allowed more flexibility in services, which suited more contemporary hymn styles and worship songs. While the 1960 hymnal remained the official hymn book of the Church of Ireland, some parishes had started to use other hymnals such as *Hymns for today*[33] and *Mission praise.* The use of these supplementary books indicated that the 1960 hymnal now required a supplement. This came in the form of *Irish church praise*, which was published in 1990 containing 146 hymns. These were a mixture of traditional hymns that had not been included in the 1960 hymnal, and contemporary worship-song-style hymns. As a response to liturgical reforms, *Irish church praise* contained metrical versions of the canticles contained in the *Alternative Prayer Book* (1984). Significantly, it included four hymns with Irish-language texts (and alternative English translations). Until this point there had been no hymns in Irish in the main hymn books in use in the Church of Ireland but an Irish-language hymnal, *Leabhar Iomann*, was in use, containing seventy-seven hymns. However, this volume suffered from the use of the *seanchló* (old typeface), which was falling out of use and was no longer taught in schools. Younger generations found this older script difficult to read. *Sing and pray* was issued in 1990 and designed for use in Sunday schools and primary schools. It was edited by Dr Harry Grindle, former organist of St Anne's Cathedral Belfast and head of music at what is now Stranmillis University College, Belfast.[34]

Irish church praise was intended as an interim measure until a full comprehensive revision of the 1960 *Church Hymnal* could be undertaken. This journey started in 1994 when the General Synod set up a Hymnal Revision Committee.

32 *Church Hymnal*, p. ix. 33 The House of Bishops authorized the use of this hymnal in 1983. 34 Harry Grindle's hymn tune '*Stranmillis*', a prize-winner in the St Paul's Cathedral Millennium Hymn Competition, is included in *St Paul's Cathedral hymnal* (London).

Bishop Edward Darling was appointed chairman and Dr Donald Davison music editor. The landscape of the Church of Ireland had changed rapidly since the publication of the 1960 book, so a radical approach was required to address new circumstances that had emerged from liturgical reform and a wide spectrum of churchmanship.

A pragmatic approach was adopted for the preparation of a new edition of the *Church Hymnal*. A church-wide survey was conducted to investigate how frequently the existing hymns were actually used. The aim was to retain all that was good in the existing hymnal but to embrace new material. In many cases small alterations to the language of some older hymns were adapted where the original language was considered to be archaic, obsolete or gender exclusive. Reflecting the decline in the use of Anglican chant, considerable new material was added to the 2000 revision to be used as alternative ways of singing texts that had traditionally been sung to that chant. This included material for the singing of canticles and music for use for liturgical texts of the Eucharist. Thirteen hymns with texts in the Irish language (and English translations) were incorporated, taking the lead from *Irish church praise*. Another new feature was the inclusion of descants for some hymns, which are suitable for churches with good choirs. The fifth edition of the hymnal is marked by a scholarly as well as a liturgically sensitive approach. Verses from hymns that had been omitted from previous editions were restored, in many cases giving the option of including them or not as desirable.

Five years after the publication of the 2000 *Church Hymnal*, a comprehensive companion was produced by Bishop Edward Darling and Dr Donald Davison.[35] No comprehensive companion had accompanied earlier editions of the *Church Hymnal*, so this meticulously researched companion (larger than the hymnal itself) is a vital resource for clergy, church musicians and others who wish to discover more about the texts and music presented in the 2000 hymnal. It is also an invaluable aid for marrying the themes of hymns to the church's liturgical year.

As with earlier editions of the *Church Hymnal*, there were calls for further publications. A supplement to the fifth edition of the *Church Hymnal* came in the form of *Thanks & praise* (2015) edited by Revd Dr Peter Thompson and Mrs Alison Cadden. This supplement restores some hymns that had been omitted from the 2000 hymnal together with more contemporary hymns, more liturgical items and some additional Irish hymns.[36]

While the *Church Hymnal* and *Thanks & praise* provide a rich resource for the church, they are primarily intended for churches where there is an organist or praise band to lead the worship. This is not always the case in more rural communities. Rather than leaving worship in these churches devoid of music, the church has supported a recorded church music scheme to fill this gap. The origins of this initiative lie with Bishop Arthur Butler when he was bishop of the

35 Edward Darling and Donald Davison, *Companion to Church Hymnal* (Dublin, 2005).   36 Edward Darling has also published *Sing to the word* (Dublin, 2015).

sparsely populated diocese of Tuam in the 1950s. He proposed the use of recorded music for hymns, psalms and canticles in churches where no organist was available. A choir was formed to make recordings of the most popular hymns together with psalms and canticles, accompanied by Revd Victor Dungan on organ. These first recordings were produced on 45 rpm gramophone vinyl. The introduction of the *Alternative Prayer Book* in 1984 created a need for further recordings and the bank of recorded music available continued to increase. The publication of the 2000 hymnal was a further catalyst for recordings. The medium of reproduction has changed to cassette tape, CD and mini-disk.

PSALMODY

The Second Vatican Council sat from 1962 to 1965 and introduced radical changes to centuries-old liturgies in the Roman Catholic Church. The most radical change was the replacement of Latin with vernacular languages. The 1960s marked the start of liturgical review in the Church of Ireland also. Until then, the version of the *Book of Common Prayer* being used in the Church of Ireland was very close to the 1662 version. The General Synod established the liturgical advisory committee in 1962 to examine desirable modifications or revisions to the existing prayer book. The first fruit of this committee's work was the introduction of an alternative Eucharistic liturgy in 1967. After much more work, the *Alternative Prayer Book* was completed in 1984. A further development was the publication of *Alternative occasional services* in 1993. Further work resulted in these strands being drawn together into a new edition of the *Book of Common Prayer*, which was authorized for use from Trinity Sunday 2004.

While the liturgical changes had a powerful impact on hymnody, they were even more profound in the case of psalmody and the canticles. These are formal parts of the authorized liturgies of the church. While hymns have allocated places in the liturgy, their actual contents are not formal parts of the liturgy.

The principal way of singing psalms in the Church of Ireland in the second half of the twentieth century was Anglican chant. While the canticles were normally sung to through composed settings in the larger cathedrals, Anglican chant was used to sing the canticles in most parish churches. Merbecke's communion service was widely used in the Church of Ireland. Merbecke's 1550 composition was the first musical setting of the Eucharist after the Reformation. It is in *The Irish chant book* (Dublin, 1938), which also includes a Eucharistic setting by Sir Robert Prescott Stewart, 'revised for use in parish churches'.[37] In addition to these settings of the Responses to the Commandments, Creed, Sanctus and Gloria (in its 1662 placement at the end of the Eucharist) the book has seventeen further settings of the Responses to the Commandments.

---

37 Stewart's tenure at Christ Church Dublin from 1844 to 1894 included a decade as organist at St Patrick's Cathedral. He was also professor of music at Trinity College Dublin.

This very comprehensive collection contains 781 chants. These are divided into chants for the psalms of the day, morning and evening, as set out in the *Book of Common Prayer*, and also chants for the psalms proper to each Sunday and to major feasts. The book has more than 100 composers represented, including Irish composers L.L. Dix, G.H.P. Hewson, J.T. Horne, J.T. Huggard, T.R.G. Jozé, J.C. Marks, John Robinson, Joseph Robinson, R. Roseingrave, J. Stevenson, C.G. Marchant, C.V. Stanford, R.P. Stewart, G. Walsh, G. Wesley (earl of Mornington and father of the duke of Wellington) and R. Woodward.

The comprehensiveness of this collection is an indication of the very wide-spread use of Anglican chant in the Church of Ireland in the twentieth century, but the fact that there has been no revision of this chant book since 1938 is also a reflection of how the use of Anglican chant has diminished considerably in the Church of Ireland in recent decades. In some cases this has resulted in the psalms being said or sung in metrical versions that are well represented in the hymnal. However the language of many of these metrical settings is somewhat outdated – fresher metrical interpretations might gain more traction.

A pointed psalter is included in the *Book of Common Prayer* (2004), which is an advantage over earlier editions where the psalter was not pointed. This makes the use of Anglican chant a little easier in places where there is not a large choir. Interestingly, the translation is that from *Common worship* rather than Coverdale's translation from previous prayer books which creates a rather uneasy marriage of words when used in the context of Morning and Evening Prayer One.[38]

Many parishes are now using alternative ways of singing the psalms, including responsorial psalm singing. There is substantial evidence that this type of psalm singing was used in the early church. Two members of the Liturgical Advisory Committee, Mrs Alison Cadden and Revd Dr Peter Thompson, have produced a very attractive responsorial setting of the psalms in *Singing psalms*, which is adaptable for various situations, including those where there is no choir available.

With a view to facilitating parish choirs wishing to sing psalms to Anglican chant, in 2019 Church Music Dublin began considering a project that will enable each Sunday's psalm, with a well-known chant, to be available online.

CONCLUSION

Ireland has probably experienced more change in the years 1969–2019 than in any other comparable period in history. The globalization of the planet with mass and instant communication and increasing migration has affected all aspects of society. The church and its musicians have seen the challenges and opportunities that these new situations have presented. The traditional patterns of music in cathedrals and parish churches have changed quite dramatically. In the case of the larger

---

38 The text of the psalms in the 1928 *Book of Common Prayer* incorporated some very minor alterations to Coverdale's translation.

cathedrals, greatly enhanced financial resources have been provided, and profes-sional structures and staff models are in place.[39] A number of cathedral choirs travel extensively and have busy recording and broadcasting schedules in addition to the provision of music at weekly (and in some cases daily) liturgies. In contrast, music in the smaller cathedrals has tended to decline somewhat, and many parish churches that supported robed choirs with regular choir practices have found it increasingly difficult to maintain this due to so many competing secular activities. It is particularly difficult for parish choirs to attract younger members.

The paucity of references to music and musicians in Church of Ireland liturgi-cal documents mentioned above is also reflected in the very sparse instructions relating to music in the *Book of Common Prayer*. This is in stark contrast to the Roman Missal, which has detailed musical instructions.

Despite challenges, church music has remained vibrant in the Church of Ireland, if in a greater complexion of manifestations. In the more evangelical parishes, praise bands and informal types of music-making attract considerable support – much of the material used is of a high musical quality. Notwithstanding larger parish churches producing service sheets for Sunday worship, an appetite for new printed hymnals has not dampened — there is no sign that this appeal is to wane in the near future. New ways of singing the psalms have been introduced so that they may still be sung in parishes that have meagre musical resources.

A musical opportunity that has not yet been addressed comprehensively is that of cultural diversity. Ireland is a rich multi-cultural society but, to date, there is very little music from non-European or North American sources in the official hymn books of the church. Africa has a strong Anglican presence and many peo-ple have come to live in Ireland from that continent and are active in Church of Ireland parishes. The rich musical heritage of Africa and other parts of the world could enhance the worship of the church and would be attractive to traditional Irish congregations as well as new migrants. Much of this music can be performed with a varied range of instruments.

The larger cathedrals in Ireland attract congregations from very diverse back-grounds. In many cases they draw people who may prefer to be more anonymous than is possible in a parish situation. The beauty of the architecture, the liturgy and its music can provide a haven for those leading very busy lives. Indeed, there has been a trend of congregations increasing in cathedrals in Great Britain and Ireland in recent decades.

The musical experience provided in our major cathedrals is captured well in a recent interview by Mark Fitzgerald with composer Garrett Sholdice in the *New Music Journal*.[40] Garrett comments on his experiences of being a chorister at St Patrick's Cathedral in Dublin:

---

39 In most cases this has become possible through increased income derived from tourism.   **40** Mark Fitzgerald, 'Sometimes the actual sound of the voice is my own', 23 May 2019, www.aicnewmusicjour-nal.com/articles/sometimes-actual-sound-voice-my-own, accessed 18 June 2019.

Singing in Saint Patrick's had an enormous influence on me. It's an experience I am deeply grateful for today. When I was a child, for me music was the theatre of the Anglican service ... What got into the blood most at this time was the evensong service. In particular, I have this memory of an evensong service sometime in late summer, perhaps an August evening with that summer dusk light. Very likely there was no one at the service! We had just finished an anthem; I can't recall what it was but I imagine it was something by Byrd or Tallis. I just remember gazing down at this piece of music and having a real out of time moment and then snapping back to reality and feeling like I had traversed the whole earth. It was my first experience of being really very deeply moved by music.

Worship and mission are core activities in the church and music has a fundamental role in supporting both of these activities. The last fifty years have been transformative in the realms of church music. Resourceful church musicians and clergy can still embrace this powerful evangelical tool – the future *will* contain 'unending hymns of praise'.

4

The development of women's ministry in the Church of Ireland

Revd Canon Ginnie Kennerley

From women's priesthood being unthinkable, to the consecration of its first woman bishop in 2013, the Church of Ireland has moved far in the matter of women's ministry in the past fifty years, even if certain challenges for women remain.

After meeting four times between February and June of 1969, the General Synod's CACTM[1] Subcommittee on Women Church Workers noted specifically that it had not considered any possibility of women's ordination, but simply full-time work at a professional level for women in the church.[2]

'Women are as much part of the church as men, and ... have heads as well as hands', read their communiqué, the implication being that women church workers at that time had only been thought of as cleaners, caterers or at most flower arrangers. Now, the subcommittee urged, women as well as men, 'with clearly recognised professional training', which might be in education, social studies, psychology or theology, should be enlisted as full-time lay workers and given appropriate training to fit them for their work. Such full-time workers, they suggested, should be offered clear salary scales, with parity in terms of minimum clergy stipends.

However, unpaid service was also on the committee's agenda. Women, it urged, 'should be encouraged to take part in Select Vestries, Diocesan Synods and Councils, General Synod and the Representative Church Body ... with a real part in decision-taking'.

On the possibility of women lay readers, the committee was circumspect. Even male lay readers were still not acceptable in some parishes, they noted;[3] so women would need to be very well selected and trained if this option were to be

---

1 The Central Advisory Council on Training for the Ministry was established in the Church of Ireland in the early 1960s. 2 CACTM Subcommittee on Women Church Workers 1969, accessed in the papers of the late Daphne Wormell in the RCB Library. The Committee, chaired by the Very Revd Victor Griffin, dean of St Patrick's Cathedral, included Revd R.H.A. Eames, Revd C.G. Hyland, Dr A.D.H. Mayes, Revd J. Hartin, Miss V. Darling, Miss M. Fitzsimons, Miss A. Ormsby, Mrs Peacocke, Mrs Wormell and Miss J. Scott. 3 Lay reader ministry in the Church of Ireland only took off in 1948–9, although the office had been revived in the Church of England in 1866. See George Leckey, *Reader ministry in the Church of Ireland* (Dublin, 2009).

considered. They concentrated instead on the idea of trained parish workers, who would be paid but not ordained.

What developed instead was a body of lay readers and part-time clergy who, though unpaid, proved hard-working and helpful to the cadre of stipendiary clergy and to the church as a whole.

Despite the CACTM subcommittee's dismissal of the idea of female clergy, and its reluctance on the matter of women lay readers, neither of these developments would be stopped for long, even though it took another twenty years before a bill to allow women to be ordained to the priesthood was presented to the General Synod.

As early as 1970, the House of Bishops, in response to the 1968 Lambeth Conference request that every national church give careful study to the question of the ordination of women to the priesthood,[4] agreed among themselves that there were no theological barriers to the ordination of women. And the momentum in this direction would be kept up by the decision of the first meeting of the Anglican Consultative Council (ACC) at Limuru, Kenya, that the bishop of Hong Kong was free to ordain two women to the priesthood with the consent of his diocesan synod.[5] Then two years later, when the national churches had finally responded to the Lambeth Conference request for study and response on the matter, the second meeting of the ACC in Dublin confirmed the decision, advising that the churches of the Anglican communion should come to their own decisions according to their own situation, and should respect one another's right to do so.[6]

THE FIRST WOMEN LAY READERS

Decision-making in the Church of Ireland General Synod would take somewhat longer; but in the meantime moves were made by two forward-looking bishops to accustom their congregations to the presence of women in the sanctuary. On 29 June 1972, the bishop of Clogher, the Rt Revd Richard Hanson, who had only

---

4 The Lambeth Conference 1968, resolution 35. 'The Conference requests every national and regional Church or province to give careful study to the question of the ordination of women to the priesthood and to report its findings to the Anglican Consultative Council (or Lambeth Consultative Body) which will make them generally available to the Anglican Communion.'   5 'The time is now', Anglican Consultative Council, first meeting, Limuru, Kenya (London, 1971). Resolution 28 b. 'This council advises the Bishop of Hong Kong, acting with the approval of his Synod, and any other bishop of the Anglican Communion acting with the approval of his Province, that if he decides to ordain women to the priesthood, his action will be acceptable to this Council; and that this Council will use its good offices to encourage all Provinces of the Anglican Communion to continue in communion with these dioceses.' Carried by 24 votes to 22.   6 'Partners in mission', Anglican Consultative Council, second meeting (Dublin, 1973), p. 41. Referring to the former resolution 28: 'The Council agrees to recommend once more that, where any autonomous Province of the Anglican Communion decides to ordain women to the priesthood, this should not cause any break in communion in our Anglican family.' Carried 50 in favour, 2 against, 3 abstentions.

been consecrated in March 1970, licensed two women lay readers, after supervising the two-year training course he designed for them.[7] The new readers were Mrs Nora Stevenson, the wife of Canon Stevenson of Clogher Cathedral, and Miss Susan Austin (later Moore), both of whom were greatly appreciated for their leadership of worship and their preaching in this cross-border diocese, clad in specially designed grey dresses. Conducting up to three, sometimes even four, services on a Sunday was challenging for them in many ways, not least because of the necessity of constant border crossings at the height of the Troubles.

The archbishop of Dublin, the Most Revd Alan Buchanan, followed suit three years later, after personally recruiting and training the first five women lay readers for the united dioceses of Dublin and Glendalough. Commissioned in Christ Church Cathedral on 16 November 1975, they were Mrs Thea Boyle, Miss Patricia Hastings-Hardy (who was also the archbishop's secretary), Mrs Joan Rufli (later Russell), Mrs Audrey Smith, and Mrs Daphne Wormell. The last of these, the wife of the TCD Professor of Latin Donald Wormell, had already made herself well known in church circles when just a year after her participation in the cautious CACTM Subcommittee on Women Church Workers, she had written an article entitled 'Women and the Church' at the invitation of Archbishop George Simms for the November 1970 issue of the recently launched *New Divinity: A Church of Ireland Journal*. In this, she declared her conviction that the ordained ministry of the church must come to include women on an equal basis with men, urging the building of '*koinonia*, where there is neither Jew nor Greek, male nor female' and asserting that 'it is now generally conceded that there is no theological barrier to the ordination of women'.

GENERAL SYNOD PROCEEDINGS

Only six months after the Dublin commissioning of these early women lay readers came the General Synod in Dublin at which the synod passed the resolution 'that this House approves in principle the ordination of women'.

The following year, 1977, the General Synod's Select Committee on Women's Priesthood was formed, under the chairmanship of the Rt Revd John Armstrong, then bishop of Cashel, who along with the Hon. David Bleakley, had represented the Church of Ireland at the crucially permissive ACC meetings of 1971 and 1973. A member of the select committee was Irene McCutcheon, who had returned from working as a theologically trained lay minister in England to her native Belfast, and was known to have a strong vocation to the priesthood.

The select committee's work failed to come up to expectations, however. Reporting to the General Synod in 1979, it was criticized for its lack of theological exploration. The question of women's ordination was referred to the diocesan synods, with a great deal of briefing material, including the Association for Promoting

7 See Leckey, *Reader ministry*, p. 44ff.

Christian Knowledge (APCK) pamphlet 'Should we have women priests?' in which the arguments in favour were put by Revd Michael Kennedy of Armagh and Daphne Wormell, while those against were urged by Bishop Walton Empey of Limerick and the Very Revd John Paterson, dean of Kildare.

Over the autumn and winter of 1979–80, all these diocesan synods returned a favourable vote, amounting on aggregate to 223 clergy in favour and 126 against (almost reaching the two-thirds majority that would be required in General Synod), and 622 laity in favour with 160 against – a comfortable majority of over 80 per cent. However, as suggested by the diocesan voting, the two-thirds majority in the House of Clergy proved elusive at the subsequent General Synod of 1980, falling short by just seven clergy votes, although 77 per cent of the laity were in favour.

Given the lack of enthusiasm suggested by the clergy vote, the select committee decided on a more cautious approach, and suggested at the General Synod of the following year that a bill be brought forward in 1982 to enable the ordination of women as deacons. Their expectation was that this, at least, would be agreed, and that women's ordination to the priesthood would follow naturally in due course.

Their proposal was accepted; but the way forward was not to prove as clear as they supposed. The bill as prepared for the General Synod did not allow for an adjustment to the ordinal, which then assumed that deacons would proceed to the priesthood the following year. Unfortunately, the need for this adjustment to allow for the ordination of women deacons, whose future priesthood was then only a remote possibility, came to light too late for the bill to be changed in time for the General Synod debate. Instead, it was only when the bill came up for discussion on 11 May that the assessor informed the synod that several valid points of order had been raised the previous week in connection with the bill. An adjournment for lunch was agreed, which would enable consideration by the House of Bishops. The upshot was that the bill was withdrawn, to the great distress of Irene McCutcheon and other potential women ordinands, but with the undertaking that a new bill 'free from all legal dilemmas' would be introduced within the next two to three years.

At the following year's General Synod, in 1983, a resolution permitting the introduction of a bill the following year to allow the ordination of women to the diaconate was brought forward, along with a second bill to make consequent changes in the ordinal. The resolution was passed by a healthy majority at that synod and the bills were passed in 1984 without further dissension, partly thanks to an explanatory booklet from the bishop of Kilmore, Gilbert Wilson, commended as 'required reading' by the primate, the Most Revd John Armstrong.[8] Thus, from May 1984, women could be accepted as ordinands at the Church of Ireland Theological College.

8 W. Gilbert Wilson, *Should we have women deacons?* (Dublin, 1984). The bishop subsequently published a companion booklet, *Towards accepting women priests* (Dublin, 1989), to prepare voters for the decision on women priests and bishops in the General Synod of 1990.

THE FIRST WOMAN ORDAINED

Katharine Poulton (née Noble) was the first woman to enter training, leading to her ordination as the first woman deacon in June 1987. Married to a fellow cleric, her experience of deployment offers something of a challenging template for the married women, and indeed the married clergy couples, who followed. Regulations did not permit a husband and wife to work in the same parish, so although Katharine and her husband initially secured curacies in parishes close to one another, his promotion to a parish 40 miles away meant that it was she who had to undertake the daily commute. Similar deployment difficulties continued for the couple for the next thirty years, just as they have done for almost all the clergy couples who have followed, the problems being most acute in the years of child-bearing and child-rearing. What has made it particularly challenging for such couples has been the traditional expectation that rectors and their families will reside in the rectory of their parish.

THE NEED FOR FLEXIBILITY

This arguably intractable problem, which applied to a similar extent to all married clergywomen, was one of the reasons for the church's hesitation about women's ordination to the priesthood. To help resolve anxieties in this area, the Women's Ministry Group in the Church of Ireland[9] conducted an investigation into how the women priests already ordained in provinces of the Anglican Communion had managed to integrate their family lives with their ministries. At the request of the Rt Revd John Neill, who as well as being elected bishop of Tuam in 1986 had been appointed chair of the Select Committee on the Ordination of Women to the Priesthood and Episcopate in 1988, the report was submitted to this committee on 23 November 1989.[10]

The report, which collated the responses of 107 Anglican women clergy from the USA, Canada, New Zealand and England (though the English women were only in the diaconate at the time) went a long way to reassure the doubters and also to point to the need for more administrative flexibility in the church if it was to make the most of all that women clergy would have to offer. The short version of this report, which was administered and compiled by this writer, was published as

9 The WMG was founded by Daphne Wormell and C of I supporters of women's ministry in 1986, with the aim of supporting women's ordination in a judicious and non-confrontational manner. At its first public event, a Conference on Women's Ministry in the Church of Ireland, on 11 April 1986, the aim was not to push for women's ordination to the priesthood, but to clarify what they would be able to contribute as deacons. Ironically, the result was that many clergy speaking from the floor contended that women would be better able to serve the church as priests than as permanent deacons. For further information on the formation of the Women's Ministry Group see Ginnie Kennerley, *Embracing women* (Dublin, 2008), pp 54–9. See also the 36-page booklet *Report of the Conference on Women's Ministry in the Church of Ireland*, 11 Apr. 1986 (edited for the WMG by Sheila Wayman and privately printed).   10 Bishop Neill had also been appointed as 'link bishop' to the WMG – a way of recognizing this self-appointed group without giving it official status in the church.

an appendix to the General Synod report of 1990, although without the final page of 'suggestions'.[11] A longer version of the research findings, allowing more detail and more personal testimony, was put together by Margaret Larminie, former education officer for the Church of Ireland.[12]

All in all it has to be said that family responsibilities and work location continue to be challenging issues for all Church of Ireland clergy and their spouses, whether these are also clergy or not. The issues for clergy couples in particular, though, have required increasing flexibility in the administrative structures of the church. The need to allow for periods of maternity (and indeed paternity) leave and paid part-time work, with the maintenance of pension entitlements and an agreed length to the average working day, has been increasingly recognized; but improvements in this area are still required at the time of writing.

VOTING ON PRIESTHOOD AND EPISCOPATE

Women being confined to the diaconate was not to last for long. The resounding vote at the Lambeth Conference of 1988 in favour of making way for women in the episcopate, in a debate ably introduced by Bishop John Neill, had blown away a good deal of caution. So the women deacons ordained in June 1988, Kathleen Brown (née Young) of Belfast and this writer, in fact only had to wait until 1990 to proceed to the priesthood.

Some anxiety was caused in advance of the presentation of the resolution for General Synod 1989 in that it proposed that the vote be taken the following year on whether or not the Church of Ireland should accept the ordination of women both as priests and as bishops. While the proposer, Dean John Paterson, may have hoped that the inclusion of ordination to the episcopate would greatly increase the 'No' vote, both the seconder, Revd Michael Kennedy, and the select committee argued that if women could not proceed to the episcopate theirs would be a 'second-class' priesthood.

The resolution was phrased as follows:

> That in accordance with the provision of Section 26(1) of Chapter 1 of the Constitution leave be granted for the introduction of a bill in the General Synod of 1990 to enable women to be ordained as priests and bishops, and to make consequential amendments to the formularies of the Church.

There followed an amendment to Canon 22 of the constitution stating that

> men and women alike may be ordained to the holy order of deacons, of priests, or of bishops, without any distinction or discrimination on grounds

11 For the suggestions arising from the research, and for the questionnaire, see appendices to *Embracing women*, pp 167–71. 12 The 40-page document, titled 'Conditions and deployment of married women clergy in the Anglican Communion', is available in the Representative Church Body Library in Dublin.

of sex, and men and women so ordained shall alike be referred to and known as deacons, priests or bishops.

Then there are four pages of amendments to the text of the *Book of Common Prayer* and the *Alternative Prayer Book* of 1984, largely concerned with putting male pronouns in italics to indicate the possibility of female ones.[13]

Bishop John Neill's introduction to the debate, urging that all the signs of the times pointed to the need for the church, being faithful to the gospel, to accept women as priests and bishops, was followed by a full three hours of lively debate, in which Archbishop Caird of Dublin suggested that an assembly voting in favour of the proposal, in defiance of tradition, could be likened to a herd of lemmings throwing themselves over a cliff. Pros and cons were evenly balanced; so evenly, indeed that Bishop Neill in his summing-up suggested that the vote about to be taken could be simply a vote 'in principle' and that he was willing to delay the introduction of the actual bill to 1991 to allow time for further reflection, if the synod so desired. This concession carried the day, with the clergy voting 131 to 47 in favour (a 73.6 per cent majority) and the laity affirming the resolution by 244 to 37 (a whopping 86.8 per cent). It was hard for those in favour to restrain their delight; yet the policy of civility and consideration held fast. Nobody wanted a split of any kind in the church.

It was just as well that this resolve was held, for an uncivilized dispute could easily have arisen over the questionnaire issued in an attempt to muster the 'no' vote for the following year, by a clerical group named the 'Concerned Clergy'.[14] The final three items of the questionnaire, which was issued to all clergy in the Church of Ireland, including retired and auxiliary clergy,[15] was found unanswerable by those not already leaning towards a negative vote, on account of the 'loaded' quality of the questions. Do you approve of the Church of Ireland moving in the matter with what seems, to some, undue haste? If in November 1989, the Church of England decides against ordaining women, would you still approve of the Church of Ireland going it alone? Should account be taken of its effect on relations with other churches?

Protests against the questionnaire were made by a number of individuals, and the Women's Ministry Group invited the Concerned Clergy to a colloquium at the Salle D'Armes in Dublin's Sandymount, in an attempt to allow feelings and fears on both sides to be expressed and heard with understanding.

---

13 For the full text of the resolutions, see General Synod 1989 report, pp 247–59.   14 Leading members of the group included Dean John Paterson, by then of Christ Church Cathedral, Dublin, Revd Victor Stacey of Santry, Dublin, Revd Peter Barrett, chaplain of TCD and subsequently bishop of Cashel and Ossory, Revd Ken Clarke of Coleraine, subsequently bishop of Kilmore, Revd John Crawford of St Patrick's Cathedral, Dublin group of parishes, and the Very Revd John McCarthy, dean of Clogher, who subsequently ministered in the United States of America.   15 The term 'auxiliary' indicates a cleric who devotes much of his or her spare time to ministry in the church, receiving no payment apart from expenses. It is used interchangeably with the term 'NSM', indicating 'non-stipendiary ministry'.

When it came to the General Synod of 1990, it seemed to be a toss-up whether the bill would be debated then or postponed to 1991. Either course gave rise to certain anxieties. In the event Bishop Neill, perhaps moved by the consideration that the triennial elections would result in new synod membership the following year and convinced that more than sufficient time had now been given for discussion, asked the synod's permission to withdraw his amendment, so that the debate could go forward in the course of the current synod. Despite some indications of discontent, permission was given, and when the final vote came the bill was passed by a resounding majority: 126 clergy voted for, with 55 against, a percentage of 69.6 per cent in favour. The laity vote was even more emphatic, at 172 for and 29 against, a percentage of 85.8 per cent. The bishops' vote, not formally declared, was said to be 9–3 in favour, which meant that two bishops had agreed with Archbishop Caird's view on the matter. However, all the bishops accepted that the positive vote was conclusive and was the mind of the church. And given the prayerful atmosphere in which Archbishop Eames had conducted the debate, it was generally accepted that the vote had been guided by the Holy Spirit.

THE FIRST WOMEN PRIESTS

Four ordinations of women to the priesthood followed this decision of 1990 in the same year. Kathleen Young and Irene Templeton (née McCutcheon) were priested by Bishop Sam Poyntz along with Connor's male deacons on 24 June in Belfast Cathedral, Kathleen for the stipendiary and Irene for the non-stipendiary ministry (she had been ordained deacon the previous year, after topping up her already impressive qualifications). There followed Janet Catterall, already ordained deacon in 1987 in England, priested by Bishop Roy Warke in late September in Cork, where her husband was an incumbent, and in late October, Virginia (Ginnie) Kennerley in Christ Church Cathedral, Dublin, with a past and a future archbishop of Dublin, H.R. McAdoo and John R.W. Neill, participating with Archbishop Caird in the ordination ceremony.

RESISTANCE

There remained determined resistance among some in the Concerned Clergy group, which resulted in a further challenge to the acceptance of women priests the following year. During the debate that should have settled matters once and for all, Dean John Paterson had made a strong request, if the bill were passed, for a 'conscience clause' to be introduced to protect clergy who felt unable to accept women priests or to work with them. The request was discounted at the time, but was to return forcefully as a proposal to General Synod the following year.

The motion in the names of Bishop John Neill and Dean John Paterson, if passed, would in effect have made the recognition of women's priesthood optional in perpetuity, permitting future as well as current clergy to refuse to accept the priesthood of women. It asked the synod to agree that clergy who objected to the ordination of women 'should suffer no discrimination or loss of respect by reason of their bona fide views, nor should such views constitute any impediment to the exercise of ministry in the Church of Ireland'.[16]

Although the motion was supported by Archbishop Eames and many of the senior bishops on the grounds that the minority had a right to their views and deserved the full consideration and respect of the majority, the synod refused to 'affirm' the motion, which was only 'noted and received'. Judging by the arguments on the floor, it was not any disrespect for serving senior clergy of the minority opinion which caused its rejection, but the consideration mentioned above, that the measure would make recognition of women priests optional indefinitely – the caveat possibly even being written into the formularies of the Church of Ireland.

A NEW ERA

Thus the 1990s began a new era for women in the Church of Ireland. Now that women could access the same opportunities as men within the ordained ministry of the church, the numbers offering themselves for ordination training rose decisively. From 1984 up to 1988, one female entrant a year to the Theological College had been the maximum; but by 1989 some had already entered the application process in anticipation of a positive final vote. Thus, by the end of 1990, Jacqueline Mould, Susan Green, Rosemary Logue, Dorothy McVeigh and Gillian Wharton were already in training. (This was the year when Sheila Zietsman from Zimbabwe was ordained deacon and appointed by Bishop Walton Empey to take charge of Geashill in Co. Offaly.) There followed an influx to the CITC of six women, along with just six men, entering in 1991: Frances Bach, Jan Hales, Paula Halliday, Nicola Harvey, Olive Donohoe and Anne Taylor.

Many women entered non-stipendiary ministry training in these early years, studying mainly at home but with regular weekend sessions at the Theological College, the syllabus being largely that of St John's College, Nottingham. On the whole such women were mature, often having raised their families. In general, they felt called to serve in parish ministry without being uprooted from their home context, and maybe also from their weekday working life, it being understood that stipendiary ministry required clergy to be willing to go wherever they might be needed. Some of these women later transferred to stipendiary ministry, completing whatever extra training was required, to become rectors or priests-in-charge, often rising to the rank of canon. That teachers, nurses, farmers' and sometimes clergymen's wives continue to give outstanding service to the church in this way puts the whole church in their debt.

---

16 General Synod, 1991, motion 3, 'Recognition of diversities of conviction of faithful members of the Church of Ireland'.

CONTINUING RESERVATIONS – AND
RISING NUMBERS

In these early years, there did remain certain reservations about women's ministry in some parishes, especially in the northern province, where the more conservative were troubled by the issue of 'headship'.[17] They suggested that women might quiet these scruples by not seeking to become rectors, or even by opting to remain as deacons.[18] Indeed such opposition continues in the late 2010s among some members of the male clergy affiliated to Reform and GAFCON. However, from the mid-1990s there was a broad welcome for women clergy in the church as they graduated into parish ministry, many of the doubters being reassured by their competence and their personal qualities.

Thus by 2007 there were already 30 women rectors and one woman dean serving in the Church of Ireland, along with 3 priests in charge, 6 bishop's curates, 17 parish curates, and 6 assigned to chaplaincy or specialist work. To these should be added 36 NSMs, plus 9 women already retired from stipendiary ministry along with 3 retired NSMs. The stipendiary women serving thus amounted to just 12 per cent of the total number of paid clergy in the Church of Ireland, while the non-stipendiary figure worked out at over 30 per cent of all NSMs.

Some of the stipendiary women clergy had come in from other provinces of the Anglican Communion, mostly from England, though the first woman dean, Sue Patterson, hailed from New Zealand and in due course returned there. In the early years, most had come in as deacons, two of them with their clergy husbands, before the Church of England voted in favour of women's priesthood in 1993.

For this first generation of women clergy, the pressure to prove oneself was considerable. If a woman preached a boring sermon, spoke too softly in the liturgy, failed to notice the absence of a faithful congregant or allowed a select vestry meeting to get out of control, there would be those who would say, 'There you are! It's as I thought. Women can't do it!' So each woman owed it to her female colleagues as well as to herself to be as good, if not better, than any man.

But gradually things settled down and the first female rectors were appointed in Belfast (St Paul and St Barnabas) in 1992 and in Dublin and Glendalough (Narraghmore and Castledermot) in 1993.

Appointments to canonries and as rural deans and to other diocesan positions followed in due course to the extent that by the mid- to late 1990s it would have been hard, in the province of Dublin at least, for clergywomen to claim that there was any discrimination against them.

17 Cf. 1 Timothy 2.12: 'I do not permit a woman to teach or to have authority over a man.' 18 Some of these anxieties were expressed later on by interviewees for Canon Desmond McCreery's 2003 survey, 'An examination of the ordination of women after eighteen years in the Church of Ireland', for his MA in religion and society for Queen's University Belfast. Available in RCB Library: thesis 94.

FURTHER REFLECTION

Reflection on women's ministry has continued down the years, and its development can be traced in particular through the following studies:

- the 'Report of the conference celebrating ten years of women priests in
  Dublin in 2000';
- the above-noted research project by Canon McCreery presented as an MA
  thesis to Queen's University Belfast in 2003;
- an appendix to the Commission on Ministry's General Synod report of
  2003 detailing the experience of women in ordained ministry as researched
  by Revd Olive Donohoe;
- a special issue of *Search: A Church of Ireland Journal* (28:3, 2005): commentary by Revd Darren McCallig, research by Revd Bernie Daly and
  reflections by Revd Grace Clunie; and
- general commentary at the time of the consecration of the Most Revd
  Patricia Storey as bishop of Meath and Kildare in 2013 – an event that
  brought women's ministry in the Church of Ireland to a certain sense of
  completion.

In general, all the above writers agreed that women priests had been increasingly well received over the period under consideration and that any occasional
personal antagonism, bullying or inappropriate behaviour had been exceptional. It
was also noticeable that the amount of clerical opposition to women priests waned
steadily as time went on. For instance, Archbishop Caird, despite his notorious
'lemmings' speech of 1989 and his advice to a woman ordinand that she would
probably have to go to Hong Kong if she wanted to be priested, went on not only
to priest a number of women but to appoint at least one as an incumbent in the
archdiocese. Bishop Peter Barrett recanted his views when consecrated for the diocese of Cashel, Ferns and Ossory, and proceeded without delay to institute a female
rector to Maryborough (Portlaoise) in 2003. Revd John Crawford, once the most
outspoken member of the Concerned Clergy, whose expostulations in the letters
columns of the *Irish Times* had cast a shadow over the celebration of ten years
of women's priesthood in Dublin, was suddenly surprised, at an early morning
celebration in St Patrick's Cathedral, to find Canon Maureen Ryan's Eucharistic
ministry was as potent as that of any male cleric. Even Dean John Paterson, having
resigned as clerical honorary secretary of the southern province when the General
Synod declined to affirm his motion of 1991, later welcomed a woman canon to
Christ Church Cathedral and to the cathedral board. (Of that cathedral's twelve
canons, three are now women, and in 2018 Dr Mary McAleese was appointed as a
lay canon and Revd Dr Lorraine Kennedy Ritchie as an ecumenical canon.)

None of this, however, means that the development of women's ministry was
plain sailing, and even in 2018 the share of female clergy in the Church of Ireland

stood only at 20 per cent of the total, whereas in the Church of England 29 per cent of active clergy are women.[19] What is more, only 15 per cent of Church of Ireland incumbents are female – forty-nine in all – as against 24.7 per cent in the Church of England.

By way of explanation, all the sources listed above noted the domestic and time-management difficulties of married women priests in full-time stipendiary ministry, especially those with children. It was also noted that these difficulties applied almost equally to male clergy with children to be cared for, and it was generally agreed that for the sake of male as well as female clergy much more flexibility must be built into the church structures, with the development of part-time stipendiary opportunities, possibly in the context of team ministry.

The requirement that incumbents live in the rectories provided by the parish has proved a serious barrier to incumbency for women whose husbands' employment is tied to their locality and whose children would be disadvantaged by moving from their home. These two family-linked difficulties have resulted in making full-time ministry less attractive to many married women, and to around a third of the total of female ordinands initially opting for unpaid part-time (NSM) ministry.

However, the proportion of female auxiliary to stipendiary clergy fell noticeably over the decade, from 28:76 (56 per cent) in 2008 to 36:64 (37 per cent) in 2018.[20] It is clear that the reason female NSM numbers have fallen off is that, in order to boost the morale and general acceptability of auxiliary clergy, the church elected in 2009 to make the academic requirements for ordination identical for auxiliary and stipendiary clergy.

The new regulations required all ordinands to complete a master's degree in theology in line with the practice of the Porvoo Communion churches, including the Anglican churches in Ireland and Great Britain and the Nordic/Baltic Lutheran churches. This was commendable in its intention to ensure that NSMs would be as well qualified as their stipendiary colleagues, but the unconsidered result was that the training became unendurably lengthy for many part-timers. The new demands particularly discouraged mature women who felt called to a ministry that would not separate them from their husbands and their homes. If a woman reckons she may have up to twenty years of useful life ahead of her, it hardly seems reasonable to spend seven years of these in preparation and training. (The time-span has recently been reduced, but the curriculum demands remain the same.)

---

19 Hattie Williams, 'More women than men enter clergy training, latest figures show', *Church Times*, 27 Sept. 2017. **20** These figures were provided by Church of Ireland House (the Representative Church Body). However, perusal of the *Church of Ireland Directory* shows just how difficult it is to define non-stipendiary ministry, which may also be provided on a house-for-duty with expenses basis or other personal arrangement by former stipendiary clergy. Thus the numbers for women in NSM ministry may be higher than the official figures suggest. For further discussion on the numbers, seniority, and proportionality of women clergy in the Church of Ireland, and their relationship to the situation in the Church of England, see the Very Revd Susan Green's article, '"Do you see this woman?" – women's ministry in the C of I today', *Search: A Church of Ireland Journal*, 42:1 (2019), pp 34–44.

This consideration has persuaded many women to offer instead for lay reader-ship, for which the preparation is not so lengthy – usually two years part-time. According to the 2018 *Church of Ireland Directory*, there are currently 79 women lay readers serving in the province of Armagh and 64 in the province of Dublin. (In most cases the numbers of male and female readers are roughly equivalent.) In addition many dioceses licence 'parish readers' and 'lay pastoral assistants' without noting this in the *Church of Ireland Directory*.[21] Even without including such lay assistants and ministers, this amounts to 143 women lay readers in the church – or 152 if we include the 9 women readers commissioned in Down and Dromore late in 2018 – against only 28 active women non-stipendiary ministers. The figures speak for themselves.

ORDAINED LOCAL MINISTRY

It is to be hoped that the new category of 'ordained local ministry', designed to prepare ordinands in a shorter time[22] for a priesthood the exercise of which will be confined to their own parish area, will go some way to remedying this situation, making the vocations and gifts of more women available to the church. That said, it would be important not to allow unpaid ministry to become in any way identified with the female gender.

In late 2018, there were 26 NSM ordinands from 8 dioceses training for ordained local ministry, 10 of them women. 12 of the 26 were hoping to be ordained dea-con in 2019 and priested in 2020. These clergy, whether female or male, will be particularly valued as team members in areas with low population densities, where clergy in charge of the increasing number of amalgamated parishes, with multiple churches set many miles apart, are unable to provide the sacramental ministry their parishioners need. The ministry of OLMs will also bring a welcome community aspect to the priesthood in the parishes concerned.

A BISHOP AT LAST

The final proof of the acceptance of women's ministry in the Church of Ireland came with the consecration in November 2013 of the Most Revd Patricia Storey, formerly the rector of St Augustine's in Derry, as the bishop of Meath and Kildare, third in seniority only to the archbishops of Armagh and Dublin.

Queries, even hopes, have been voiced down the years about how women in the priesthood might somehow 'do ministry in a new way', so as to liberate the church from patriarchal attitudes and structures. On the whole, though, women have been

21 For instance the diocese of Cork Cloyne and Ross lists 7 'lay liturgical assistants', 5 of whom are women, with another 5 women counted among the 8 'lay local ministers'. Other dioceses recognize similar areas of lay ministry.   22 For those who are already lay readers or who have completed the foundation course, the part-time course runs for two years, with ordination to the diaconate after one year and priesting after two. Other entrants study part-time for three years.

content simply to be themselves and get on with the job of teaching, pastoring, encouraging and inspiring the flock assigned to them. No feminist agendas as such have come into play.

Bishop Pat Storey is very much one of those. She gets on with the job, working hard and praying hard, but not afraid to take time off for her family and friends. She is refreshingly herself, does not stand on her dignity, speaks frankly and is instantly available when needed. Solemnity is alien to her; sincerity is her hallmark – and occasionally a bit of fun. These are not particularly female qualities and indeed are shared by many male bishops. Yet having such a woman in such a senior position in the leadership of the church has been a great encouragement to women clergy. The call is simply to be your best self and do the best job you can for the people who need you. Playing roles, whether as bishop or dean, priest, deacon or lay reader – or feminist symbol – is simply not what is required.

It will take the election of a second woman bishop for the ratio of female to male clergy in the episcopate to be roughly equivalent to the ratio in the ordained ministry as a whole. However, given that already five women have proved themselves as deans of cathedrals, three have risen to the rank of archdeacon, many more to that of canon and another has been clerical honorary secretary to the General Synod for some years, there is no reason to suppose it will be long before another woman is consecrated.

There does remain one particular problem, though, however helpful church structures may become: the traditionalism of Irish family life. Will the next woman bishop's husband and family be willing and able to move?

5

Pastoral care

Revd Canon Daniel Nuzum

Pastoral care and ministry at its heart involves relationship. Relationship for the person of faith is a continuously interpreting dynamic between on the one hand the pastoral minister and God, and on the other between the pastoral minister and the person with whom he/she is ministering and called to serve. Pastoral care is woven throughout the biblical narrative of God and God's people and has been an integral part of the life and witness of the church from the time of Jesus Christ. This care is most potently expressed in the Jewish sense of '*shalom*' which translates as wholeness, well-being, completeness, and forms a theological and redemptive backdrop of creation and salvation for the person of faith. '*Shalom*' is closely bound up with a deep understanding of the dignity of the human person, a dignity that is expressed in how the church values and cares for the human person, most especially in times of challenge, illness, frailty and distress. This care is expressed in the Scriptures, sacraments, prayer and pastoral ministry.[1] From a Christian perspective, we draw inspiration and motivation from the life, ministry, command and witness of Jesus Christ during his earthly ministry and continued through his great commission (Matthew 25) and the ongoing indwelling and presence of the Holy Spirit in our day. Pastoral care is perhaps best captured in the command to love: '[A] new commandment I give to you, that you love one another: even as I have loved you, that you love one another.'[2]

The Church of Ireland, in common with sister churches of the Anglican Communion, understands itself – at least in common parlance – as 'a pastoral church'. This claim is built on centuries of pastoral polity where the church cares for and supports all who are in need. The self-understanding of the church as rooted in the ancient parochial model has in no small way shaped a broader pastoral approach and identity where literally every part of the island of Ireland is served by a parish. Indeed there has traditionally been an expectation that parish clergy – and bishops – are at heart pastoral ministers among the people they are called to serve. (Anecdotally it is not unusual to hear that such pastoral qualities are measured by the barometer of parochial visiting!) As a minority and relatively small church numerically, the capacity to form close pastoral relationships between

---

1 'Notes to ministry to those who are sick', *Book of Common Prayer* (Dublin, 2004), p. 440. 2 John 13:34–5.

clergy and people has been possible and has in many ways been inspired by the pastoral image of Jesus as 'Good Shepherd' ('I know my sheep and my sheep know me' – John 10:14). In addition to being a biblical imperative, the importance of pastoral care is also affirmed in the ordinal for deacons, priests and bishops. Both in the charge to those to be ordained and in the declarations made at ordination, pastoral care is an integral part of the understanding of holy orders. It is significant that the same question is put to deacons, priests and bishops by the ordaining bishop: 'Will you be faithful in visiting the sick, in caring for the poor and needy, and in helping the oppressed?'[3]

In the charge to deacons the bishop proclaims:

> Deacons have a special responsibility to ensure that those in need are cared for with compassion and humility. They are to strengthen the faithful, search out the careless and the indifferent, and minister to the sick, the needy, the poor and those in trouble.[4]

Priests are enjoined to work 'as servants and shepherds among the people to whom they are sent ... to minister to the sick and to prepare the dying for death'.[5] Bishops are called 'to have special care for the sick and for the outcast and needy'.[6]

It is noteworthy that the collect prayed at the ordination of deacons, priests and bishops prays that those to be ordained would be 'instruments of your love'.[7] The ordinal, as a foundational document of Anglican identity and theology, therefore affirms a fundamental understanding of pastoral ministry and care at the heart of ordained ministry.

The fifty years from 1969 to today have seen some fundamental changes in the life of the Church of Ireland. These changes have been both within the church itself and also in wider Irish society in both Northern Ireland and the Republic of Ireland. The ordination of women to all three orders of deacon, priest and bishop was a momentous watershed that brought with it a pastoral gender balance to what had been a male preserve. While pastoral ministry and care is not a gender-driven enterprise, nonetheless the inclusion of women as equal partners in pastoral care brought a refreshing balance and its success has been that it is now unremarkable.

In wider society various social changes have provided impetus for the Church of Ireland to evolve pastorally and the General Synod has been the midwife of new pastoral liturgies to respond to changing social realities; among these was the remarriage of divorced persons in church. Other social changes in the Republic of Ireland such as the extension of marriage to same-gender partners in 2015 and the introduction of the Termination of Pregnancy Act 2018 are proving more

---

3 Ordinal, *BCP* (2004), pp 556, 567, 577.   4 Ordination of deacons, *BCP* (2004), p. 555   5 Ordination of priests, *BCP* (2004), p. 565.   6 Ordination of bishops, *BCP* (2004), p. 577.   7 Ordinal collect, *BCP* (2004), p. 554.

challenging as the church seeks to provide a pastoral response. The General Synod in 2019 approved the service of prayer and naming and the funeral service in cases of miscarriage, stillbirth and neonatal death. Of significance, the church recognized the pastoral complexities of pregnancy loss that also includes trauma and necessary termination of pregnancy and explicitly names these painful realities in the pastoral and liturgical guidelines for these new services.

PASTORAL CARE IN PAROCHIAL MINISTRY

Pastoral care in the Church of Ireland is most commonly expressed and experienced in the parochial context. While society has changed considerably in the period from 1969, the value, importance and need for pastoral care has not. Each generation navigates afresh the current complexities and challenges it finds itself amid where the message of the gospel is forever contemporary. This dynamic understanding of ministry and pastoral care equips the church to respond afresh to contemporary needs, challenges and opportunities in a meaningful and transformative way.

Pastoral care alongside the celebration of public worship has been the mainstay of parochial ministry in the Church of Ireland. In addition to responding to particular pastoral need the Church of Ireland has always enjoined a proactive approach to pastoral ministry where a faithful pastoral relationship is built between clergy and people. While this is regarded as a strength it is also an inherent weakness that can be overly clericalized not just by clergy themselves but also by parishioners. In the increasing reality of longer vacancies in incumbencies, the role of the parish community, the 'laos' is highlighted. This remains an evolving area as the church discerns how pastoral care can be supported in a non-clericalized way where the whole people of God, by virtue of baptismal covenant, has a pastoral role in a generic way alongside and in collaboration with deacon, priest and bishop.

PASTORAL CARE IN CHALLENGING TIMES

The wider societal challenges experienced during the Troubles in Northern Ireland were a traumatic crucible wherein the pastoral ministry of the Church of Ireland (in common with other churches) was both a response and witness in tremendously challenging circumstances. The many experiences of pastoral ministry crossing boundaries of division provided much witness to the healing and reconciling power of the gospel expressed in the care extended to those in need. Undoubtedly the opposite was also true where pastoral ministry was experienced as chaplain to one side or another. However, on balance the public and private witness and ministry of pastoral care, much of it done ecumenically, provided prophetic spiritual and community balm and hope in the most devastating of contexts.

In the Republic of Ireland the difficult decisions concerning parochial reorganization and church closures were among the most exigent experiences and threats to self-identity in what was still a young state and society maturing in self-identity and place in the European Union and on the global stage. The closure of church buildings and the amalgamation of parishes, with the associated reduction in clergy, was the evolving landscape upon which pastoral ministry was exercised and new directions forged. This was a traumatic time of considerable loss to sense of identity and place as well as attachment to much loved places of worship that held many sacred memories and associations. It was a community bereavement with all the associated feelings associated with any bereavement. For some it was too much to bear and resulted in a fractured relationship between them and the church. The inevitable increase in administration and geographical spread provided a thinner presence of clergy, which no doubt increased the pastoral workload. The increasing administrative tasks associated with running any organization such as a parish added further to the demands placed on clergy and consequently their potential pastoral availability for what was a quintessentially Anglican approach of proactive rather than reactive pastoral care and polity.

SCHOOLS

The parish school has always had a treasured place in the life of a parish community. The pastoral importance of the parish and school link cannot be overemphasized. Although it comes at an administrative cost, the presence, support and care provided to generations of children and their parents is not insignificant. The fact that most Church of Ireland parish primary schools in the Republic of Ireland are small schools provides a nurturing and pastoral environment for the flourishing and support of each pupil. The pastoral witness of the church has shaped the distinctive ethos of our parish schools and what they offer to children of all faiths and none in a modern pluralist society.

YOUTH WORK AND CHILDREN'S MINISTRY

Related to the role of the church in education, the Church of Ireland has shown a particular pastoral care of young people primarily through formal parish ministry (for example, sacramental preparation for confirmation and parochial youth ministry) and also through the work of the Church of Ireland Youth Department nationally and locally. The contact that youth groups have with teenagers and young adults as well as the pivotal role that secondary-school chaplains have in the support and accompaniment of young people cannot be overestimated. The challenges faced by young people are immense and this level of pastoral care is worthy of recognition. While much of it is provided in a voluntary capacity, it is supported and resourced by committed professionals, youth officers and school chaplains working together.

Alongside the development of youth ministry has been the important growth in the recognition of children's ministry as a dedicated area of ministry and pastoral care in a parochial context. This development has contributed much to the engagement and participation of children in an age- and developmentally appropriate way as well as nurturing the spirituality of children.

The care and protection of children and vulnerable adults has been at the forefront of pastoral ministry and development in recent years and the introduction of legislation civilly and canonically in this regard has enshrined the importance of the trust placed in all who provide pastoral ministry and care on behalf of the church. In addition to the self-evident culture of trust, good practice and governance that is promoted, the introduction of the Church of Ireland's own safeguarding policy, 'Safeguarding trust', has also undergirded an important pastoral-care dimension of all ministry with children and vulnerable adults. Highlighting the dignity of each human person, it calls us to uphold and nurture that dignity: values that are at the core of all pastoral ministry.

PASTORAL CARE IN HEALTHCARE

The church has always had a particular sense of care for those who are ill and, as demonstrated in the ordinal, the Church of Ireland places a particular importance on this ministry. As an episcopal church where matters of ministry ultimately lie with the diocesan bishop, each bishop has traditionally appointed a chaplain to each healthcare institution in her/his diocese. For the most part this is usually the local rector and/or curate-assistant within the parish where the healthcare institution is located. This approach served the church and healthcare well, especially where good working relationships were established – often integrated in smaller local/community hospitals where there were many existing connections. In larger hospitals, however, the demands of chaplaincy were considerably more onerous. Addressing a forum of the Royal College of Nursing in 1984, Canon Jack Rolston, chaplain at the Mater Infirmorum Hospital, Belfast, reported that during one of the worst years of the Troubles in Belfast he was called to the casualty theatre 'at least ninety-six times between the hours of 2.30am and 7.30am' – a considerable out-of-hours pastoral commitment on top of parish ministry.[8]

One of the challenges of automatically appointing the local incumbent as the de facto chaplain was the challenge of suitability where the chaplaincy demands were onerous or requiring specialist skills in, for example, acute psychiatry, intellectual disability, maternity, palliative care or paediatrics. While traditionally it was usually deemed that by virtue of ordination the appointed chaplain was the appropriate person and sufficiently qualified to carry out this ministry, it has long been recognized by chaplains themselves and more recently by healthcare facilities that this is not always the case. The expectations of suitability and education in modern healthcare apply as much to the chaplain as they do to the medical or wider healthcare team.

8 'The hospital chaplain', *Church of Ireland Gazette*, 9 Nov. 1984.

The other reality was fiscally driven, where the remuneration received for chaplaincy was (and is) in a number of cases used to support a broader benefice and a knock-on implication was that paid chaplaincy ministry was invariably the preserve of those in stipendiary ministry and supported the appointment of a priest in a local parish. In both the National Health Service in Northern Ireland and the Health Service Executive in the Republic of Ireland, chaplains have been remunerated for their work either through direct employment or through a service-level agreement with the local bishop or diocese.

In some places lay people were trained as hospital or pastoral visitors but this was very much seen as an adjunct to the formal/official ministry of the ordained chaplain and was very much a volunteer ministry.

As healthcare has evolved in recent decades so too has the understanding of the significance of the spiritual dimension of illness and the importance of spiritual care as a recognized professional healthcare discipline. The introduction of clinical pastoral education (CPE) in Ireland in the early 1980s provided the first formal recognition of this evolving landscape for chaplaincy. The Church of Ireland has embraced these changes in varying ways and recognizes the place of CPE as an essential element of training for those who wish to become healthcare chaplains.[9] CPE is an intensive action-reflection-action form of supervised ministry programme that develops the personal, pastoral and professional identity and awareness of the pastoral minister in preparation for ministry. In addition it provides focused education and training in healthcare ministry to recognized international standards and competencies. As a form of education CPE has evolved over the decades to equip both lay and ordained chaplains to minister as competent healthcare professionals, nurturing both the vocational and the professional dimensions of what is now a discipline in its own right.

As with all healthcare disciplines, healthcare chaplaincy requires an evidenced-based, research-informed approach where the professional chaplain can identify, assess and meet the spiritual needs of patients and service users alongside fellow healthcare professionals in the wider multi-disciplinary team. The formal certification of healthcare chaplains to agreed and expected standards is an important commitment in this regard. While initially the Roman Catholic Church was in a position to provide formal certification of chaplains through the Healthcare Chaplaincy Board for those who met the required standards for healthcare chaplaincy, this ceased to be the case in 2007 when the Roman Catholic Church felt it could no longer provide certification to members of other churches or faiths and thereafter could only provide certification of Catholic healthcare chaplains. This changed reality, while impacting relatively few Church of Ireland candidates, nevertheless paved the way for the Church of Ireland to address this by establishing

9 House of Bishops (HOB) protocol 2014 1003.

the Chaplaincy Accreditation Board in 2008. This was a significant development for the Church of Ireland in the recognition of the professional role of healthcare chaplains, both lay and ordained.

THE CHAPLAINCY ACCREDITATION BOARD

The House of Bishops established the Chaplaincy Accreditation Board (CAB) in 2008 as a means to provide a professionally robust form of accreditation for Irish healthcare chaplains. This was the first time that the Church of Ireland set out the professional competencies, education and standards expected of those who would be appointed as healthcare chaplains. The standards are equivalent to those of the Healthcare Chaplaincy Board. Although the Chaplaincy Accreditation Board is run under the auspices of the House of Bishops, it also provides professional certification to chaplains from other traditions with the support of the appropriate faith body. This approach has been a significant contribution to the Irish health service by way of recognizing the increasing diversity of Irish society and spiritual practice.

In addition to the standards for certification, the Chaplaincy Accreditation Board also provides a code of conduct and registration process for those in health-care-chaplaincy positions.[10] This commitment by the Church of Ireland is an important demonstration of how the church recognizes the particular importance of healthcare chaplaincy and spiritual care in a modern healthcare environment and in no small way enables the church to engage in a professional and credible way in a modern pluralist healthcare milieu.

One of the more significant changes in recent decades is the growing reality of religious diversity, which is representative in both civil demographics and also church attendance. As a pastoral church with a proactive pastoral approach, the Church of Ireland is well placed to respond meaningfully and sensitively in this regard. In practice, this means that increasingly healthcare chaplaincy is no longer purely to one's own denomination but to those of various expressions of faith, belief and no belief. This is characterized by how increasing numbers of patients in hospital describe themselves as 'spiritual but not religious'.[11] Indeed through the multi-faith approach of CPE, the professional chaplain is trained and equipped to minister with those across the faith/philosophical spectrum while at the same time respecting denominational and religious boundaries appropriately. This expanding understanding of and approach to pastoral care can be described as one of increasing specialization and depth, where insights from the human sciences and societal change have been responded to meaningfully by a minority church that seeks to confidently minister alongside and with sister churches in modern Ireland.

---

10 Ibid.   11 D. Nuzum, A. Skuse, K. Keaney, 'Healthcare chaplaincy: a contemporary Irish perspective', *Search*, 40:1 (2017), pp 40–9.

EXPANSION OF HEALTHCARE CHAPLAINCY

In tandem with similar developments in other churches, the Church of Ireland has broadened its expression of healthcare chaplaincy to support and resource the education, training and employment of professional lay healthcare chaplains. The diocese of Dublin and Glendalough has led the way in this regard with the opening of healthcare chaplaincy posts (funded by the health service) in some of the larger acute hospitals in Dublin to accredited lay chaplains who are professionally employed and supported. Of importance is that the same standards of education, training and professional accreditation are in place for both lay and ordained healthcare chaplains who present to the Chaplaincy Accreditation Board for accreditation. Although lay chaplains have been employed in other sectors such as education, this development in approach from the church has been an important step in the formal recognition of ministry and pastoral care in healthcare chaplaincy. The appointment of lay chaplains is also an important statement of the place of pastoral ministry alongside sacramental care and provision which continues through ordained colleagues. This collaborative approach to pastoral care is one that holds much promise for future exploration in parochial settings.

Other dioceses, notably Cork, Cloyne and Ross, and Connor have supported the expansion of pastoral ministry by providing designated pastoral skills training and development to train lay pastoral assistants who serve both in parish and in some healthcare contexts alongside parish clergy and chaplains. In addition the Northern Ireland Healthcare Chaplains' Association also runs hospital pastoral visitors' training in conjunction with Edgehill Theological College. Our covenant relationship with the Methodist Church in Ireland also holds potential for the development of shared pastoral care and ministry, a venture which has begun structurally with the development of shared ordained local ministry training. While the Church of Ireland has long recognized the ministry of lay readers and parish readers in the provision of liturgical ministry, these new developments in the provision of pastoral care are welcome and innovative in a changing ministerial context. Indeed the ministry of reader in itself has a pastoral dimension by virtue of leading worship and prayer.

PRISON CHAPLAINCY

As in healthcare, the church has traditionally appointed clergy to serve as chaplains in prisons. In earlier days, similar to the approach taken with hospitals, it was the local clergy who were de facto appointed as chaplains to prisons in their parishes. This system evolved to a situation where the prison services in both jurisdictions now advertise and recruit their own chaplains. In some cases these chaplains represent their own faith community and require the endorsement of their bishop and in other cases the chaplain is recruited and appointed by the prison authorities to provide generic pastoral care to all without endorsement from any particular faith community. Prison chaplaincy has also evolved to include both lay and ordained chaplains.

MILITARY CHAPLAINCY

Military chaplains have a long and distinguished reputation of service and care to the army, naval and air personnel in both Northern Ireland and in the Republic of Ireland. By virtue of demographics, there are relatively few Church of Ireland chaplains serving in the defence forces in the Republic of Ireland, with chaplains usually nominated by the diocesan bishop to serve local military barracks and corps in the army, the naval service and the air corps. In Northern Ireland, once again by virtue of demographics, there are greater opportunities for military chaplaincy in the British armed forces. In both jurisdictions military chaplains provide valuable pastoral care and support to military personnel and their families. This pastoral care and service also extends to overseas duty and deployment with the United Nations in some cases.

IN CONCLUSION

The trajectory of pastoral care in the fifty years since 1969 can be characterized as a broadening recognition of the place of pastoral ministry and care as being the business of the whole people of God. Pastoral ministry is exercised in diverse contexts, from parish to healthcare, school, prison, the military – wherever the people of God are to be found. This is incarnational ministry in action.

In tandem with immense internal change – from disestablishment through the formation of a new state, the turmoil of the Troubles and the pain of internal reorganization – the Church of Ireland has in the last fifty years found a growing and more confident and self-assured voice in pastoral care. This growing confidence has been characterized by how the church has engaged with many challenging social and ethical issues in a primarily pastoral way. Although the debates on sensitive issues where the church has evolved its practice or polity have at times been painful, especially in the public debating chamber of General Synod, the church has nonetheless sought to be pastoral even when agreement was not possible. Being pastoral is not an artificial panacea of contentedness; more often than not, being pastoral calls us to remain committed to the tensions, disagreements and the brokenness of reality, recognizing that it is in this brokenness and vulnerability that Christ is to be found. In this regard it can be argued that the pastoral dimensions of sensitive issues have given the church the confidence to be courageous, responsive, prophetic and incarnational with integrity and care.

The challenges of the last fifty years have laid important foundation stones for a confident and ongoing commitment to pastoral care across the strata of a diverse and pluralist society in both Northern Ireland and the Republic of Ireland as an all-island church. It has been a formative half-century for the Church of Ireland to continue to build upon.

6

The development of youth work

The Most Revd Patricia Storey, bishop of Meath and Kildare

It is without doubt that there have been huge swathes of change in society and culture throughout the island of Ireland, and alongside this irrefutable fact the same can be said of youth work in the Church of Ireland. Youth work in churches does not look anything like it did in 1969 when the church had been disestablished for one hundred years. It has changed, like this island, beyond recognition. In this chapter we will look at the principal changes in the last fifty years along with their causes and effects, and try to outline where we are now in faith-based youth work, and where indeed the trajectory might be from here.

Firstly, why does youth work merit a chapter in a series of essays on the history of the last fifty years in the Church of Ireland? Why is youth work so important? If we did not have parish youth work, would anyone notice the difference? This author would of course vehemently say 'Yes!' and hopes to demonstrate this in the following pages. We should also not shy away from the unpalatable truth that it is getting much harder to attract young people and young adults to the institutional church, and it can be discouraging, particularly in rural areas, to see perhaps a 'lone ranger' young person in worship, or at best two or three young people. A mention should be made here of the impact in the Republic of Ireland of Church of Ireland boarding schools. Up until fairly recently, most Church of Ireland families in rural areas sent their children to Church of Ireland boarding schools. The impact of this of course was that there were no young people able to participate in church life during the week, and very often they had to be back in their schools by early Sunday evening. Therefore there was very little point in running events either during the week or after lunch on Sunday for young people as they quite literally were not there. There were particular challenges therefore for youth work in the rural areas in the Church of Ireland.

Participation in church life in all the institutional churches is declining, and with that, young families in particular are under pressure in their personal and professional lives, and church attendance does tend to take a back seat. Young adults, and in particular those with small children, can feel so exhausted on arrival home from work, and after putting their children to bed, that the last thing they want to do is to attend a church event during the week. All organizations complain of the increasing difficulty in getting anyone out to a midweek event. The culture is changing and commitment to any organization is being affected. It is not solely a problem for youth work, but it certainly should raise our awareness of the issues that impact upon any church activity.

In secular circles 'young people' are defined as those 'between the ages of 11–25' and so our Church of Ireland definition of a young person as 'under 45' seems rather ludicrous. An 18-year-old does not see someone of 45 years of age as young. We will come to challenges later on in this chapter, but suffice it to say at this point that one of our major challenges in youth work in the Church of Ireland is harnessing the energy of very few young people in a parish, who may be scattered around several churches. How do you plan youth work for such a scenario? How do you even establish any kind of group? We will explore this shortly.

In 1969 and in the ten years that followed, youth and children's work in churches was primarily witnessed in the activities of uniformed organizations. Parishes would run Church Lads' Brigade, or the Girls' Friendly Society. Many churches used their halls for Girls' Brigade and Boys' Brigade, Scouts and Guides. Through much of the 1970s and early 1980s, the energy and volunteer hours garnered from church leaders were ploughed into the uniformed organizations. These served a wonderful purpose before the advent of informal youth work, which took hold in the institutional churches towards the end of the 1970s. Indeed, for a long time, the uniformed organizations and informal youth work existed side by side and there were still significant numbers of young people in each. Much of youth leadership owes its origins to the uniformed organizations and to their training of young people for leadership roles.

While the uniformed organizations still exist in many parishes, it would be fair to say that the numbers are not encouraging, and the activities are less attractive to a generation that has a hundred things from which to choose.

DEVELOPMENT

The environment has changed enormously from the days in the 1960s and 1970s when the parish church was the hub of all social activity, including clubs for children and young people. Young people now have a range of choices regarding how to spend their spare time. Sport is an increasingly looming spectre on the feast of Sunday worship for instance – many sports clubs and activities operate primarily at weekends and often the matches are set for Sunday mornings. This, of course, inevitably affects the attendance at church of our children and young people. Even if they would be inclined to stay involved in church life after confirmation, they have choices to make and their love for sport often vies with their familial pull to the local parish. Indeed many youth workers would say that the key challenge in youth work is to provide an attractive alternative at a different time from Sunday mornings that would keep young people invested in church life.

To define 'informal youth work', it would be understood to include mainly youth clubs and youth fellowships. The main difference between the two was that the youth club was principally there to bring young people into a safe space for an evening (perhaps in Northern Ireland, particularly during the Troubles, but also for all of the island) – there may have been an epilogue, but the entertainment was principally sport and games. A youth fellowship was more likely to involve worship and biblical teaching and focus more specifically on a young person's spiritual life and relationship with God.

During the 1970s and '80s it would probably never have occurred to anyone that you would pay someone to take care of youth work in your church. There was no culture of salaried youth workers and the vast majority of clubs were organized by volunteers. In many churches, uniformed organizations thrived for a long time because of the vast number of volunteer hours that people in churches were prepared to give to their young people. Many adults are thankful for their upbringing in the uniformed organizations throughout their childhood and into their teenaged years.

Another manifestation of investment in young people in the Republic of Ireland was the proverbial 'Protestant disco' at the Green Isle Hotel on the Naas Road and other venues. One correspondent with whom I spoke declared that this primarily existed as a way of preserving the Protestant tribe. It wasn't so much youth work as a marriage bureau! While many could look back and see this as a rather sectarian initiative, it is also understandable when you are in the minority and you have an impetus for survival.

As the late 1970s progressed, the youth culture began to change. The Church of Ireland Youth Council set up an office and employed staff. There was an annual conference north and south of the border and youth work officially became more central to church life. Many churches started youth fellowships in order to further disciple their young people and prepare them for a life of faith. These often ran alongside confirmation classes in the hope of keeping the confirmation candidates involved in church life. Indeed it is quite legitimate to say that confirmation is, in itself, a vital part of youth work, as it too aims to help young people to retain an active faith into adulthood. It would be fair to say that where youth work was active and healthy and had enthusiastic leadership in parishes, those parishes were more successful in retaining young people in church life. Where parishes did very little to encourage youth work, very often they encountered a low level of interest in any ongoing relationship between those young people and any investment in their church.

In the mid- to late 1980s something interesting began to happen. Firstly, and there is no way to overestimate the impact of this, in 1987 the first Summer Madness festival took place. Summer Madness originated in the Church of Ireland and is a Christian youth festival that has been run in several locations in Northern Ireland. Young people and their leaders come and camp for five days and there is a range of events to encourage Christian faith in young people. There is the 'big top' event where worship takes place both morning and evening, and it is one of the only times I have ever seen queues to get into worship. During the day there will be seminars and debates on topical issues. There will also be a lot of sporting activities, and fun and games laid on, and indeed, inevitably, the odd mishap. The onset of Summer Madness on the youth scene in Northern Ireland (although attended over the years by many from the Republic too) was, and remains, utterly seminal. Many of our present-day rectors, lay readers and volunteer leaders point back to Summer Madness as a pivotal point in their spiritual journey. The festival has generated a generation of leaders that serve in many parishes around the island. Many ordained clergy would say that their living faith originated and was encouraged through attendance at Summer Madness and similar events. We should be eternally grateful for the work of Summer Madness, whether or not it is everyone's 'cup of tea'. Much tribute should be paid to John Kee, who piloted and then steered Summer Madness from those early days right through to this year, when thousands of young people will camp at Glenarm Castle and queue for Christian teaching and worship. Who knew?

Alongside Summer Madness, and probably partly due to the festival's impact, there emerged the 'parish youth worker', who was actually paid to work with the young people. The Church of Ireland Youth Council had been set up several years before this and it continued to respond to the needs of young people and to staff and coordinate much of the excellent work that was beginning to take place. It should be added that before the advent of the salaried youth worker, the rector or the curate was responsible for the spiritual health of young people and many did a fantastic job of this. Of course it was in general only the larger parishes that could afford youth workers – so smaller parishes had no choice but to do the best they could. Many adults look back on their discipleship by rectors and curates with great thankfulness. There is also a myriad of volunteers in the rural dioceses who plug on with youth work without a paid officer at all. However, the landscape did begin to change and there began to be a pathway for a young adult to begin to do some training that would equip them for this work. YouthLink in Northern Ireland and diocesan youth councils all around the island encouraged training and equipping youth workers who felt that ministry to young people was their vocation. YouthLink was established in Northern Ireland in 1992 by the four main churches as a response to its divided society at youth level. Father Paddy White was the first training and development officer and he now leads the organization. YouthLink was formed and still exists to resource church-based youth work and to encourage a model of effective collaboration. While the purpose of the organization was to complement denominational youth work, as the years have progressed there is more and more integrated youth work happening in all the church-based organizations.

Diocesan youth councils were established in most dioceses by this time, and the Church of Ireland Youth Council had already been established to oversee and encourage training for both paid staff and volunteers in youth ministry. They appointed staff, North and South, to encourage and build up those who felt that they wanted to serve young people across the land. At one time rectors began to employ youth workers instead of curates. They could not afford both, and some chose to invest primarily in their youth work.

The early 1990s brought the first diocesan youth officer. This enabled a diocese to invest heavily in young people and to have a dedicated officer for youth work. While this new initiative took time to embed itself in the Church of Ireland, at the present time almost every diocese in the Church of Ireland has a diocesan youth officer. It is a big financial commitment – but it also demonstrates a seriousness about young people and their future. Between 1993 and the present day, having a diocesan youth officer in a diocese has almost become the norm.

In 1999 the Church of Ireland Youth Council became a recognized body of General Synod. It was rebranded as the Church of Ireland Youth Department and established a central board where every diocese continued to be represented around the table. Out of those meetings came many new initiatives including Anois, which was a kind of 'mini Summer Madness'. It took place for the first time in 2006 and there have been eleven Anois events since then in different venues. While it did not attract large numbers (180 to 280 people), it was again a very seminal influence on the young people and the volunteers who attended. It was a victim of its own success to some extent, as all its volunteer leaders moved on to do other things in their own dioceses and parishes.

PROGRESS

It would be fair to say that there has always been a little tension between North and South in terms of funding and resources. There has always been an understandable request for financial parity and equality of resources, and even though the Church of Ireland Youth Department has always tried to be absolutely fair, this fearfulness does still exist if you scratch the surface. It has become incumbent upon all of us to ensure that whatever one part of the island gets for their youth work, the other part feels equally resourced, but there remains some tension under the surface which arises when any grant money is available. However, we are definitely in a much better place than we used to be and we are thankful for that. It probably mirrors other church organizations in this respect.

It was recognized in the Christian churches that more energy and money needed to be invested in serious training for youth workers. At Belfast Bible College, encouraged by YouthLink, a new degree course was started in 2008 offering a BA Hons in youth and community and practical theology, and this was the first of its kind on this island. Those who showed serious interest in a career in youth work took this study option and faith-based youth work was rather suddenly and rightly recognized as a viable career option. The course gave recognition and skills to those who had passion and a vision for young people. At this point over 120 people have completed the degree course, many of whom have gone on to be involved in youth ministry. Salaried youth workers do complain that due to the fact that they get involved in church life, they are always asked if they are considering ordination. It is almost as if youth ministry cannot be a serious option or vocation in itself, and surely if you are getting involved in study for church life, you must want to be ordained? I have heard many youth workers disavow the questioner in no uncertain terms. You can be called to youth ministry, and have no intention of getting ordained.

I really would like at this point to salute the ministry of parish and diocesan youth officers. They give not just their time and talents, but often their own social lives, to the care of their young people, which is why so often they burn out rather quickly. When adults are tucked up in bed, youth workers are still investing in their young people, often long after midnight. In my experience of managing youth workers, the rector very often does not understand why the youth officer is reluctant to turn up at a staff meeting at nine o'clock in the morning, and I have often heard youth workers described as 'lazy'. However, I feel that this often disregards the timetable under which youth workers operate – they often work when the rest of us are asleep and they do have to recover at some time in the day. They need to find the energy and passion for the next long meeting at unsociable hours, and their own social lives certainly suffer. They are often working when their friends are available and their own self-care needs to be addressed. I often feel that there is a lack of understanding of a youth worker's investment in their young people and the toll that this takes on them as people. The vast majority of youth workers that I have met are dedicated, industrious and care for those around them to their own detriment. They are most certainly not 'lazy'. Their ministry is just different.

However, there is an issue around a career in youth ministry that does need to be examined. One of the youth workers I contacted about this chapter bewailed the lack of career progression in youth ministry. He felt that salaried youth workers, both parochial and diocesan, were not really seriously regarded. Their voice was not really heard. They did not feel called to ordination, and even the pathway to ordination they felt would not have suited their temperament and skills. They also felt that for those who would have considered ordination, the present method of selection and training would not have been either easy or suitable. So after a few years in the job a parish or a diocesan youth officer can become uninspired and see no career plan ahead. At one time when I worked for the Church of Ireland Youth Department, the average lifespan of a youth worker in a parish was 18 months. Inevitably, youth workers got older, got married, had children and needed a more secure and a better-paid career. It is rare that someone makes a lifelong career out of youth work.

CHALLENGES

Are we serious about discipling our young people? Are we just heaving a sigh of relief when we get them to confirmation and then we can feel that we have done our duty – whether we are parents, grandparents, godparents or clergy? When you look around your churches, in thirty years' time, who do you think will be there? It has been my experience that where there have been central, diocesan and parochial funds and personnel made available specifically for youth work, our young people inevitably benefit. They are taken seriously and included. Their voices are heard. The Church of Ireland Youth Department now runs an annual Youth Forum for the whole of the Church of Ireland and each diocese is invited to send three to six young people. They are encouraged to influence policy, to get elected on to vestries and committees, to attend synods and to find a way to be included and for their voices to be heard.

In a 2017 survey by the Barna group in the Republic of Ireland about the attitudes of young people to Christian faith, called 'Finding faith in Ireland', there were some very interesting findings and indeed some sober statistics. Half of young adults say that they are less spiritual today than when they were 12 years old. Their church attendance has declined over time and 67 per cent say that they are less active in church than when they were children. Young adults feel increasing conflict between progressive values and Christian morality as it is traditionally taught. However, interestingly, 71 per cent of young practicing Christians in Ireland want to find a way to follow Jesus that connects them to the world they live in. The Barna Report asks: who will help them? Young adults worry more about their world and their prospects. It would be interesting for the church to harness the drive in young adults to make a difference to the world – they are concerned about climate change, overseas relief and international politics. They are also extremely anxious about social media, their self-image and their mental health. For them, as for us, the world is changing and that can be a frightening prospect. The Barna Report indicates that young adults feel deep insecurities about themselves and about their world. Again, is not the church in a position to teach and to offer help? Should we not be addressing the issues that face our young people, rather than the issues that we feel they need to know and we want them to address?

We all complain that young people do not attend our churches or get involved in the church at a central level. However, for the most part, we hold our central and diocesan events at times which do not suit young adults. If I want young adults involved in my diocesan synod or council, and I want them to influence policy, the worst way I can effect that is to schedule a meeting during the day. Young adults work. If they are teachers and office workers and health workers, they cannot drop everything to attend a church meeting. I was asked recently to nominate a representative for a central committee and to make an effort to find a young adult. I found a fantastic young adult who is a teacher – however, the meetings were at 2 o'clock in the afternoon and no one mooted changing the time to suit the young adult. So that young adult, who has immense passion and skills, is not able to contribute to that committee. We need to change this if we are serious about hearing the voices of young people, and so sometimes I am tempted to ask: are we?

What are the key challenges of youth work in the average parish? That of course depends on many things – is the parish small or large, Northern or Southern, urban or rural? Does the diocese have a dedicated officer for its young people? In rural areas, are parents or volunteers willing to commit to travel in order to take young people to events? Parents need to play some part too in the discipleship of their sons and daughters. However we view it, investment in youth work is the only answer. For we know what happens when we do not invest: nothing. Our youth work never stands still for long – if there is no investment then it moves backwards. Most people who attend worship feel that we have lost enough. If we are adamant in refuting decline, the next generation and the one after that should be the target of our money, energy, volunteering and imagination. Young people and young adults are brimming with ideas, enthusiasm, spirituality and passion for the world. We need to harness it. We need to care.

HOPES

So what are the signs of hope? I have already referred to Summer Madness and Anois, and it is true to say that the youth stream at New Wine, held each year in Sligo, commits to encouraging lifelong faith in children and young people. There are many diocesan youth officers and parish youth and children's workers who are giving their lives to the young people in their care. The central church finances the Youth Department so that our youth leaders can be trained and encouraged in their vocation. Numerous volunteers plug away in their own corners encouraging youth ministry in their parish and in their diocese.

I will finish as I started by reflecting on the changing societal culture in Ireland, both North and South. We can no longer hold missions that expect non-believers to come to us. Our churches are not necessarily viewed as accessible entities by many in the community. It is no longer the case, for instance, in the Republic, that the Protestant population is 3 per cent and the other 97 per cent are Roman Catholic. In the last census the rise of the 'nones' has made the whole village or town the mission field. Talking about our faith is no longer proselytizing another faith. We might need to bring imagination to how we can reach out into our communities. Many, many parishes are doing this extremely well. It is, of course, not all about the young people. Many parishes have targeted initiatives at older people, young parents, the bereaved, the recently divorced – young people are only one part of the family, albeit a rather vital part.

In the same way, youth work has to bring more imagination to bear and reach out into the community, providing for all young people. It would be wise to ask what young people in our areas actually need and want, before we embark on such a task. How we measure success is really very difficult as it may not be solely assessed by numbers. New initiatives like Messy Church principally aimed at children do not for the most part increase attendance at Sunday worship, although they have proven popular for new growth. Messy Church is worship based around crafts: there is praise time followed by crafts around tables where the Bible story for that day is taught and then a free, cooked meal; for some in deprived areas the free meal has been welcomed. Parishioners and rectors have had to get their heads around the fact that for those at Messy Church, that is their church (albeit perhaps at entry level). The challenge is: how do we begin to disciple those children and their parents in a different way? Is the measure of our success only greater numbers at church? Or do we have to think creatively, in youth work and in all our outreach, about meeting people where they are at and learning to have the confidence to share our faith in their environment, and not only in ours. The landscape is changing.

CONCLUSION

The moral of the story is: listen to young people and include them. Take them seriously and allow them to be heard, including at central level. Never was this more important than now in the institutional churches. It is not too late. We often hear the phrase 'young people are the future of the church', and I have a particular antipathy to that phrase – young people are not the future of the church. Young people are the present.

Fifty years of youth work has brought a richness of faith to a great number of young people. I am proud of our church and its continuing investment in our youth and children. If we counted up over the fifty years the money, the volunteers and the volunteer hours invested in our young people, we would see that the church would be a greatly impoverished place had this wonderful investment not taken place. So as president of the Church of Ireland Youth Department, I want to end with a thank you – thank you to the Church of Ireland for taking young people seriously and making an extremely worthy investment. Although there are very significant challenges, we look forward, with the help of God, to what the next fifty years will hold.

7

The Church of Ireland:
politics and social change

The Rt Revd John McDowell, bishop of Clogher, and
the Rt Revd Michael Burrows, bishop of Cashel,
Ferns and Ossory

In the archives of the Standing Committee for the year 1975 there is a short paper written by the Queen's University historian and parishioner of St Thomas', Belfast, Professor J.C. Beckett. The paper is entitled 'Religion and politics in Ireland: the position and responsibility of the Church of Ireland'. Written during a year of deepening violence and political sclerosis in Northern Ireland, it sets out with admirable brevity 'where we are' as a society and goes on to suggest what the Church of Ireland's vocation might be in the circumstances. It is worth quoting at some length:

> [T]he Church of Ireland is in a position to take an important part. Alone among the Protestant denominations it has a substantial stake in the Republic, where it is, for most purposes, the natural mouthpiece of the Protestant minority. Unlike the Presbyterians it has never had a distinctively 'Ulster' character. Though a large majority of its members now live in the North, it maintains its administrative headquarters in Dublin; and Southern churchmen play, in relation to their numbers, a very influential part in its affairs. The only other religious denomination with a comparable 'cross border' character is the Roman Catholic Church; and its position is, in one important respect, quite different. For all practical purposes it is politically committed; it is identified with the policy of bringing the Six County area under the control of a government in Dublin ... In other words Roman Catholics on both sides of the border represent, on this critical issue, a single point of view. The Church of Ireland has no such political commitment. An overwhelming majority of its members in the North are unionists; but those in the South have no distinctive political label. And on whichever side of the border they may be, Churchmen accept the legality of the constitution under which they live. The Church of Ireland, then, represents in a unique way the idea of a non–political unity – the only kind of unity that Ireland seems likely to attain in the foreseeable future.

It is a vision of a church with a distinctive role to play in both Northern Ireland and the Republic of Ireland by using its character, moulded by its historical experience, to help shift political discussion away from what we would now call 'binary' or 'zero-sum' constitutional concepts and towards the difficult business of living together while accepting the inevitability of a certain tension to be used creatively towards a union of diverse hearts and minds.

Thinking of the church in terms of its synods, committees and official spokespeople rather than its 'ordinary' members, we can ask how far has the Church of Ireland lived up to Beckett's vision? Or has the opposite happened? In the words of one of the founder members of the Corrymeela Community (speaking about Northern Ireland), has 'society influenced the Church much more than the Church has influenced society'?

The period with which we are dealing begins with an organizational failure within the Church of Ireland. After many years of work a committee dominated by lay people from both jurisdictions had produced a report entitled *Administration*. The report was a thorough and thoughtful attempt at examining how the Church of Ireland should organize itself to face outwards towards the modern world. It was extraordinarily wide-ranging, looking at diocesan administration, synods, boundaries and the resourcing of bishops, which it identified as crucial for speaking clearly into a rapidly pluralizing society. By slow degrees, successive General Synods crept away from its conclusions. One permanent archdeacon was appointed in a single diocese and even that innovation lapsed when he was elected as bishop a few years later. One diocese was detached and added to another, the ripples of which cataclysm continue to be talked about around the coffee tables of the General Synod.

Even had *Administration* been implemented in full it would not have changed the ineluctable reality that as a church we disperse our resources and what might be called our social capital across twelve diocesan centres with a minimally equipped central organization compared to the research and specialist capabilities of more centrally organized bodies. Such diffuse organization makes for interesting and varied debate but reduces the possibility of focused executive follow-through.

In some ways the church made a good start in the turbulent '60s. Contemplating the rapidly deteriorating security and political situation in Northern Ireland the diocesan synod of Cork, Cloyne and Ross sent a resolution to the Standing Committee of the General Synod asking it to establish a body to consider the role of the church in relation to what was happening in society north and south of the border.

The result was the creation of the Role of the Church Committee (ROCC) in April 1970, which was responsible for addressing the many social and political issues emanating from the ferment of the 1960s. Its members could by no means be considered *soixante-huitards* but it included and soon attracted clergy such as Dean Victor Griffin (who along with future Bishop Samuel Poyntz was to have substantial experience of leadership in both jurisdictions), Robin Eames, Jim Mehaffey,

Gordon McMullan, Eric Elliott, David Bleakley (a future executive minister in Northern Ireland), J.A. Young, J.L.B. Deane and David Bird, the latter both leading laymen in Cork.[1]

The ROCC provided an opportunity for the first time for clergy and lay people from both jurisdictions to have space and time outside the crowded agendas of the Standing Committee and the General Synod to *consider together* the social and political issues arising in both jurisdictions. Its terms of reference were 'to study the positive role of the Church in all aspects of political, social and economic life in Ireland and report back from time to time'. Moreover, its members accepted that there was no point in addressing contemporary society *de haut en bas* or in a manner which society had long since surrendered a desire to hear.

At a special meeting of the Standing Committee held immediately following the pre-General Synod evensong in May 1970, the ROCC presented its first report which affirmed 'the personal dignity of all human beings, their right to be free to know and serve the truth and their responsibility for the general welfare of the whole community in which they live'.

Moreover, it alone of Church of Ireland committees appointed a dedicated, though part-time secretary/researcher, Mr J.T. McGaffin, who throughout the life of the committee produced very high-quality papers for each meeting and at a time when the body to which it reported (the Standing Committee) met ten times per annum.

The committee was most fruitful in the 1970s, producing substantial documents on a wide range of matters, some of which continue to vex the Church of Ireland. Although the Troubles in Northern Ireland continued to dominate the church and society interface, the ROCC made sure that other social developments were kept in sight.

For instance its report to the Standing Committee for March 1972 includes, inter alia, an encouragement to greater contacts between Northern and Southern parishes; a critical note on Pope Paul VIs recent *motu proprio* on mixed marriage; some scepticism about the increasing use in NI of the term 'institutional violence'; an expression of regret at the introduction of internment in NI along with a hope that releases would soon happen; and an affirmation of the right of 'individual priests or deacons' to join the Orange Order, but also a wariness of the consequent link with a political party.

None of these can be considered as radical comment and may to some degree serve to underline the Church of Ireland's ability to identify issues without directly

1 Jim Mehaffey became bishop of Derry (1980–2002) and exercised a personal and costly ministry of reconciliation in that city and diocese during days of appalling violence and destruction. Gordon McMullan was elected bishop of Clogher (1989–6) and translated to Down and Dromore (1986–96). In both dioceses he brought a measured and academically robust analysis of socio-economic issues. Canon Eric Elliott was a distinguished educationalist and teacher as well as a much-loved rector of St Thomas, Belfast. John Young, Barry Deane and David Bird brought a fearless, experienced and open-minded commitment to the affairs of the Church of Ireland.

addressing them. However, they were at least a beginning in bringing them to the church as matters requiring honest consideration. The last item on Orange Order membership also helps to underline that, in NI at least, the task of disentangling or at least bringing to the surface a number of informal but very deep-seated connections between the church and society would have to take place alongside encouraging a more distinctively Anglican contribution to the analysis of contentious issues and an emphasis on the common good.

Although space does not permit, an analysis of the weekly columns written in the *Church of Ireland Gazette* by Canon John Barry under the pseudonym 'Cromlyn' would give an indication of the struggles of a very self-consciously Anglican writer steeped in Northern society to work out his convictions with great honesty and integrity in the face of changing the realities of modern Ireland.

For instance, the Standing Committee papers for April 1975 contain what is probably the first reference to gay rights, in the form of a letter, appended to which was a forthright report from the first International Gay Rights Movement Conference, which had taken place in Edinburgh. By February 1976 a majority ROCC report recommended the decriminalizing of homosexual acts and urged church members not to approach the subject in a condemnatory manner, while also encouraging further medical research in the 'hope that effective treatment can be found'. A minority on the committee argued that 'homosexual relationships are the best possible for a number of people, the only relationship they can hope to achieve' and urged greater acceptance.

As will be noted a little further on in this chapter, the debate on human sexuality has moved on to a great degree in the Republic of Ireland, but attitudes in Northern Ireland, including within the Church of Ireland, have not conspicuously changed. However, within the Northern Ireland Assembly the paradoxical situation exists whereby a majority of the representatives of the nationalist/Catholic population have consistently voted in favour of same-sex marriage, contrary to the teaching of the Roman Catholic Church, while the majority of the representatives of the unionist/Protestant community have voted against marriage equality, in keeping with the teaching of their churches.

As might be imagined, the security and political situation in Northern Ireland was a significant (though not a dominant) feature of the work of the ROCC, the Standing Committee and the General Synod at least up to the signing of the Good Friday/Belfast Agreement, all taking place against a background of an almost anarchic society for much of the 1970s and an 'acceptable level of violence' in the 1980s and early '90s.

In relation to the Troubles and the permanent political crisis that existed in Northern Ireland throughout much of the period it is probably true to say that the Church of Ireland, in common with the other churches, made its greatest contribution unseen, by its pastoral care of victims and their families and by the unremitting moderation shown by its public representatives at times of crisis locally and province-wide. Many clergy and laypeople were quiet peacemakers in extraordinarily difficult circumstances, beginning with the establishment of an Information Centre at St Anne's Cathedral in 1969–70, whose principal spokesperson was the forthright Archdeacon Billy McCourt of Down, and on through to the witness made by Canon Stuart Lloyd standing in solidarity with worshippers at the Roman Catholic Church in the Harryville area of Ballymena while they endured sectarian harassment by groups of militant Protestants during the late 1990s.

If the early 1970s were marked by what became known as the 'Ripon Affair', when threats from an ultra-Protestant organization caused the dean of Belfast to cancel a visit of the bishop of Ripon (who had been the official Church of England observer at the Second Vatican Council), and when the bishop of Clogher, theologian and Patrician scholar R.P.C. Hanson felt unable to continue in his episcopal ministry (because, he believed, of hostility generated by what he had said about Northern Ireland's brand of Protestantism), it was also the decade of the Feakle meeting between church leaders and the senior members of the Provisional IRA,[2] and the initiative that led to Protestant and Catholic Church leaders meeting and speaking together in a formal way through the Ballymascanlon conferences.

However, the note of the Feakle meeting in the report of the ROCC to the Standing Committee in February 1975 exposes the inner tensions of the moment, outlining 'respect' for 'the courage and dignity of the churchmen, clerical and lay, who, acting on their own responsibility, engaged at the meeting in Feakle and subsequent contacts with Provisional Sinn Fein'.

A certain degree of evasion in more straightforward ecclesiastical matters was also evident. For instance in April 1975 a notice of motion was tabled at the Standing Committee to amend a number of references in the 39 Articles which might reasonably be thought to be gratuitously offensive to Roman Catholics. The proposer agreed to withdraw his motion in favour of another by Dean Victor Griffin of St Patrick's, Dublin that 'an explanatory statement of the 39 Articles in the Church of Ireland be published'. However, by the meeting of 27 January 1976 it was decided that a query on how best to deal with the 39 Articles should be sent to the Anglican Consultative Council (ACC). It was not until 2008 that a declaration along the lines proposed by Dean Griffin in 1975 was adopted by the General Synod to be prefixed to the articles in the 2019 reprint of the 2004 *Book of Common Prayer*.

In some areas the nuancing of attitudes to social change was slow but it was steady. The October 1969 meeting of the Standing Committee had received a very

---

2 On 10 December 1974 a group of church leaders including the bishop of Connor (Arthur Butler) and Revd William Arlow met representatives of the republican movement in Smyth's Hotel, Feakle, Co. Clare to explore in what way it might be possible to bring peace to Northern Ireland. The representatives of the republican movement included not only the president of Sinn Féin (Rúairí Ó Brádaigh) and the chief of staff of the Provisional IRA (Dáithí Ó Conaill) but also all but one member of the Provisional Army Council. The discussions lasted only for a few hours until the hotel was raided by Garda Special Branch and Irish Army personnel. The members of the republican movement escaped just before the police and army arrived.

lengthy report called 'Women church workers', and by 1975, in response to a request for its opinion from the ACC, the House of Bishops declared unanimously that there were 'no valid theological objections to the ordination of women'. The first ordination of a woman to priest's orders took place in 1980 in St Anne's Cathedral in Belfast, and of course the archbishop of Armagh, Robert Eames, chaired the Anglican Communion commission that set an official communion seal on the ordination of women. During his brief (1970–3) and controversial episcopate in Clogher R.P.C. Hanson noticed that the canons governing the matter did not specify that diocesan readers should be men, so he immediately licensed women.

Not everyone shared in even this slow *aggiornamento*. During the 1970s when some of the more radical policies of the World Council of Churches in relation to liberation struggles around the world were causing deep concern in other denominations in Ireland, a motion was brought to Standing Committee condemning the WCC for providing 'an unsupervised gift of soya bean meal to the Provisional Government of South Vietnam (Viet-Cong)'. A seconder could not be found.

In short, political progress towards a more genuinely pluralist society in Northern Ireland, and the Church of Ireland contribution to that progress, was (sometimes literally) painfully slow. For instance, the deep concern of the unionist community at the signing of the Anglo-Irish Agreement by the governments of the Republic of Ireland and the United Kingdom, which formally recognized a consultative role for the Republic in the affairs of Northern Ireland, is reflected in correspondence between the primate, Archbishop John Ward Armstrong, and the prime minister appended to the Standing Committee minutes of the period.

The stand-off at Drumcree (1995–8), when a Church of Ireland parish church became the focus of a bitter loyalist confrontation with the government and the security forces about rights of assembly, horrified and perplexed many observers around the world and was the cause of sharp exchanges at all levels within the church. Although virtually powerless to correct what was amiss, the episode became a protracted nightmare for the church and what Robin Eames, the archbishop of Armagh, called his personal Calvary.[3]

Drumcree also gave rise to a good deal of soul-searching within the church as a whole and also to what became the Hard Gospel project (2005–9). This project, benefiting from considerable public funding, generated a good deal of useful study material and a degree of strategizing on how to address the issue of 'dealing with difference'. As with most centrally organized initiatives it was hampered in its success by the structural weaknesses within the Church of Ireland for delivering any strategy, and is something of a case study for the change-management adage that 'culture eats strategy for breakfast'.

However, beside that has to be placed the central contribution of Archbishop Eames to the Downing Street Declaration around the whole idea of the principle

3 Quoted in a *Belfast Telegraph* interview with journalist and Eames biographer Alf McCreary, 26 Dec. 2006.

of consent, which was to be the foundation of future Anglo-Irish negotiations leading up to and including the Good Friday/Belfast Agreement. Eames dominated
both the church and the image of the church throughout Ireland and in the wider
world during the years of his long primacy (1986–2006). His cautious yet focused
diplomacy was a considerable asset in a church that could so easily have torn itself
apart over political differences. His was a crucial voice of moderation respected
throughout Ireland and internationally.

South of the border the disestablishment centenary in 1969 took place almost at
a 'time between the times' in the experience of the membership of the Church of
Ireland in the Republic. The 'new' state was more than a generation old; a younger
generation looked nowhere else to bestow their political loyalty. The relative economic prosperity of the 1960s had boosted the morale of many and the Republic
was on the verge, in a somewhat paradoxical way, of rediscovering its independence
from Britain through enthusiastic participation in the bigger world of the EEC.
The Troubles in the North were in their infancy and there was as yet little sense of
how elongated or painful they would prove to be.

So the Church of Ireland in the South could aspire to be that 'confident minority' of which Bishop Arthur Butler famously spoke.[4] An improving ecumenical
climate in the aftermath of Vatican II of course aided this confidence. Apart from
the small Jewish community, the Protestant minority was really the only significant
minority that existed within the Ireland of *c.*1970, and the state could afford not
just to be kind to it in a patronizing sense, but to cherish it in a more receptive and
generous sense.

There were many symptoms of the 'confident minority' syndrome at that time.
The 'special position' of the Roman Catholic Church was deleted fairly controversially from the constitution in 1972 – and with it went old fears that, for example,
the civil law might be used to aid and abet the upholding of Roman Catholic canon
law in relation to mixed-marriage discipline. State funding was poured into the
provision of new school buildings, particularly in the primary sector.

At the multitudinous openings of new schools and school extensions, prelates
such as Archbishop Simms and Bishop McAdoo charmed and impressed the political cohorts by speaking in mellifluous Irish. In 1973 Erskine Childers, a member
of the Church of Ireland of unimpeachable Republican credentials, was decisively elected as president in succession to the retiring Eamon de Valera. Childers'
inauguration symbolized many of the paradoxes of the time. He insisted that the
preceding service in St Patrick's Cathedral would be a Eucharist. He received the
sacrament; his Roman Catholic wife did not. Most members of the government
attended a separate pre-inauguration Mass in the Pro-Cathedral. The English-
educated president-elect had no Irish, although his literary-cum-political father
had been executed by the pro-Treaty side during the Civil War for possession of a

---

4 Butler used these words in a sermon preached in St Patrick's Cathedral, Dublin on the eve of the
General Synod of 1963.

firearm. The younger Erskine could only take the prescribed presidential oath in Irish when it was written out for him phonetically.

In retrospect, it is easy to forget that the Church of Ireland community of the time were still essentially conservative. W.B. Yeats' earlier anger over the prohibition of divorce did not seem to vex many, and it would not be until the 1990s that the church resolved its own agonizings over the remarriage in church of divorced persons. The young women who took the famous contraception trains to Belfast in the early '70s did not include many prominent Anglicans in their number, and when shortly afterwards Taoiseach Liam Cosgrave voted against his own government's attempt to legislate very modestly for the provision of contraception (the bill was defeated), there do not seem to have been seismic protest waves across the Church of Ireland.

By the mid-1970s Archbishop McQuaid's famous 'ban' on Roman Catholics attending TCD without special dispensation on account of its threat to faith and morals had at last been lifted. The University's representatives in Seanad Éireann, some but not all members of the Church of Ireland, became renowned for their use of law reform in the pursuit of what they saw as basic human rights, and were prepared to make their cases in the European courts. Names such as David Norris (an Anglican) and Mary Robinson (not an Anglican but married to one) are well written on the pages of history in relation to the rights of women and gay people. They came out of a TCD, which continued to be, although in a somewhat diminishing sense, a true meeting ground of North and South. Most members of the Church of Ireland outside the college walls were not quite so passionate.

The early '80s were years of great political uncertainty, partly on account of extremely disturbing events in Northern Ireland, including the infamous hunger strikes at the Maze prison. The elections both to the House of Commons and the Dáil of convicted imprisoned hunger strikers can in retrospect be seen as the moment when the combination of the gun and the ballot box became strategically powerful in a manner that was to transform politics. The quest not just to take guns out of politics but also to decommission them became the great issue in Anglo-Irish relations up to the late 1990s, by which point the essential nature of everything from policing to political participation in Northern Ireland was being transformed. Looking back at those years, it is remarkable how the concerns of the Anglicans of the South remained in many ways much more domestic. Constant prayers for peace were offered in churches, no doubt with great sincerity, and there was a real sense of the unending travail of co-religionists not many miles away. Yet the North remained, as Archbishop Gregg had once perhaps unhappily put it, 'a strange land spiritually and politically'.[5] Polite Southerners frowned when they felt the *Church of Ireland Gazette* was dominated by news from 'up there', and they were at pains to assure their neighbours of their embarrassment at some of the excesses of the Orange Order.

5 G. Seaver, *John Allen Fitzgerald Gregg: archbishop* (Dublin, 1963), p. 217.

There was no doubt sectarianism in the South too, usually of a more subtle and less visible kind, but it fuelled the relative ghettoization of education and the tendency of a small minority at times to define its spiritual identity in negative terms over and against the beliefs of others. However, in the early 1980s there was something of a public clash over the so-called 'pro-life amendment'. During the political turbulence of the period, which included three general elections in rapid succession, politicians of varying hues sought to garner the support of a powerful emerging movement that aspired to copper-fasten the statutory prohibition on abortion by inserting in the constitution an amendment guaranteeing the right to life of the unborn. A fear lurked in certain quarters that without such an amendment abortion might be foisted on the people by a judgement in the courts, as had happened in the USA. While most of the Church of Ireland bishops were reluctant to join vociferously in the campaign, and the archbishop of Dublin[6] was reputed to have hastily approved the wording, the general feeling in the Church of Ireland was that the pro-life amendment represented the absolutist position of the Roman Catholic Church, a position repeatedly emphasized by Pope John Paul II, whose 1979 visit to Ireland had been greeted with such rapture. The anti-amendment campaign found a leader in Victor Griffin, the outspoken and popular dean of St Patrick's Dublin, who saw himself as a latter-day Swift, not least through his determination to improve the quality of life of inner-city residents. Griffin, whose Christmas sermons advocating a society of tolerance and pluralism were published annually in the *Irish Times*, contended that the amendment was unnecessary, divisive and even sectarian. The constitution, he argued, was no place for addressing complex moral issues, and while Anglicans might hesitate to condone abortion except in exceptional medical circumstances, nevertheless giving 'the unborn' a right to life equal to that of the mother was a bridge too far. After a bitter campaign the 8th amendment was endorsed by a 2:1 majority of voters. When it was repealed in 2018, by a similar majority, it was ironic that more bishops appeared to favour its retention than had endorsed its insertion in 1983.

The next great 'liberal' campaign was to achieve the removal of the constitutional prohibition on divorce, again a favoured theme of Griffin's in his sermons on festal days. The first attempt to do this was made by the government of Garret FitzGerald in a referendum in 1986, a component of the taoiseach's 'crusade' to make the constitution more inclusive. The ground was ill-prepared, particularly in the farming community, and all sorts of fears concerning the inheritance of land were inflamed. It was only in 1995 that civil divorce was introduced by the very narrowest of voting margins. The amendment of 1995 made it constitutionally mandatory that divorce should be preceded by a period of at least four years of separation, a restriction that over time became regarded as excessively restrictive. In a relatively uncontentious referendum in 2019, the constitution was further amended to remove its cumpulsory four-year waiting period.

6 The Most Revd Henry Robert McAdoo, archbishop of Dublin (1977–85).

The evolution of modern Irish society was largely shaped by a series of referendums between 1995 and 2018 which dealt, inevitably, with aspects of the relationship between civil law and private morality. Thus Irish public debate coincided with a period of agonizing global discussion within Anglicanism concerning human sexuality. The formal decriminalization of male homosexual acts in 1993 was followed in the early years of the new century by the provision in law of civil partnerships for same-sex couples. Gay people emerged from the shadowy margins of society to be greeted with remarkable affirmation and empathy. The Church of Ireland was frankly ill-prepared for, even wrong-footed by, the pace of events and changing public opinion. What pastoral response, if any, was it to make to the presence of committed same-sex couples in its midst and what was it to do if a serving priest chose to enter a civil partnership? These questions came to a head at the General Synod of 2012, for many the most divisive synod in living memory. While it is wrong to make sweeping statements, particularly concerning perceived North /South divisions, and while a significant number of Southern Anglicans remained firmly conservative in their view of sexual ethics, there was a clear sense in several of the Southern dioceses that some positive pastoral response needed to be made to the requests of same-sex couples for prayer and blessing. The issue continues to texture the life of the church in a manner that is at best exhausting and at worst divisive, and in the eyes of many it is a constant distraction from other matters pertaining to the building of the Kingdom. While the church argued, the pace of social change accelerated. In 2015, by a substantial majority, voters endorsed the amendment of the constitution to permit equality of access to civil marriage regardless of gender. Church of Ireland bishops were active on both sides of the campaign, although the House of Bishops sought to make a public utterance to which those of both points of view could assent in the context of the church's own unaltered marriage discipline.

As one reviews the last fifty years, one sees a church now largely tolerant of social change in a society hugely different to that of the late 1960s. The Republic has become a transformed 'liberal', largely secular, even anti-clerical place. While the Church of Ireland has taken no pleasure in the discomfiture of the Roman Catholic Church, particularly in the wake of the scandals surrounding clerical sexual abuse of children, it finds itself in the strange position (shrewdly prophesied by Fr Michael Hurley SJ almost half a century ago),[7] of helping to teach a once self-confident majority church what might be the virtues and possibilities of itself being a minority. Increasingly, the church faces the challenge of witnessing in two radically different political contexts, and this tension is only emphasized by the current implications of Brexit. The end of the Troubles in Northern Ireland had perhaps the peculiar consequence of reducing the empathy of the Southern church with the Northern church. In the days of violence and mayhem, there was constant prayerful empathy with co-religionists bearing the brunt of suffering; now there

7 Michael Hurley SJ, *Irish Anglicanism, 1869–1969* (Dublin, 1970).

can be a more detached impatience with how the North is perceived (very often unfairly) as inhibiting the church in the South from responding pastorally to its own social and political context. Thus, as never before, North/South engagement across the church is vital. One of the reasons why a scheme to reorganize diocesan boundaries in more recent years ran into difficulties was because of a fear that it might reduce the number of dioceses that straddled the political divide.

However, church people in the South should be cautious about over-enthusiastic patting of their own backs when it comes to social and political engagement. In many ways the church has maintained a caring pastoral 'chaplaincy' role in relation to its own members, striven to uphold its best traditions of worship and responsibility for built heritage, and provided a genuine if less than proactive welcome for wanderers and seekers, usually of a liberal disposition, who come from other backgrounds seeking to take refuge under the shadow of its wings. As one scans the histories and the newspapers of the past half-century, it is hard to decide what precisely the church has offered to national political and economic life by way of prophetic contribution. Any distinctively Anglican contribution to the dominant issues of economic injustice, particularly in the areas of housing, homelessness, the working poor and the monopolizing of economic policy by an unthinking neo-liberalism has been so negligible as to be microscopic.

In terms of social theology Roman Catholics still leave Anglicans rather at the starting blocks. Precious few voices have made a real and lasting impression on the Southern public square – one can only look to a few individuals such as Victor Griffin, and perhaps more recently Kenneth Kearon in the area of medical ethics, Kenneth Milne in the context of the church's engagement with the European institutions and Trevor Sargent in the environmental sphere. The banking crisis of the early years of the new century which threw the political fabric of the country into disarray provoked remarkably little comment from within the church beyond discussion of its impact on the holdings of the RCB. The challenges of migrancy provoked various benign local attempts to offer hospitality, and indeed many parishes and schools would not be themselves now without their 'new Irish' members, but a hasty glance at the membership of the General Synod would hardly give the impression that we are a church characterized by multi-ethnicity. One of the leading Church of Ireland contributors to the architecture of the peace process, Dr Martin Mansergh, was known to hold the view that religious conviction was personally influential, but publicly private.[8]

It is probably true to say, to sum matters up, that the contribution of the Church of Ireland to political life has evolved into the formation of individual Christian citizens, persons able to add their contributions to public discourse in a manner that is infused with a characteristic spirit of Anglicanism which informs the style and tone, if not necessarily always the outward substance, of their contribution.

---

8 Martin Mansergh, advisor on Northern Ireland to Taoiseach Charles Haughey. Unpublished contribution to a conference held in the diocese of Cashel, Ferns and Ossory.

Observers tend to search in vain for the Church of Ireland 'view' on particular subjects, and certainly the bishops are no longer treated as obvious oracles in that context. The reluctance to express a particular 'view' on behalf of a specific 'community' is accentuated by the procedural challenges of articulating such a view in the first place. Only the General Synod, or its Standing Committee, can articulate a Church of Ireland position on political/social matters, and this is rarely considered expedient or even achievable. It was noteworthy that at the time of the debate over the repeal of the 8th amendment (guaranteeing the right of life of the unborn) the Standing Committee said little beyond the repetition of old utterances dating back, for example, to the Lambeth Conference of 1958, and otherwise individual church members were left to follow their own judgements and consciences.

So how has the Church of Ireland measured up against J.C. Beckett's outline of its vocation in modern Ireland? As an institution perhaps at best a beta minus. Yet North and South, in their quite distinctive ways the people of the Church of Ireland have made their own contribution to a vision not so much of a world that is fair, as to the fructification of a Kingdom which is more than fair.

8

The church and media and communications[1]

Lynn Glanville

We are living through a communications revolution – the digital world of the internet and social media is transforming the ways in which we interact with as well as inform and educate one another. Attention spans are generally considered to be getting shorter, with visual media often trumping the written word, while a 'sound bite' (and often very adversarial) culture can make it difficult to convey nuance and complexity; there is much talk of 'echo chambers'. Mainstream media is being forced to change in a variety of ways, radically challenged by the concepts of 'fake news' as well as the powerful role of 'influencers', not to mention advertising and the cold reality of economics. In all of this, individuals, businesses, organizations and institutions have to adapt to survive and be heard, including the churches. The pace of change can seem bewildering.

Whatever the communications landscape and the Church of Ireland's connectivity within it may look like in 2019 (more on this later), in fact, looking back, the past fifty years has been marked by many very significant developments by the church in response to the desire and necessity to have greater engagement with the world beyond itself. Arguably, and in response to developments in both mass communications and societal circumstances, much more change has taken place in this domain in the past five decades than during the previous one hundred years since disestablishment.

EVOLVING STRUCTURES, 1969–90

In 1969, the Church of Ireland communications structure consisted of the News and Information Service operating as a committee of Standing Committee, with four press officers; a Publications Committee; and a Sound and Television Broadcasting Committee (with northern and southern subcommittees). The magazine *Church of Ireland Monthly*, produced under the aegis of the News and Information Service and published by the Christian Knowledge Press, had a circulation of 6,000.

In 1970, the General Synod amended this structure, creating a Communications Committee (1970–85) and began the first phase of development towards an

---

1 The author is indebted to Paul Harron, Janet Maxwell and Peter Cheney for their assistance in writing this essay.

integrated church-wide communications infrastructure, forming the basis for that which is still largely in place. Alongside the Communications Committee was a Radio and Television Committee and a Publications Committee. *Church of Ireland Monthly* did not survive, and following several efforts at restructuring, by the 1980s took the form of a monthly news sheet called 'Newstime' containing non-confidential material from the Standing Committee and other church boards, which was circulated to diocesan and parish magazine editors. Eventually, this, in turn, became the Standing Committee News (and Committee News), which was published following meetings by the *Church of Ireland Gazette* and, after the establishment of the Church of Ireland website, then both in the *Gazette* and on the website; it is still issued electronically by the Press Office.

In 1981, the General Synod appointed a Commission on Communications to report to the Standing Committee in November 1982 and to the General Synod of May 1983. In 1983, a major report on Church of Ireland communications was produced – 'Time to tell'. The report had two foci – modernizing church communications infrastructure and using that infrastructure to clearly communicate the voice of the church. In 1984, the General Synod adopted a resolution setting up a new communications structure, which established the Central Communications Board, with the subcommittees of the Broadcasting Committee (replacing the Radio and Television Committee) and the Literature Committee (replacing the Publications Committee). The new structure made its first report in 1986.

Almost immediately, the board and its subcommittees took up the challenge of communicating in new ways. In 1988, the literature and broadcasting committees supported CACTM (as the ordination selection process group was then known) in producing a video on vocation for use in secondary schools and parishes. Communications training became established, with the first training event for church communicators being hosted by the press officer in 1987.

In 1990, a small broadcasting studio was established in the theological training college at Braemor Park, partly with the aspiration to produce some material, although this was perhaps ambitious, but on a more practical level, providing the possibility of training clergy and ordinands in dealing with broadcast interviews. (It was later given up during redevelopment of the building.)

The move to actively develop communications was not confined to the Church of Ireland. In the same year, the Church of Ireland, Methodist, Presbyterian and Roman Catholic churches came together to establish the Irish Churches Council for Television and Radio Affairs (ICCTRA). This body lasted several years and acted jointly to support public-service broadcasting, particularly religious broadcasting, in Ireland, and to respond on a sectoral basis to consultations on broadcasting by the state.

The Literature Committee was also facilitated in its work by the establishment of a fund that had its origins in royalties arising from sales of the *Alternative Prayer Book*. This led to the foundation of the General Synod Royalties Fund, as the initial sum has been added to over the years since, by royalties and, to a lesser degree, income from the publication of successive editions of the *Book of Common Prayer* and hymnals. In turn, the fund has been able to provide grants to, and support publication of, liturgical resources and Church of Ireland historical, pastoral and educational materials, sometimes under the imprint of Church of Ireland Publishing.

The mid-1980s was a very significant period for Church of Ireland communications, as much as for the wider church, as a number of notable events and projects demanded new skills and expanded vision. In 1984, the launch of the *Alternative Prayer Book* was extensively supported through the Press Office and the first print run of 70,000 copies sold out within one month of publication. In 1985, the General Synod met in Belfast, the first time since disestablishment that it had moved outside Dublin.

THE CHURCH OF IRELAND PRESS OFFICE

The Church of Ireland established its Press Office and the role of press officer in Belfast. The first of these was Charles Freer, and then Bobby Byers, followed by Alan Johnston,[2] and they responded to the developing press and communications needs of the church set within the turbulent context of the Troubles in Northern Ireland. The role of press officer became much more developed with the formation of the Central Communications Board, and from 1986 onwards the importance of this position was emphasized by its location in Belfast, at a time when so much of the domestic and international media was reporting on the conflict.

The 1972 Book of Reports sets the formation of the Press Office in the context of those turbulent times. Mr Freer was appointed by the Standing Committee in March 1971, and took up the role on 1 April 1971. 'The unrest in Northern Ireland has meant that since appointment the major part of the work of the press officer has been concentrated in that area. He has, however, attended eight diocesan synods and has found these to be a useful method of getting to know both clergy and laity.'[3]

With relief and gratitude, we can look back and appreciate the tangible transformation from that unrest to our current peace, while also understanding that, for many, a sense of deep loss remains. For the record, the report also notes the appointment of Revd R.H.A. Eames as a member of the Communications Committee.

The work of the press officer largely involved providing information about the Church of Ireland, promoting the work of the General Synod and Standing Committee and providing media support to the archbishop of Armagh. (In the dioceses at this period, a group of diocesan information officers, mostly part-time clerical appointments, provided media support to the local activity of bishop and

---

2 Alan Johnston, aside from his time as press officer, is a survivor of the Kegworth air disaster of 1989. An avid traveller, he authored a photography book *Should I bring an umbrella? Celebrating weather in photographs* in 2009, raising funds for the RNLI, whose members had been instrumental in helping save his life.   3 Standing Committee Report, Book of Reports (1972), pp 76–7.

diocese.) The role of providing media support to the primate became an increasingly essential one.

The Church Leaders' Meeting in Northern Ireland (made up of the four main denominations' most senior clerics – the Roman Catholic archbishop of Armagh, the Church of Ireland archbishop of Armagh, the Presbyterian moderator and the Methodist president) at this time became very important in articulating the voice of the churches in the face of violence and division. In particular, the work of Archbishop Robin Eames was often front and centre. For an extended period, he became one of *the* people to whom the media looked in the first instance for comment, observation and a steadying voice, effectively aided by Bishop James Mehaffey in Derry and Bishop Brian Hannon in Clogher, both of whom shared Archbishop Eames' capacity to catch and articulate the emotions of their communities.

In 1987, Elizabeth (Liz) Harries (later Gibson-Harries) was appointed to the role of press officer. A dynamic and energetic communicator, Liz worked throughout the difficult period of the 1990s, before leaving in 2000 to set up her own business in England. The 'Church of Ireland Notes' in the *Irish Times* remarked upon her retirement:

> During her period of office, the job expanded considerably. This was due in part to Ms Gibson-Harries' perception of communication which involved being constantly available and ensuring that the Church of Ireland view, where appropriate, was always heard.
>
> The expansion of the job was due also to the escalation of the Northern troubles. The seemingly endless torrent of tragedy, political and personal, demanded a constant response from the church, and the press officer was to the fore in advising bishops and clergy on how to respond. Heart-rending funerals, controversial political developments and the protracted problem of Drumcree were all part of the daily fare at the press office.[4]

Indeed, the (often international) media attention on the contentious situation involving the annual Orange Order march to/from Drumcree church near Portadown was a difficult running story between 1995 and 2000.

While much press attention tended to focus attention on Northern Ireland during the Troubles, tribute must also be paid to Dr Valerie Jones, who acted as diocesan communications officer for Dublin and Glendalough during this time. Dr Jones was a fluent Irish speaker, an able academic and a shrewd but kindly diocesan communicator, who was known for being equally at home guiding archbishops of Dublin through complex church and political matters, and reporting on parish fêtes.[5]

4 'Church of Ireland Notes', *Irish Times*, 21 Jan. 2000, www.irishtimes.com/news/church-of-ireland-notes-1.238942, accessed 24 June 2019. 5 Valerie Jones carried out notable research into Protestant radical nationalists, which was published posthumously: *Rebel Prods: the forgotten story of Protestant radical nationalists and the 1916 Rising* (Dublin, 2016).

FROM 2000 TO 2019

Brian Parker (later Revd Brian Parker) succeeded Liz Gibson-Harries as press officer in 2000, having come from a senior position in the Government Information Services in Northern Ireland. Notably, Brian managed the church's media interface with the Anglican Communion and was actively involved in providing media support to the Lambeth Commission chaired by Archbishop Eames and to the Primates' Meeting held at Dromantine in 2005. Brian retired as press officer in 2005 (and served for some time as a non-stipendiary clergyman).

In 2000, following several years during which the Central Communications Board had promoted the idea unsuccessfully within the synodical structures and the Representative Body, the decision was taken to create a director of communications. The role was to be jointly supported by the allocations process and by the Priorities Fund for the first three years, and thereafter to be the responsibility of the Allocations Committee through its provision for the General Synod. In 2001, Janet Maxwell was appointed to the new role. Janet came from having held the position of head of the School of Media and Performance and head of the Department of Journalism at Technikon Natal, Durban, in South Africa. In addition to her academic career, Janet had experience in business journalism in Ireland, Australia and South Africa as well as in public relations, media management, publishing, training and administration.

As a member of the RCB's senior management team with executive responsibility for the church's communications strategy and for coordinating its public relations, media relations and publishing activities, Janet's work was supported by the press officer in Belfast, who continued to provide (inter alia) national-level media support to the archbishop of Armagh. Additionally, a central financial contribution was established to facilitate a press and communications officer based in Dublin and Glendalough, in respect of media support for work at a national level undertaken by the archbishop of Dublin, as well as administrative support provided by a press office assistant in the Press Office in Belfast.

Garrett Casey was to undertake the role of Dublin communications officer for several years, working closely with Archbishop John Neill before his appointment as synod officer and subsequently pursuing a legal career. He was succeeded in the current Dublin communications officer role in 2011 by the author, working with Archbishop Michael Jackson. Archbishop Jackson brought with him to Dublin his interest and experience in interfaith engagement. His arrival coincided with a significant time for interfaith development in Dublin, with the establishment of the Dublin City Interfaith Forum in 2012.[6] Communications in this area has been

---

6 DCIF works with interested members of faith communities to deliver interfaith gatherings and activities in Dublin city. Recognizing the diverse nature of the backgrounds of the residents of Dublin, DCIF seeks to provide the space and opportunity for faith communities to build relationships with and between Dublin city communities, statutory and voluntary organisations and the residents of Dublin city.

enriched through cooperation and relationship-building with DCIF and consequently with members of many of the world faiths who contribute to the diversity and vibrancy of the city which is now home to people from about 200 different countries.

Jenny Compston had been appointed as press office assistant in 1998, reflecting the increasing busyness and output of the Press Office and also tied in with the promulgation of the Church of Ireland's highly outward-facing reconciliation initiative – the Hard Gospel project.[7] Jenny served in this role with great warmth and efficiency for seventeen years, until her retirement in 2015. She was known especially for providing an annual haven for print and broadcast journalists as well as diocesan communications officers in the media centre at each year's General Synod, and for the smooth running of the church's annual communications competition, which is aimed at encouraging innovation and good practice in communications across the church, from parishes to dioceses to affiliated organizations.

Janet Maxwell has continued in the role of head of communications since her appointment; however, a resignation at senior level in the synod area in 2003 enabled the church to merge the director of communications function to create the role of head of synod services. When the new structure was put in place, the dioceses outside Dublin and Glendalough were mostly still operating with part-time, largely voluntary support from diocesan clergy acting as information officers, rather than communications officers. Even the central Church of Ireland website, which had been established by a small working group during the late 1990s, was in its infancy. This team was led by Revd Michael Graham of Drogheda, with Bob Sherwood, chief officer of the RB, and a recently appointed IT member of the RB staff, Michelle Carter. While, in 1999, the central church website was unfurling like a newly hatched butterfly, diocesan sites were still in their cocoons. They emerged slowly but steadily over the next decade. This development was acknowledged by the Central Communications Board, with the establishment of a special award for website design and content in the annual communications competition.

Following Brian Parker's retirement as press officer, Sarah Williams, who had been a press officer to Archbishop Rowan Williams in Lambeth Palace, took on the role for the Church of Ireland between 2005 and 2006. Following a short gap, Dr Paul Harron took up the press officer position based in Belfast in 2008, holding it for the following ten years. Paul came from a managerial role with the Arts Council of Northern Ireland (with an arts and architecture specialism) but had a background in both book publishing and freelance journalism and writing on cultural subjects, and he was also 'a son of the rectory', familiar with Church of Ireland structures and people. During his tenure, working first as media advisor to Archbishop Alan Harper and then to Archbishop Richard Clarke, he was responsible, along with

7 'Hard Gospel', www.ireland.anglican.org/archive/hardgospel/index.php, accessed 27 June 2019.

a team of others including IT colleague Charlotte Howard, for taking forward the sizeable project to redevelop the church's website as a contemporary, mobile-responsive communications tool; for the creation of a popular monthly Press Office e-bulletin; for the development of new social-media guidelines; and for the genesis of the Daily Worship app. He also led on providing regular media training for church spokespeople, as the prospect of engagement with 'the media' became increasingly daunting for all but the most confident, and communications training for a network of diocesan communications officers in areas such as creating video content on mobile phones, and social-media engagement.

These developments reflected the by-now rapidly changing world of communications. In truth, right across the island, including in Northern Ireland following the Troubles, media interest in church news and affairs was waning into the new millennium. Mainstream media coverage was usually hard-won, unless the subject was controversial, even sometimes scandalous. And during this period, the Church of Ireland and its press officer and communications staff did find themselves dealing with media interest in difficult societal, ethical and theological areas and on contentious matters – reputation-management being a key element of public relations. The Church of Ireland, as a member province of the Anglican Communion, was also regularly drawn into matters that were proving complex for the communion as a whole. Dr Harron, like Brian Harper, was also to serve the media and communications needs of a Primates' Meeting held in Ireland, this time in Swords in 2011, and of the visits to Ireland of two archbishops of Canterbury, Rowan Williams and Justin Welby.

It is worth noting one particularly significant event during this period, however, which garnered widespread and international media attention for positive reasons: the election and consecration of Ireland's first woman bishop, the Most Revd Pat Storey, as bishop of Meath and Kildare in 2013. Bishop Storey was subsequently to become chair of the Church's Central Communications Board and highly engaged with the work of the Press Office and communications.

As a published writer and editor, Paul Harron brought a new dimension to the Press Office, increasing the capacity within the communications team to tackle substantial publishing projects, including the *Illustrated history of the Church of Ireland* (2013), and the *Commentary on the constitution* (2018), as well as this current publication. A further aspect of his time as press officer was his active participation in regular learning fora with other mainstream church communicators and the Irish Council of Churches (in an echo of the efforts of ICCTRA in the 1990s).

Following Jenny Compston's retirement in 2015, Peter Cheney – a journalist by training – joined the Press Office as assistant press officer. Among his various contributions to his role and an increasing emphasis on producing e-bulletins, reflecting stories from across the whole church and island, he has developed innovative resource materials for church engagement with migrants and refugees, reflecting the increasingly fractured global picture. Peter is currently acting as the church's press officer, with the Press Office still based in Church of Ireland House, Belfast.

The period 2000–19 saw a transformation of communications technology as electronic platforms and mobile technologies changed how the church communicated its message and attempted to tell its own stories more and more. Technological change has been very much demand-led. The church was constantly in danger of getting left behind if it did not maintain its investment in technology and people.

Focus on technology masks an even greater challenge with content. Since 2000, public broadcasting services began to reduce religious programming content in Northern Ireland, and to a lesser degree in the Republic of Ireland. The result is that the accepted place of churches and faith in the public square can no longer be assumed. Churches, consequently, have to climb further in order to reach the mountain top so they can be heard. When they speak, they cannot assume that people understand their vocabulary or sympathize with their ethos.

Reflecting wider change, the General Synod amended the terms of reference once more in 2019, so that the internet and broadcasting subcommittees will merge back into the Central Board, which, in turn, will take more direct interest in these areas and also consider what is needed by way of permanent subcommittees to best serve the interests of the church in the next decade.

EFFECTIVE COMMUNICATIONS INTO THE FUTURE

From the turn of the century, dioceses began to set up their own websites, which in turn required additional support both to keep the content updated, and to write the additional content required. A proliferation of online media and news meant there was increased demand for content. Slowly, the part-time clerical information officers, who had served the church so well for most of the twentieth century, began to give way to part-time and full-time (mostly) lay appointments of people with previous media experience.

Today, most dioceses have a paid diocesan communications officer and the Church benefits from a strong network of 'DCOs'. Each diocese (with one or two exceptions) produces a magazine and a website, and many have moved onto a range of social-media platforms to ensure that church activity is made known to members. The church has begun to explore locally produced audio-visual material and podcasts, with a live audio feed now established as a regular feature of the General Synod – albeit, still sometimes balancing precariously on the edge between affordability and quality.

Communications has been more appreciated and studied during the last fifty years than ever before. The world of communications can feel overcrowded and jumbled, but it is a very human environment and, in that sense, it is very recognizable. The church has risen to the challenge of keeping its voice in this modern public square and has maintained its place there, even during the recent years of financial crash and recession. At their best, the church's communications personnel capture the mood of the times and support the clergy and laity to produce articulate Christian responses to life in our time.

The challenges facing communications ahead are, firstly, internal – keeping people in the parishes and church communities throughout the dioceses in touch with what is happening at both diocese and parish level and in the wider Church of Ireland; secondly, external – informing people in the wider Church of Ireland and Anglican Communion and those, locally, nationally and internationally, with no particular connection to the church, about what we are doing and handling media enquiries and issues; and, thirdly, missional – by enabling the message of the church, either through reports of parish and diocesan events, or comments and statements, to reach a wider audience via the church's websites, diocesan magazines, social media and mainstream media. The time has never been more right to let people in both small communities and large communities across the island know that they are part of something bigger.

A NOTE ON THE *CHURCH OF IRELAND GAZETTE*

Finally, it would be remiss not to mention the role of the *Church of Ireland Gazette*, founded in 1856, and which has often functioned as the regular source of news and information about the Church of Ireland to itself and the wider world, as well as a forum for critique, reflection and lively discourse in its letters pages. Importantly, and this sometimes comes as a surprise to people (including journalists), it is not an official publication or organ of the Church but rather has always guarded its editorial independence. It has often been a paper that has 'punched above its weight', being consulted by those in the mainstream media who wish to 'take the temperature' on church affairs from a reliable and articulate source from time to time.

In 2018, the *Gazette* moved from its weekly newspaper format to become a magazine-like publication published monthly (also published in an electronic for-mat), and in 2019 – breaking yet new ground – its first female editor was appointed: Karen Bushby.

In this current time of flux and negativity, it is notable that the vast majority of 'church news' continues to be 'good news' for parishes from one end of the island to another.

9

The Church of Ireland and ecumenical relations

Revd Canon Ian M. Ellis

In the late 1960s, the Church of Ireland found itself in the midst of significant ecumenical developments both at home and on the international stage. Experience has shown very clearly that what happens in the international church context has a direct influence on events in the church at home. The local and universal aspects of church life are inextricably linked.

The universal church brings different perspectives on which the local church can reflect and by which it can assess its own life and faithfulness. There are immense horizons here which bring promise and yet also the daunting demand to examine oneself against standards that come from outside and are not purely or more comfortably from within.

This overview of the Church of Ireland's relations with other churches during the past fifty years cannot be exhaustive and so it will proceed relatively briefly in relation to the international and national contexts.

THE INTERNATIONAL CHURCH CONTEXT

The two major developments in international church life that fundamentally influenced the situation of the Church of Ireland in the mid-1960s were the formation of the World Council of Churches (WCC) in 1948 and the Second Vatican Council, held from 1962–5 (Vatican II). This is the wider context in which we must situate our consideration of the Church of Ireland's relationships with other churches.

The World Council of Churches

The WCC brought together two international church movements that were of the highest significance: the Faith and Order, and Life and Work movements. The former dealt with theological as well as structural and ministerial church issues, and the latter with Christian witness in terms of social and political involvement.

The Church of Ireland has been involved in the WCC since its inception and has followed closely the multilateral dialogue of its Faith and Order Commission, a high point of which was its 1982 'Baptism, Eucharist and Ministry' report (also known as the 'Lima Report'), adopted by the commission's plenary meeting in Lima, Peru in that year, and exploring the growing agreement as well as remaining differences between the churches. It has been hailed as the most widely distributed and studied ecumenical document and as having formed a basis for many mutual recognition agreements between churches around the world. Indeed, the Roman Catholic Church, while not a member-church of the WCC, has been a full member of the council's Faith and Order Commission and this fact alone rendered the document all the more significant.

The Lima Report was the culmination of over fifty years' work of the Faith and Order Commission. The Church of Ireland in its response to the text noted its 'descriptive' nature, aiming to draw out convergences that had been reached. The document had a novel approach of setting out convergences along with commentary that stated differences that still needed to be resolved.

The Church of Ireland commented: 'As to the text itself, because it is largely descriptive in character, there is little or nothing in it with which we should want positively to disagree. Such reservations as we have would centre around details of emphasis.'

The church also noted that the Lima Report seemed to be saying to the churches that living in a time of change was also to live in a time of opportunity, which in turn highlighted the urgent need for the Church of Ireland to respond 'not only in an official written statement but at the deeper levels of the Church's life'.[1]

The Lima Report – with which the 'Lima' Eucharistic liturgy is associated (as it was first used at the 1982 commission meeting) – thus provided a rather heartening boost to ecumenical relations generally, and in particular to the work of dialogue. Focusing on convergence rather than difference created an optimistic mood and it is probably true to say that, since Lima, ecumenists have focused less on trying to agree on contentious issues of doctrine and more on building up a life of common witness based on what the churches share. Perhaps one might venture to suggest that through this approach, and with time, the divergences will come to be seen in a different light and may, as it were, take care of themselves.

Whether or not Lima was the spur to this change of approach from a narrower and more purely institutional view of church unity to a more dynamic concept, or expressed a change of emphasis that was already taking shape, is unclear. However, a shift in perspective did occur and Lima at least contributed to it.

If Lima signalled such a change, because of its open and creative approach, the difficulties that arose following the Anglican-Roman Catholic International Commission's 1984 Final Report (ARCIC-I) showed how intractable the older approach to dialogue, in terms of institutional unity, actually was, thereby creating an awareness of the need to be less focused in that direction.

Vatican II and bilateral dialogues

Vatican II (held from 1962–5) was called by Pope John XXIII and was to open up the church to the wider world, representing a less 'sealed' understanding of the

---

1 Response, *Journal of the General Synod* (1985), p. 92ff.

church. This purpose came to be widely described as *aggiornamento*, a word encapsulating the intentions of John XXIII himself. There had been many pressures driving this change of approach away from central control and the promotion of neoscholasticism as the theological norm. Principal among those pressures was the modernist movement that sought to relate the church more directly to the modern world.

From an ecumenical perspective, Vatican II's Dogmatic Constitution on the Church (*Lumen Gentium*) and its Decree of Ecumenism (*Unitatis Redintegratio*) represented a shift in the Roman Catholic Church's self-understanding away from previous isolationism and self-sufficiency, now seeing authentic Christian life and what it regarded as elements of catholicity in other denominations, specifically citing the Eastern churches and the Anglican Communion as having special positions.

While other denominations certainly would not see such a concept as doing justice to their ecclesial nature, it was a change of heart and mind that would drive the Roman Catholic Church into ecumenical life. Its ecumenical 'conversion' at Vatican II in effect demanded that its new teaching had to be lived out in the church around the world. This in turn led to local Roman Catholic hierarchies taking various initiatives.

At the international level came the formation of bilateral dialogues. Following a visit in 1966 by the archbishop of Canterbury, Michael Ramsey, to Pope Paul VI (who succeeded John XXIII in 1963), the two leaders called for 'a serious dialogue which, founded on the Gospels and the ancient common tradition, may lead to that unity in truth, for which Christ prayed'. There then followed the establishment of the Anglican-Roman Catholic Commission on the Theology of Marriage, which was to be particularly concerned with interchurch marriages (or 'mixed marriages' as they were then known), and a Joint Preparatory Commission which in turn led to the formation of the Anglican-Roman Catholic International Commission (ARCIC).

The Church of Ireland was directly involved in both the marriage commission and ARCIC. Dr George Simms, archbishop of Armagh 1969–80, was co-chair of the former, while Dr Henry McAdoo, archbishop of Dublin 1977–85, was co-chair of ARCIC-I (there have been subsequent ARCICs).

While Archbishop Simms' appointment was hardly controversial, the background to the appointment of then Bishop McAdoo was not as straightforward. Given the tensions between Protestants and Roman Catholics, particularly in Northern Ireland, the involvement of a Church of Ireland bishop in ARCIC was bound to be controversial.

The Jesuit ecumenist, Fr Michael Hurley, recounted in his memoirs how, in an article he wrote in the pastoral journal, *The Furrow*, in 1966, he had echoed editorial criticism in the *Church of Ireland Gazette* of the fact that the Anglican team on the Anglican-Roman Catholic Joint Preparatory Commission did not include a member of the Church of Ireland. The editorial had stated:

We venture to suggest that the omission of the Church of Ireland from the list is worthy of note and difficult to understand. There is probably no other Church in the Anglican Communion that ought to be so deeply concerned with relationships with Roman Catholics and any consideration of ways and means to improve these relationships might be said to be very much our business.[2]

Fr Hurley wrote that Lambeth Palace had been aggrieved by all of this because the Anglican authorities had in fact wanted to include Bishop McAdoo as a member. He, Fr Hurley, went on to suggest that it was 'apparently the Church of Ireland which had objected'. Nonetheless, he recorded that Bishop McAdoo did become a member of the Preparatory Commission after its first meeting, and went on to be co-chair of ARCIC-I.[3]

The Church of Ireland's response to the 1981 Final Report of ARCIC-I, which dealt with Eucharistic doctrine, ministry and ordination, and authority in the church, managed to be both extensive in scope and lukewarm in its verdict. Asked by the Anglican Consultative Council to respond to the co-chairs' questions as to whether the text was 'consonant in substance with the faith of Anglicans' and whether it offered 'a sufficient basis for taking the next concrete step towards the reconciliation of our Churches', the General Synod took the view that it was not possible to reply with 'a general Yes'. There were certain issues that did need further work and this was also to be the Vatican's view.

While the Church of Ireland responded to the Final Report in 1986, the Vatican's response did not come until 1991 and it requested certain clarifications. These were published by ARCIC in 1993, together with a letter from Cardinal Edward Idris Cassidy (then president of the Pontifical Council for Promoting Christian Unity) stating that in the light of the clarifications, no further work was needed in relation to Eucharist and ministry 'at this stage' – which presumably meant that the state of affairs was not yet fully acceptable to the Vatican – and noting that ARCIC would be continuing to study the issue of authority. Over the years, ARCIC has produced a series of agreed statements, but without the same degree of controversy as surrounded its initial work.

The Church of Ireland has also been represented in international bilateral dialogues with other communions. Archbishop Richard Clarke is a co-chair of the international Anglican-Orthodox Commission, which was established in 1973, and Archbishop Michael Jackson has been involved in the Anglican-Oriental Orthodox Commission, established in 2001 but suspended from 2003–14, at the initiative of the Oriental Orthodox, due to inter-Anglican tensions relating to sexuality issues. Dr Jackson has also been involved in international interfaith bodies, and is a co-chair of the Porvoo Communion (see further below). Interfaith relations are the subject of a separate essay in this volume.

---

2 *Church of Ireland Gazette*, 11 Nov. 1966.
3 M. Hurley, *Healing and hope: memories of an Irish ecumenist* (Dublin, 2003), p. 43.

The Conference of European Churches

Following the Second World War, the churches in Europe felt the need for closer relationships and particularly so as the Cold War took hold around them. Formed in 1959, the Conference of European Churches (CEC) brought Orthodox and Protestants together in a single body. The Church of Ireland was a founding CEC member-church.

There have been fifteen CEC assemblies addressing various aspects of church life and witness. Notably, the fourth CEC assembly, in 1964, was held in the Baltic Sea on board the MV *Bornholm*, due to visa issues for representatives from eastern Europe.

While the Roman Catholic Church is not a CEC member-church, a close collaboration has grown between the CEC and the Roman Catholic Council of the Bishops' Conferences of Europe (Consilium Conferentiarum Episcoporum Europae, CCEE). There have been three CEC-CCEE European Ecumenical Assemblies which have marked the growing nature of ecumenical collaboration.

CEC focuses a considerable amount of its work on European Union issues, having been based in Brussels since 2014, but nonetheless remains a body with a much wider scope of interest. The Church of Ireland has played committed roles in both the CEC and the WCC.

Lutherans, German Protestants and the Old Catholics

Dialogue with Lutheran churches bore fruit in the 1992 Porvoo Common Statement, which was published in the following year. It led to the formation of the Porvoo Communion, in which Bishop Paul Colton played a founding role, between the Anglican churches in Ireland and Great Britain, the Nordic/Baltic Lutheran churches, the Church of Iceland, the Lusitanian Church of Portugal, the Reformed Episcopal Church of Spain, the Evangelical Lutheran Church of Latvia Abroad and the Lutheran Church in Great Britain (all joining at various stages between 1996 and 2014, the Evangelical Lutheran Church of Latvia having observer status).

This new communion relationship, which was built on the work of previous Anglican-Lutheran dialogue and a common understanding and mutual recognition of apostolic succession in episcopal ministry, has enabled the interchange of ordained ministry. However, at least as far as Ireland is concerned, that interchange has been more Lutheran to Anglican than vice versa, language issues having undoubtedly been a factor. On the other hand, there have been new diocesan links, visits in both directions, attendance at episcopal ordinations and joint learning ventures. The diocese of Cork, Cloyne and Ross currently uses confirmation resources from the Church of Sweden and is considering a youth exchange programme.[4]

4 Correspondence with Bishop Paul Colton.

Writing on the subject of the Porvoo Communion, Revd Helene Steed has indicated that while it is a fellowship of Anglicans and Lutherans, both church traditions retain their identities, adding: 'It is important to underline that all Churches in the Porvoo fellowship retain their independence and have their own constitutions. Hence, rules and requirements may vary from Church to Church.'[5]

German Protestants are often considered all to be Lutherans, because Martin Luther was a German, but the situation is somewhat more complex. The German Protestant churches are called '*Landeskirchen*' (regional churches); some are of the German Lutheran tradition, others Calvinist ('Reformed') and others are Lutheran-Calvinist 'United' churches. The *Landeskirchen* together form the structure of the Evangelische Kirche in Deutschland (EKD, the German Protestant church). The EKD, despite its name, is not a conservative evangelical church. (The German word for 'evangelical' in that sense is '*evangelikal*'; the German word '*evangelisch*' is better translated as 'Protestant'.)

The EKD has been very aware of the Porvoo developments but, because of church order issues, in particular episcopal ministry, a similar relationship has not been possible between the EKD and Anglicans. However, it is instructive to note that an agreement between the Church of England and the EKD, known as the 'Meissen Agreement', in fact preceded the Porvoo development. The Meissen relationship also involves the Anglican churches in Ireland, Scotland and Wales.

The Meissen Agreement, signed by Archbishop Robert Runcie in Westminster Abbey, London, and by Bishop Johannes Hempel in the Kaiser-Wilhelm-Gedächtnis-Kirche in Berlin in 1991, created space for an enhanced relationship between the Church of England and German Protestants (whose country was still divided at the time). The Church of England and the EKD have a particular common interest due to their special, although by no means identical, relationships with their respective states.

The role of Archbishop Runcie in this is especially noteworthy. During the Second World War he had fought through Normandy, Holland and Germany as a tank commander and after the war was concerned with promoting British-German reconciliation. In 1983, as archbishop of Canterbury, he visited the EKD and the then separate Federation of Protestant Churches in the German Democratic Republic to take part in celebrations marking the 500th anniversary of the birth of Martin Luther.

Bishop Christopher Hill, who at the time was a member of the archbishop's staff, has recalled how Dr Runcie had wanted his ecumenical and other visits to be strategic and that this lay behind soundings taken on his behalf regarding his 1983 visit to both parts of Germany. Bishop Hill has written:

> He preached about contemporary reconciliation but he also picked up
> Caroline affirmation of the reality of the Protestant churches in Europe

(Lancelot Andrewes and Archbishop Laud). From this the Germans were very positive and there was a mutual desire for the tripartite conversations which led to the Meissen Agreement.[6]

The Church of Ireland, the Scottish Episcopal Church and the Church in Wales have an observer place in the ongoing Meissen Commission meetings, which has been shared on a rotating basis.

There was an earlier, informal but nonetheless quite structured contact in the late 1970s and early 1980s between the Church of Ireland and the EKD in the Herne, North Rhine-Westphalia district, organized by the then dean of Cashel, David Woodworth.

As well as ecumenical involvement in the Porvoo and Meissen relationships, the Church of Ireland was a signatory to the 2001 Reuilly Agreement between Irish and British Anglican churches and the French Reformed Church. Janet Barcroft, a laywoman and then teacher of French at the High School, Dublin, was involved in earlier years in joint meetings on behalf of the Church of Ireland and, most recently, Revd Dr Christine O'Dowd-Smyth attended in 2017. Both have affirmed the value of the engagement.[7]

The 1931 Bonn Agreement between the Anglican and Old Catholic churches (of the Union of Utrecht) led to a relationship of communion between Anglicans and Old Catholics. The extent of Irish interest in this relationship is instanced in that Bishop Michael Burrows is currently co-chair of the official Anglican-Old Catholic dialogue.

IRELAND AND BRITAIN

The British Council of Churches (BCC), formed in 1942, included the Church of Ireland and the Methodist and Presbyterian churches in Ireland as full member-churches. The Church of Ireland ecumenist, Bishop Samuel Poyntz, was deeply involved in the 1980s. While the Roman Catholic Church was not in membership of the BCC, the visit of Pope John Paul II to Britain in 1982 was to have a profound effect on ecumenical relations. Unlike the papal visit to Ireland in 1979, the British visit had a very considerable ecumenical dimension. The pope's encouraging of the churches to walk 'hand in hand' was taken to heart and, following an inter-church process of discussion, the BCC was transformed into the then Council of Churches for Britain and Ireland (CCBI) – now known as Churches Together in Britain and Ireland (CTBI) – with the Roman Catholic Church in England and Wales, and in Scotland, in full membership.

This decision was the result of the Swanwick Declaration of 1987, which was the fruit of a major conference on the ecumenical future in these islands, held at

6 Correspondence with Bishop Christopher Hill.   7 Correspondence with J. Barcroft and Dr C. O'Dowd-Smyth.

Swanwick, Derbyshire. It was an in-depth meeting and at it the churches made a decisive commitment to move from 'cooperation to clear commitment' and to establish the necessary ecumenical structures. It was an especially big step for the Roman Catholic representatives, but the mood at Swanwick changed in a positive direction when Cardinal George Basil Hume stood up and made an unambiguous and quite historic speech of commitment. Roman Catholic attendees remarked that it was an example of the 'GBH factor' at work!

The Church of Ireland and the Methodist Church in Ireland were the only two Irish churches to join the new CCBI, but the Irish Roman Catholic hierarchy agreed to observer status. At the CCBI's 1990 inaugural assembly in Liverpool, Bishop John Neill (later archbishop of Dublin) was elected as one of the council's four presidents.

Such considerable ecumenical advance suffered a setback in 1998 – coincidentally or not, the year following a controversy over then President Mary McAleese's decision to receive Holy Communion in the Church of Ireland's Christ Church Cathedral, Dublin – with the publication by the Roman Catholic hierarchies in England and Wales, Scotland and Ireland of the document, *One bread, one body*, which indicated that under no circumstances should a Roman Catholic receive Holy Communion in a Protestant church and that only in extremely limited circumstances should a Protestant be allowed to receive in the Roman Catholic Church.

The controversy over the document's reactionary approach, while intense, was short-lived, perhaps because it had merely stated what already was the Vatican's policy, although often honoured in the breach. The bald terms of the document, in the context of general ecumenical progress, had given rise to the intensity of reaction. However, if the intention behind the publication of *One bread, One body* had been to stop a trend towards a more relaxed popular approach to Eucharistic sharing, it succeeded only to a limited extent; while perhaps tide-stemming to some extent, it was not tide-turning.

In terms of development aid, the organization Christian Aid is sponsored by a range of churches in Britain and Ireland, including the Church of Ireland, but not the Roman Catholic Church, which has its own development aid structures. This aspect of church work was a complication in the development of CCBI, in particular because of the strength and independence of Roman Catholic aid efforts, but satisfactory and realistic agreement was reached on the aid framework.

IRELAND

The ecumenical progress in establishing the CCBI, and parallel national structures also with Roman Catholic representation in England, Scotland and Wales, led to a serious attempt to establish a similar ecumenical body for Ireland. Representatives of the member-churches of the Irish Council of Churches and of the Irish Roman Catholic hierarchy came together to try to agree a new structure that would bring together the ICC and the Irish Inter-Church Meeting (IICM, bringing together the Roman Catholic Church and the ICC in membership) into a new, single body. That story requires some background.

The ICC, which had been formed in 1923, had not included the Roman Catholic Church due to that denomination's pre-Vatican II stance on ecumenism. However, following the change of direction at Vatican II in terms of ecumenical relations, the leaders of the Church of Ireland, Methodist, Presbyterian and Roman Catholic churches started to meet together. Subsequently, the ICC and the Irish hierarchy established two joint committees – the ICC-RC Joint Group on Social Problems and the Violence in Ireland Working Party – and, ultimately, high-level meetings that were held at the Ballymascanlon Hotel, Dundalk, which came to be known as the 'Ballymascanlon Talks' and then more formally as the Irish Inter-Church Meeting (IICM).

The Irish Presbyterian Church historian John Barkley recorded:

> On 17th July, 1972, the Episcopal Conference of the Roman Catholic Church responded to an overture from the ICC and issued an invitation to the member churches to attend a 'joint meeting at which the whole field of ecumenism in Ireland might be surveyed'.[8]

The Ballymascanlon talks set up working parties on particular issues and, following a paper by Micheál Ledwith, then of St Patrick's College, Maynooth, and David Poole, a leading Irish Quaker, were restructured in 1984, in particular now having an Irish Inter-Church Committee, which would carry on the work of the IICM at church-leadership level, meeting several times a year.

Irish ecumenism, structurally viewed, now had two formal national instruments, the ICC and the IICM, both having executive bodies but only the latter having Roman Catholic membership. The emergence of CCBI and parallel bodies in England, Scotland and Wales, embracing Protestant and Roman Catholic representation, led to the consideration of merging the ICC and IICM into a single instrument. An ICC-Roman Catholic review group accordingly drew up a formal proposal for the new Conference of Churches in Ireland (CCI). This was approved by all the ICC member-churches' governing bodies in 1999, except for the Presbyterian General Assembly. The voting at the General Assembly was 144 votes for and 224 votes against, with 96 members recording their dissent, a relatively rare move in the assembly and intended to signify protest.

Reviewing the proposal in light of the decisions of the ICC member-churches, and not wanting to drive any wedge between the churches over the matter, the Irish hierarchy announced that it did not wish to proceed. The hierarchy did not

---

8 J.M. Barkley, *The Irish Council of Churches, 1923–1983* (Belfast, [1983]), p. 26ff; for further background, see M. Hurley, 'The preparatory years' in *The Irish Inter-Church Meeting: background and development* (Belfast, 1998).

want to damage what had been achieved in terms of ecumenical relations among the Protestant churches.

In its report to the General Assembly in 2000, the Presbyterian Church's Inter-Church Relations Committee stated that the hierarchy had 'decided not to proceed with proposals to form the Conference of Churches in Ireland, therefore, the existing structures will remain'.[9] However, had the General Assembly agreed to the proposal in 1999, it was widely foreseen that the hierarchy would not have turned it down. The ICC's Executive Committee was so perturbed by the Presbyterian Church's 1999 decision that it wrote to the denomination expressing its disappointment. The Presbyterian Church's Inter-Church Relations Committee replied stating that it did not wish, as a result of the decision, to be 'misconstrued as being not committed to whole hearted inter-church engagement' and citing the problem, 'for some of those who were against', with the CCI proposal as having been its proposed constitution.[10] However, the review group that drafted the constitution had done so with the express aim of avoiding potential Presbyterian objections, particularly on doctrinal grounds.

Nonetheless, there did follow a streamlining of the administration of the ICC and IICM, with the two bodies working more closely together while remaining technically distinct. Eventually, there was a 're-branding' of the two bodies, by now with a single administration, known as Churches in Ireland Connecting in Christ. As this is essentially only a strapline, although a very effective one, its use did not require the churches' individual approval.

Quite apart from this *dénouement*, the Church of Ireland had been involved in tripartite conversations with the Methodist and Presbyterian churches. The 'Tripartite Consultation' started its work in 1968. There had been earlier, bilateral 'reunion' talks among the three churches which had come to naught. With the Presbyterian Church, the problem had been the ordained ministry and the issue of ministerial itinerancy had brought Church of Ireland-Methodist talks to an end. In 1973, the Tripartite Consultation produced the report, 'Towards a united church', but in particular Presbyterian concerns over the historic episcopate ended this approach. In 1988, the Presbyterian Church rejected proposals to set up a successor body to the Tripartite Consultation, a new Joint Theological Working Party, and in the following year the Church of Ireland and the Methodist Church formed a bilateral group. This led to a joint covenant in 2002, which in turn led in 2014 to a groundbreaking bilateral interchange of ministry scheme, enabled by a mutual recognition of personal episcope in the president of the Methodist Conference.

Church of Ireland-Moravian discussions have flourished for a period in recent years, under the Church of Ireland leadership of Bishop Michael Burrows, but a particular problem has been the fact that the Moravian Church in Ireland is part of the British province of that denomination and it has been difficult to coordinate

9 General Assembly annual reports, 2000, p. 153.   10 Ibid., p. 154.

advances in Church of Ireland-Moravian discussions with the Church of England. At the time of writing, there are hopes of a resolution of this issue following communication with the Church of England by the chair of the Church of Ireland's Commission for Christian Unity and Dialogue, Bishop John McDowell.

The development of the Irish School of Ecumenics – inaugurated in 1970 and led by Bishop Kenneth Kearon from 1999–2004, before he became secretary general of the Anglican Communion – was a remarkable and very successful venture, gaining international renown and attracting students from around the world. Fr Michael Hurley, the pioneering Jesuit ecumenist who edited *Irish Anglicanism*, this volume's predecessor marking one hundred years from disestablishment, was instrumental in the formation of the ISE.[11]

Ecumenism in Ireland has a chequered history over the past fifty years and there were many unofficial contacts arising from individuals' ecumenical commitment, such as the Glenstal and Greenhills conferences and the work of the Christian Renewal Centre in Rostrevor, Co. Down, which was founded by the Church of Ireland clergyman, Cecil Kerr.

The Troubles in Northern Ireland clearly had a religious dimension and no doubt the churches could have been more proactive and bolder in the cause of reconciliation, being held back in this by close religious-political identities. However, sectarianism was always a great concern for the churches and there were, indeed, outstanding examples of reconciliation work, such as in the Corrymeela Community, of which Bishop Trevor Williams is a former leader, the Columbanus Community, founded by Fr Hurley, and the Cornerstone Community.[12]

Various church-related peace initiatives have been supported by churches abroad as well as by government agencies and the European Union; the churches' own thinking on the subject was set out in two landmark documents: *Violence in Ireland: a report to the churches* (1976) and *Sectarianism: a discussion document* (1993).[13]

The German churches took a particular interest in Irish ecumenism, especially during the years of the Troubles. The Presbyterian historian John Barkley records that in 1977, through the generosity of the German churches, there was the possibility of new offices for the ICC being obtained. Thus, the Inter-Church Centre, at 48 Elmwood Avenue in Belfast, was opened in November of that year by Dr Eberhard Spiecker of the Protestant Church of the Rhineland. Professor Barkely adds that the gift provided the ICC with 'its own headquarters, facilities for its administrative, consultative, and committee work, well equipped offices, and accommodation for a resource-centre'. He also records that the Conference of European Churches established an emergency fund for Ireland in 1972, that

11 Cf. M. Power, *From ecumenism to community relations: inter-church relationships in Northern Ireland, 1980–2005* (Dublin, 2007), pp 166ff. 12 Cf. I.M. Ellis (ed.), *Peace and reconciliation projects in Ireland* (Irish Council of Churches, 1986). 13 *The report of the working party on sectarianism: a discussion document for presentation to the Irish Inter-Church Meeting* (Belfast, 1993).

in 1977 the ICC set up an Irish National Committee for the 1946-established and Geneva-based Ecumenical Church Loan Fund, and that the National Council of Churches of Christ, USA, had an Irish desk 1975–9, with financial support being channeled to the ICC.[14]

The book *Christians in Ulster: 1968–90* by the distinguished Methodists, Eric Gallagher and Stanley Worrall, sets out with particular vividness the ecumenical story of the churches and the Troubles in their stated period. Writing in 1982, they point out that during the 1970s the churches 'achieved considerable innovations and development in their relationships', and add:

> There have been setbacks and disappointments in the ecumenical field, but they must not be allowed to obscure the fact that there is now more contact, more mutual respect and understanding, between the Churches than at any earlier period of Irish history.[15]

Neither Eric Gallagher nor Stanley Worrall looked at the churches through rose-tinted spectacles and, for that reason, such observations are reassuring. The years from 1990 saw the churches further building up their ecumenical life and witness in many local and national initiatives that promoted dialogue and peace as well as a deeper ecumenical experience.

Ecumenism is about the people of God sharing together, as much as possible, in faith and witness. However, the issue of all Christians being in communion in a canonical sense remains largely unresolved. It is somewhat ironic that issues of ministry, which is essentially about service for the good of God's people, have been one of the main factors impeding this aspect of unity.

Despite certain advances, such as on this island in the Church of Ireland-Methodist relationship, the churches globally have largely moved on from canonical communion matters to focus on more practical aspects of ecumenical life. It is to be hoped that this deeper working together will nourish the longer-term ecumenical vision of mission in complete communion.

---

14 J.M. Barkley, op. cit., p. 15 and pp 25ff.   15 E. Gallagher and S. Worrall, *Christians in Ulster: 1968–80* (Oxford, 1982), p. 211; see also I.M. Ellis, *Vision and reality: a survey of twentieth-century Irish inter-church relations* (Belfast, 1992), ad loc.

10

A Methodist perspective on the Church of Ireland: the pursuit of unity in mission

Fergus O'Ferrall

I have been doubly privileged to have benefited from membership of both the Church of Ireland and of the Methodist Church in Ireland. I was brought up in a Church of Ireland family which also frequently worshipped in our local Methodist Church. I treasure memories of being confirmed by the late Archbishop George Simms in St Peter's Church when a pupil in Wesley College, Dublin on 13 March 1963. I equally value my membership of the Methodist Church, which has provided great Christian riches in my life. It has, therefore, been a further privilege to have been a member for significant periods of the Joint Theological Working Party between the two churches in the 1990s, and of the succeeding body, the Covenant Council, established following the signing of the covenant between the Church of Ireland and the Methodist Church in Ireland in 2002. To have had a 'ringside' seat when an historic new theological understanding emerged transforming the relationship between my two formative churches, given the ecclesiastical separateness that existed prior to these recent developments, is indeed to be specially blessed.

I provide my personal background to this Methodist perspective on the Church of Ireland since 1969 so that the critical comments I may express may be understood to stem not only from my love of both churches, but from concern and indeed impatience – given the urgency of an effective Christian mission in Ireland – that the full fruits of the covenant and the 2014 agreement on the interchangeability of ordained ministries in both churches may be harvested as quickly as possible. First, however, it is important to trace how the covenant and interchangeability of ministries emerged before suggesting what the future might hold for both churches.

TOWARDS THE COVENANT, 1968–99

When Frederick Jeffrey wrote on Anglican-Methodist relations in 1970, he described the churches' relationships since John Wesley's missionary movement evolved into a separate church. Sadly his account is largely one of separate development by each church.[1] This separateness stemmed from theological disagreements,

---

1 See Frederick Jeffery, 'Anglican-Methodist relations' in Michael Hurley, SJ (ed.), *Irish Anglicanism, 1869–1969* (Dublin, 1970), pp 79–92.

especially that concerning the 'historic episcopate', and from negative attitudes held by, and indeed actions by, many Anglicans and Methodists as they understood or misunderstood each other down the years until the 1960s.

During the 1960s some steps were taken by the Church of Ireland – with significant leadership from Archbishop Simms – and by the Methodist Church and the Presbyterian Church to form a Tripartite Consultation, having previously had bilateral contacts in the new ecumenical era, which developed slowly in the twentieth century but gathered pace after the Second Vatican Council, which ended in 1965. In March 1968 came the significant declaration of intent in which the three churches acknowledged each other as being within the Church of God and affirmed the intention to together seek the unity that is both God's will and his gift to the church. In 1973 a significant report of the Tripartite Consultation was produced, entitled 'Towards a united church'. This report highlighted the level of agreement reached and proposed a new united church bringing together the major traditions of each of the three churches. This foundered over concerns of the Presbyterian Church about accepting the 'historic episcopate'. The three churches were able to recognize the ordained ministries in each church as real and efficacious ministries of word and sacrament but also recognized that each church had different forms of church order: interchangeability of ministries remained work for another day. Nonetheless, progress had been made given that this mutual recognition had been withheld in the past.

The Presbyterian Church in Ireland for a variety of reasons – political, social and theological – from the 1970s gradually withdrew from a number of ecumenical bodies. Sadly, this process has continued. For example, it later ended the level of joint training for ministry that had long existed between Presbyterians and Methodists and recently it has moved to distance itself from the Church of Scotland, with which it has had such a strong and historic relationship. With this trend in Irish Presbyterianism becoming evident, the Tripartite Consultation moved in 1988 to become a theological working party. The Church of Ireland and the Methodist Church approved this proposal, but the Presbyterian Church decided to withdraw from any theological discussion with either church. In 1989, the General Synod and the Conference established a new Joint Theological Working Party with six members from each church, with the remit:

- to consider the implications of the work of the Tripartite Consultation in the new bilateral context;
- to relate the work of the proposed Anglican- Methodist International Commission to Anglican/Methodist relations in Ireland;
- to explore opportunities for developing Church of Ireland-Methodist relationships and to make appropriate recommendations for the furtherance of the visible unity of the church; and
- to report annually to the two churches.

From what appeared to be more retrenchment than radical progress there gradually developed a new understanding and trust between the two churches, particularly gaining impetus from documents issued from the Anglican/Methodist International Commission, which first met in 1992. In particular, the 1996 report of this commission, 'Sharing in the apostolic communion', was influential especially as it said that 'it is important that we do not demand of each other a greater uniformity of interpretation than we experience in our own separate communions'. Clarifying expectations and being more realistic about the pluralism *within* each church helped the dialogue progress. It needs to be recalled that the Methodist-Anglican proposed scheme of reunion in Britain, which had received the required approval in the Methodist Conference in 1972, had not been approved by the General Synod: Methodists became wary of Anglicans following this and feared that Anglicans were more interested in developing relationships with the Roman Catholic Church than with them. In 1982 a 'Covenanting for unity' proposal involving the United Reformed Church, the Moravian Church and the Methodist Church also did not receive approval in the General Synod of the Church of England. Despite these ecumenical setbacks there was slowly germinating a new missionary mentality in the 'decade of evangelism' – the 1990s. In 1994 informal conversations began between the Methodist Church in Britain and the Church of England, leading a report in 1996, 'Commitment to mission and unity'. In 1999 the Church of Ireland and the Methodist Church in Ireland endorsed the measure of agreement reached in the Joint Theological Working Party and 'encouraged it to hasten on with its work'.

In 1999 new terms of reference were approved by the Church of Ireland and the Methodist Church for the Joint Theological Working Party:

- to examine and express the theological issues involved in the promotion of visible unity between the Methodist Church in Ireland and the Church of Ireland and make appropriate recommendations;
- to explore opportunities for developing Church of Ireland/Methodist understanding and relationships at all levels, local, regional and national;
- to study the work of conversations involving Anglican and Methodist churches in England, Scotland and Wales, and relate these to the relations between our two Churches in Ireland;
- to relate the work of the Anglican/Methodist International Commission and of any other major Methodist/Anglican conversations to the work of the JTWP in Ireland; and
- to report annually to our two churches.

This set a new capacity for progress which rapidly culminated in an agreed covenant in 2002.

DEVELOPING THE COVENANT, 1999–2002

As the new millennium dawned there was a fresh emphasis on mission. The rapidly changing context in Ireland characterized by the Good Friday Agreement of 1998 bringing an end to the decades of terrorism in Northern Ireland, 1969–98, an increasing secularism in the Republic during the Celtic Tiger boom, and the collapsing authority of the Roman Catholic Church in the face of institutional and clerical abuses, led many to ponder how best to witness to the Gospel in a different and rapidly changing society. Early in 2000, at a residential meeting attended by the then primate, the Most Revd Dr Robin Eames, and the then president of the Methodist Church in Ireland, Revd Dr Kenneth Wilson, this missionary emphasis was stressed: how to best witness to the Gospel together. This, it was felt, would be facilitated by a public and formal recognition of what Archbishop Eames memorably described as 'the special relationship between the two Churches'. Work began on drafting a covenant text, with the Fetter Lane Declaration of the Church of England and the Moravian Church of Great Britain as a model.

The draft covenant was presented to the General Synod and the Conference at their meetings in 2000. The Joint Theological Working Party asked that it be sent to parishes and circuits for response and comment and this was agreed, with the Conference asking that explanatory notes be included. A total of sixty-five responses were received, the majority of which came from Methodist circuits. As a result, small amendments were made in the interests of clarification. The revised draft was presented to the General Synod and the Conference in 2001, urging that 'the journey of exploration be continued'. The covenant was presented for a final vote to the General Synod and the Conference in 2002. The synod, after a very moving discussion, passed the resolution 'to enter into a covenant relationship with the Methodist Church in Ireland' unanimously. Three weeks later, the Methodist Conference passed the same resolution in respect to the Church of Ireland with an overwhelming majority.

In a preface to the printed revised draft of the covenant in 2001, Archbishop Eames and Revd Dr Harold Good, then president of the Methodist Church in Ireland, stated that the covenant outlines

> what we are already able to say of each other, based on years of theological exploration between our Churches both nationally and internationally. On the basis of that acknowledgment, we would enter into a new commitment to worship, work and witness together.

It is important to observe how in the new century Anglicans and Methodists, in Ireland and internationally, had through dialogue put themselves in a position to accept from each other those gifts and insights that sadly had not been acceptable to these churches in the past era of separate ecclesiastical development.

Now they were not immediately proposing institutional or organic union or seeking assimilation – rather it was an 'agenda of unity in mission based upon the commission of Jesus Christ and to make visible that unity which has already been given to us by Christ himself'.[2] The understanding of 'visible unity' being offered in the covenant was one of visible evidence of working together in witness and mission.

WHAT DOES THE COVENANT SAY?

The covenant contains six affirmations as a basis for the belief that God 'is calling our two Churches to a fuller relationship in which we commit ourselves

- to share a common life and mission,
- to grow together so that unity may be visibly realized.'

The six affirmations are:

1. We acknowledge one another's churches as belonging to the One, Holy, Catholic and Apostolic church of Jesus Christ and as truly participating in the apostolic mission of the whole people of God.
2. We acknowledge that in each of our churches the Word of God is authentically preached and the sacraments of baptism and Holy Communion authentically administered according to the command of Christ.
3. We acknowledge that both our churches share in a common faith set forth in the Scriptures and summarized in the historic creeds.
4. We acknowledge our common inheritance in traditions of spirituality and liturgy. We rejoice in our diversity from which we may mutually benefit as we continue to develop varied forms of worship as appropriate to different situations.
5. We acknowledge each other's ordained ministries as given by God and as instruments of His grace by which our churches are served and built up. As pilgrims together, we look forward to the time when our ministries can be fully interchangeable and our churches visibly united.
6. We acknowledge that personal, collegial and communal oversight is embodied and practised in both churches, as each seeks to express continuity of apostolic life, mission and ministry.

The covenant then sets out ten agreed steps towards the goal of sharing a common life and witness and of growing together so that unity may be visibly realized. The first five steps are to be implemented in local circuits and parishes:

2 See preface by Archbishop Eames and President Harold Good in printed *Revised draft covenant between the Church of Ireland and the Methodist Church in Ireland* (Joint Theological Working Party, 2001).

1. To pray for and with one another and to avail of every opportunity to worship together.
2. To welcome one another's members to receive Holy Communion and other ministries as appropriate.
3. To share resources in order to strengthen the mission of the church.
4. To help our members to appreciate and draw out the gifts which each of our traditions has to offer the whole people of God.
5. To encourage the invitation of authorized persons of each church to minister in the other church, as far as the current disciplines of both churches permit.

The sixth to the ninth steps were more structural and are to be implemented by the governing bodies of the churches:

6. (a) To encourage united Methodist/Church of Ireland congregations: (i) where there are joint church schemes, (ii) where new churches are to be planted, (iii) where local congregations wish to move in this direction; (b) to encourage united Methodist/Church of Ireland chaplaincy work.
7. To enable a measure of joint training of candidates for ordained and lay ministries of our churches where possible and appropriate and to encourage mutual understanding at all levels in our churches.
8. To establish appropriate forms of consultation on matters of faith and order, mission and service.
9. To participate as observers by invitation in each other's forms of governance at every possible level.

The tenth step was 'to learn more about the practice of oversight in each other's Churches in order to achieve a fuller sharing of ministries at a later stage of our relationship'. This refers to the key element of the ongoing theological dialogue that occurs in the new Covenant Council, which succeeded the Joint Theological Working Party in 2003.

THE SIGNING OF THE COVENANT

On a wet Thursday afternoon on 26 September 2002 some twenty-five Anglicans and Methodists met at Chrome Hill House, outside Lisburn, County Antrim. They stood at the foot of two beech trees joined halfway up the trunk and growing together as one. The ageing John Wesley had intertwined two beech saplings, saying as he did so, that this is how he hoped the then established church and 'the people called Methodist' would be – in relationship with each other and growing as one. Here, after a short worship service, the primate of the Church of Ireland and the president of the Methodist Church in Ireland signed the historic covenant.[3] The era of ecclesiastical separation, which so often had been character-ized by mutual antagonism, was ended and it remained to be seen whether this 'intertwining' of these more mature branches of the Church of Jesus Christ would result in a real impetus for unity for mission in the challenging soil of Ireland in the twenty-first century.

TOWARDS INTERCHANGEABILITY OF MINISTRIES

A key focus of the work of the Covenant Council, alongside giving support and encouragement to local initiatives seeking to implement the covenant, has been exploring episcope and interchangeability of ministries. In 2007 the churches were presented with an interim statement of episcope and interchangeabil-ity for discussion throughout both churches. In 2010 interim proposals were endorsed by the governing bodies of both churches. More developed proposals were presented and received by synod and conference in 2011. Ten years after the signing of the covenant, in 2012, final approval was given by the Methodist Conference to the scheme of interchangeability and in 2013 the necessary legis-lation to enable the scheme passed its first stage at General Synod, amounting to another historic breakthrough following these years of patient work within the Covenant Council. In 2014 the General Synod passed the second and final stage of the legislation.

The key to the breakthrough on this the most neuralgic issue which had bedev-illed Anglican and Methodist relationships since the eighteenth century was the recognition of the historic episcopate within each church. As a consequence, the Church of Ireland recognized that the office of the president of the Methodist Church gives specific and personal expression to the historic episcopate as gifted to the whole Church of God. The title 'episcopal minister', embraced by the Methodist Church in Ireland, expresses the role of serving and former presidents in a manner consonant with, and parallel to, that in which the Church of Ireland describes the personal oversight exercised by a bishop. It was agreed that in future the president of the Methodist Church in Ireland and at least two former presi-dents (and at least two episcopal ministers thereafter) would participate fully in the ordination/consecration of Church of Ireland bishops to symbolize and effect the consonance between the understanding by both churches of personal and collegial episcopate. It was also agreed that at least three Church of Ireland bishops in the first instance (and at least two thereafter) would participate fully in the installation and consecration of the president of the Methodist Church in

3 The Chrome Hill worship service used on 26 Sept. 2002 is printed in Gillian Kingston, *A shared spiritual heritage* (Dublin, 2009). This booklet is part of a series published under the rubric 'Working out the covenant', which also includes Peter Thompson, *The journey so far* (2007) and Gillian Kingston, *Guidelines for the journey* (2008). Publications and materials relating to the covenant may be found at www.covenantcouncil.com.

Ireland to symbolize and effect the consonance between the understanding by both churches of personal and collegial episcope. When these ceremonies had taken place, as they have now done, it was agreed that the presidents of the Methodist Church and Church of Ireland bishops should participate fully – as often as practicable – in the ordination of priests or presbyters in each church. This sharing is now the regular occurrence and all presbyteral ministries in each church are now interchangeable. It remains, however, to work out and agree the detailed protocols or juridical instruments to govern, and give practical effect to, ministerial interchangeability in the two church polities. Models and protocols need to be agreed by the Church of Ireland and the Methodist Church and introduced through the constitution of the Church of Ireland and the manual of laws of the Methodist Church, thus creating ecclesial space for local covenant partnerships to flourish, which will be 'extra-parochial' and 'extra-circuit' units: this requires senior church leadership committed to new missionary endeavours *together* and so far, regrettably, this is not much in evidence. Agreeing doctrinal statements has been significant progress but they are only a means to the end – fulfilling the mission of the Church of Jesus Christ.

Both churches continue through the Covenant Council to explore the mutual recognition and interchangeability of local preachers and diocesan readers and also the full meaning, role and function of the diaconal ministry. In broad terms it has been agreed that under the scheme of interchangeability individual clergy/ ministers will come under the polity and discipline of the church in which they serve.

UNITED IN DOCTRINE, DIVIDED BY CULTURE, STRUCTURES AND CHURCH PRACTICES

The new era heralded by the agreement of the covenant and interchangeability has, as yet, not significantly influenced the 'unity in mission' goal to the extent that throughout the island the whole is greater than the sum of the two separate churches. Most Anglicans and Methodists continue to maintain their own churches at local level, without much or even any thought of their covenant partnership with another church. As far back as the Joint Theological Working Party it was recognized that fuller communion could not leave current church structures intact: unity in mission would require closer integration, and full communion 'must mean a full integration of each Church with the other'; the report of the Joint Theological Working Party to the Churches in 1998 affirmed that 'we can find no theological objections to full visible unity between our Churches'. It is the powerful non-theological factors, such as culture, structures and practices, that are keeping the churches apart from comprehensively and at all levels reinvigorating the mission of Christ in the island of Ireland.

That said, there are a few encouraging local examples of the two churches working together where the mission has been significantly more effective because of this shared endeavour. These include the Church of the Good Shepherd in the diocese of Connor which sought to be a 'prototype Church of the Covenant'. Here it was understood that missional unity is more at risk from administrative issues than from doctrine or liturgical practice. The Covenant Council produced a booklet, 'Local covenant partnerships', in 2005, with a view to assisting the churches to come together for more effective witness and mission. It emerged that the Church of Ireland did not have the relevant ecumenical canons required to have protocols approved by General Synod. This is a recognized danger to ecumenical advance where legal normativity – and indeed an attitude of 'this is always how we have done it' – acquires the pretence of doctrinal normativity. The constitution of the Church of the Good Shepherd as a single-congregation local covenant partnership is effectively based on guidelines that were not considered appropriate to be passed into law by the Church of Ireland.

Other local covenant partnerships have developed, such as that agreed for the Methodist and Church of Ireland chaplaincies at Queen's University Belfast in 2013. This forms a 'single centre', under the chaplain approved by both churches, ministering across the student body, through the Hub café, and conducting worship in the Church of the Resurrection, recognized by both churches as a 'covenant church'. This partnership was signed by the bishop of Connor and the district superintendent of the Methodist Church. This is a most encouraging development, seeking to serve students through a common witness to the Gospel and is well placed to exert a positive Christian influence on future generations. The model is already proving influential in developing shared third-level chaplaincy at other universities in Northern Ireland.

Further encouragement may be taken from a new partnership that was developed in 2017 between Longford Methodist Church and the Edgeworthstown Group of Church of Ireland parishes in County Longford under Revd Christian Snell. This combination of what is, in effect, two part-time charges, has resulted in a full-time appointment and demonstrates that at local level the two churches together are able to provide scattered country parishes with a vigorous ministry and a link with ministry in Longford town. Other older partnerships such as those at the Church on the Hill at Maghaberry and the sharing of buildings at Movilla Abbey and Primacy continue to present joint opportunities for unity in mission.

Another fruit of the covenant is the fruitful relationship that has developed between the Church of Ireland Theological Institute in Dublin and Edgehill Theological College in Belfast. An annual two-day integrated seminar is proving very successful, and the two colleges are seeking to enhance their cooperation and to collaborate in teaching on some Queen's University Belfast Open Learning Centre courses, which will contribute to the programme of training for local ordained ministers and lay preachers.

A major challenge now facing the Covenant Council and the two churches, while providing an impetus to these ongoing projects, is discerning how to overcome the widespread institutional lethargy concerning 'unity in mission'. Indeed, even communicating to congregations the story of the covenant and an under-standing of how it might facilitate a fresh missionary outreach in every county in the island has proved very difficult in local churches many of which are in decline and are focused on maintenance and mere survival.

MEETING THE MISSIONARY CHALLENGE: A UNITING CHURCH OF IRELAND

The positive connections between the Joint Theological Working Party and subsequently the Covenant Council and the Anglican–Methodist International Commission are a new factor in the story of the growing relationship between the Church of Ireland and Methodist Church in Ireland. The value of 'Sharing in the Apostolic Communion' report in the 1990s has been noted. Later, when an impasse arose in the Anglican–Methodist dialogue in 2007, after significant input from members of the Covenant Council, a meeting of international repre-sentatives was held in London. This meeting resulted in a new framework and agenda being agreed leading to the establishment of the Anglican–Methodist International Commission for Unity in Mission (AMICUM) which began its work in 2009. It was the Irish churches' initiative that made the difference and a particular debt is owed to Ms Gillian Kingston and to Rt Revd Harold Miller, who co-chaired the critical meeting in London; later Bishop Harold Miller co-chaired AMICUM, which published the 2014 important report 'Into all the world: being and becoming apostolic churches'. Both the Church of Ireland and the Methodist Church in Ireland would greatly benefit by giving more detailed consideration to this report, particularly the questions it posed in what it called 'tool kits' for further conversations in part three.

The Anglican Consultative Council, representing Anglican churches and about 85 million Anglicans (or Episcopalians) worldwide, and the World Methodist Council, representing Wesleyan, Methodist, United and Uniting churches and over 80 million worldwide, who received this report, have overseen the develop-ing global relationships between the two communions. Both communions have recognized their common confession of the apostolic faith and a common par-ticipation in God's mission. In the preface to 'Into all the world', Bishop Miller and his Methodist co-chair Revd Professor Robert Gribben wrote, noting that the churches are 'awash with ecumenical reports':

> If we are honest, we are often willing to be friendly as long as nothing changes. If we do act ecumenically, we do it minimally, watching every care-ful step. Or, in our unity discussions we ask of each other an impossible perfection. Scripture reminds us however, 'Not that we are sufficient of ourselves to claim anything as coming from us; our sufficiency is of God' (2 Cor. 3:5). We do not name the problem: the churches themselves are in

need of repentance and conversion, of *metanoia*, which means a willingness to turn from our own self-absorbing, restricting concerns, to Christ alone. What we continually seem to miss is that the unity we seek is precisely not of our own making, but for us to receive as a gift of Christ himself. It is in fact the very nature of the Church of Jesus Christ which impels us.

As soon as interchangeability of ministries was agreed, some members of the Covenant Council in 2014 proposed that the council invite the Church of Ireland Council on Mission and the Home Mission Department of the Methodist Church to consider *together* advancing the covenant between our two churches by jointly planning and hosting a major Irish conference on the mission of God to be undertaken by our churches in Ireland. It was envisaged that the conference would mark an historic new departure by our churches *together.*

The objectives of the conference, it was proposed, should include:

- setting out the new frontiers in mission which confront our churches in a radically changing Ireland;
- assisting our churches to focus on discipleship-making in order for disciples to be effective in everyday mission;
- spreading examples of effective mission in the Church of Ireland and in the Methodist Church in Ireland so as to assist other churches in their renewal of their mission;
- engaging the media so as to create a better understanding of the mission and contribution of the churches to the common good; and
- bringing together how the growth by each disciple in the love of God, the use of the spiritual disciplines and means of grace, the sharing of fellowship and engaging in mission are linked in healthy nurturing and worshipping local churches.

It was suggested that such a major conference would have to be well planned over two years so that it would become a seminal turning point in the new era of the covenant and interchangeability of ministries. It would require a major investment of resources, human and financial. It would seek to mark a new and shared missional consciousness and avoid the danger that the covenant being perceived as a 'technical' theological advance, which thereby fails to make visible our new 'unity in mission' at local level. The conference would only be one focal point in building a whole new programme of Methodist and Church of Ireland leaders and members working *together* and learning to share a common analysis of our radically changed societal context in which we communicate and witness to the Gospel. If the proposal were to be adopted, it would be additional to the continuing local covenant partnerships, the agreeing of protocols on interchangeability of ministries, representation on each other's church committees, the developing of effective relationships between Edgehill Theological College and the Church of

Ireland Theological Institute and so forth under the covenant. This proposal ought to be jointly considered or, if not this proposal, from where is the 'unity in mission' imperative to arise?

'Into all the world' put the aim concisely: 'visible unity in a common mission must be our goal'. Yet the Church of Ireland and the Methodist Church in Ireland are not equipping each other to be *visibly* united. In the last two decades each has developed or adopted separate new liturgical and worship books – such as new hymnals and the revised *Book of Common Prayer* (2004) and the *Methodist worship book*. Given our shared spiritual heritage surely we must arrive at a stage where *together* we approve and use common liturgical and worship resources, ones which will facilitate diversity and difference reflecting our very changed population in Ireland, if *visible unity* is to be realized at local level. Each church produces its own mission strategies or statements such as 'God's mission, our mission', the major Methodist Church in Ireland conference statement approved in 2014. This statement indeed used the Anglican Five Marks of Mission as a helpful summary of Methodist understanding of mission illustrating how much both churches agree in regard to Christian mission. 'God's mission, our mission' did state that 'deepening the Covenant with the Church of Ireland and enriching our ecumenical relationships will give rise to historic opportunities for Christian witness and more effective mission in the period ahead'. The challenge of separate parish and circuit buildings must be confronted *together* not as an exercise in decline and retrenchment but as good stewards of God-given resources that ought to be used for more effective mission and service in our new societal conditions with so many withdrawing so rapidly from institutional religion but continuing to have deep but unmet spiritual hungers. A growing Irish church will depend on outreach, witness, service and effective mission – making new disciples who themselves are shaped and influenced by mission. The challenge for the Church of Ireland and for the Methodist Church in Ireland for the next fifty years is the radical one of giving practical evidence of faithfulness to what both have already discerned and expressed as God's will and call. This will, in my view, require a Uniting Church of Ireland that will embrace fully and wholeheartedly the gifts of the Methodist Church and, in particular, its missionary imperative, as both institutional churches prune and discard all that is no longer relevant or necessary for effective worship, mission and service.

II

The Church of Ireland and
the Anglican Communion

The Rt Revd Kenneth Kearon,
bishop of Limerick and Killaloe

In 1969, as Fr Michael Hurley finalized the text of *Irish Anglicanism*, the Anglican Communion did not figure in the consciousness of the average Irish church member, unless one happened to be involved in missionary work. That has changed dramatically in the fifty years since that publication, and so, in this chapter, an attempt will be made to recover the stories of Church of Ireland involvement in the communion over a longer period than just the last fifty years, and so present a fuller picture over the two volumes.

The Anglican Communion has often been described as a work in progress, a family of churches whose origins lie in one of the expressions of church that emerged from the political and ecclesiastical turmoil of the sixteenth and seventeenth centuries in England and Ireland, and to a lesser extent, in Scotland and Wales. It travelled with the rapidly expanding British empire from the seventeenth century onwards, a missionary expansion given shape and focus with the founding of a number of missionary agencies, especially the Society for the Propagation of the Gospel (SPG) in 1701 and the Church Missionary Society (CMS) in 1799, and numerous others such as the Society for Promoting Christian Knowledge (SPCK), which brought specific focuses to the missionary enterprise.

Throughout the seventeenth and eighteenth centuries, the churches of the British Isles sent clergy to all corners of the British empire, both to serve as chaplains to the expat communities, and to bring Christianity to the local people. Bishops soon followed, and dioceses were created in response to need. It is from this expansion that the early diocesan structures of what we know of today as the Anglican Communion emerged. The Church of Ireland's involvement in this is to be found through the involvement of a number of individuals who engaged with the needs of this global expansion, and made a distinctively Irish contribution.

In the Church of England, the eighteenth century has been described as a time when the church entered into its role as an established church and as a participant in the life of a global power, but it was not until the nineteenth century that the 'Church of England abroad' began to take shape as the Anglican Communion we can recognize today. As is so often the case in the history of Anglicanism, it was controversy or the threat of division that triggered theological and institutional structural reform.

The first major challenge was the American Revolution and the Declaration of Independence in 1776, and the consequent autonomy in that country of what had been up to then the 'English' church. The Protestant Episcopal Church was set up in 1789 and modelled its democratic polity closely on the political structures of the United States, published its own version of the *Book of Common Prayer*, and committed itself to maintain apostolic succession – in effect becoming the first province of the Anglican Communion.

JEBB AND THE ANGLICAN RENAISSANCE

Later that same century, much of the theological identity of Anglicanism was worked out in the controversy surrounding the high church Oxford Movement and the evangelical revival in the Church of England during the nineteenth century.

The Oxford Movement (many of its founders were associated with Oxford University) emerged in the early nineteenth century, and its followers were soon labelled 'Tractarians' because of a series of tracts published between 1831 and 1844 which argued for a high ecclesiology rooted in the early church fathers, and in liturgy and devotional practice drew close to Roman Catholicism. A major impetus for the movement was the Irish Church Temporalities Act (1833), which reduced the number of Irish bishoprics and introduced changes to the management and ownership of ecclesiastical property in Ireland, and which led to John Keble's sermon in 1833 when he perceived the act as an attack by the state on the established church.

The theology of evangelicals, which included many parish clergy and the majority of the laity, found expression in the great sermons of preachers of the time, and in a growing sense of identity as part of the wider evangelical movement, and often looked to John and Charles Wesley for inspiration.

These two movements of the nineteenth century, which shaped so much of the theological identity of Anglicanism, did not leave the Church of Ireland untouched, with the church depressed by the movement of many of its key lay leaders to London after the Act of Union in 1800, yet during the nineteenth century it experienced greater organization and management within the church.

When one looks to a Church of Ireland influence in all of this, the name of John Jebb, bishop of Limerick (1823–33), comes to mind. He was a great friend of Alexander Knox, the high churchman, and yet Jebb related to evangelicals as much as to the high churchmen, and stated that there were 'more congenialities between me and the better order of evangelicals, than between me and the high churchmen'.[1] He is commemorated by a white marble statue in St Mary's Cathedral,

---

1 Quoted in A.R. Acheson, *Bishop John Jebb and the nineteenth-century Anglican renaissance* (Toronto, 2013), p. xiv.

Limerick. Writing in 1958 about Jebb and his statue, Robert Wyse Jackson, bishop of Limerick (1961–70), wrote:

> Placid cultured, an intellectual, a little remote; the statue suggests these things, and so he was. But he was also a man beloved of simple people. He was a scholar, whose paths were set in quiet ways; a thinker, who, from a remote rural Irish rectory, wielded an influence which altered a world church; a saint who infused the Spirit of God into the dry bones of the theological antiquarianism, a man of humility and modesty, whose mind was to mould the beliefs and the faith of many generations.[2]

Jebb's influence on emerging Anglicanism was twofold. The first was his version of high churchmanship. Through his lifelong friendship and correspondence with Alexander Knox, Jebb marked out what is sometimes called the Anglican Renaissance. Knox was an Irish lay theologian and correspondent with John Wesley, who, together with Jebb developed a style of high churchmanship which respected many of the elements of evangelicalism. Acheson writes of these high churchmen as those who

> stressed the primitive and catholic aspects of their churches heritage, and generally taught what they called 'church principles' or 'sound churchmanship' … The daily offices, early Communion, Lent and Holy Week observances, sung Eucharist and choral evensong were restored to the church's life.[3]

Yet this was combined with his respect for evangelical piety and devotion, and a strong sense of pastoral commitment and evangelical outreach: 'his High Churchmanship had about it a warm-heartedness, a depth of spirituality and devotion, which were distinctly evangelical in tone'.[4]

Jebb and Knox are often said to have been precursors of the Oxford Movement, though the extent of this and the manner of that influence is often debated. Jebb knew several of the leaders of the Oxford Movement, though he died in 1833, the year of Keble's assize sermon. Some of these same leaders were aware of Knox's writings, though most do not acknowledge his influence.

The second way in which he influenced Anglicanism was through his effect on the emerging and self-confident Protestant Episcopal Church in the United States. This appears to have begun with a meeting over dinner with Bishop John Henry Hobart of New York. Hobart was eager for learning from those in leadership across the Atlantic, and so Jebb was able, through Hobart, to present copies of several of his publications to ten American bishops. Jebb's writings became an

2 Ibid.   3 A.R. Acheson, *A history of the Church of Ireland, 1691–1996* (Dublin, 1997), p. 154.   4 Quoted in Acheson, *Bishop John Jebb*, p. xiv.

immediate success in the United States and American editions of his books were circulated widely. In later life Jebb was invalided, a restriction that enabled him to write prolifically, and many of his writings from this period received wide circulation in the United States. His high church theology and ecclesiology found a resonance especially among the bishops of that church, and was in contrast to the attitudes of many high churchmen in England, who did not share Jebb's positive and enthusiastic support of the transatlantic church.

THE FIRST LAMBETH CONFERENCE

The decision to convene a conference at Lambeth in 1867 gave the beginning of a structure to the Anglican Communion. The background was a controversy in South Africa, when the bishop of Natal, William Colenso, was keen to indigenize the Gospel into local culture but his radical theological writings soon led to accusations of heresy and eventually he was deposed by Robert Gray, archbishop of Capetown. Colenso, who had been consecrated bishop by the archbishop of Canterbury, challenged the right of the archbishop of Capetown even to try him and appealed to the Judicial Committee of the Privy Council in London. In 1865 the Privy Council upheld the appeal, confirmed him in office and secured his stipend. Gray appealed to the archbishop of Canterbury (Longley), who already had a number of problematic issues concerning 'overseas dioceses' on his plate. The Canadian bishops proposed to the archbishop that he call a synod of bishops of these overseas dioceses to deal with the Colenso affair, and this suggestion was taken up in 1867 when Longley invited all Anglican bishops (except Colenso), bishops with whom he was in communion, to a meeting at Lambeth Palace. The purpose was expressly stated by Archbishop Longley:

> It should be distinctly understood that at this meeting no declaration of faith shall be made, and no decision come to that shall affect generally the interests of the Church, but that we shall meet together for brotherly counsel and encouragement ... I can assure my brethren that I should enter on this meeting in the full confidence that nothing would pass but that which tended to brotherly love and union, and would bind the Colonial Church, which is certainly in a most unsatisfactory state, more closely to the Mother Church.[5]

Despite this assurance, several bishops did not attend for a variety of reasons. Irish bishops generally attended, though the bishops of Cashel (Daly) and Tuam (Bernard) withdrew their acceptances of the invitation when they saw the agenda, over which there had been further controversy.

Another Irish input to the formation of the Anglican Communion can be found in the objection by the bishop of Meath (Plunket, later archbishop of Dublin) to

---

5 Quoted in A.M.G. Stephenson, *Anglicanism and the Lambeth conferences* (London, 1978), p. 31.

the use of the term 'Anglican Communion'. In a letter to the *Guardian*, which he wrote soon after the second Lambeth Conference (1878), he outlined his reasons.

> I should be glad … through the medium of your paper, to suggest to those more competent than myself for such a task, the desirability of finding, if possible, some more appropriate term than 'Anglican' whereby to describe the great communion from which the Conference at Lambeth has taken, hitherto, its name.
>
> As an Irish Bishop I have a special reason for desiring some change. It is the habit of certain Roman Catholic controversialists in this land to try and enlist the patriotism of their fellow-countrymen against the claims of our communion by asserting that our church is the church of the Anglo-Saxon invaders …
>
> So far as the Irish Church is concerned, the term 'Anglican' does not seem an altogether accurate description. And may I be permitted, with all deference, to ask whether it be altogether wise or right that the English church should on her part entirely ignore those early centuries of British Christianity which preceded the mission of St Augustine? As regards the Episcopal Churches of Scotland and America, I may, I think, with confidence add that there are many in those churches who are not quite satisfied with the name by which the communion to which we all belong is at present described.[6]

The name 'Anglican Communion' remained – support for a change of name was not as strong as Plunket had imagined.

IRELAND AND THE IBERIAN CHURCHES

The churches on the Iberian Peninsula first surfaced on the agenda of the Anglican Communion in 1878. Prior to this, since the 1850s several groupings had broken away from the Roman Catholic Church on a number of doctrinal issues, usually concerning questions of papal authority and primacy, and many styled themselves 'Old Catholic'. The best known of these are the Catholic Churches of the Union of Utrecht, which emerged after the First Vatican Council in 1869–70. Other Old Catholic groups emerged during this period and two of these – one in Spain and the other in Portugal – were set up after a degree of religious liberty had been granted in the peninsula. These churches petitioned the bishops at the first Lambeth Conference (1867) to consecrate a bishop for them. The request at that time was not granted, but by the second Lambeth Conference (1888) the cause of the Iberian churches had been taken up by the archbishop of Dublin, Lord Plunket. Plunket's championing of their cause led to a more favourable response,

6 Quoted in Stephenson, op. cit., p. 7.

so that Plunket could hope that 'by lawful and cautious means the two Churches might secure an episcopate of their own according to the principles of primitive jurisdiction, each limited to his own flock and without territorial title'.[7]

Plunket initially received little support from his fellow Irish bishops, but, supported by the bishop of Clogher (Stack) and the bishop of Down (Welland), he announced to the Irish bench that, 'in view of altered circumstances and unless formally forbidden either by the Bench or by the General Synod, they would consecrate as bishops for those Churches native priests elected by their own synods if approved by the three bishops themselves'.[8] The three bishops then went on to consecrate Juan Cabrera as first bishop of the Spanish Reformed Church.

Not everyone welcomed this initiative, and Lord Halifax, a prominent layman in the Church of England, wrote to the cardinal archbishop of Toledo apologizing for the presumption of the archbishop of Dublin 'without the sanction of your Eminence and of the bishops of your Province of Toledo, to consecrate a certain schismatic named Cabrera to the Episcopate'.

Plunket's response is recorded. He is said to have put his head between his hands and with a sob said

> to think of it – an English churchman addressing in this manner the head of the most intolerant part of the Roman church, because a body of Spaniards wish to have what English Churchman believe to be a spiritual privilege, and I helped them to obtain it. Surely, surely, there is something very wrong.[9]

Plunket's enthusiasm for these embryonic churches was taken up by Archbishop Gregg when in 1920, as archbishop of Dublin, he became a member of the advisory council of Irish bishops, along with Armagh and Meath. By this time the churches were again without a bishop, and remained so until 1954 when the then bishop of Meath joined with two American bishops to consecrate Bishop Santos Molina Zurita. Gregg first visited in 1924, conducting several confirmations and ordinations and generally encouraging the newly emerging churches during his several visits. He learned to read and speak both Spanish and Portuguese and conducted liturgies in these languages.

Gregg was aware of the anomaly being created by supporting this indigenous Spanish church when much of Spain was part of the Church of England diocese of Gibraltar, itself formed out of the many English chaplaincies of southern Europe. Gregg met the recently consecrated bishop of Gibraltar, Bishop Harold Buxton, in London before visiting Spain. Gregg stated the position succinctly:

> Naturally, as I am *not* visiting your diocese, and as you *don't* approve of my activities, I shall not embarrass you, and I will not intrude into your

7 G. Seaver, *John Allen Fitzgerald Gregg Archbishop* (London, 1963), p. 131.   8 Ibid., p. 131.   9 Ibid., p. 132.

Chaplaincies. We shall keep at arm's length if we meet in Madrid. I'll have nothing to do with *your* Embassy, mind you. *We* have our own.[10]

The anomalous position of these churches was partly resolved in 1980, when both were incorporated into the Anglican Communion as 'extra-provincial dioceses', with the archbishop of Canterbury exercising the function of primate.

VATICAN II AND ECUMENISM

As is well known, relations between the Roman Catholic Church and the Anglican Communion changed dramatically at Vatican II. In a new spirit of openness to ecumenism and dialogue, Anglicans received special mention in the documents of Vatican II. This opened the door to meetings between Pope Paul VI and Archbishop Michael Ramsey in Rome in March 1966. While it did not have the sense of momentous change as the first meeting of an archbishop of Canterbury with the pope (Archbishop Fisher's meeting with Pope John XXIII in 1960 was far more historic, as the first such meeting since the Reformation), the 1966 meeting was much more productive. A common declaration issued from the meeting, stating an intention to set up a major dialogue between the two communions, a dialogue to include scripture, tradition, liturgy and practical difficulties. The major dialogue became known as ARCIC, the first phase of which was co-chaired by Bishop Henry McAdoo of Ossory.

What is not as widely known is that one of the 'practical difficulties' identified was 'mixed marriages', and Archbishop George Simms of Dublin was appointed as co-chair of that commission. Simms' profile was already high in the Anglican Communion, as he had played a significant role in the Lambeth Conference of 1958, a fact noted by Archbishop Michael Ramsey, who became archbishop of Canterbury in 1961. Simms also preached in Trinity Church, New York (a prestigious invitation) before the Anglican congress in Toronto in 1963, and was the only Irish person invited to give a paper at the congress.

Another outcome from the meeting in Rome in 1966 was the setting up of the Anglican Centre there. It was to be an Anglican presence, a place where Rome could become familiar with Anglicanism, and Anglicans could come to know the heart of the Roman Catholic Church. The centre's fifth director in 1995 was Canon Bruce Ruddock, originally from the Church of Ireland. By that time the centre had been in existence for almost thirty years, but it had to move to larger premises and it fell to Canon Ruddock to oversee this move. His time in Rome was a time of change, not only of location, but of image and profile in Rome, as Ruddock developed and deepened relations with Cardinal Cassidy, president of the Pontifical Council for Promoting Christian Unity and other influential leaders there.

10 Ibid., p. 140.

OUTSTANDING SERVICE TO
THE ANGLICAN COMMUNION

The 1960s and '70s began a period of rapid change and expansion for the Anglican Communion as national churches in many parts of the world, but especially in Africa, became autonomous provinces of the communion. This welcome development required more formal structures to set alongside the Lambeth Conference which only met every ten years, and anyway comprised only bishops, which didn't sit well with the democratic synodical governance model that was becoming the norm within the communion. The Anglican Consultative Council came into being as a result of a resolution of the Lambeth Conference 1968, and first met in 1971 in Kenya. The ACC meets approximately every three years. This was followed by the Primates' Meeting, a proposal made by the archbishop of Canterbury during the Lambeth Conference in 1978 for primates of the communion to meet regularly for 'leisurely thought, prayer and deep consultation'. It meets at the discretion of the archbishop of Canterbury every two years or so.

Archbishop Robin Eames was elected archbishop of Armagh in 1986 and as such became the Church of Ireland's representative at the Primates' Meeting, one of the 'instruments of communion' of the Anglican Communion. Before that his formal involvement with the communion had begun in 1984 when he attended the 6th Anglican Consultative Council meeting in Nigeria as one of two Church of Ireland representatives. At that meeting he supported a motion on Anglican-Roman Catholic marriages that encouraged engagement on the matter with the Secretariat for Christian Unity in the Vatican.

Thus began Eames' involvement with the structures of the Anglican Communion that lasted for over twenty years, and included membership of the ACC, the Primates' Meeting, and the Joint Standing Committee of the ACC and the Primates' Meeting, as well as a prominent role in successive Lambeth Conferences during that period.

The extraordinary diversity within the communion so evident at these meetings and rightly celebrated puts strain on a fellowship of churches, each deeply embedded in its own social and cultural contexts. As each autonomous church took responsibility for decisions appropriate to its own context, so the potential for misunderstanding and incompatibility grew.

As a result, themes such as communion, koinonia, authority and collegiality were to become major issues in the Anglican Communion during Eames' time, and it was precisely in these areas that he made his greatest contributions to the life of the communion.

About his first Primates' Meeting in 1986, Eames wrote:

> The Anglican Communion is a constantly evolving part of the world Church. It is a relationship rather than a set structure. It involves consensus

rather that confrontation. It embraces diversity rather than conformity. It rejoices in comprehensiveness rather than rigid policy.[11]

A major controversy was already on the agenda. The Lambeth Conference in 1978 had noted that many provinces had already ordained women to the priesthood, and recognizing that the prospect of women in the episcopate was an imminent possibility, requested members of churches not to proceed with ordination to the episcopate until a wider consultation with the whole communion episcopate had taken place. By 1985 it was clear that the Episcopal Church of the USA was moving towards such an ordination. The opinion of the Primates' Meeting in 1986 was sought.

The issues were complex. The Episcopal Church of the USA has a constitutional right to proceed with the ordination of a woman to the episcopate. By contacting the Primates' Meeting in this way they were consulting with a representative body of the communion episcopate. After extensive discussions at the meeting, a primates' working party on the matter was set up to continue the process of consultation.

The issue was discussed again at the 1988 Lambeth Conference in an atmosphere of tension and division, with dire warnings from both the Roman Catholic and Orthodox churches about the implications for ecumenical relations. In the end, it was decided to appoint a commission, and so Eames was invited to chair the Commission on Communion and Women in the Episcopate. The purpose of the commission was clear – while it must acknowledge and respect different theological perspectives, the main task to be addressed was how communion within the Anglican Communion was to be maintained given the diversity of opinion within the church and the mutual incompatibility of many such opinions. It's interesting to note that this is the same topic that was the first item on the agenda of the second Lambeth Conference, in 1878, so it certainly wasn't a new one. Clarifying the task before the Commission in this way proved prescient, as that question returned again, especially surrounding the issue of same-sex relationships.

The report was completed in 1989, and presented to the Primates' Meeting that year. They warmly commended it to the provinces for study and endorsed the guidelines as a means of furthering 'the highest degree of communion, in the spirit of the Lambeth Conference of 1988'. Two further reports followed, in 1990 and 1993.

Meanwhile, that same Lambeth Conference requested 'further exploration of the meaning and nature of communion'. The work began at a consultation at Virginia Theological Seminary in 1991, again chaired by Eames and the group, soon to be called the Inter-Anglican Theological and Doctrinal Commission (IATDC), produced the Virginia Report, which explored concepts of primacy, oversight and

11 R.H.A. Eames, 'Towards agreement', *Search*, 9:2 (Winter 1986).

the nature of communion. It was considered by the ACC in 1996, and played an important part in the agenda of the 1998 Lambeth Conference.

Both of these documents, one facing the immediate issue of division within the communion caused by the ordination of women to the episcopate, and the other addressing the underlying issue of the maintenance of unity in the increasingly diverse and rapidly growing Anglican Communion, steadied the Anglican Communion at a time of extreme challenge and crisis, and shaped it for the succeeding decades. Each was widely welcomed within the communion and that successful achievement in both cases was put down by most to the exceptional and skilful chairmanship of Archbishop Robin Eames.

Those skills were again brought to bear on what is possibly the most divisive issue that has faced the Anglican Communion so far – that of same-sex relations, which came to a head in 2003 with the decision of the 74th General Convention of the Episcopal Church (USA) to consent to the election of Gene Robinson, a bishop of New Hampshire, and in the same year the authorizing by the diocese of New Westminster in the Anglican Church of Canada of a public Rite of Blessing for same-sex unions. The response on the part of some was equally difficult, when bishops from other provinces intervened in the Episcopal Church (USA) and the Anglican Church of Canada and performed episcopal functions without the consent of the diocesan bishop.

The origins of this controversy go back at least as far as the Lambeth Conference of 1978, which addressed the issue of sexuality by calling for, among a number of issues, a 'deep and dispassionate study of the question of homosexuality, which would take seriously both the teaching of Scripture and the results of scientific and medical research'.[12] The Lambeth Conference of 1988 reaffirmed that call,[13] and also in a separate resolution reaffirmed 'the historical position of respect for diocesan boundaries and the authority of bishops within those boundaries'.[14]

By 2003 the focus was on the 1998 Lambeth Conference's Resolution 1.10, which states that the conference, 'in view of the teaching of scripture, upholds faithfulness in marriage between a man and a woman in lifelong union, and believes that abstinence is right for those who are not called to marriage,[15] and 'cannot advise the legitimising or blessing of same sex unions nor ordaining those involved in same gender unions'.[16]

It was no surprise that after an emergency meeting of primates in 2003 the then archbishop of Canterbury, Rowan Williams, turned to Archbishop Robin Eames to chair the Lambeth Commission on Communion, which produced what is commonly called the Windsor Report. The report was published in October 2004. The task was by now a familiar one – the maintenance of the highest degree of communion possible given the level of division evident in the Anglican Communion at the time. The mandate from the archbishop of Canterbury was specific:

12 Lambeth Conference 1978, res. 10.3.   13 Res. 64.   14 Res. 72.   15 Res. 1.10.1.   16 Res. 1.10.5.

to examine and report to him .... on the canonical understandings of communion, impaired and broken communion, and the ways in which provinces of the Anglican Communion may relate to one another in situations where the ecclesiastical authorities of one province feel unable to maintain the fullness of communion with another part of the Anglican Communion.[17]

The report is a carefully argued thesis, exploring the common self-understanding of Anglican churches, their celebration of diversity, the concept of interdependence and the meaning of and limits to provincial autonomy. It recommended the Episcopal Church (as it was now called) and the Anglican Church of Canada express regret for breaching 'the bonds of affection' in the communion and offer an explanation to one of the instruments of communion. It called for an immediate cessation of interventions by bishops into provinces which were not their own. It also recommended a number of initiatives that should be taken to strengthen the common life of the Communion.

Eames received many awards and much recognition for his varied work, especially within the context of the Northern Ireland peace process. He was created a life peer as Baron Eames of Armagh in 1995 on the recommendation of the prime minister, John Major, and in 2007 received the Order of Merit from Queen Elizabeth. In 2006 he received the Archbishop of Canterbury's Award for Outstanding Service to the Anglican Communion, only the second person to receive it (the other was Archbishop Desmond Tutu). In presenting that award in St Patrick's Cathedral, Armagh, Archbishop Williams said:

> [W]e have in the Anglican Communion various ways of recognizing distinguished service. There are awards given at Lambeth, there is the Cross of St Augustine. But once in a while somebody comes along for whom this doesn't seem completely adequate and when Desmond Tutu retired, the then archbishop of Canterbury invented the archbishop of Canterbury's Award for Outstanding Service to the Anglican Communion. Tonight it is a huge privilege to present that award for the second time.

AN IRISH SECRETARY GENERAL

The author was appointed secretary general of the Anglican Communion in July 2004 and took up office on 1 January 2005, two months after the Windsor Report had been published. The position of secretary general had evolved from the appointment of Bishop Stephen Bayne from the Episcopal Church of the USA as executive officer of the communion in 1959. When the ACC was formed in 1971 the then executive officer, Bishop John Howe (Scotland), became secretary general of the ACC, followed in 1982 by Canon Sam Van Culin (ECUSA) and by Canon

17 Windsor Report, para. 13.

John Peterson (also ECUSA) in 1994. The author therefore became the first person from the Church of Ireland to hold that position.

The officer is described as having two distinct roles: an 'ambassadorial' role, representing the Anglican Communion to its constituent parts by visiting and often addressing General Synods and Conventions and other important provincial meetings and gatherings; and representing the communion to other world churches and bodies, through regular contacts with the Vatican (through the Pontifical Council for Promoting Christian Unity), the Ecumenical Patriarchate in Istanbul, the Lutheran World Federation, the World Council of Churches and so on. An important vehicle for this is the little known but important Conference of Secretaries of Christian World Communion (CSCWC) of which he was the president for two years. The secretary general is also the formal representative of the Anglican Communion at the United Nations (though an observer is appointed) and is a governor of the Anglican Centre in Rome.

The other part of the role is as secretary and executive officer to the ACC, and by invitation of the archbishop of Canterbury, secretary to the Lambeth Conference and the Primates' Meeting. In this he is administrative head of the Anglican Communion Office in London, an office of twenty to thirty people, working on issues such as ecumenism, communications, mission, women's role in church and society, interfaith and so on. In all of this the office seeks to implement the decisions of the instruments of communion and is immediately answerable to the standing committee, which meets annually for three to four days.

As the instruments of communion address widely varying issues, the demands on the office change and evolve with every meeting, and part of the role of secretary general is both to manage expectations as to what is administratively and financially possible, and also enable the evolving changes in structures and staffing that this demands.

The Windsor Report presented the first set of challenges. It made several recommendations. There were recommendations to the Episcopal Church and to the Anglican Church of Canada to express regret for the damage they had done to the bonds of affection within the communion, coupled with a request to set out the scriptural and doctrinal reasons for the actions that had been taken. This was paralleled by a request that those bishops who had intervened in other provinces should desist immediately.

Other recommendations were addressed to the communion as a whole, and fell to the Anglican Communion Office to steer and support. Chief among these was a recommendation that an Anglican Communion Covenant should be developed. Unhelpfully, as it turned out, a suggested draft was included with the report as an appendix, and for a time the content of this very preliminary draft was a matter of further controversy. A commission to draft such a covenant was set up, ably supported by Canon Gregory Cameron of the Anglican Communion Office.

After a few years' work a text emerged in four parts – the first three sections represented a modern restatement of the nature and shape of Anglicanism and the Anglican Communion as it was at the beginning of the twenty-first century. Not only were these three sections uncontroversial, they were widely welcomed. Section four was another matter.

Section four of the draft covenant, which deals with the consequences of acting in ways deemed incompatible with the covenant, went through several drafts, each of which was made public with comments invited. The special commission that finalised the text of section four, taking on board many of the comments and criticisms of earlier drafts, was ably chaired by Archbishop John Neill (Dublin).

In 2009, the Standing Committee of the General Synod appointed its own Anglican Covenant Working Group to guide the church in its response to the emerging covenant text. The Church of Ireland received the final text in January 2010. The House of Bishops' opinion was sought, and they concluded that 'The Anglican Covenant is consonant with the doctrines and formularies of the Church of Ireland.' They further suggested that the term 'subscribe' rather than 'adopt' would be more appropriate for use in the proposed motion for the 2011 General Synod.

The thinking behind the church's decision to subscribe to the covenant is helpfully explained in a document circulated before the General Synod. In so deciding, the church

> would be saying that in the context of its own clear and unchanged self-understanding, the covenant provides a means, not of altering the character of the Church of Ireland, but of regulating our external relationships with other churches in a manner which we freely acknowledge to have value and from which we indeed have the capacity to withdraw should external circumstances change. The covenant does not lock us into an arrangement that undermines our autonomy, but passing the motion before the synod does display our willingness to display generosity and faithfulness and our acknowledgement that in making major or innovative decisions no Anglican province can simply walk alone. It will be the role of the General Synod in the future to assess the extent to which the covenant has borne fruit in terms of the purposes for which it was gestated.[18]

Framed in terms of inevitable consequences for those who failed to respect Anglican principles and structures, it was quickly seen by its detractors as penalties and punishments for member churches who failed to 'toe the line'. While many churches supported the adoption of the covenant, including the Church of Ireland, it soon became clear that the necessary majority did not exist for its communion-wide acceptance. Hopefully, the very valuable and widely accepted first three sections will find a lasting acceptance as a description of the foundations of the modern Anglican Communion.

18 *Journal of the General Synod of the Church of Ireland* (2011), p. 239. The full document is to be found on pp 238–40. See also p. 219.

It is the secretary general's responsibility to steer all of this through the various instruments of communion under the overall direction of the Standing Committee.

Other recommendations found varying degrees of acceptance. The proposal that instead of four instruments of unity (the archbishop of Canterbury, the Lambeth Conference, the Anglican Consultative Council and the Primates' Meeting), the archbishop should be described as 'focus of unity', with the other three described as 'instruments of communion' was welcomed.

The report recommended that the Primates' Meeting be named the 'Primates' Conference – the Lambeth Standing Committee', but this was not accepted as it was felt it gave an ongoing status to the Lambeth Conference between its meetings every ten years, when in fact the conference meets too infrequently and is too large to have an authorative role within modern Anglicanism, and instead should remain as a consultative and relational body, expressing the mind of the communion at a specific time. The proposal for a 'council of advice' for the archbishop was considered but it was recognized that that purpose is best expressed by the already existing Primates' Meeting.

The Joint Standing Committee (of the ACC and the primates) that met annually was strengthened by making the primates' standing committee ex-officio members of the ACC and of its standing committee, giving a stronger role to this body, which meets annually, with the archbishop of Canterbury present, for three to four days. Its name was changed from the Joint Standing Committee of the ACC and the Primates' Meeting to the Standing Committee, often with the words 'of the Anglican Communion' added.

All of this had to be undertaken alongside the normal work of the Anglican Communion Officer (ACO) in ecumenism and faith and order, mission, theological education, communications and administration. Archbishop Rowan Williams had placed an emphasis on theological education as part of his ministry as archbishop, and so this work had to be strengthened. Interfaith issues were a growing priority, as were gender issues. The Mission Department was strengthened and was given a major boost when Archbishop Welby made mission and evangelism priorities. The setting up of the Anglican Alliance after Lambeth 2008 also absorbed a lot of energy. And all of this together with the organization of the Primates' Meeting, and ACC meetings every three years, and preparations and follow-up for Lambeth 2008, with all of the controversy that entailed.

The author stepped down as secretary general at the end of 2014 to become bishop of Limerick and Killaloe, a welcome return to the Church of Ireland.

AN ONGOING COMMITMENT TO THE ANGLICAN COMMUNION

As was noted at the beginning of this chapter, the Anglican Communion had not featured large in the consciousness of the Church of Ireland when Fr Hurley was editing his book *Irish Anglicanism* in 1969. That has changed in the intervening fifty years and today, through positive engagement with the ACC, the Primates' Meeting and the Lambeth Conferences, the profile of the Church of Ireland in the Anglican Communion has been raised significantly.

Before that, it was through the individual contributions of figures such as Plunket, Gregg, Simms, McAdoo and Eames that the Church of Ireland's involvement was experienced.

The growing involvement of the Church of Ireland in recent years has been noted by other Anglican churches, which respect the Church of Ireland's ancient history, which is so different from the comparatively short history of many Anglican churches. These mainly smaller churches can relate easily to a church that is small in comparison with the dominant size and role of the Church of England within Anglicanism.

They can look to a church whose experience is something they can recognize in their own very different contexts – that of being a minority church, a church that has known and lived through violence and religious and social division, a church struggling with secularism and issues of relevance, a church that has demonstrated wisdom in its nuanced responses to many potentially divisive social and ecclesiological challenges, especially in recent years.

That engagement with the Anglican Communion has never been higher than today: Archbishop Clarke is a member of the Primates' Standing Committee and chair of the Anglican-Orthodox Dialogue; Archbishop Jackson is involved in Anglican interfaith work and chairs the Anglican-Oriental Orthodox Dialogue; Bishop Miller is chair of the Anglican Methodist International Commission on Unity and Mission; and Bishop Burrows is chair of the Anglican-Old Catholic International Commission. This is an exceptional level of commitment from one small church, and is also a continuation into the future of a long and diverse contribution from the Church of Ireland to the Anglican Communion.

12

The Church of Ireland and
dialogue with other faiths

*The Most Revd Michael Jackson, archbishop of
Dublin and primate of Ireland*

The years 1969 to 2019 are a time frame during which events outside the churches have moved rapidly and forcefully. These changes have altered our perceptions of ourselves, others' perceptions of themselves and their perceptions of us. We are now, as members of the Church of Ireland, very clearly part of a range of options within the expression of faith and faiths and also inside lived Christianity. This situation is less predictable and potentially more exciting. It means that we who call ourselves Church of Ireland and Anglican have a lot more work of understanding, explanation and witnessing ahead. No longer do we have an entitlement; no longer are we privileged. As institutions in and of themselves weaken, they become more accessible to others who previously saw themselves excluded, but they also become more in need of advocacy on the part of those who carry the tradition within and who previously saw no need to explain themselves to anyone, and they need friends outside who understand them and can give voice to their worth. Things are different and, as a church, we too are different from who and what we were in 1969.

PERCEPTIONS

Perceptions are never quite enough. Perceptions can all too easily slip into the realm of what we can set to one side and lose and what we think we can do without – once we get back to 'the real business before us'. Events change our understanding of what we can grasp conceptually and what we can control physically, changing the environment we have long understood to be ours by entitlement. And, sooner rather than later, events create new contexts in which our values and our principles and our generosities and our phobias are tested. External events change us as well. Since 1969 so many things have happened that were deemed impossible: the collapse of totalitarian communism, itself so destructive of the spiritual in the human person; the dismantling of the Berlin Wall, with all of the emotional energy this brought to a still new European self-understanding and cultural confidence; the Troubles in Northern Ireland, as a result of which incalculable heartbreak continues to be carried deep inside individuals and communities throughout Ireland,

North and South; the collapse of Apartheid and the ongoing experiment that is today's South Africa; the unseating of Robert Mugabe and the birth pangs of a new Zimbabwe; the rise of Vladimir Putin and the phenomenon of North Korea; the enigma that is President Donald Trump. And these are only snapshots of a continuing cycle of change that is not going to change back. To these, within Ireland and the Church of Ireland we might add the still unclear outcome of Brexit. Such changes result in differences in our perception of the size of the world and of the importance of our place in it.

STRUCTURAL CHANGES IN THE INTERFAITH LANDSCAPE

Three things in particular have helped to shape the landscape of interfaith relations in Ireland during this period. The first is the outworking of the European Convention on Human Rights (Article 9) regarding freedom of thought, conscience and religion. Jacques Delors, when European Commission president in 1994, established, under 'A Soul for Europe', structured dialogue with representatives of faith communities and humanists to a noble purpose: contributing to the spiritual and ethical perspectives of the European Union and promoting the participation of civil society in the ongoing integration. Article 17 of the Lisbon Treaty (2009) ushered in for the first time a legal basis for regular, open and transparent dialogue between the EU institutions and churches, religious associations and philosophical and non-confessional organizations. The Reflection Group on the Spiritual and Cultural Dimension of Europe, established in 2003, has developed its brief since 2005. It engages annually with the Commission of the Bishops' Conferences of the European Community (COMECE), the Council of European Churches (CEC), Muslim communities, the European Jewish Congress and the associations of the Hindu, Sikh and Mormon communities. Areas discussed have included the combating of terrorism, fighting poverty and social exclusion, promoting democratic rights and liberties, solidarity across generations and demographic challenges. Similar meetings have been held in Ireland between leaders of faith communities and politicians. Members of the Church of Ireland will need to work this vein of communication and commitment assiduously, cleverly and with commitment of personnel and of resources in the fifty years ahead if we are to move from passive to active contribution to the common good within the new emerging religious framework. Enhanced social integration will also be urgent in the next fifty years.

The Northern Ireland Inter Faith Forum, founded in May 1993, has sought to promote mutual understanding across faith traditions and to educate people in Northern Ireland beyond the exclusivities of 'the two communities' into an understanding that there is a vibrant community of many faiths whose adherents come from varied religious and ethnic backgrounds. In many ways, while it predates the 'A Soul for Europe' initiative, it goes further in its expressed aims, which include: to provide a forum for dialogue on matters of religious, civic and national

importance; to support a wider interfaith dialogue; to be the representative platform of the constituent faith communities for faith matters in Northern Ireland
and to advise government on the same; to encourage and facilitate education and
training on faith diversity in Northern Ireland; to organize and promote interfaith
activities and events in Northern Ireland. Membership is very open and is not
confined to faith leaders or those who might be seen as official delegates. Activities
include the provision of training and training materials for public and private
sectors as required by section 75 of the Northern Ireland Act 1998; a travelling
exhibition entitled 'In good faith'; facilitating schools, colleges and faith communities to talk about various faith traditions; maintaining the Quiet Rooms in Belfast
International and Belfast City Airports.

The Dublin City Interfaith Forum (DCIF) began in 2012. Its documentation
expresses its mission as follows: '[T]o build understanding, respect and cooperation between different religious denominations and faith groups in our local
community, our nation and the world.' This expresses itself in the following aims:

> [S]upport and strengthen the contribution made by all faith communities
> in Dublin; educate and encourage people of different faiths to engage in
> dialogue, reflect and work together on matters of policy, strategy and action;
> promote and support the participation of third country nationals in the
> civic, community and public life of the city; contribute to a fully integrated
> city; and challenge all forms of injustice and discrimination.[1]

On 16 December 2016 Dublin launched the Dublin Interfaith Charter and was the
first city in Europe to do so. The charter was taken up within seventy-two hours by
the Council of Europe. As well as speaking of freedom of religious practice, peace,
justice, solidarity and the defence of the dignity of each human being, the Charter
explicitly sees dialogue across the different communities of belief as enabling people generally to build a better society, city and country. The emphasis on young
people offers an important challenge: 'To focus our efforts on encouraging the
young towards real acceptance of religious diversity by developing programmes
which reflect the joint fundamental values of our faiths while retaining our own
individual beliefs.' It therefore requires of the Church of Ireland that we be a more
theological church with vigorous and informed discipleship programmes, some at
least clustering around the Five Marks of Mission of the Anglican Communion, as
approved by the Lambeth Conference of 1988, and aiming to empower the active
discipleship of all members of the community through the dialogue of life as well
as through the dialogue of ideas. Again, the emphasis on developing 'our appreciation of religious differences and diversity to focus on our similarities, shared
values and common respect for humanity and planet' well illustrates what we in

1 Both quotations come from Dublin City Interfaith Forum Strategy 2018–21, launched 10 Dec.
2018.

the Church of Ireland were taught repeatedly through the Hard Gospel project by John Paul Lederach. Throughout his many publications on conflict transformation, he has consistently and generously taught that diversity is our friend. Such an emphasis combines reconciliation and justice with environmental and ecological responsibility in the spirit of Marks 4 and 5.

DCIF makes the confident assertion that it is the most religiously diverse body in Ireland. It works with European agencies, the Council of Europe and the European Commission. It is clear that the concentration on diversity includes the focus on engagement and inclusion; DCIF is concerned to encourage everyone to see communities as assets to be realized and not as problems to be solved, managed or placated and to see faith communities as a potential resource to the city in this quest.

SOME OF THE WAYS MEMBERS OF THE CHURCH OF IRELAND HAVE BEEN ENGAGED

In 2002 a meeting was convened in The Palace, Cork by Bishop Paul Colton, involving people of a range of world faiths. This was a joint initiative of the bishop and the St Fin Barre's Cathedral Steering Committee to the Immigrant Support Centre, Nasc. Also in that year the archbishop of Armagh, Dr Eames, and the archbishop of Dublin, Dr John Neill, welcomed senior Muslim and Christian leaders from Egypt to Ireland as part of a programme to create and develop understanding between the two religious communities. A number of publications in this period has contributed to knowledge and understanding on the part of members of the Church of Ireland through a range of networks and these have enabled our church to add its voice to understanding of the issues in Ireland. They include: 'Guidelines for interfaith encounter', developed by the churches of the Porvoo Communion at a conference in Oslo in November–December 2003; 'Life beyond boundaries', a publication of the Hard Gospel project prepared by the Committee for Christian Unity and the bishops of the Church of Ireland 2006; 'Guidelines for interfaith events and dialogue', again prepared by the Committee for Christian Unity and the bishops of the Church of Ireland, January 2007 (this was the first of its kind in the provinces of the Anglican Communion); 'Embracing difference: the Church of Ireland in a plural society', written by Canon Patrick Comerford on behalf of the Church in Society Social Justice and Theology Group (Republic of Ireland), which recognizes that the Church of Ireland takes its place within a pluralist society in Ireland today.

As bishop of Clogher (2002–11), Michael Jackson took these insights into the Anglican Communion, most widely understood, in a number of ways. Through chairing NIFCON, he began with a consultation on Christianity and citizenship in Kaduna, Nigeria (2005) and, following a visit he made with the then archbishop of Canterbury in 2006 to the churches in Pakistan, he presented a petition on the blasphemy laws to the Pakistani high commissioner in London, together with Dr Musharraf Hussain, chair of the Christian Muslim Forum in England. Through NIFCON, Jackson led a day of exploration at the Lambeth Conference (2008) around interfaith issues for all participating bishops. This resulted in bishops embarking on discussion of the document 'Generous Love' as well as their sharing insights around their own living as part of a Christian minority in a multi-faith environment with fellow bishops from other and different minorities. Jackson also led the sections on ecumenism and interfaith relations in the first workshop of the Episcopal Church of the Sudan's Commission for Inter Faith and Ecumenical Relations, assisted by the Reverend Dr Johnson Mbilla, general adviser to the Programme for Christian-Muslim Relations in Africa (PROCMURA) in 2009.

The period 2010–13 also was a time when the Inter Faith Working Group of the Church of Ireland, chaired by Bishop Jackson, with the Reverend Darren McCallig as its secretary, brought a range of interfaith workshops to various parts of Ireland. The first was a conference held in the Church of Ireland Theological Institute in 2010 on the challenges and opportunities of interfaith relations in the twenty-first century. The conference featured expert national and international speakers along with visits to local Jewish and Islamic places of worship. The two booklets previously alluded to – 'Life beyond boundaries' (2006) and 'Guidelines for interfaith events and dialogue' (2007) – formed the basis of the conference. In 2011, Archbishop Jackson and Bishop Williams (Limerick and Killaloe) led a group of more than a dozen people from the Church of Ireland to take part in an interfaith training programme in the St Philip's Centre, Leicester. The group learned a range of useful lessons around the interaction of civic and religious bodies, not least when tensions rise because outsiders come to the city of Leicester for marches and rallies of a racist character. In such circumstances, the religious community leaders have the telephone numbers of the young people locally in their communities and keep closely in touch. They also call an all-night vigil in Leicester Cathedral on the day before rallies and protests. The group stayed with families in Leicester and visited the Masjid Umar, one of the most prominent mosques in Leicester, which is close to the St Philip's Centre, and the Shree Sanatan Mandir, a large Hindu temple in a former Baptist church, and had discussions with leading members of Leicester's Sikh community in the Amritsar Restaurant. Perhaps the most fascinating insight of the whole visit was the observation of the director of the centre to the effect that, if you read your newspaper from an interfaith perspective, you will probably find up to five faith issues in it every day without any difficulty.

In Ireland, two further conferences were held in Belfast in 2012 on the themes of 'Educating for understanding', which addressed the theological, pastoral and practical implications of such educating for understanding, and 'Engaging diversity, staying faithful', which addressed aspects of how one can and must remain faithful to one's own faith tradition while developing an engaged generosity towards the Other as a friend in the wider diversity. In the same year, NIFCON published: *Land of promise? An Anglican exploration of Christian attitudes to the Holy Land, with special reference to Christian Zionism*. Successive pilgrimage groups from Dublin and Glendalough have used and studied this with representatives of the Israeli embassy and the Palestinian mission to Ireland before going on pilgrimage. In 2013, the conference called 'Building the common household: gender and inter-faith dialogue' was held in Mary Immaculate College, Limerick by the Inter Faith Working Group. It examined ways in which the gender of those engaged in inter-faith dialogue impacts on their involvement. Interesting was the fact that students and staff of Mary Immaculate joined in the seminars. The final seminar in this series was held in NUI Galway, an intensive workshop on ways to develop inter-faith dialogue locally based around the Porvoo Communion's 'Study guide: keys to interfaith engagement'. In 2014, the archbishop of Canterbury's Anglican-Jewish Commission, established in 2006 with Dr Jackson as co-chair, met in Dublin and discussed themes of identity including the person of Leopold Bloom in James Joyce's *Ulysses*.

The year 2015 saw the lord mayor of Dublin, Ms Críona Ní Dhálaigh, host an interfaith forum in the Mansion House, examining religion's role in global con-flict. The discussion was organized by the Dublin Three Faiths Forum, chaired by Professor Linda Hogan, vice provost of Trinty College Dublin, and introduced by the Reverend Canon Desmond Sinnamon, founding member of the forum. In the same year, Mr Philip McKinley, a lay member of the Church of Ireland, was appointed a member of the multi-denominational and interfaith chaplaincy team in Dublin City University, which celebrated thirty years of its existence in 2018. And in 2016 DCU was designated a 'university of sanctuary' in recognition of its commitment to welcoming asylum seekers and refugees into the academic and intellectual life of the community. This designation has been extended to Christ Church Cathedral, the first among Irish cathedrals, St Patrick's Cathedral (Dublin), University College Dublin and University College Cork. The year 2015 also saw the publication of the M.Th. dissertation of the Reverend Suzanne Cousins on the application of generous love to the life of the Church of Ireland: 'Generous love in multi-faith Ireland: towards mature citizenship and a positive pedagogy for the Church of Ireland in local Christian-Muslim mission and engagement'. The author said:

> [T]he aim behind the book was to identify hindrances to Christian-Muslim engagement in Church of Ireland parishes and dioceses, with a view to stim-ulating the future development of a contextualized teaching resource on Christian-Muslim engagement for use by clergy and laity in the Church's changing mission context.

The year 2016 saw a number of developments in the year during which the Republic of Ireland commemorated one hundred years of independence. 'Commemoration' as a term brought a degree of reflection and a sense of responsibility for those for whom there was and remains, a different reading of history. In this way, it has released energies that are constructive, sober and free of triumphalism. A 1916 remembrance wall was unveiled at an interfaith commemoration in Glasnevin Cemetery. The archbishop of Dublin (Michael Jackson) represented the Church of Ireland. This type of worship is based on the highly successful annual National Day of Commemoration customarily held in the Royal Hospital, Kilmainham or Collins Barracks. For this, representatives come from all thirty-two counties and the religious service is conducted by the main Christian denominations followed by prayers by a rabbi and an imam and a reflection by a representative of the Irish Humanist Society. As well as the Interfaith Charter, Irish faith leaders issued in 2016 a joint Declaration on the Dignity of Human Life in the Holy Land. Seventeen representatives of the three Abrahamic faiths, including the Church of Ireland archbishop of Dublin who introduced the day and the former archbishop of Armagh Alan Harper, signed the declaration and presented it to the Anglican archbishop of Jerusalem, the Most Reverend Dr Suheil Dawani, at an event that was a 'first' for Glencree Reconciliation Centre. In the same year, the Cork Three Faiths Forum was founded to bring together representatives of Judaism, Christianity and Islam to develop strategies of understanding and a shared society.

The year 2017 was the year in which worldwide the 500th anniversary of the Protestant Reformation was marked. Through the joint working of the Lutheran World Federation and Pope Francis, this became a significant ecumenical event in Lund in Sweden. The Ahlul Bayt Islamic Centre, the Shia mosque in Milltown, Dublin 6, invited the Church of Ireland archbishop of Dublin to give a lecture entitled: 'Reformation 500: whence and whither?' in the course of which he drew out the importance of interfaith dialogue as follows:

> The Reformation is rightly lauded for offering choice in the public expression of faith in God. The contemporary world has shown us that choice can and does foment competition and cause chaos. The ecclesiastical world now has the opportunity to embrace choice with the pivotal recognition that The Other is essential to our setting our agenda, individually and corporately, and that your margin is the centre of my world. Connecting Others and margins is the calling of all churches together. The Reformation took place in a world where Christianity had no option but to rub shoulders with World Faiths other than itself. Some things it got spectacularly and disastrously wrong. We too in our day have no other option than to rub shoulders and to shake hands with those of World Faiths other than our own. Ecumenism simply is no longer sufficient. Reconciliation, in which Ireland, North and South, has sought to specialize, and to which the Irish School of Ecumenics has contributed so significantly, demands of us as responsible citizens interfaith dialogue and understanding and respect.

Also in 2017 the archbishop accompanied the lord mayor of Dublin, Brendan Carr, to Jerusalem to observe first-hand the work of Judaism, Christianity and Islam in Israeli-Palestinian society at the invitation of Archbishop Suheil Dawani.

The year 2018 saw the celebration of the fifth active year of the Dublin Interfaith Forum. As part of this, the archbishop of Dublin was invited to develop from a Christian and an Anglican perpsective Five Marks of Interfaith Understanding as an offering into a secular civic space. Inspired by the Interfaith Charter, the Five Marks initiative offers a practical way for Irish churchgoers to reach out to and to be met by their neighbours of all faiths in order to dispel the mistrust that can all too easily lead to the isolation of minority religious groups. The exploration had the full backing of the lord mayor of Dublin, Micheál MacDonncha. In 2018, the Reverend Dr Yazid Said, who had lectured in Mater Dei Institute, Dublin before gaining a full-time position in Liverpool Hope University, and had led explorations of *A common word* in Mater Dei, edited and published *The future of interfaith dialogue* with Cambridge University Press. That same year also saw the inaugural meeting of the Network for Inter Faith European and North American Concerns (NIFENAC) in the Church of Ireland Centre (CIC), All Hallows Campus, Dublin City University. It is chaired by the archbishop of Dublin. It was co-hosted by the Reverend Professor Anne Lodge, director of the Church of Ireland Centre, and Dr Eithne Regan, head of the School of Theology, Philosophy and Music, DCU. NIFENAC is one of the five regional groups which, while operating independently, feed into the work of the Anglican Inter Faith Commission launched at the Primates' Meeting in Canterbury in October 2017. The inaugural meeting drew together representatives from the Anglican provinces in these islands. It is intended that NIFENAC will include representatives from Canada and the Americas, from the Porvoo Communion of Churches, along with the Anglican dioceses of Spain and Portugal, both of which are closely allied with the Church of Ireland.

Many aspects of the Church of Ireland's engagement with interfaith life in the Anglican Communion came together in the NIFENAC meeting. The first is the doctrine of subsidiarity: those who form the context of Anglican interfaith life in Ireland locally and from other world faiths were present and contributed. Subsidiarity is a recognition of the specific and the local as essential in understanding and assessing the generalized and the global. It is a fundamental principle of Anglican living because subsidiarity requires the honouring of the local in the building up of the global as we live out communion. The second is that the meeting was centred in a place of learning and education. CIC prepares teachers for primary education in the reformed Christian traditions, learning in a modern secular and multi-faith university, DCU. These students mostly go on to work in schools with an Anglican ethos and often serve a population that is very diverse in faith and culture. The third is that, while being an Anglican body, NIFENAC from the outset includes and incorporates the voices of those of other world faiths as valued members and not as observers.

PRESENT AND FUTURE

I want us to look at four things that are here to stay: communications; ecumenism; migration; encounter. They are interconnected and, in a fast-moving world, interdependent. Communications have advanced with significant rapidity and happen relentlessly. Virtual reality can readily triumph over real-life accountability. The entitlement to violence and the invasion of personal space combine with a sense that, because we preside over who we are by means of smart technology, we are impervious to danger. We are slowly realizing our immaturity around the novelty of self-generated and self-related social media. We nonetheless have the opportunity to 'speak truth to power' and to give power to truth. We need to use this to counter extremism and to prevent caricature. We also discern that future wars will be about resources such as water and the holding of data as much as about anything else. While ecumenism is not uniform across the Church of Ireland, rapport and relationships with a range of Christian churches other than our own have become a settled part of our life and identity. We need to face the question: are not interfaith encounter and dialogue the next stage of our shared Christian life together – and, if not, why not? Migration is another non-theological factor. It is one that has wave after wave of people of all ages entering Europe and Ireland, ranging from those in need and destitute to professionals moving in pursuit of career opportunities in a highly globalized economy. While the presenting symptoms of this complex movement of people include economics and warfare at home, alongside the needs of multi-national industries, the causes are more intricate. The danger for us in Ireland is that they bring us to the heart of contemporary instability around resources and can exacerbate cultural vandalism. It is a shock to many in the Ireland of 2019 that those who migrate for whatever reasons bring also their faiths with them. This sits ill with an Ireland increasingly angry with its own faith inheritance and institutional churches. It complicates the assumed move by Ireland from the pre-secular to the secular and already living in part at least in the post-secular. It also presents a challenge to those in the indigenous population who wish to silence any public discussion about or declaration of faith. Encounter generally, and interfaith encounter in particular, is inescapable and unavoidable. But if we have learned anything from the exploration of our sectarianism and from the Hard Gospel project, we need once again to take to heart the words of John Paul Lederach to the effect that diversity is our friend. It is for these reasons that communications, ecumenism, migration and encounter are key components in any realism we bring to bear on the urgency of interfaith engagement for the future.

Such recognition brings us to the heart of what is throughout the period in question work in progress and still remains work to be implemented right across the Church of Ireland in the next fifty years of our life – the Church of Ireland in regular dialogue with other world faiths. This needs to run in tandem with building up the core of our Christian faith, the positives of our denominational identity

1. President Erskine Childers and Archbishop Alan Buchanan of Dublin with Archbishop Dermot Ryan (his Roman Catholic counterpart, at left) and visiting Anglican archbishops Allen Johnston (second left) and Michael Ramsey (at right), July 1973. (Lensmen)

2. Primate George Simms makes a presentation to archbishop of Canterbury Michael Ramsey as President Childers looks on, July 1973. (Lensmen)

3. Archbishop McAdoo of Dublin and Archbishop Simms of Armagh at a meeting of the Standing Committee of the General Synod. (Church of Ireland Press Office)

4. Dean Victor Griffin with Archbishops Robert Runcie and Henry McAdoo outside St Patrick's Cathedral, Dublin. Archbishop McAdoo chaired the Anglican-Roman Catholic International Commission (ARCIC). (Church of Ireland Press Office)

5. Archbishop Robin Eames at an early Standing Committee meeting during his primacy, 1986. Archbishop Donald Caird also pictured, at left. (Irish Times)

6. The first ordination of women priests in the Church of Ireland, Kathleen Young and Irene Templeton, June 1990. (Pacemaker Press International)

7. Bishop Pat Storey makes history as the Church of Ireland's first woman bishop, 2013. (Church of Ireland Press Office)

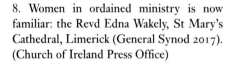

8. Women in ordained ministry is now familiar: the Revd Edna Wakely, St Mary's Cathedral, Limerick (General Synod 2017). (Church of Ireland Press Office)

9. Bishop Harold Miller with Pam Rhodes of the BBC's *Songs of praise* at the launch of the 5th edition of the *Church Hymnal* at St Patrick's Cathedral, Dublin, 2000. (Maxwells)

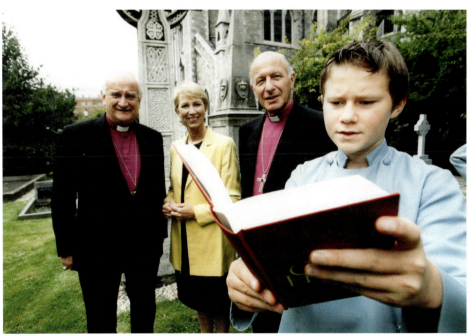

10. Bishop Edward Darling (centre), editor of the *Church Hymnal*'s fifth edition, at its launch in Dublin, 2000. (Maxwells)

11. Revd Peter Thompson and Alison Cadden, authors of *Singing psalms*, at the launch of the first volume in 2008. (Church of Ireland Press Office)

12. Dean Samuel Crooks – the original 'Black Santa' – collecting outside St Anne's Cathedral, Belfast, in the run-up to Christmas. (Church of Ireland Press Office)

13. Dean Crooks with some early recipients from the wide-ranging charities that benefited from the annual 'Black Santa' sit-out. (Church of Ireland Press Office)

14. St Ann's, Dawson Street, Dublin also established an annual Advent sit-out – Revd Canon Tom Haskins with choral back-up. (Church of Ireland Press Office)

15. Signing the Church of Ireland–Methodist Covenant, September 2002. (Church of Ireland Press Office)

16. The Northern Irish Troubles brought many dark days: Archbishop Robin Eames at the funeral of Corporal Robert Crozier at St John's Church, Kilcluney, Co. Armagh, June 1991. (Church of Ireland Press Office)

17 & 18. The colourful Summer Madness Christian youth festival was begun by the Church of Ireland and has blossomed into the largest gathering of its type attracting young people from across the island each summer; events are both outdoors and under canvas. (Summer Madness)

19. The service of remembrance at St Anne's Cathedral, Belfast, following the Kegworth air disaster, 1989. (Church of Ireland Press Office)

20. Secretary of State for Northern Ireland Tom King and British Prime Minister Margaret Thatcher at the Kegworth air disaster service of remembrance at St Anne's Cathedral. (Church of Ireland Press Office)

21. Archbishop Walton Empey of Dublin and Archbishop Robin Eames of Armagh outside Belfast's Waterfront Hall during the General Synod held in the city in 2000. (Harrison)

22. Church leaders coming together: the Revd Harold Good (Methodist president), Archbishop Sean Brady, Dr Alistair Dunlop (Presbyterian Moderator), and Archbishop Robin Eames on a walkabout at Forestside Shopping Centre, Belfast, Christmas 2001. (Church of Ireland Press Office)

23. Dean of Belfast Houston McKelvey (right) shortly after his installation in 2001 with Monsignor Tom Toner from St Peter's Cathedral, Belfast. Strong ecumenical links have been established between the two cathedrals. (Church of Ireland Press Office)

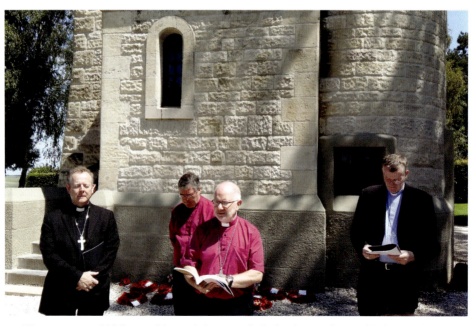

24. The present archbishops of Armagh have worked closely together and led two joint cross-community pilgrimages to the sites of the First World War, in 2016 and 2018 – Archbishop Richard Clarke reads war poetry at the Ulster Tower, June 2016, with Archbishop Eamon Martin. (Church of Ireland Press Office)

25. Archbishop Michael Jackson (second right) with Lord Mayor Nial Ring, Archbishop Diarmuid Martin, and representatives from the Dublin City Interfaith Forum at the launch of its strategy for 2018 to 2021. (Lynn Glanville)

26. Canon Lady Brenda Sheil, a barrister, was for many years the Northern lay honorary secretary of the General Synod and was installed as a lay canon of St Patrick's Cathedral, Armagh in 2008 – seen following the service chatting with Bishop Michael Mayes (Church of Ireland Press Office)

27. The church and higher education: Queen's University Belfast chaplains seen reunited in a photograph (L–R): Revd Stephen Forde, Bishop Harold Miller, Bishop Trevor Williams, Revd Cecil Kerr, Very Revd Maurice Carey and Canon Edgar Turner (undated). (Church of Ireland Press Office)

28. The Anglican Primates' Meeting at the Emmaus Centre, Dublin, 2011. (Church of Ireland Press Office)

29. RCB Head of Synod Services Janet Maxwell, Bishop Richard Clarke (as he then was) and Ruth Handy at a ministry summit held in Church of Ireland House, Dublin, 2003. (Church of Ireland Press Office)

30. Church of Ireland Press Officer Liz Gibson-Harries (left) with press office assistant Betty McLaughlin (right) – Liz was the press officer from 1987 to 2000, working during the Troubles in Northern Ireland and the protracted Drumcree marching tensions. (Church of Ireland Press Office)

31. Church communications continue to be transformed over the years: Press Officer Brian Parker with General Synod magazine competition judges Dianne Harron, Graham McKenzie and Rodney Miller, *c.*2001. (Kelvin Boyes)

32. Church of Ireland Publishing has published a number of titles including the Braemor Studies series in conjunction with the Church of Ireland Theological Institute. Dr Maurice Elliott, Bishop Kenneth Kearon, Dr Susan Hood and Dr Patrick McGlinchey with Revd Abigail Sines (author, second right) at the launch of her Braemor Studies title, *Let us celebrate the feast – Holy Communion and building the community*, November 2016. (Lynn Glanville)

33. Belfast Cathedral at dawn from Academy Street. The building of St Anne's Cathedral, Belfast, was finally completed with the installation of the stainless steel Spire of Hope in 2007. The North Transept was completed in 1981 and features an emphatic Celtic cross. The cathedral plays an important civic and ecumenical role in the life of the contemporary city and has given its name to Belfast's lively 'Cathedral Quarter'. (Paul Harron)

34. St Mary's Cathedral, Limerick, was restored from the early 1990s onwards in various phases; in 1991 the interior walls were completely stripped of plaster creating an ancient atmosphere. (Paul Harron)

35 & 36. Two views of the interior of Down Cathedral, Downpatrick, showing the extensive reordering of 2015, following much previous restoration work carried out from the 1980s. The new installations include elegantly crafted stalls with high backs creating a reredos effect, an oval communion table and mosaic roundels in the stone floor. (Annette McGrath)

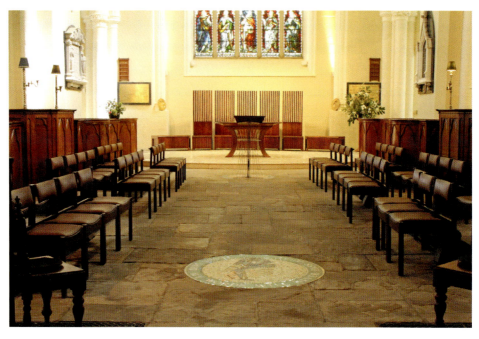

37 & 38. Two views of Lisburn Cathedral, showing the 2015 reordering of both the chancel and the area under the gallery to accommodate contemporary musical worship and community-based functions, carried out by Des Cairns Architecture. (Paul Harron)

39. The exterior of Armagh See House, completed in 2012 and designed by Leighton Johnston Associates, which replaced the see house of 1975 on the same site. The gable-ended single-storey annexe houses the Primate's private chapel with views over the city and towards the Observatory and Royal School – both primatial foundations. (Paul Harron)

40. Stained glass panels of episcopal coats of arms taken from the original Archbishop's Palace, Armagh, and subsequently displayed in the hall of the new see house. (Paul Harron)

41. The fine Music Room at Christ Church Cathedral, Dublin, with a wooden wagon roof and a large neo-Gothic fireplace, was restored and refurbished in 2014 and is used by the cathedral choir and for numerous events such as this historical centenaries seminar in 2016. (Paul Harron)

42. Episcopal portraiture remains a relatively lively source of artistic commissioning within the Church of Ireland. Clogher Diocese has a fine continuous collection of bishops' portraits, the latest of which is of Bishop John McDowell, painted in photo-realistic style by the emergent Irish artist Stephen Johnston in 2018. (Image courtesy of and © Stephen Johnston)

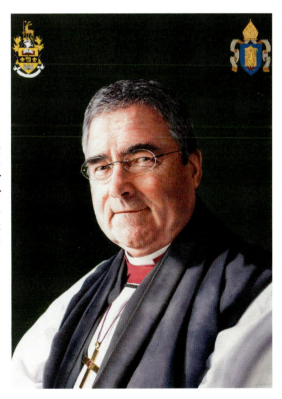

43 & 44. St Elizabeth's Church, Dundonald, built a fine pavilion-like hall on a podium attached to the front of its 1960s church building, designed by Hall Black Douglas in 2015. (Paul Harron)

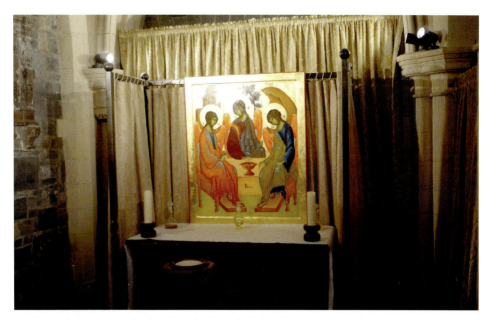

45. The Trinity Icon in Christ Church Cathedral, Dublin, written by Georgetta Simion (2009), forms one of a series of icons introduced to the cathedral over the past decade. Christ Church Cathedral has revived a healthy artistic commissioning tradition over the past three decades. (Church of Ireland Press Office)

46. Dáithí Ó Maolchoille of Cumann Gaelach na hEaglaise (left), Donald Caird as archbishop of Dublin, and Canon Cosslett Quin at the launch of a book of collects in Irish to accompany the Church of Ireland's *Alternative Prayer Book* in 1994.

47. 'The *Titanic* Pall' at St Anne's Cathedral, Belfast (2012), the work of Helen O'Hare and Wilma Kirkpatrick of the nearby University of Ulster. When not used as a pall, it is displayed on the wall of the south aisle adjacent to the tomb of Sir Edward Carson. Its delicately sewn silver crosses and Stars of David commemorate the lost souls of the *Titanic* sinking tragedy of 1912. (Karen Bushby)

and our contribution as disciples and citizens to the political and societal life of both Northern Ireland and the Republic of Ireland. The gaze needs to be turned outwards much more vigorously towards a complex world of participation in a civic society where the human membership now constitutes people from at least two hundred nationalities. Many of us find that a more sophisticated world gobbles up time a lot faster. It is not without good reason that the University of Cambridge commissioned a chronophage to mark the start of the new millennium. Survival is rarely enhanced by looking inwards.[2] I say this out of obedience to the words of Holy Scripture as found in 1 John 3.2: 'Dear friends, we are now God's children; what we shall be has not yet been disclosed, but we know that when Christ appears we shall be like him, because we shall see him as he is.' Decades of experiencing unexamined sectarianism, inside and outside the Church of Ireland, have forced us to ask of ourselves the very awkward and open-ended question: who, then, is my neighbour? The reality of interfaith encounter on the street, at baptisms, weddings and funerals, asks of us the same question. It forces us back to asking questions of institutional obedience and fundamental theology and in the direction of an expanding generosity towards and understanding of every neighbour. The very phrase I have just used – who, then, is my neighbour? – is in itself an expression of the problem posed to a church prone to inward-gazing. Neighbours are people we cannot control as well as people with whom we share cups of sugar when either of us runs out. During the period 1969–2019, the Church of Ireland has been learning to grow out of an understanding of itself as some sort of local Christendom. We are an 'other faith' to more and more people in Ireland today rather than being part of the only public faith, accustomed, somewhat strangely, to being a privileged and a pilloried minority at the same time. The old methods of self-protection will not help us sufficiently for the future; and the future is already fast and furious in the present.

INTERFAITH ENGAGEMENT AND SCRIPTURAL LIFE

A few cobwebs of misperception need to be cleared away around the discipline of interfaith studies and engagement. The Letters to the Thessalonians draw our attention to the fact that early in the life of the nascent Christian Church there were those who were beginning to fear how they would fare if they died before the Second Coming of the Lord. There was also unresolved concern about salvation before the coming of Christ and where the Christian message had not gone. The apologists in the second and third centuries held a positive view of other world religions through the doctrine of the universal presence of the Divine Logos.

---

2 The Cambridge chronophage is a metal sculpture on the wall of Corpus Christi College, Cambridge. It eats time (*chronos* and *phage*) and looks like a grasshopper atop a sphere moving beneath it. See johnctaylor.com/the-chronophage.

This was because there was direct experience of living alongside not only Jews but also Buddhists and Brahmins in Egypt, which was a great melting pot of culture and commerce and therefore of religion. It was under Constantine that the great catchcry went up: no salvation outside the church. What previously had applied to Christian heretics and schismatics was extended to pagans and Jews. It could readily be assumed that everyone would have a chance to hear the Christian message in the empire. The encounter in the seventh century with Islam confirmed Christianity in its need for exclusivism, not least because Islam, unlike Judaism but like Christianity, is a missionary religion. Therefore, the advance of both Christianity and Islam met with the resistance of the Other. The Council of Florence in 1442 endorsed the belief that salvation was confined to the church. It seemed that the battle lines were well and truly set.

This background is important because it sets the scene for many Christian assumptions about people of other world faiths. The one thing that has been added in the time frame under our consideration is a popular caricature that 'the Muslims are often international terrorists'. Not only is Islamophobia sometimes a feature of casual Christian discourse but so also is anti-Semitism. Neither redounds to the credit of our understanding or strengthens our hand in engagement. Interfaith studies received a fresh breath of urgency in the second half of the twentieth century, exactly our period, with decolonization, greater travel and enhanced communications. This engagement requires a very specific shift in mindset on the part of everyday Christians like ourselves. It is no longer adequate to think that we explain ourselves (or simply assume ourselves to be explained by default) and others have to catch up. This engagement requires of us that we can and do give an account of our faith and of our practice to those for whom we are the Other and will remain the Other. It therefore, by implication, forces us to make hard choices about the understanding of mission and proselytization. And so it asks of us that we become and remain thoroughly scriptural and biblical Christians. The document *Nostra Aetate* (1960) was part of Vatican II and the Roman Catholic tradition led the way in encouraging its members to value what is holy, good and true in other religions. The World Council of Churches established (1979) the Sub-Unit on Dialogue with People of Living Faiths and Ideologies. The Anglican Communion, through the Network for Inter Faith Concerns (2007) produced 'Generous love: the truth of the Gospel and the call to dialogue – an Anglican theology of interfaith relations'. NIFCON developed this document in response to a request that had come from the 1988 Lambeth Conference for more materials in interfaith issues. Every bishop then serving in the Church of Ireland had the opportunity to participate with bishops from right across the communion in a full day of witnessing to their personal faith and to the faith of their dioceses in regard to the complex issues of interfaith encounter locally at Lambeth 2008. The Anglican principle of subsidiarity was respected as was the healthy Anglican understanding of the dynamic of 'a range of voices'. Bishops shared their experiences and their fears and their need for engagement.

NIFCON: 'GENEROUS LOVE'

In the early years of the twenty-first century, Anglicans worldwide found themselves in a dilemma. As suggested above, the Roman Catholic tradition had offered *Nostra Aetate* in 1960. The eirenic Dr Williams, archbishop of Canterbury, suggested to NIFCON that we do something in an Anglican idiom in the following clear terms: '[Generous Love] is offered for study to the Anglican Communion – and more widely – in the hope that it will stimulate further theological thinking among Anglicans who share that double conviction that we must regard dialogue as an imperative from Our Lord, yet must also witness consistently to the unique gift we have been given in Christ.' The key words of Anglican and Christian orthodoxy here are: that dialogue is an imperative from our Lord and: witness consistently to the unique gift we have been given in Christ. Dialogue and witness hold together in and through the divine imperative and the divine gift. This is not a 'selling out' of principles to a multi-faith soup; this is mission as dialogue and witness, and a significant move away from the coercion and disrespect of the past.

'Generous love' begins with God unequivocally: 'Whenever as Christians we meet with people of different faiths and beliefs, we do so in the name and the strength of the one God who is Lord of all.' The Trinitarian belief of the Creeds is given expression in the following terms: '[W]e seek to mirror the Father's generous love; we proclaim Jesus Christ as the one who shows us God's face; we celebrate the work of the Holy Spirit made known through the fruit of the Spirit.' It is worth noting that across the provinces of the Anglican Communion, the Anglican tradition is a minority and therefore context and partnerships with those other than ourselves, while retaining an honourable distinction, are important. 'Generous love' encourages encounter as a possible renewal of our life in Christ as we meet with people of different faiths. The interesting consideration is that it advocates faith-explosion rather than faith-implosion as a way of personal and institutional faith-understanding. It lays down the challenge that in meeting other people who are self-evidently different from ourselves, rather than more and more people similar to ourselves, we will renew our life in Christ. This will happen through witness and advocacy, through friendship and hospitality, through difference and respect. I suggest that for many of us this will be a new and exciting experience if we dare to risk. Once again, this will work itself out in an entirely orthodox and Trinitarian way. In Anglican understanding, nothing lies without the concern of God the Creator; everything is held together by a loving providence; this is a recipe for hope and for relationship and for re-creation. The historical and earthly life of God the Son ties Anglicans into living history and specific context and fuels our doctrine of subsidiarity (the understanding that you build up the central thinking from the local practice). I quote from 'Generous love':

> It [Anglicanism] has treated with caution generalized claims made for timeless and ahistorical systems, preferring to make its judgements – including

those relating to other religions – through seeking to discern the implications of the catholic faith within particular historical and social situations.[3]

Institutional churches need to resist the urge to domesticate and control God the
Spirit. The Third Person of the Trinity provides rigorous compassion for relationships within the body of Christ but also provides the working conditions for
a flourishing life of the society. If for no other reason than this, interfaith engagement is a spiritual imperative. This is the other side of implosive care within the
churches; explosive care, as found in freedom and truth and justice, requires from
Christians liberty and order as a contribution to society and its flourishing outside our churches. This is the basis of the public good. Interfaith engagement in
Ireland, following sustained work around the Hard Gospel and significant strides
in the recognition of our own sectarianism, will enable us to take up again the
challenge of engaging in the public forum actively and positively with those who
are secular and those who are of other world faiths as well as with those who are
Christian.

An innocent person might ask: but is Holy Scripture not all about God and
Jesus? Holy Scripture is the definitive expression of the work of God in the world
from within the inspired perspective of those who follow Judaism and Christianity.
Christianity recognizes the ongoing and independent role that the Scriptures (to
Christians: the Old Testament) have in Judaism. Christianity also recognizes their
role in the revelation of the God whom Christians themselves worship as One God
in Three Persons. Anglicanism rejects supersessionism, the view that Judaism is a
living fossil, effectively superseded (literally sat upon) by Christianity. The doctrine of supersessionism was codified in the nineteenth century by a clergyman in
the Church of Ireland who went on to found the Exclusive Brethren, John Nelson
Darby. This perspective is anathema to interfaith dialogue and witness. We recognize that those who lived in Old Testament and in New Testament times lived in
a world of religious plurality and that such experiences have shaped the formative
texts of Holy Scripture. Israel worshipped the one Lord their God among the
varied nations of the ancient Near East both in and out of exile. Jesus taught and
healed in the context of a range of faiths as he brought the Incarnation to bear on
the lives of all he met and touched; the first followers of the Way confessed the
name of Jesus among the many cults and philosophies of the Roman empire and
within the kingdoms of the east of the same empire. Our contemporary context,
while vastly different, contains continuities of concept in the midst of vast differences of expression. While it is with one faith in particular that Christianity works
out its self-understanding in the pages of the New Testament, the New Testament
itself tells us that Christianity has a context, that it has a need for living history and
that convictions about the love of God and the person of Jesus are for sharing with

3 NIFCON, 'Generous love: the truth of the Gospel and the call to dialogue – an Anglican theology
of interfaith relations' (2007), p. 4.

others, whoever they are and whoever they might yet be. Holy Scripture speaks of engagement with and not withdrawal from the world. The ecological agenda, so courageously taken up within The Eco-Congregation Movement in Ireland and globally by Pope Francis, is something that is yet to be developed in an interfaith direction by the Church of Ireland. It enhances civic life; it is theological (after all, care of creation is the Fifth Mark of Mission); it is of common human value; it does everyone and everything good.

SCRIPTURAL REASONING

'Scriptural reasoning' has been developed in Cambridge and by a son of the Church of Ireland, David Ford, as a way of helping people of different faiths to come together to read and to reflect on their Scriptures. Once again, it is a thoroughly Christian and scriptural way to live and to witness to Christ the Word made Flesh. People read their own Scriptures and expound them; others then react to them from within their own tradition; and the conversation begins in earnest – with equivalence of respect in the shared dynamic engagement. It is not about seeking agreement or about scoring points, but about exploring the texts and their possible meanings and interpretations across faith boundaries, and about learning to disagree better. Living too long in one's own religious bubble militates against seeing things from the perspective of others and imperceptibly makes it less and less attractive to try. The aim is that of a deeper understanding of one another's Scriptures. Scriptural reasoning is used across the world, including places which are deeply affected by religion-related tensions and conflicts. Over the next fifty years of disestablishment, I should hope that it might be used in an Ireland that knows all too much of such conflicts before and after disestablishment, used as a means of grace and as a deepening of understanding of ourselves and of others by Church of Ireland people. The 'Guidelines for scriptural reasoning' are very useful in other church contexts too. One is to stick to the texts and not to stray in an unstructured way into generalized discussion on religion. Another is to invite others to explore your texts and ask them to allow you to explore their texts; scriptural reasoning, like all dialogue, is not about competitive cleverness but about hospitality. Scriptural reasoning is an invitation to cross boundaries in a creative and uncomfortable way: getting to know yourself and your Scriptures better and allowing and inviting others to do the same. Intense concentration and respect for the other person and his/her Scriptures are the way forward in this engagement. It accords with an inalienable principle of interfaith dialogue: do not compare the best of yourself with the worst of the Other. Scriptural reasoning draws us into the heart of generosity and trust through what matters to us most as members of the Church of Ireland: the Scriptures. It does so by encouraging informed vulnerability, gracious hospitality and critical understanding. I suggest that it can be a fresh expression of the spirit of disestablishment as expressed in 1869: freedom to shape our own future.

Interfaith encounter involves the dialogue of life every bit as much as it involves the dialogue of ideas. In the northern hemisphere we all too frequently assume that a superficial level of literacy brings a social and a spiritual superiority. This is a dangerous fallacy and it cuts right across the pastoral practice that is and must remain the heartbeat of the Church of Ireland. 'Generous love' has drawn together three ways of approaching interfaith engagement in everyday life:

- Presence and engagement: among communities of other faiths, as is the case in every Province worldwide, we are present and active as signs of the body of Christ in each place. Presence and engagement invite Christians out of their churches and into direct involvement in political and civic life, leading to transformation through the energy and the mission of the Holy Spirit. In matters interfaith and in light of the Church of Ireland-Methodist covenant signed during the half-century of disestablishment just concluding, we can take our inspiration from John Wesley, Anglican and Methodist, who said that though we may not think alike yet we may love alike, and that we may be of one heart though we are not of one opinion. Encounter with others brings out the best in us and it is the work of the Church of Ireland in the next fifty years to equip its people, who are now more diverse than ever they have been, for Christ-like encounter with the Other. This is where the Gospel comes to life.

- Embassy and hospitality: these point us to service as at the heart of belief and of practice. I wonder if, as we look back at the last fifty years, we will wonder if somehow we overemphasized leadership to the detriment of service in our understanding of church life, lay and ordained. The corporatization of society, along with the almost unquestioned emphasis on the economic definition of the human person and of human life in general has put tremendous pressure on the inherited understanding of service as the yardstick of lived faith. The type of confident understanding of ourselves as children of God that comes through service to others in ways that open us up not only to giving but also to receiving is a definition of being ambassadors of Christ. This is precisely because of our dependence on other people and on God in the following way: 'We do not proclaim ourselves; we proclaim Jesus Christ as Lord and ourselves as your servants for Jesus' sake.' Embassy takes us straight into the area of reconciliation because the giving and receiving of hospitality of whatever form and the trust involved is embassy in action. This is because the tent of meeting belongs to God and not to either host or guest. This is the transformation of relationship between friend and stranger that God makes happen. These are the public spaces of public life. Again, Christians are called by God out of their churches and out of their parochial halls to witness in the contested space and to redeem it as community space for all. Economic necessity will force us sooner rather than later to live our church life in such external spaces.

True hospitality is about the practical expressing of our convictions rather than fudging or concealing them.

• Sending and abiding: our witness is ever giving and ever replenished in the life of God that is beating at the heart of the Trinity. We are sent apostolically as disciples of Jesus Christ to connect once again those who are the Other to one another. In every situation, there are those who are other to us and to whom we are other. Sending and abiding are not only activities. They are states of being. And again I wonder if those looking back at the last fifty years of Church of Ireland life will marvel at our instinct for exhaustion in activity rather than for seeking the presence of God in the rhythm of work, rest and prayer. They will at least wonder what we did with the divine gift of Sabbath. 'Father, Son and Spirit abide in one another in a life which is a dynamic, eternal and unending movement of self-giving.' It is this sending and abiding that we are invited to share in a life of discipleship on earth. This will become possible if we avoid the call to hypocrisy in terms of exclusivity and division because the reality of outward engagement is that you are always being watched. None of this is a work of our own. It is a formation in and by God in newness of life and through prayer and worship.

PROSPECT

I have tried to show that a concern for and an engagement with interfaith matters is entirely Christian. The picture before us in the media of 2019 is one in which Muslims can be seen as terrorists, but the picture we have conveniently forgotten is that the Reformation engendered, in part at least, one of the most bloody and cruel series of wars in Europe in its time and the Crusaders might be viewed as religiously driven warriors. Christianity is not immune from criticism. I revert to my earlier dictum: it is important not to compare the best of ourselves with the worst of another. I have tried to show how an appropriate immersion in our Judaeo-Christian Holy Scriptures develops a proper fear of the Lord, which is the beginning of wisdom and, furthermore, the starting point of encounter with others around the things that matter most to us – the things of God in the world. I wish also to suggest that adherence to the Five Marks of Mission of the Anglican Communion (now widely used across the Church of Ireland as an expression of our identity and adopted by the Lambeth Conference of 1988) is a witness to faith in God and a portal of the Holy Trinity at work in the world of today and that those Five Marks are compatible with and essential to the free flow of an interaction with all others which is incarnational – where God meets creation and humanity with grace and redemption. I have offered as working examples of relationship with others both in giving and in receiving the three principles of interfaith engagement – presence and engagement, embassy and hospitality, and sending and abiding – as ways of developing, discovering and disclosing relationships applicable to all facets of a Christian life lived in accordance with the method of Anglicanism: scripture, tradition and reason. I do so not to suggest them as clever things to do but as faithful things to do in the world of God's creation and recreation. Mission studies are increasingly recognizing that interfaith and mission march together and have done so for a long time in the dialogue of lived experience.

The above suggested way forward does mean that we will have to become a more self-consciously theological church, by which I mean that at every level of our life we will have to become more confident about giving an account of ourselves to others. Giving an account of ourselves, or rather giving accounts of ourselves in all our healthy diversity, ought not to alarm us. Many of us take this in our stride as a matter of course. Educational methods have been turned on their head. We now take as normal lifelong learning, at whatever level of participation and difficulty, as a gift for personal development and public sharing. We take also as normal the fact that information is available to all through a range of mass media. What is urgently needed is the living criteria of interpretation and application. We will have to become also a more self-consciously politically and socially engaged church, embroiled in issues of justice and peace as the connections between the institutions of the church and the people of God who are outside the church itself widen and deepen. The next fifty years will see the Church of Ireland becoming a more Apologetic church, not in the sense of being self-effacing, but in the sense of being willing to give an account of ourselves in the places where we live and work. Ireland will continue to be a destination for people of other nationalities – for opportunities for work, for escape from warfare and trafficking and from unthinkable but tangible human cruelty. This is what happens in island cultures: we constantly attract new people and we constantly change our human dynamic. New people bring their cultures and their religions. This is a shock, while we have accustomed ourselves to a broadly monochrome Christian culture followed by a diverse post-Christian culture with no certainty as to how the latter will develop in the next fifty years. There is no option to do nothing.

If we can learn about others in dialogue, then others can learn about us also. The gift of God's grace and the vision of God's glory were not given to us alone. We have an exciting challenge before us: mission without proselytization, our faith, an 'other faith', with those of other faiths, seeking the common good. The broad sweep and the intense detail of our life of faith continue to take us from Genesis to Revelation. The commissioning of disciples to make disciples of all nations continues to hold and to inspire. It is set alongside the gift of reconciliation whereby we are also commanded to love God and to love our neighbour as we love ourselves. Both send us out asking the question, in our hearts and in our hands: who, then is my neighbour? The challenge that presents itself to us is surely this: is my neighbour the person in whom God next encounters me and in whom I next encounter God? And: how much choice do I really have in this? This will require of us that we be a humble church and that our communities be a mixed flock. And in all our relations with others, personal, ecclesiastical, ecumenical and interfaith, the words of St Paul to the Galatians which we use in the peace at Pentecost and at confirmation ring out:

> The fruit of the Spirit is love, joy, peace.
> If we live in the Spirit, let us walk in the Spirit.[4]

4 Galatians 5.22.

13

Law and the disestablished Church of Ireland: fifty years of accelerating change

The Rt Revd Paul Colton, bishop of Cork, Cloyne and Ross

Since 1969, when the centenary of disestablishment was commemorated, the Church of Ireland has changed and continues to change at a gathering pace. In the midst of all this change, it endeavours to remain faithful to its apostolic, scriptural and canonical inherited tradition as set out, for example, in the preamble and declaration to the Constitution of the Church of Ireland (CCI). Such was the importance of continuity with that tradition that on the fifth day of the General Convention (Saturday, 19 February 1870) the members of the convention stood, removed their hats, and the preamble and declaration was read solemnly by the bishop of Cork.

The Church of Ireland, having been an established church, is rooted, not only in its canonical tradition (itself grounded within the ancient apostolic faith), but also in centuries of law-making (ecclesiastical law) governing its life and activity. The archbishop of Armagh emotionally expressed the importance of that continuity at the General Convention:

> Our Church still retains all that is essential to its existence ... In doctrine and in discipline we are unchanged. We have not, therefore, to create, but to restore; not to build up a new Church but to supply such supports as the State has taken away from the old.[1]

In the fifty years that have followed the centenary commemorations in 1969, there have been discernible and dramatic changes in the governance of the Church of Ireland, changes that are fundamentally altering the church itself and the way it fulfils its calling. Changes in polity in recent decades are setting the church on new and uncharted paths. These need to be observed and noted. Members of the Church of Ireland need to recognize and come to terms with them.

The first of these is the ever-increasing impact the law of the state is having on the day-to-day work of the Church of Ireland.[2] The second change is in the

---

1 *Journal of the General Convention of the Church of Ireland* (1870), p. 2. 2 For the purposes of treating of this aspect of the essay – the impact of law of the state on the Church of Ireland – the principal focus will be on the Republic of Ireland and examples given will, in the main, be from

way the church regulates its own business internally, much of which is now done by what may be styled as quasi-legislation or soft-law instruments. Such quasi-legislation may be low in the hierarchy of laws, but it is, nonetheless, formative, pervasive and, most of all, it is resulting in change.

The first of these – the impact of the law of the land – has increasingly consumed the time of the central committees of the church, and, in terms of administrative overload, is now widely commented upon by clergy and lay church workers. Is this subjective observation borne out by empirical scrutiny? This essay argues that it is. The second of these factors has been the subject of little comment, but again, it is demonstrable.

This essay illustrates the accelerating pace of these changes in the years between 1969 and 2019. In part II, the ever-increasing impact of state law on the Church of Ireland is set out. Part III deals with the phenomenon of quasi-legislation and soft law, a means of law-making that the church increasingly utilizes. Part IV sets out some of the implications of these two new dynamics. The conclusion highlights some of the practical challenges that ought to be addressed. First, in part I, the context of law-making at the time of disestablishment and in the years that followed needs briefly to be described.

I. DISESTABLISHMENT

In the period between the passing of the Irish Church Act 1869 and its coming into force on 1 January 1871, there was a flurry of law-making and administrative activity. The Irish Church Act 1869 (32 & 33 Vict., c. 42) was given Royal Assent on 26 July 1869. As and from 1 January 1871, the union between the Churches of England and Ireland would be dissolved, and the Church of Ireland would be disestablished. The ecclesiastical courts would be abolished from that date, and the ecclesiastical law of Ireland, except that relating to matrimonial causes and matters, would cease to exist as law. However, the ecclesiastical law of Ireland in place on 31 December 1870 (the eve of disestablishment) would continue to bind members of the Church of Ireland as a matter of consensual compact or contract between them. In disestablishing the Church of Ireland, the act also set up the means of transition to a new ecclesiastical polity.

With only a year and a half to get organized, the 'Church of Ireland was thus left free to shape her future course, independent altogether of state control',[3] a restructuring to be 'accomplished by clergy and laity who were inexperienced in the workings of a voluntary church ... [It] was an architectural experiment and a hazardous one at that.'[4] They rose to the challenge. Within a month (18 August),

within that context. However, it should be noted that the phenomenon and trend set out pertains equally in Northern Ireland.   **3** *Journal of the General Convention* (1870), pp v and vi.   **4** Donald Akenson, *The Church of Ireland: ecclesiastical reform and revolution, 1800–1885* (New Haven, 1971), p. 276.

the old National Synod was summoned and met 14–17 September. The first resolution established the mechanism for continuity:

> That this Synod deems it its duty to place on record that it is now called
> upon not to originate a constitution for a new Communion, but to repair a
> sudden break in one of the most ancient Churches in Christendom. And
> they further desire to state that, under the present circumstances of the
> Church of Ireland, the cooperation of the faithful Laity has become more
> than ever desirable.

Some days beforehand (on 31 August 1869) the laity met and requested that a lay
conference be convened (held 12–14 October 1869) with a view to determining the
extent and manner of such lay cooperation. Therefore, an organization committee[5]
was formed and met 5–28 January 1870. (The bishops met as a caucus two days
earlier.) Meeting for only four days each week, it accomplished an amazing feat. At
the outset the primate proposed six subjects: standing orders, the Representative
Church Body, the constitution, finance, the election of bishops and diocesan
courts. A seventh was added by amendment – a preamble and declaration[6] – and,
consequently, seven committees set to work drafting on each topic.[7]

When disestablishment took effect on 1 January 1871, the church had standing
orders, a preamble and declaration, a constitution, and a Representative Church
Body. Work on canons had been initiated, and revision of the *Book of Common
Prayer* was soon also under way.[8]

All of this was but the start of a prodigious law-making process by the General
Synod.[9] Since 1870, 1,095 statutes have been passed by the General Synod: affecting the constitution of the Church of Ireland (500 statutes), relating to the *Book of
Common Prayer and Revised Services* (325 statutes), and covering a variety of other
areas (270 statutes).[10]

---

5 Representative Church Body Library, General Convention Papers, MS 1/6: minute book of the
'committee of organisation', which met during January 1870, including first draft 'Act of constitution of
the Church of Ireland' (Jan. 1870).   6 Ibid. (5 Jan. 1870), p. 20.   7 Ibid. (5 Jan. 1870), p. 21 – names
of the members of the subcommittees.   8 The revision of the *Book of Common Prayer* following disestablishment is a full study in itself, and may be pursued in William Sherlock, 'The story of the revision
of the Irish prayer book', *Irish Church Quarterly*, 3:12 (1910); Richard Clarke, 'The disestablishment
revision of the Irish book of common prayer' (PhD, TCD, 1989); and Michael Kennedy, 'The theological implications of recent liturgical revision in the Church of Ireland' (PhD, TCD, 1987).   9 In
exercising its law-making jurisdiction, the General Synod follows a parliamentary bills procedure and
Standing Orders of the General Synod 22 to 30. Bills may be either ordinary bills or special bills (dealing with modifications in doctrine or formularies, in which case the procedure for ordinary bills is
elongated over a two-year period, commencing with a resolution seeking leave to introduce the bill in
the first year and completing the bills procedure in the second year), and the procedure encompasses
a first reading, a second reading, a committee stage, a consideration on report, a third reading, after
which, if passed, the bill becomes a statute (certified by the Records Committee and published in the
Journal of the General Synod).   10 See *Journal of the General Synod* (1871–2018).

II. THE INCREASING IMPACT OF CIVIL LAW

When it comes to law and religion, members of the Church of Ireland should be in no doubt about the fact that the church, like every voluntary association, is governed by the law of the land. Against the backdrop of disestablishment Fitzgerald, J in *O'Keeffe v. Cullen*[11] emphatically asserted the supremacy of the law of the state and stressed that no one could be above that law:

> There can be no doubt that if the rule in question, or the rule of any Church, had for its object the exemption of the clergy from secular authority, or their immunity from civil jurisdiction or civil punishment, it would be our duty at once to declare that such a rule was utterly illegal. Upon this there ought to be, as there is, no doubt. No Church, no community, no public body, no individual in the realm, can be in the least above the law, or exempted from the authority of its civil or criminal tribunals. The law of the land is supreme, and we recognise no authority as superior or equal to it. Such ever has been, and is, and I hope will ever continue to be, a principle of our Constitution.[12]

After Irish independence this was cited with approval by Kennedy, CJ in *O'Callaghan v. O'Sullivan*[13] and he said:

> In my opinion, all law is foreign to these Courts other than the laws which these Courts have been set up under the Constitution of Saorstát Éireann to administer and enforce, that is to say, other than the laws given force and validity by Article 73 of the Constitution and the enactments of the Oireachtas made after the coming into operation of the Constitution.[14]

More recently, this understanding was underscored in the Ferns Report.[15]

That noted, the current time in the Church of Ireland is one of unprecedented preoccupation with the law of the state. Civil law is, in recent decades, having a greater impact on the life of the church; resulting in uncertainty, vulnerability, and revision of some key components of internal church law. All of this is changing the church and its work quite radically.

These changes coincide with a period of controversy about religion in Irish public life. The current experience is distinguishable from the energetic legal activity of the early post-disestablishment period when, uniquely, the implementation of the Irish Church Act 1869 was the all-consuming concern. The focus then was creating a framework for the continuity of the Church of Ireland. It would be

---

11 *O'Keeffe v. Cullen*, IR 7 CL 319.   12 *O'Keeffe v. Cullen*, IR 7 CL 319, 371.   13 *O'Callaghan v. O'Sullivan* (1925), 1 IR 90.   14 *O'Callaghan v. O'Sullivan* (1925), 1 IR 90, 108.   15 Ferns Report (Dublin, 2005) pp 37–8; an official government, but non-statutory, inquiry into the sexual abuse of children by Roman Catholic priests in the diocese of Ferns.

wrong, however, to assume that the newly disestablished Church of Ireland was introspective to the point of introversion. The *Journal of the General Synod* attests to a church consistently engaged with issues of the time from 1871 until this day. Outward-looking concern characterizes responses to major world events and political situations.[16]

In the intervening years the Church of Ireland is seen engaging with law reform debate;[17] responding to legislation that impinges on a Christian

16 Home Rule: *Journal of the General Synod* (*JGS*) (1893), pp lix–lx; *JGS* (1893), p. lxxv; *JGS* (1893), pp 178–9; *JGS* (1911), p. 223; see also petition of 12 Apr. 1912 in *JGS* (1913), pp 238–9; San Francisco earthquake: *JGS* (1906), p. lxxvii; sinking of the Titanic: *JGS* (1912), p. lxiv – resolution of 17 Apr. 1912; Irish political situation: see e.g. primate's address in *JGS* (1914), p. xlvi; and in relation to War of Independence see *JGS* (1920), p. liv and 202 (condemnation of outrages in Ireland); and also concerning the murder of members of the Church of Ireland see *JGS* (1921), pp lviii–lx; First World War: outbreak – *JGS* (1915), pp xlvi–xlvii; casualties – *JGS* (1917), p. li and *JGS* (1918), pp lii–liii; ending of war and reconstruction of society – *JGS* (1919), pp li–liii; Easter Rising: *JGS* (1916), p. l: 'the rebellion, which has brought sorrow and shame to our beloved land'; Irish independence: *JGS* (1922), pp liii–liv; Great Depression: *JGS* (1931), pp liii–liv; communism: *JGS* (1933), p. lviii; rise of Nazism: *JGS* (1939), pp lxxiv–lxxv; outbreak of the Second World War and Irish neutrality: *JGS* (1940), pp lxxiv–lxxvii; Second World War: *JGS* (1941), pp lxxiv–lxxix, *JGS* (1943), pp lxxv–lxxviii; the evacuation of schoolchildren: *JGS* (1940), pp 203–4; emerging awareness of the Holocaust: *JGS* (1945), p. lxxv; World Council of Churches: *JGS* (1945), pp cxix–cxx; devastation following war: *JGS* (1945), p. cxxiv, *JGS* (1946), p. lxxx; atomic bomb and atomic power: *JGS* (1947), pp 161–5, *JGS* (1950), pp cxiv–cxv; Middle East: *JGS* (1949), p. cxix; Cold War: *JGS* (1952), p. cxviii, *JGS* (1953), p. lxxxiii; nuclear weapons and disarmament: *JGS* (1956), p. cv, *JGS* (1960), p. 90, *JGS* (1978), pp lix and lxxv, *JGS* (1981), p. 111, *JGS* (1983), pp 163–6, *JGS* (1986), p. 186; Suez Crisis: *JGS* (1957), p. lxxxv; apartheid: *JGS* (1958), p. 164; relations between Northern Ireland and the Republic of Ireland: *JGS* (1966), p. lxiii, *JGS* (1977), pp 89–92, *JGS* (1978), pp 98–100; the Troubles in Northern Ireland: *JGS* (1970), p. xlvii, *JGS* (1972), pp 250–2, *JGS* (1974), pp 253–4 NS 262–4, *JGS* (1976), pp xli–xlii, *JGS* (1980), p. 108, *JGS* (1981), p. 84, *JGS* (1983), pp 154–60, *JGS* (1986), pp xliii–xlvii, *JGS* (1987), pp li–lv, *JGS* (1994), p. lxxiv, *JGS* (1996), pp lxxiii–lxxv; constitutional amendments in Ireland: article 44 (religion) – *JGS* (1973), p. 75; divorce – *JGS* (1987), p. 84; articles 2 and 3 – *JGS* (1990), pp 167–8; 8th amendment – *JGS* (1992), p. 93 and *JGS* (1993), p. 103; Dublin bombings: *JGS* (1974), p. xciii; papal visit to Ireland: *JGS* (1980), pp 84–5; H-Block hunger strikes: *JGS* (1981), pp 80–3 and 107; New Ireland Forum: *JGS* (1984), pp 132–4 and 183–4; the Anglo-Irish Agreement: *JGS* (1986), p. 86, *JGS* (1991), pp 132–9, *JGS* (1992), pp 155–60; AIDS: *JGS* (1987), pp 145–8, *JGS* (1989), pp 119–20, *JGS* (1991), pp 127–9; environmental issues: *JGS* (1987), pp 148–6, *JGS* (1989), pp 128–33, *JGS* (2003), pp 208–9 from when it was subsumed in the work of the Church in Society Committee; the European Single Market: *JGS* (1990), pp 162–5; first Gulf war: *JGS* (1991), pp 105–6; biotechnology: *JGS* (1991), pp 130–2; Sellafield: *JGS* (1992), pp 165–6; parades in Northern Ireland: *JGS* (1996), pp lxxv–lxxvii, *JGS* (1997), pp lviii–lxi, *JGS* (1999), pp 137–60; Northern Ireland peace process: *JGS* (1998), p. 123, *JGS* (1999), p. l; and engagement with trends in society generally: *JGS* (1986), pp 188–90.   **17** Abortion: *JGS* (1983), pp 100–1, *JGS* (1988), pp 162–6, *JGS* (1993), p. 103, *JGS* (1993), p. 131, *JGS* (1993), pp 185–7; adoption: *JGS* (1973), p. 333, *JGS* (1977), p. 61; children (care and protection) bill 1985: *JGS* (1986), pp 91–2; child care bill 1988: *JGS* (1990), p. 113 and 135–6; commercial legislation (e.g. Shops Act 1911): *JGS* (1913), p. lxxix; criminal justice bill 1969: *JGS* (1969), p. lxxiii; elementary education: *JGS* (1896), p. lxix; family law bill 1994: *JGS* (1994), p. 83; family planning bill 1973: *JGS* (1974), p. 250; health (family planning) bill 1978: *JGS* (1979), p. 65; Health (Family Planning) outlook;[18] addressing legislation with a particular import for the church;[19] making representations about the implementation of legislation;[20] petitioning government or urging legislative change;[21] anticipating legislative change, and proffering views on it;[22] seeking clarification on administrative implementation of legislation;[23] relying on legislation for routine transactions;[24] and framing resolutions or statements articulating the view of the church on the regulation of issues.[25] In one instance, the fear was of increased costs for the church.[26]

Amendment Act 1985: *JGS* (1985), p. 72; illegitimacy: *JGS* (1984), pp 87–8; intoxicating liquor: *JGS* (1895), p. lviii, *JGS* (1896), p. lxviii, *JGS* (1903), p. lxi; judicial separation and family law reform bill 1987: *JGS* (1988), pp 93–4; licensing laws: *JGS* (1900), pp lxxiii–lxxiv; local taxation (customs and excise) bill 1891: *JGS* (1891), p. lxxiii; marriages bill 1963: *JGS* (1966), p. 68; marriages bill 1972: *JGS* (1971), p. 81; Marriages Act 1972: *JGS* (1973), p. 83, *JGS* (1975), p. 80; marriages (nullity) bill 1976: *JGS* (1977), pp 70–5; national school system: *JGS* (1896), pp 178–86; prohibited degrees of marriage and age of marriage: *JGS* (1978), pp 67 and 76–7; rules for national schools: *JGS* (1890), p. lxxv; selective employment tax: *JGS* (1966), p. lxiii; Sexual Offences Act 1967: *JGS* (1976), p. 91; status of women: *JGS* (1976), pp 91–2; and taxation: *JGS* (1981), p. 21.   **18** Abortion: *JGS* (1983), pp 100–1, *JGS* (1988), pp 162–6, *JGS* (1993), p. 103, *JGS* (1993), p. 131, *JGS* (1993), pp 185–7; divorce: *JGS* (1987), pp 84 and 121–30; marriage breakdown (white paper): *JGS* (1992), p. 96, *JGS* (1993), pp 146–51.   **19** Adoption Act 1974: *JGS* (1976), p. 59; Amendment Act 1875: *JGS* (1876), p. 32; Public Records (Ireland) Act 1867 (31 & 32 Vict., c. 70); Trustee Churches (Ireland) Act 1884 (47 & 48 Vict., c. 10): *JGS* (1885), pp 27–8 and 36, *JGS* (1886), p. 115, *JGS* (1908), p. 25.   **20** See e.g. Social Welfare Act 1952: *JGS* (1973), p. 89.   **21** Alcoholism: *JGS* (1907), p. lxiv; Divinity School: *JGS* (1876), p. 41, *JGS* (1879), pp 20–1; family planning: *JGS* (1971), p. lxxxviii; hygiene: *JGS* (1923), p. xcvi; illicit distillation of alcohol: *JGS* (1923), pp xcvi and cxi; intemperance: *JGS* (1875), p. 53; intoxicating liquor: *JGS* (1897), p. lxv, *JGS* (1898), p. lvii; intoxicating liquor in colonies: *JGS* (1891), p. lxxiv; licensing laws: *JGS* (1902), p. lxv, *JGS* (1936), p. lxviii; marriage age: *JGS* (1959), p. cxix; marriage law: *JGS* (1893), p. lxxv, *JGS* (1895), p. 177f, *JGS* (1900), p. 180; mixed-(interchurch) marriages re *Ne Temere* decree: *JGS* (1908), p. lxi, *JGS* (1911), pp lviii–lix; opium trade: *JGS* (1911), p. lxvii, *JGS* (1914), p. xcvi; poverty: *JGS* (1928), p. lxxxvi; the sale of alcoholic drink to children: *JGS* (1906), p. xc; Sunday closing: *JGS* (1872(2)), p. 23, *JGS* (1875), p. 23, *JGS* (1876), p. 15, *JGS* (1891), pp lxix and lxxii; and toxic substances: *JGS* (1891), p. lxxiii, *JGS* (1908), p. lx.   **22** Denominational education: *JGS* (1885), p. xcix; homosexuality/gay rights: *JGS* (1976), p. 91; marriage breakdown: *JGS* (1984), p. 87, *JGS* (1986), pp 165–71, *JGS* (1987), pp 84 and 121–30, *JGS* (1992), p. 96, *JGS* (1993), pp 146–51.   **23** National Insurance (Northern Ireland) Social Security Pensions Act 1975: *JGS* (1979), p. 105; Social Welfare (Amendment) Act 1978: *JGS* (1979), pp 105–6.   **24** See e.g. reliance on legislation for the purposes of setting fees in registers: Friendly Societies Act 1896 (59 & 60 Vict., c. 25); Unemployment Insurance Act (NI) 1936; Factories Act (NI) 1945; Shops Act (NI) 1946; Elections and Franchise Act (NI) 1946; National Insurance (Industrial Injuries) Act (NI) 1 Family Law (NI) Order 1992; Family Law (NI) Order 1992; Education Act (NI) 1947; Exchequer and Financial Provisions Act (NI) 1950; Trustee Savings Bank Act 1887 (50 & 51 Vict c 47); Widows' and Orphans Pensions Act 1935; Workmen's Compensation (Amendment) Act 1953; Social Welfare Acts 1952–60 – all referred to in *JGS* (1964), pp 73–4.   **25** Blood sports: *JGS* (1969), pp lxxvii and lxxxiii; hare coursing: *JGS* (1931), p. lxxxiii; homosexuality/gay rights: *JGS* (1975), p. 79, *JGS* (1976), p. 91, *JGS* (1991), pp 146–7; humane slaughtering of animals: *JGS* (1932), p. lxxxi; intoxicating liquor in colonies: *JGS* (1891), p. lxxiv; raffles and bazaars: *JGS* (1902), p. lxii; licensing laws: *JGS* (1938), p. xcii.   **26** See e.g. fear of rising insurance costs arising from the malicious injuries (amendment) bill 1986, *JGS* (1986), p. 32, *JGS* (1987), p. 28, *JGS* (1988), p. 30.

In addition the *Journal of the General Synod* embodies much comment and briefings on issues of the day, including: adoption;[27] agriculture;[28] capital punishment;[29] child abuse;[30] the death penalty;[31] disability;[32] education;[33] the elderly;[34] emigration;[35] Europe;[36] euthanasia;[37] gambling;[38] the general state of the country;[39] homelessness;[40] human rights;[41] human sexuality;[42] hygiene;[43] intemperance;[44] international peace conferences;[45] the Irish language;[46] mixed marriages;[47] migration from the land;[48] poverty;[49] racism and race relations;[50] religious equality;[51] Saturday closing of public houses;[52] school hygiene;[53] school transport;[54] social housing;[55] stress;[56] Sunday observance;[57] Sunday trading;[58] terrorism;[59] unemployment;[60] and the import of legislation for the church.[61]

It is crucial to note that the distinguishing dynamic of encounter with state law throughout those years has been that it was overwhelmingly outward in tendency: this was the Church of Ireland endeavouring to be prophetic, engaging with society and attempting to pronounce on it, or, to influence or change it. In contrast, in the current time, we see a church reacting, oftentimes fearfully or reluctantly, to the advances of civil law, and the dominant dynamics are compliance, implementation and consequent changes required locally and nationally in administration and practice.

Since the 1990s the civil law is having a greater impact than ever before, necessitating changes in the church's own internal legal framework, giving rise to uncertainty and a sense of vulnerability. New areas of legislative interest are

---

27 Foreign adoptions: *JGS* (1991), pp 141–5. **28** *JGS* (1992), pp 163–4; *JGS* (1999), pp 230–2. **29** *JGS* (1990), pp 172–7. **30** *JGS* (1988), pp 159–62; *JGS* (1995), pp 133–4; *JGS* (1996), pp 135–6. **31** *JGS* (1981), pp 107–8. **32** *JGS* (1981), p. xlii; *JGS* (1988), pp 154–7. **33** Each year since 1873 the journals contain a full report of the education work of the Church of Ireland. **34** *JGS* (1992), pp 150–5. **35** *JGS* (1909), pp lxiii and lxxvii; *JGS* (1990), pp 170–1. **36** *JGS* (1992), pp 160–2; *JGS* (2003), p. 203 from when it was subsumed in the work of the Church in Society Committee. **37** *JGS* (1993), pp 192–9. **38** *JGS* (1901), p. lxxiii; *JGS* (1989), pp 120–8; *JGS* (1990), p. 171. **39** *JGS* (1882), p. lvii. **40** *JGS* (1988), pp 149–54. **41** *JGS* (1978), p. 97. **42** *JGS* (2004), p. liii. **43** *JGS* (1923), p. xcvi. **44** *JGS* (1876), pp 10–11. **45** *JGS* (1899), p. lxxi. **46** See e.g. the compulsory teaching of Irish in schools at *JGS* (1927), p. 189. **47** Mixed marriages or interchurch marriages: *JGS* (1973), pp 97–8, *JGS* (1975), pp 94–5, *JGS* (1976), p. 92. **48** *JGS* (1920), p. xcvi. **49** *JGS* (1899), p. lxxvi; *JGS* (1906), p. 291; *JGS* (1907), p. 290; *JGS* (1987), pp 157–61; *JGS* (1989), pp 133–7; *JGS* (2006), pp 148–49. **50** *JGS* (1976), pp 70 and 85–7; *JGS* (1986), pp 190–1. **51** E.g. Protestants in workhouses: *JGS* (1910), p. lxxvii. **52** *JGS* (1888), p. lxxv. **53** E.g. *JGS* (1934), p. 225. **54** *JGS* (1924), p. 218; *JGS* (1961), pp 111–12. **55** *JGS* (1925), p. cxxv. **56** *JGS* (1987), pp 301–14. **57** *JGS* (1902), p. lxii; *JGS* (1903), p. lxii; *JGS* (1907), p. lx; *JGS* (1912), p. lxxxvi. **58** *JGS* (1990), pp 168–70. **59** *JGS* (1991), pp 139–41. **60** *JGS* (1906), p. 292; *JGS* (1907), p. 291; *JGS* (1978), p. 100; *JGS* (1981), p. 110; *JGS* (1982), p. 124; *JGS* (1983), pp 161–2; *JGS* (1986), pp 194–7; *JGS* (1988), pp 157–9; *JGS* (1993), pp 189–92. **61** See e.g. the Purchase of Land (Ireland) Act 1885 (48 & 49 Vict., c. 73): *JGS* (1889), p. 48; Saorstát Éireann Land Act 1923: *JGS* (1924), p. 21, *JGS* (1936), p. 22; Workmen's Compensation Act 1906 (6 Edw. 7, c. 58): *JGS* (1908), p. 25, *JGS* (1909), p. 36.

emerging such as medical ethics,[62] sectarianism,[63] toxic waste,[64] ethical investment, climate change and care of vulnerable adults.

That the 1990s marked a turning point was captured at the General Synod in 1996 by the primate, who said that his 'call to the synod this year is to be unafraid of change'.[65] The following year (1997) was significant. In that one year, the report of the Secondary Education Committee (SEC), for example, concerns itself with four major developments: the education bill 1997, the education (no. 2) bill 1997, the employment equality bill 1997 and the equal status bill 1997.[66]

This author initiated a survey in June 2011 of clergy and lay people in the Church of Ireland to test a variety of propositions concerning the law of the Church of Ireland.[67] The survey indicated that there was a definite perception that the present period was different and that, as never before, the civil law was impacting on the work of the Church of Ireland in key, determinative areas. The survey confirms that all of the bishops and all of the chancellors were of the view that state law was having a greater impact on the life of the church than it had ten years beforehand. Moreover, all of the bishops and 75 per cent of the chancellors believed its impact to be greater even than five years before. Of the registrars, 91 per cent believed its impact to be greater than ten years before and 73 per cent than five years before. Among clergy, 81 per cent sense the impact to be greater than ten years before and 70 per cent than five years before. Laity have a similar perception: 77 per cent than ten years before and 65 per cent than five years before. There was then an overwhelming sense that the law of the state was impacting on the life of the church to a greater extent than it had ten years before or five years before. This is more than an impression. Those surveyed identified specific areas where they perceived the civil law to be having that greater impact.

Moreover, these perceptions and experience are supported by an examination of the church's reported work in the same period of time. There is a consistent pattern. The state enacts new legislation. Sometimes there is consultation with the church (e.g. in the field of education). Sometimes the church engages with a consultative process (e.g. marriage-law reform). On other occasions, the law changes and the church simply responds. In all cases, the church finds that significant changes have to be made in the way it exercises ministry in particular areas or in its life in general, nationally and locally.

---

62 *JGS* (1996), pp 228–30; *JGS* (2000), pp 171–4; *JGS* (2003), p. 205 from when it was subsumed in the work of the Church in Society Committee. **63** *JGS* (1997), pp lxi–lxii; *JGS* (1997), p. lxxxv; *JGS* (1999), p. li; *JGS* (1999), pp 168–98. **64** *JGS* (1992), pp 166–7. **65** 'Presidential address of the Most Reverend R.H.A. Eames', *JGS* (1996), p. lxxxiii. **66** 'Report of the Secondary Education Committee', *JGS* (1998), pp 205–7. **67** The samples were as follows: 360 clergy and 174 lay people. The response rate was 64% and 82% respectively. In addition, each person in all of the following categories were surveyed separately: all the bishops of the Church of Ireland (all of whom responded); all the chancellors (all but one of whom responded); all but one diocesan registrar and assistant registrars (the one being unavailable, and eleven others responded).

Some of the areas in which there have been significant legislative changes as a result of which the Church of Ireland has faced change in its own life and ordering are: broadcasting;[68] charity law;[69] child protection;[70] civil partnerships and marriage equality;[71] copyright;[72] data privacy;[73] disability;[74] education;[75] employment law; environment law; equality law;[76] the European Convention on Human Rights; finance and investments;[77] health and safety;[78] heritage and planning law;[79] human rights law; immigration law; insurance law; family law; marriage law;[80] pensions law;[81] and ongoing changes to tax law. Some particular examples are illustrative.

There is immense consciousness of cases argued on the basis of human rights and equality legislation.[82] The ongoing debate about human sexuality is a particular locus

---

68 Broadcasting Act 2001.   69 Northern Ireland: Charities Act (Northern Ireland) 2008; Ireland: Charities Act 2009.   70 United Nations convention on the Rights of the Child 1989 (ratified by Ireland 21 Sept. 1992); European Convention on the Exercise of Children's Rights 1996 (signed by Ireland 25 Jan. 1996, but not yet ratified); European Convention on Human Rights and Fundamental Freedoms; European Convention on Human Rights Act 2003; Charter of Fundamental Rights of the European Union (adopted 7 Dec. 2000); Hague Child Protection Convention 1996; Protection of Children (Hague Convention) Act 2000 (passed but not commenced); *Putting children first* (Dublin, 1997); Child Care Act 1991; Children Act 2001; *A code of good practice – child protection for the youth work sector* (Dublin, 2003) – revised edition: *Children first: national guidelines for the welfare and protection of children* (Dublin, 2009); Protection of Persons Reporting Child Abuse Act 1998; Sex Offenders Act 2001; Criminal Justice Act 2006; Criminal Law (Sexual Offences) Act 2006; Criminal Law (Sexual Offences) Act 2007; Criminal Justice (Withholding of Information on Offences against Children and Vulnerable Persons) Act 2012; National Vetting Bureau (Children and Vulnerable Persons Act), 2012–16; Children First Act 2015; Criminal Law (Sexual Offences) Act 2017; *Children first: national guidance for the protection and welfare of children* (Dublin, 2017); *Child protection and welfare practice handbook* (Dublin, 2011); *Child safeguarding: a guide for policy, procedure and practice* (Dublin, 2018).   71 Northern Ireland: Civil Partnership Act 2004; Ireland: Civil Partnership and Certain Rights and Obligations of Cohabitants Act 2010; and the Marriage Act 2015.   72 Copyright and Related Rights Act 2000; Copyright and Related Rights (Amendment) Act 2007.   73 Initially, the Data Protection Act 1988 and the Data Protection (Amendment) Act 2003, which have repealed and replaced by the Data Protection Act 2018.   74 Northern Ireland: Disability Discrimination Act 1995; Ireland: National Disability Authority Act 1999.   75 Education Act 1998, Education (Welfare) Act 2000; Qualifications (Education and Training) Act 2000; Teaching Council Act 2001; Education of Persons with Special Educational Needs Act 2004; Teaching Council (Amendment) Act 2006; Education (Miscellaneous Provisions) Act 2007; Education (Amendment) Act 2012; Education and Training Boards Act 2013; Education (Miscellaneous Provisions) Act 2015; and Education (Admissions to Schools) Act 2018.   76 Employment Equality Acts 1998–2015; Equal Status Acts 2000–15.   77 Pensions Act 1990; Finance Act 2001, s. 45.   78 Occupiers Liability Act 1995; Safety, Health and Welfare at Work Acts 1989–2005.   79 Principally, the Planning and Development Act 2000.   80 Since the 1990s: Family Law Act 1995; Civil Registration Act 2004; and Marriage Act 2015.   81 Pensions Act 1990; Pensions Act 1995 (UK); Pensions (Amendment) Act 2002; Civil Partnership Act 2004.   82 See e.g. *Norris v. Ireland* (1989) 13 EHRR 186; *Foy v. An t-Árd Chláraitheoir & Others (No. 2)* (2007) IEHC 470; *Zappone and Gilligan v. Revenue Commissioners, Ireland and others* (2008) 2 IR 417, (2006) IEHC 404; for cases involving other European countries, see e.g. *Lautsi v. Italy*, app. no. 30814/06 (ECtHR, 18 Mar. 2011); see also 'State drops transgender challenge', *Irish Times*, 6 June 2010; Shiranikha Herbert, 'Religious rights given priority in Belfast Pride advert case', *Church Times*, 13 May 2011; 'Court fight on gay adoption ban in Northern Ireland', *Belfast Telegraph*, 13 Dec. 2011.

for tensions arising from human rights and equality issues.[83] The Civil Partnership Act 2004 came into force in Northern Ireland in January 2006.[84] Likewise, in Ireland, the Civil Partnership and Certain Rights and Obligations of Cohabitants Act 2010 had force from 1 January 2011 and the Marriage Act 2015 gave effect in that year to the marriage-equality referendum in Ireland on 22 May 2015.

There is perhaps no area of the civil law that illustrates more the anxiety of the church about the encroaching influence of civil law in recent time than the employment status of clergy. The principal driving forces of this preoccupation are changes in the law in both jurisdictions, and awareness of such cases as have been taken, in the main, in the United Kingdom.[85] Academic argument that 'religious or spiritual duties are not incompatible with a contract of employment' has also fed this fear.[86] In parallel, the church's internal debates provide a measure of the change in this area: part-time stipendiary ministry,[87] mediation and severance, payments to auxiliary clergy and, more recently, a 'dignity in the life of the church' charter and policies At all times there has been a manifest determination to avoid the language of 'employment', with few notable exceptions.[88]

Closely related to 'personnel' matters is the issue of discipline. Between 2003 and 2009 there was an intensive focus on a revised scheme of ecclesiastical discipline and tribunals which emerged, in part, from the prevalent uncertainty about the employment status of clergy, and also from concerns about constitutional justice. This latter preoccupation was specifically outlined in 2005: the independence of the complaints body; the minimizing of the adversarial element; a system not based in the diocese to ensure 'fairness and independence'; the availability of enough people to sit on tribunals; and openness to public scrutiny.[89]

In the area of pensions, the civil law – the Pensions Act 1990, the Pensions Act 1995 (UK), the Pensions (Amendment) Act 2002[90] and the Civil Partnership Act (NI) 2004 – together with the economic climate, have necessitated a complete revision of the church's approach to clergy and staff pensions.

---

83 See e.g. Olivia Kelly, 'Senior cleric in same-sex ceremony', *Irish Times*, 5 Sept. 2011; 'Gay row "may split church"', *Belfast News-Letter*, 7 Sept. 2011; Alf McCreery, 'Bishop under fire over cleric's gay marriage', *Belfast Telegraph*, 13 Sept. 2011; and 'Clerics unite against civil partnership', *Portadown Times*, 20 Sept. 2011; for the debate in wider Anglicanism, see generally e.g. Stephen Bates, *A church at war: Anglicanism and homosexuality* (London, 2004). 84 *JGS* (2007, p. 178. 85 See e.g. *Reaney v. Hereford Diocesan Board of Finance* (concerning youth workers), unreported, but made available unofficially at thinkinganglicans.org.uk/uploads/herefordtribunaljudgment.html, accessed 25 Jan. 2012; see also Frank Cranmer, 'Casebook' (2007), 159 *Law and Justice* 153; 'Ruling won by Croydon organist', *Church Times*, 13 May 2011. 86 See e.g. Emma Brodin, 'The employment status of ministers of religion' (1996), 25 *Industrial Law Journal* 211. 87 'Report of the Commission on Ministry', *JGS* (1998), pp 252 and 251–5. 88 See *JGS* (1975), p. lxxviii. A member of the clergy 'who has been in the paid employment of the Church of Ireland shall not so far as possible, be left without alternative employment, and that the RCB be asked to report on the question of making suitable payments to any clergyman whose office has been terminated.' 89 'Report of the Courts and Tribunals Committee', *JGS* (2005), pp 216–19, 218. 90 Provided for the introduction of Personal Retirement Savings Accounts (PRSAs) in Ireland.

Since 1998, the impact of the civil law has been encountered strongly in the field of education (a crucible of ongoing controversy in Ireland).[91] This has been referred to as 'a dormant crisis in waiting'.[92] It has preoccupied the Church of Ireland.[93] The transition to a new legal dispensation has shaped the education agenda of the church throughout the last twenty years, most recently with the commencement of sections of the Education (Admissions to Schools) Act 2018.

The impetus for legislative and social change in the area of child protection arose from an horrendous litany of crimes and malpractice, including within churches, exposed in the 1990s.[94] In the years since 1996 the development, implementation and review of 'Safeguarding trust' have been a key feature of the church's work, resulting in extensive changes at local level. In 2006, a new chapter was inserted in the constitution of the Church of Ireland entitled 'Ministry with children'. Complete revisions of this work were required in 2018 by legislative changes.

In Northern Ireland, new marriage legislation came into force in 2004, and, in Ireland, the Civil Registration Act 2004 became law on 5 November 2007. Until then the formalities of marriage within the Church of Ireland were governed principally by nineteenth-century legislation. Now there were major changes to the substantive requirements for marriage.

An emerging area with immense legal implications relates to people with disabilities. The first legislative influences on the church in addressing disability came from the UK in 1995.[95] This exemplifies how legislation emerging in one jurisdiction, and affecting life there, has affected the mindset of the church in the other.

There have been major changes governing protected structures and heritage properties (many of which are owned by the Church of Ireland). A principal force for change has been the Planning and Development Act 2000, which consolidated all

91 See e.g. 'Suburbs full of empty promise', *Irish Times*, 26 Aug. 2006; 'Is your child Catholic enough to get a place at school?', *Irish Times*, 5 May 2007; 'Is denominational education suitable for 21st Century Ireland?', *Irish Times*, 4 Apr. 2008; 'Protestant bishops fear cuts will close schools', *Irish Independent*, 1 Nov. 2008; see also Oran Doyle, 'Article 44: privileging the rights of the religious' in Eoin Carolan and Oran Doyle (eds), *The Irish constitution: governance and values* (Dublin, 2008), pp 476–89.   92 Claire Hogan, 'A veiled problem: religion in Irish schools' (2005), 8 *TCD Law Review* 5–31 at 29.   93 See e.g. Paul Colton, 'Schools and the law: a patron's introspection', *Irish Educational Studies*, 28:3 (2009), p. 253; Paul Colton, 'Religion in public education in Ireland' in Gerhard Robbers (ed.), *Religion in public education* (Alcalá de Henares, 2011), pp 227–56; Richard Clarke, 'What do we want from denominational education?', *Search: A Church of Ireland Journal*, 29:3 (2006), p. 228.   94 See June Goulding, *The light in the window* (London, 2005); Andrew Madden, *Altar boy* (London, 2004); BBC, 'Suing the pope', 19 Mar. 2002, news.bbc.co.uk/1/hi/programmes/correspondent/1879407.stm, accessed 20 Mar. 2012; Bernadette Fahy, *Freedom of angels: surviving Goldenbridge orphanage* (Dublin, 1999); Frances Finnegan, *Do penance or perish: Magdalen asylums in Ireland* (Oxford, 2004); Kilkenny Incest Report, 1993; Madonna House Enquiry, 1996; Mary Raftery and Eoin O'Sullivan, *Suffer the little children: the inside story of Ireland's industrial schools* (Dublin, 2000); RTÉ, '1 in 4 founder settles high court action', 9 Apr. 2003, www.rte.ie/news/2003/0409/37073-abuse01, accessed 20 Mar. 2012.   95 Disability Discrimination Act 1995. Although amended by subsequent legislation in Great Britain and ultimately repealed in Great Britain by the Equality Act 2010, the act still applies in Northern Ireland.

planning legislation in Ireland from 1963 to 1999.[96] While the Property Committee of the RCB reported its role and transactions annually to the General Synod, significantly, its first specific reference to its obligations as legal trustees and those as custodians of property was in 1998.[97] Annual reference has subsequently been made to areas of concern, the availability of grants, the implementation of advice from state bodies and the development of new internal guidelines and an advisory framework.

Very much on the current agenda, and illustrating very clearly the increasing impact of the law of the state on the life of the church in both jurisdictions are changes in charity law.[98] This has involved, and will continue to necessitate, an extensive programme of consultation, education, training and legislative changes to the internal laws of the Church of Ireland.

III. RELIANCE ON QUASI-LEGISLATION AND SOFT LAW

The legal ordering of an institution frequently depends on sources of law not found among the primary and secondary sources, either of the civil law, or of its own internal legal system.

Quasi-legislation and soft law embrace not only decisions made under delegated functions, but also categories such as codes of practice, circulars, executive orders, guidelines,[99] schemes,[100] 'mutual arrangements',[101] forms,[102] handbooks, explanatory booklets,[103] policies,[104] protocols, checklists,[105] advice,[106] local practice, local interpretations[107] and procedures.[108] They are much in evidence within the administrative activity of the Church of Ireland.

According to Ganz, the line between law and quasi-law is 'blurred'.[109] Quasi-law has to be distinguished from both primary, and secondary/delegated legislation. Houghton and Baldwin offer a three-tiered distinction:

---

96 The planning system was introduced on 1 Oct. 1964 following the enactment of the Local Government (Planning and Development) Act 1963.   97 *JGS* (1998), p. 21.   98 Charities Act (Northern Ireland) 2008; and Charities Act 2009.   99 E.g. Church of Ireland dioceses of Down and Dromore (D&D): 'Revised Guidelines for Institution Services' – form 'D' (Feb. 2002); D&D: 'Guidelines for orders of service' – form 'E' (Jan. 2002); D&D: 'Guidelines regarding faculties and dedications for furnishings, plaques and flags' – form 'B' (Oct. 1999); D&D: 'Guidelines for funerals' – form 'C' (Jan. 2002); D&D: 'Confirmation guidelines' – form 'A' (Feb. 2002); Church of Ireland dioceses of Cork, Cloyne and Ross (CCR): 'Guidelines for nominators'; CCR 'Guidelines for ecumenical and interfaith services in Cork'.   100 CCR: 'Training for ministers of the Eucharist'.   101 CCI, ch. I, s. 3, s. 4.   102 CCR: 'Marriage application and notification form'.   103 'Benefit structure of the Church of Ireland Clergy Pensions Fund'.   104 E.g. CCR: 'Annual study leave and retreats for clergy'; CCR: 'Sabbatical leave'; CCR: 'Policy on lay liturgical assistants'.   105 See e.g. CCR: 'Confirmation checklist'.   106 See e.g. CCR: 'Infection control – advice for hospital chaplains and visitors'.   107 D&D: 'Remarriage of divorced persons' – form 'F2' (Feb. 2002).   108 Church of Ireland dioceses of Derry and Raphoe (D&R): 'The proposed procedure for boards of nomination'.   109 Gabriele Ganz, *Quasi-legislation: recent developments in secondary legislation* (London, 1987), p. 24.

Three types of rule can be distinguished from primary legislation. First, there is delegated legislation, in the case of which it is usual both for the parent statute to confer power on a minister to make rules and regulations and for the statute to make clear that such rules shall have full legislative force. Second comes sub-delegated legislation where it may not be clear whether Parliament has delegated a power to an individual, nor is it always plain whether the authorisation runs to making prescriptions of full legal force. Finally, there is the huge group comprising all those rules, guides or other statements of general applicability that are promulgated by administrators or others without express legislative mandate: these might be termed 'unsanctioned administrative rules'.[110]

Megarry is credited with an innovative use of the phrase 'quasi-legislation' – what he called 'administrative quasi-legislation' – to describe 'law which is not-a-law'.[111] He labelled it an 'expanding universe' of instruments that 'are technically not law'.[112] Megarry nominated two forms of what he styled 'administrative quasi-legislation':

First, there is the State-and-subject type, consisting of announcements by administrative bodies of the course which it is proposed to take in the administration of particular statutes. [...] The second category [...] is the subject and subject type, consisting of arrangements made by administrative bodies which affect the operation of the law between one subject and the others.[113]

Megarry articulated anxiety about statutes acquiring 'an administrative gloss' or their words being 'emasculated', or 'modifications by concessions and by gentlemen's agreements' and concluded that administrative quasi-legislation is:

somewhat of a curate's egg. On the one hand, announcements by official bodies on points of procedure and the way in which it is proposed to deal with doubtful points of interpretation have much in their favour, while on the other hand there are substantial objections to administrative quasi-legislation which overrides clear law or seeks to deal with matters between subject and subject.[114]

---

110 John Houghton and Robert Baldwin, 'Circular arguments: the status and legitimacy of administrative rules', *Public Law* (1986), pp 239–84, 240.   111 R.E. Megarry, 'Administrative quasi-legislation' (1944), 60 LQR 125–9, 127; and Gabriele Ganz, *Quasi-legislation: recent developments in secondary legislation* (London, 1987), p. 1.   112 R.E. Megarry, 'Administrative quasi-legislation' (1944), 60 LQR 125–9, 126.   113 Ibid., 126–7; as examples of the former (state-and-subject type), he gave the 'practice notes' of the War Damage Commission; and of the latter (subject-and-subject type), he cited an announcement of the home secretary in relation to the implementation of section 29 of the Workmen's Compensation Act 1925.   114 Megarry, 'Administrative quasi-legislation', 127–8.

Megarry's prediction that '[n]o doubt this kind of near-law will be with us for some years to come; in its benign form, that is to be hoped for, in its malignant form feared' was well-founded. He warned that as long as such instruments remained,

> great importance should be attached to it being readily ascertainable as stat-
> ute- and case-law proper. The same applies to its jurisprudential sister, the
> body of quasi-law resulting from the decisions of the various administrative
> tribunals.[115]

Half a century later, Rawlings described Megarry's article as a 'path-breaking contribution in the field of public law', 'a stepping beyond the formal sources of primary and secondary legislation and judicial decisions', an 'expanding universe' with which lawyers would need to come to terms.[116]

This is true in the life of the church also. In a seminal article published in 1998, Doe noted that regulation within the church is increasingly being effected by what he styled 'ecclesiastical quasi-legislation'.[117] He posited the view that informal rule-making is 'a normal function of ecclesiastical government'.[118] Detailed analysis of the sources of law of the Church of Ireland, undertaken by this author, establishes that the Church of Ireland is, indeed, in more recent times, relying increasingly on quasi-legislation and soft law to fashion and enliven its legal framework.

The *Principles of canon law common to the churches of the Anglican Communion*, published in 2008, illustrates that this is not only a Church of Ireland trend. Churches of the Anglican Communion rely on 'other instruments',[119] which contain 'principles, norms, standards, policies, directions, rules, precepts, prohibitions, powers, freedoms, discretions, rights, entitlements, duties, obligation, privileges and other juridical concepts'.[120]

Delegated legislation has always formed part of the internal legal methodology of the Church of Ireland, as have, to some extent, quasi-legislative instruments. A thorough analysis of the two volumes of the General Convention 1870 and all 147 volumes of the *Journal of the General Synod* since 1870 not only illustrates this but indicates a recent and emergent tendency to augment delegated legislation with quasi-legislative and soft-law instruments. In this respect it can be seen that the Church of Ireland, consciously or unconsciously, is mirroring the state.

There is a pattern. Figure 1 shows how the enactment of primary legislation has ebbed and flowed over each twenty-year period around a similar mean point, without dramatic variation. The high points reflect those years in which there has been liturgical revision and, of course, the initial flurry of legislation necessitated by disestablishment.

---

115 Ibid., 128.   116 Richard Rawlings, 'Concordats of the constitution' (2000), 116 LQR 257–86.   117 Norman Doe, 'Ecclesiastical quasi-legislation' in Norman Doe, Mark Hill and Robert Ombres (eds), *English canon law* (Cardiff, 1998), pp 93–103.   118 Ibid.   119 The Principles of Canon Law Common to the Churches of the Anglican Communion (2008), PCLCCAC, principle 4(2).   120 Ibid., principle 4(4).

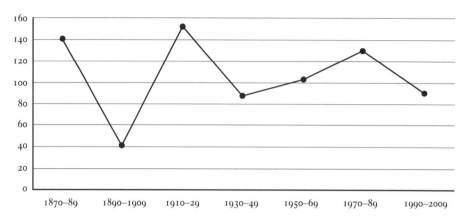

Fig. 1. Statutes passed by the General Convention and General Synod,
1870–2009

This undulating pattern has continued in the nine years since 2009, in which
there have been a further 53 statutes passed by the General Synod.

In contrast, of the 250 quasi-legislative instruments tabulated, 163 (65 per cent)
were put in place since 1990. Indeed, 80 (32 per cent) came into being in the last
ten years. In the twenty-year period between 1989 and 2009 there were 92 such
instruments. Already in the eight years since between 2009 and 2017 there have
been 71 more (see fig. 2).

In 2010 there were a further seventeen such instruments. The slightly higher
level in the initial years after 1871 is accounted for by the periodic issuing of mem-
oranda to make known, and explain, aspects of the newly adopted constitution of

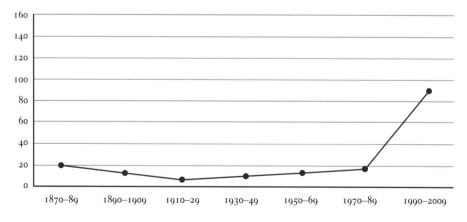

Fig. 2. Quasi-legislation generated by the General Convention, General Synod
and RCB and their committees, 1870–2009

the Church of Ireland as well as other aspects of the transition from establishment to disestablishment. Among the journals, 27 report no delegated or quasi-legislation in the given year; all of those are prior to 1983.

The graph shows that the church has had recourse increasingly in the last twenty years to soft-law instruments. The Church of Ireland, it would appear, in common with trends in the civil law, is relying increasingly on soft-law instruments to regulate significant areas of its life.

IV. IMPLICATIONS AND CHALLENGES

The law of the state, more than at any time in the history of the Church of Ireland since its disestablishment, is impacting on the church in new ways. The range of responses of the church includes acceptance and cooperation, as well as fear and opposition. Legislation has necessitated amendment of church law, retraining (marriage formalities and education) and changes in local communities (education management). Pastoral and liturgical adjustments have been required (marriage, and children's and youth work). Compliance has been a principal concern (pensions, health and safety, data privacy and ecclesiastical discipline). The Charities Act 2009 is causing major administrative upheaval at every level of church life.

State legislation has exposed shortcomings in the church's praxis (disability legislation and child protection). New church law has been necessitated (child protection). Some legislation potentially brings the church into conflict with the state (planning and development law). Other legislation mirrors contemporary controversy within the church (equality, human rights, civil partnerships, constitutional reform) and is likely to continue to do so. Much legislation is tacitly embraced and implemented.

Most significantly, uncertainty endures concerning areas in which the law itself is still unfolding (equality, sexual orientation, human rights and the employment rights of clergy). This uncertainty and the associated debates, of themselves, vindicate the assessment that, more than at any other time, the law of the state is having such an impact on the church that it is preoccupied, more than ever before, with law.

In many ways, the growing use by the Church of Ireland of quasi-legislative materials should come as no surprise. The attractions are clear: flexibility, cost-effectiveness, efficiency, ability to react, lack of technicality, informality and the saving of time at General Synod. Many permit of a more pastoral approach and several permit of a variety of interpretations.

Much of this will, naturally, sit comfortably with those in the church who have a predisposition against law and where the teaching of canon law has been weak. As has been seen in this analysis, quasi-legislation/soft law is utilized, consciously or unconsciously, to address a vast array of subjects. Many relate to compliance with state law and there is no question, in general, of a need to incorporate into church law itself. Others are routine elucidations or commendations of niches of primary or secondary sources. Still others clearly relate to the margins of difficult subjects and the need to implement best practice where the state law on an issue is not immovably determined: the best example of this relates to the employment status of clergy and their conditions of service. Breaking new ground and tackling hard subjects on which there is no theological or socio-political consensus would appear to be the basis of others such as children and communion, flags, the historic formularies, sectarianism and the Masonic order.

Routinely, such instruments are communicated to the church at large and they may affect church life generally. Many are directed at clergy and other office holders such as diocesan secretaries, diocesan councils, select vestries and church-wardens, teachers and youth workers.

Alongside advantages and attractions there are, however, disadvantages and concerns. The principal question is the extent to which, if at all, such quasi-legislative/soft law instruments are legally binding. Houghton and Baldwin suggest that 'government by informal rules' is 'a new device' by government when confronted with 'a difficult regulatory task'.[121] Their primary concern is that informal rules are 'too free of control by Parliament [in the case of the church, the General Synod], executive, judiciary or any other source and that this freedom is increasingly open to exploitation'.[122]

CONCLUSIONS

In two ways, the law and administration of the Church of Ireland have changed significantly since 1969. The pace of those changes is accelerating. The result is that the church itself is changing or finds it has no option but to change. Against that backdrop, and in conclusion, three challenges may be highlighted for action, two concerning each of the areas delineated, and one overall concern.

The increasing impact of civil law on the work of the Church of Ireland, presents not only an opportunity constantly to affirm the priority of the law of the state, but also, to engage with that law-making in a prophetic way. To this end, more time and resources need to be devoted to this engagement with and to the monitoring of legislative proposals and developments on behalf of the church in both jurisdictions, and where appropriate to join the public discourse about them. The Standing Committee of the General Synod is charged with this responsibility, as is the Board of Education of the General Synod in that field. All too often, however, this core activity is an adjunct to an already busy member of staff's existing burdensome portfolio, or is left entirely to the voluntary interest and engagement of a few church members, lay and ordained.

In the case of the accelerating reliance upon quasi-legislation and soft law, there needs to be vigilance. Useful as these tools are, not least, in terms of flexibility,

---

121 John Houghton and Robert Baldwin, 'Circular arguments: the status and legitimacy of administrative rules', *Public Law* (1986), p. 239.   **122** Ibid., p. 240.

ease and speed of use, ready revision and promulgation, as well as in addressing in broad ways contentious areas, the church needs to be alert to their potential shortcomings. Are they an accurate articulation of the law? Are they consistent with the primary sources of law of the church? Do they risk being one person's (or one group's) interpretation of the law? Have some individuals or interest groups influenced their making behind the scenes without transparency? Should some not be subject to synodical scrutiny? Some may be vague or their provenance may be unclear. All should be published and readily accessible. Do they give church members too much leeway in choosing whether to give effect to them or leave them alone? How are they to be appealed or challenged? Do they displace the role of the General Synod in making general policy?

In all of this, education and training are vital. Given that these two dynamics are shaping the way the Church of Ireland now is, awareness on its own is insufficient. Too much in this respect is left to chance, and to the hope that much of the education in this area will 'rub off' on people in curacies, or as time goes by. A haphazard approach, or learning, in the main, 'on the job' or by osmosis, fails to take account either of the scope of the changes or the pace of change. More formal and thorough patterns of initial and ongoing training and education are needed, not only of ordained members of the Church of Ireland, but also of the lay volunteers and staff of whom so much is also expected.

Those who shaped the continuity of the law of the Church of Ireland at disestablishment would recognize much at the core of today's church as it commemorates the 150th anniversary of the Irish Church Act 1869. So too would those who celebrated the centenary in 1969. What is new in terms of the impact of civil law, and the reliance on quasi-legislation shaping the mission and ministry of the Church of Ireland, would astonish them.

14

Changing structures of the church

Ven. Robin Bantry White, Ven. George Davison,
Canon Gillian Wharton, Ken Gibson,
Hazel Corrigan and Adrian Clements

GENERAL SYNOD

In reviewing the operation of the General Synod over the past fifty years, it is first worth noting that, as of 1971, the General Synod was already a century old, having evolved out of the General Convention that began meeting once disestablishment had been enacted under the Irish Church Act of 1869. Our synodical structures were among the first in the Anglican Communion in the modern era. To relive the early synod meetings in the 1870s through the *Journal of the General Synod* and the newspapers of the day is to find much that would have been familiar in 1970, and indeed in 2019, even in terms of size. Our synod has a larger number of members for our much smaller church membership than that which has evolved in recent decades in the Church of England. Indeed, it was a constant criticism by that doyen of the office of honorary secretary of the synod (1970–94), lay canon J.L.B. Deane, that it should legislate to reduce its membership by about one-half. This has not happened. It may well be that the ever-present background of the Troubles made it desirable that a large number of church members from all corners of the island of Ireland would know, understand and respect each other in some measure. It is also one of the few cross-border institutions, only paralleled by some of the sporting organizations. This is of some importance in an island politically divided for the last century. But the large numbers prepared to participate also indicates a dedication, particularly among the laity, to the church as an institution.

The bills procedure, by which changes are enacted in the liturgy, the constitution, the disciplinary code of the church and many business matters, together with cathedrals and their chapters, has sometimes seemed ponderous and reminiscent of parliamentary procedure at the time of disestablishment 150 years ago. However, its careful balancing of principle and detail, and its avoidance of doing things in a precipitate manner has probably on occasions saved the church from its own foolishness. The highly skilled professionalism of those who prepare bills, notably the first woman to be elected a lay honorary secretary, Canon Lady Sheil, and the attention of a skilled canon lawyer, the Rt Revd Dr Paul Colton, bishop of Cork, in his years as chairperson of the Bills Committee (2005–18), has helped greatly. The General Synod has been enormously assisted, in particular, by the very longstanding assessors to the primate, Mr Michael Davey and Mr Lyndon MacCann, SC.

Changed times

One great change in the period under review has been the growth in the number of women who are members. Women were admitted to parochial offices in 1920, but to synods only in 1949. Only one was elected in 1951. This had grown only to 15 by 1972, and it then increased to 38 in 1982, to 75 in 1992 and to 97 in 2002, being joined by then by eight women from among the clergy. The membership of women now stands at 198.

Up to 1982, the synod met in its own Synod Hall adjoining Christ Church Cathedral, Dublin. However, the building had become dilapidated beyond the capacity of the generous endowment provided by Henry Roe, when he had had it built in the nineteenth century. Archbishop Armstrong, in his presidential address in 1982, solemnly pronounced: 'Ichabod – its glory is departed.' The normal meeting place was for some time in the Royal Dublin Society, Ballsbridge, then the Royal Hospital, Kilmainham. The synod has also visited other places on this island: Armagh on many occasions, Belfast, Cork, Galway, Limerick and Kilkenny, and, in 2019, synod was held in Derry/Londonderry for the first time. During the recent recession, it returned on a number of occasions to Christ Church Cathedral, Dublin. However, many hotels now have elaborate conference facilities, which usually prove the most convenient.

In 1971, the Church of Ireland and its General Synod was already in reformist mood. A ground-breaking report on its structure had been presented, *Administration '67*. Liturgical revision and modernization had been commenced. Clergy retirement issues were being tackled. The Role of the Church Committee brought a new focus on the church in the modern world. In the 1970s, a new generation emerged among the clergy, who later became bishops; the most notable of this talented generation was the Most Revd R.H.A. (now Lord) Eames. Communications had become a pressing issue. Residential training of the clergy had become a reality with the opening of the new Divinity Hostel in 1963, later becoming the Church of Ireland Theological College and then the Church of Ireland Theological Institute.

Normally, a good part of the synod's work is routine, receiving reports, passing resolutions, and deliberating upon financial, investment and property matters. The presidential address by the primate sets the tone, but there is not an opportunity to discuss the issues raised, unless they pertain to the contents of the reports or other business. Nevertheless, because of the nature of the Troubles, and, in particular in the time when attention focused on the annual Battle of the Somme service at Drumcree Parish Church in the 1990s, the synod found itself at the centre of debate, and of media attention.

Progress and contention

In legislation and accompanying reports, the church moves and progresses in frequently controversial areas. During the last half-century, there have been two long
processes of legislation concerning liturgy, the first, from the beginning of the
period until the publication of the *Alternative Prayer Book* in 1984 and the second leading to the revision of the *Book of Common Prayer*, published in 2004.
Liturgical change, because it pertains to the doctrine of the church, requires a
special bills procedure, by which notice of the proposed legislation must be agreed
in the annual session of the synod preceding that at which the final enactment takes
place. In the years between the publication of the *APB* and the revised *BCP*, the
constitution was amended, which greatly facilitated the orderly conduct of this
business, requiring amendments to the text of liturgy being proposed to be notified
not later than one month after the notice being given by resolution. This gives the
Liturgical Advisory Committee ample time to decide whether to accept or oppose
such an amendment, and prevents the synod being ambushed by ill-considered
last-minute amendments.

   In the period, the synod was presented with three important and inter-related
reports. These were *First of all*, by the Priorities Committee (1979), *Ministry
today – a calling for all* (1981) and *Time to tell* (1983). It is often said that such
reports gather dust. However, most of the substantive recommendations did get
accepted. Most importantly the wholesale support for the ordination of women
contained in the ministry report was seen to come to fruition in provision for
the ordination of women to the diaconate in 1987 and to be priests and bishops
in 1990. In many ways, this most serious of processes had a less difficult time
in synod than the other reformist issue of the day, the remarriage in church of
divorced persons. This met successive defeats and upsets. A committee that had
sat since 1973 brought successive proposals, which were rejected or withdrawn.
In 1993, the committee was disbanded. However, proposals were brought in 1996
that found acceptance. Repeated attempts have been made over time to make progress on issues to do with the shape of the dioceses and episcopate. A great deal of
sincere effort has been put into these topics, which effort has not been a criticism
of episcopacy as currently exercised, but of the structural and geographical issues
surrounding it.

   In the last two decades, the church has been troubled in finding a common way
though issues of human sexuality arising from Resolution 1.10 of the Lambeth
Conference of 1998. This has tended to place in stark relief divisions over churchmanship, of theology, of differing perceptions across the island of Ireland, and of
the relative strength within the church of liberal and conservative agendas.

   If this writer[1] may give a personal view of synod during this half century, it may
be said that nowadays there are fewer bores, but also fewer skilled debaters. There

---

1 R.B. White.

are fewer people among the general membership adept at using the Standing Orders. In some ways the synod has become more an annual conference than a parliament debating great matters. On the other hand, the General Synod has stood the test of time and continues to serve the church well. In particular, we are blest with the bishops, clergy and laity, who are prepared to be generous with time, travel and commitment to make it work, and the staff, who loyally give of their professional expertise and commitment.

Governance and the state

By the centenary of disestablishment, some of the strains of modern life were beginning to affect the Church of Ireland. As noted, there emerged a series of reports to the General Synod beginning just before the period under review – on administration, support for outreach projects and communication.

A reader looking at today's General Synod agendas may smile ruefully at the realization that some of these issues remain without full resolution fifty years on and continue to reappear like old friends. For instance, under the 'Summary of main recommendations' in the *Administration* report, the synod was urged to consider 'reduction of House of Representatives from 648 to 501 and the redistribution of seats'. There was a recommendation for the rearrangement of dioceses and a proposal that dioceses should have combined regional offices.

Many of the proposals encouraged a degree of centralization of resources that did not find support or wider consensus, as can be seen by the continuation of the earlier diocese-based model of administration with which we remain familiar today. This forward-looking report also considered whether the traditional parochial unit was likely to be good for the church of the future (chapter 6). Looking around today, we see increased diversity in how ministry is delivered: pioneer ministry, ordained local ministry and mission areas have emerged as responses to changing needs.

The period following this report on church administration saw an expansion of the committee structure under the General Synod and Standing Committee, including the current range of committees serving the church on the island of Ireland and the launch of the Bishops' Appeal – the church's world aid and development programme.

Developing our structures

Funding and resourcing these new undertakings has continued to be something of a challenge. Prior to 1967, there were no dedicated General Synod staff and the 1969 proposal for the appointment of specialist officers was not fully realized. The assistant secretary to the General Synod and secretaries to the Boards of Education, both north and south, were joined by a press officer. Later, the Role of the Church Committee (created in 1970) was allocated a part-time researcher in the form of Dr

Jim McGaffin. In 2000, the decision was taken to create a head of communications, but this was subsequently merged back into the role of head of synod services and communications. Further cutbacks were made in the synod and other departments of Church of Ireland House following the financial crash of 2008, which markedly reduced central church funds and the clergy and staff pension funds.

By 1990, a pattern was emerging of three types of committee, a distinction which continues to the present day. The first group of committees are the constitutional committees, most of which have been in existence since the General Synod took shape in the 1870s. These include the Bills Committee, Legislation Committee, Standing Orders Committee, and Petitions Committee, whose work relates specifically to the General Synod meeting (and which meets only occasionally, as need dictates).

The second group are the long-standing committees of General Synod and the Standing Committee. At present, eight committees report directly to the General Synod – the Board of Education (comprising the boards of Education for Northern Ireland and the Republic), Church of Ireland Youth Department, Commission for Christian Unity and Dialogue, Liturgical Advisory Committee, Council for Mission, Commission on Ministry and the Church of Ireland Marriage Council. The Standing Committee, in turn, oversees committees including the Central Communications Board, Bishops' Appeal Advisory Committee, Church and Society Commission, Consultative Group on Disability, Priorities Fund Committee, Safeguarding Trust Board and Legal Advisory Committee.

Finally, there are groups set up to address specific tasks. In this last group may be found the current General Synod Representation Working Group, the Charities Registration Monitoring Working Group, the recently disbanded Parish Development Working Group (Church 21), the Select Committee on Human Sexuality in the Context of Christian Belief, the Hard Gospel Committee (and the Hard Gospel Implementation Working Group, which had a forerunner known as the Sectarianism Education Working Group), the subsequent Northern Ireland Community Relations Working Group (now merged with the Church and Society Commission) and, until 2016, the Commission on Episcopal Ministry and Structures, which was succeeded by the Facilitation Committee and the Historical Centenaries Working Group.

Serving God through voluntary commitment

A succession of church members has volunteered to serve on church committees over the years, without whom nothing would have been done that was done. The church is ever grateful to those who give up their time and talents unstintingly as part of their Christian service. From among these, some were called on to serve as honorary secretaries. In this demanding role, they served the church, managing not only the work of General Synod but also that of the Standing Committee. A number of outstanding stints of service were recorded, including Canon Barry

Deane (mentioned above), Mr Samuel Harper (lay honorary secretary from 1994 to 2016) and Lady Brenda Sheil (lay honorary secretary from 1999 to 2010)

Some of the most notable achievements of the members of the General Synod who served on various committees over the period include:

- the *Church Hymnal* (2000);
- the *Book of Common Prayer* (2004 edition);
- the Hard Gospel and Church 21 projects;
- *Thanks & praise* – a supplement to the *Church Hymnal* (2015); and
- a revised edition of the *Book of Common Prayer* (2018).

Significant legislation and resolutions have provided for the admission of women to ordained ministry and the remarriage of divorced persons (as previously indicated), the Environmental Charter, support for the establishment of the Eco-Congregation organization in Ireland, and the creation of safeguarding policies and structures.

During the last fifty years, the General Synod worked through a long period of turmoil and change in society. The years of the Troubles in Northern Ireland were years of strain and yet years of tremendous opportunity to offer pastoral care in the most difficult of circumstances. The vocal and consistent opposition to violence, expressed by all churches, and the pastoral leadership given by successive archbishops of Armagh and diocesan bishops, no doubt helped to hold back the potential for an escalation in the conflict. The ceasefires took place half-way through the time frame considered by this volume, and the Church of Ireland has subsequently continued to encourage Northern Ireland's communities along the long road to reconciliation, not least through the Hard Gospel project, and strong friendships between clergy and lay people in parishes and dioceses. Since the millennium, there has also been a divergence between increasing liberalism in government policy in the Republic of Ireland and lesser change in Northern Ireland, partly reflected in the need for consensus within the power-sharing devolved government, the operation of which has often been suspended due to political disputes.

In the Republic of Ireland, the Church of Ireland often found itself fêted as the progressive religious voice. Inevitably, these different experiences of being church from the 1970s through to the 1990s resulted in the Church of Ireland developing a variety of response on some issues – although as has been remarked by the working group currently considering aspects of representation on General Synod, there is no homogeneity in any one diocese nor does the perception of identity relate to the national border in any way that might help the outsider to understand. The Celtic Tiger, the economic crash, the emergence of the congested commuter society with its impact on family life and individual volunteering capacity, and the backdrop of historical social issues around the treatment of unmarried mothers and children in care, have all contributed to a sense of social upheaval – and it is impossible at the time of writing to guess whether Brexit will emerge as a blip or a significant issue on that list. In an effort to restore order, the state has prioritized the creation of legislation and regulation to prevent harm through safeguarding and equality legislation, data protection, charities regulation and employment and health and safety law.

The General Synod, along with the parishes and dioceses, has had to step up its effort in order to keep pace with the rapidly changing regulatory framework as the world of voluntary activity has become increasingly regulated. Looking forward, the General Synod may find it necessary to look back to 1967 and consider if another report on administration of the church is now needed to take us forward for the next fifty years.

HISTORICAL REFLECTIONS ON THE RB

When Gladstone was contemplating how the disestablishment of the Church of Ireland might work, he was able to refer to a Canadian model as a possible solution. The Anglican Church in Canada had been endowed with lands in the reign of George III. The terms of the endowment were not very precisely drawn and this gave rise to claims by other churches for a share in the bounty. In 1853 the necessary authority was granted to remove the Anglican clergy of Canada from the state payroll. Subsequently, it was decided that a capital sum be provided to buy out the entitlements of the then current Canadian population of clergy and later these amounts were transferred to diocesan funds, which guaranteed their stipends for their lifetime.

The Canadian model proved very useful, and some Canadian clergy and bishops campaigned in Ireland to support the concept for the Irish church. Gladstone was convinced, and the Irish Church Act was passed in 1869, with considerable implications for the temporal and material aspects of the church – for the act not only disestablished but also dis-endowed the church.

In September 1869, the National Synod of the Church of Ireland – i.e. all the senior clergy – assembled in the Antient Concert Rooms in Dublin and passed two resolutions, the second of which was very significant. It stated that 'under the present circumstances of the Church of Ireland the cooperation of the faithful laity has become more than ever desirable'. This resolution recognized the need for the laity to come to the aid of the church, and in due course the synod became predominantly lay, while retaining the ability on important topics for clergy or bishops to apply a restraining influence, as the voting is by the three 'orders' (lay, clerical and episcopal), each having to assent.

This was not the case in the newly chartered Representative Body. While chaired by the primate of all Ireland, the body was fully democratic in its decision-making, and predominantly lay when coopted members were included. The Representative Body (RB) of the Church of Ireland was enabled by its 1870 royal charter to undertake the responsibility of holding and safeguarding the assets of the church and, as in Canada, the capital value of the lifetime incomes of clergy at the time of disestablishment.

The act of settling the responsibility on a representative body and the fact that most property was held centrally, which was not the case in other churches in Ireland and Britain, supported the concept of clerical independence, and also the idea that the property of the church was there for the general benefit and support of the wider church and not confined to or 'disposable' at the will of the parish.

The first years of the church following disestablishment were worrying enough for clergy and it is impressive that the vast majority agreed that the value of their future income be transferred from the security of national government to a newly established, and untried, church body. This process was known as commutation, and dioceses that managed to obtain the agreement of more than 75 per cent of clergy to commute were rewarded with a 12 per cent bonus in the capital sum provided in compensation.

While churches and associated schools were passed to the new body at no cost, glebes had to be purchased, albeit at a very reasonable rate. Indeed, as in most cases the annual value of the glebe was included as part of the commutation calculation, the capital compensation included more than enough value to enable the RB to purchase and vest 896 glebes in the period immediately following disestablishment, and thus house the rectors of the church.

Despite all the arrangements for compensation of the active clergy at the time it was clear that, without careful management and generous financial support from the laity, the transfer of an amount that was calculated to expire as the living clergy passed away was not going to cater for the future stipends of clergy or the maintenance costs of church property.

The first RB

At the meeting of the General Convention of the church on 15 February 1870, Archbishop Beresford, after asserting that disestablishment was a 'rude shock but not a vital injury', went on to state that the most important matter to be dealt with was the formation of the 'representative body' of the church, otherwise property and commutation amounts would not be passed into the ownership of the church.

Early days

The RB was entrusted with the property of the church, to be held for the benefit of the church and for such objects and purposes as the General Synod of the church should direct.

A royal charter of 1870 had established the body as an incorporated charitable trustee, with perpetual succession. As such, it is unusual in Ireland and has the great advantage that the charitable liability is the responsibility of the incorporated body and not the members, for the time being. It was empowered to form subcommittees, make by-laws and appoint employees.

To an extent the process of disestablishment allowed the state and the church to recognize the anomalous situation of having Church of Ireland churches where there was no need or demand. Some were never vested, and, in the end, 1,628 churches and 1,400 graveyards were vested in the RB. The overall success of the Church of Ireland model was complimented by being replicated, fifty years following disestablishment, in the foundation in the Anglican Church in Wales of a Welsh RB, based broadly on the Irish model.

Sustentation fund

One of the first central actions of the RB was prompted by the acceptance of the laity of the church that they now had to provide for the material future of parishes and clergy, without the guarantee of tithe income from the general population. The minutes of the RB in December 1870 record a decision to launch an appeal to create a fund to finance the stipends of future clergy. The message to people and parishes was:

> Give to the Central Fund, that the poorer districts may share with the
>   richer
> Give largely if you are rich
> Give willingly if you are poor
> Give regularly your much or your little
> Give thankfully for the love of God
> Give unselfishly for the general good
> Give with prayer for a blessing on your gifts.

In the first twenty years following disestablishment, contributions towards the Sustentation Fund totalled £3,733,180, a huge sum then and not inconsiderable even now, without conversion to modern purchasing power.

Then to now ...

The fact that the RB still exists and is still composed in the same way of representatives of the dioceses, the bishops and twelve coopted specialists is, presumably, testimony to the durability and practicality of the original concept. It has adapted to the changes democratizing land ownership in Ireland, to home rule agitation and resistance, wars, civil war, partition and the Troubles. It has survived also the difficulties and disruptions caused by depression, recession, the introduction of the punt and the introduction of the euro.

In 1997, the RB commissioned consultants PWC to advise on its structure and created the RB Executive Committee, which now carries on more of the day-to-day oversight of activity, reducing the burden on the full membership of the Representative Body, which now meets in full three or four times a year under the chairmanship of the archbishop of Armagh. A group of specialized committees exercises oversight of various specific areas of work: property, investments, library and archives committees, as well as the Allocations Committee, the Audit Committee, the Stipends Committee and the Legal Advisory Committee. Departments were created in Church of Ireland House and staffed with specialists to support the various areas of work. These include the finance, investment, property and trusts, and legal departments.

The delegation by the General Synod to the Standing Committee of responsibility for day-to-day synodical governance is mirrored in the retention by the General Synod of the concept that the RB takes responsibility for the real and financial assets of the church. Apart from the general funds of the RB, which are utilized to fund central activities, clergy training and episcopal costs among other elements of church life, the RB retains responsibility on behalf of parishes and dioceses for in excess of 20,000 individual trusts and a portfolio of more than 3,000 individual properties.

Associated with these and other central responsibilities the RB administers clergy stipends and pensions, supports the legislative process and the archbishops and bishops and represents the church legally.

The RB focuses faithfully and exclusively on the trust responsibilities it acquired on inception and inherited since. At times, the conservation and preservation of the material assets of the church have been almost ends in themselves, and this has been interpreted by some in the General Synod and the Standing Committee of the church as being unduly single-minded, to the exclusion of any consideration of the church's spiritual or societal mission.

To avoid this accusation or pitfall the RB and the Standing Committee, encouraged by office holders in both, have been consciously working more closely together in recent years, illustrated by the expansion in 2012 of the role of chief officer of the RB to be also the secretary general of the Church of Ireland. The first secretary general was Mr Adrian Clements, formerly head of finance, and, on retirement, he was succeeded by Mr David Ritchie. This is a welcome manifestation of the fruitful coordination of the utilization and conservation of material resources for the use and benefit of the mission of the church, which is indeed the absolute object of the RB.

A decade of deficits

The global financial crash of 2008 took the world by surprise, but hit the Church of Ireland particularly hard. Irish banking shares had been regarded as blue-chip, prudent investments, and not only were central funds heavily invested in this class of share, but also the funds of many parishes and other charitable bodies associated with the Church of Ireland. The result of the collapse of the Irish banks was little short of catastrophic for the church and magnified the effect of the global crash. The seismic events in financial markets had dramatic consequences for available income and, within a few years, for the capacity to maintain pension schemes.

The RB was faced with a decade of deficits – woods from which the trustee body is only beginning to emerge. Given the scale of the difficulty confronting the RB, there was no option but to retreat and regroup. Cutbacks were the order of the day in Church of Ireland House and a number of staff were offered voluntary redundancy packages. The staff pension scheme was initially closed to new members and subsequently wound up. The RB fought unsuccessfully to maintain the clergy pension scheme, eventually contributing €25 million from already depleted coffers and agreeing a financial scheme with the Pensions Authority. As part of this scheme, parishes put a huge effort into raising additional funds annually towards a new levy so that accumulated clergy service could be honoured up to the point of closure.

While the aftershocks of 2008 continue to rumble through the global economy, the RB has been assisted in recent years by a recovery in markets and by the efforts of clergy, laity and staff throughout the church. Conservative management of resources continues to be necessary to delivering the services required by the wider church as it confronts increased legislative compliance and the economic ripples and exchange-rate volatility triggered by the Brexit conundrum. Looking back at the decade, the members of the RB, and particularly those who served on its Executive Committee, have steered the church's finances through a tough period and are ready for the fresh challenges that lie ahead.

'What, we may ask, is the Spirit saying to the churches?'[2]

The Representative Body is sometimes referred to as 'the business side of the House', and the function of Church of Ireland House itself as providing 'the civil service of the Church'. In 2015, Mr Robert Neill, then chair of the RB executive, put forward an alternative vision of the work of the RB, not just as protector of the heritage of the church, but as the salt in the seasoning of the future mission of the church. 'We are very focused on preserving our assets and investing for the future – often bypassing the needs of the here and now. We are conditioned to preserve what we have inherited and to pass it on. But, to quote one senior prelate, we end up with "conservation and preservation leading to fear and withdrawal",' he reflected.

Let us invest in the future, not just for the future

Analysing the way in which it functioned, the RB argued for the need for greater discernment and more proactive application of funds to support the active mission

2 Mr Robert Neill, in a speech to the General Synod in 2015.

of the church. One key outworking of this was the redefinement of the Church Fabric Fund into the Church Fabric and Development Fund by means of a bill brought to the General Synod in 2016 to loosen the restraints imposed by the constitution on the use or disposal of church property, whether real estate, church silver, paintings or other material or financial assets. The idea of the redefined fund was to share resources and put church assets to work to improve ministry and out-reach – investing in the future to create a system to support initiatives in building the church for the future.

Now and the future

Mr Henry Saville became chair of the RB executive in 2017 at a time of increasing legislative compliance. Under his leadership, the RB has aspired to be a central resource for the church, advising on best practice and undertaking representa-tions on behalf of the church in two jurisdictions. Most recently, it has been able to increase its provision for college-level chaplaincy through the careful financial management of resources by the Allocations Committee, modelling the RB's con-cern to invest in the future of the church.

The careful (and creative) stewards

The work of the Allocations Committee, under the chairmanship of Canon Graham Richards, has been notable for the number of initiatives that have been accommodated beyond the traditional funding model, which focused on episco-pal ministry, the work of the RB, ministerial training and the support of synod and other activities. The Allocations Committee, supported by the work of the Finance Department, always faces a significant challenge in stretching the income that remains after the fixed requirements are satisfied, to accommodate as many of those 'other activities' as possible.

In recent years, the committee gratefully received some additional support from Allchurches Trust, which enabled a number of projects to be completed. These included the development of the Parish Resources website,[3] to assist select vestries and clergy in managing the parishes. This service is a vital part of ensuring that volunteers in parishes and dioceses are supported and is enhanced by regular island-wide seminars run by Church of Ireland House staff when new provisions, such as charity law, safeguarding legislation or data-protection rules are introduced.

Ethical investment and climate action

Another key initiative in recent years was the development of an ethical investment strategy. Initially, this emerged from a policy of the Investment Committee that

---

3 www.ireland.anglican.org/parish-resources.

precluded investment in shares in companies dedicated to gambling, immorality or armaments. Under the successive chairmanships of Mr Richard Hewat, Mr Robert Neill, Mr Henry Saville and Mr Kevin Bowers, this evolved into a broader policy to encourage environmentally positive investment and to move away from investment areas that are related to harmful outcomes, such as fossil-fuel extraction. This initiative found widespread support among members of the executive, the full RB and the General Synod, which approved an environmental charter in 2015 calling all parishes and members of the Church of Ireland to consider their duty to care for creation. This charter also reflects the wider Anglican Communion commitment to the Five Marks of Mission: 'To strive to safeguard the integrity of creation, and sustain and renew the life of the earth.'[4]

The RCB has continued its commitment to address the problem of climate change in the broadest way possible. The RCB's offices seek out new projects and sustainable solutions under the #RCBEGREEN initiative and, in 2018, it became a supporter of the All-Ireland Pollinator Plan. Pollinators are vital to creating and maintaining the habitats and ecosystems that many animals rely on for food and shelter and also for crop production.

The RCB, as a founding signatory and supporter of the Climate Action 100+ initiative (launched in December 2017 at the One Planet Summit), is monitoring the engagements being undertaken with the world's most carbon-intensive companies to curb emissions, strengthen climate disclosures and improve climate governance. The RCB is also a supporter of the Transition Pathway Initiative (also launched at the end of 2017), an excellent resource for establishing which companies are taking seriously their responsibilities in relation to the transition to a low-carbon environment, and in particular in relation to a 2 degree alignment.

Gloine

In the 1990s, the Property Committee initiated another outstanding, and long-term project, which was funded by the RB's Allocation Committee with a grant of €548,000 over the twenty-five years of the project, with additional funding of €242,000 from the Heritage Council, together with support from Allchurches Trust and the Department for Communities (formerly the Northern Ireland Environment Agency). Known as Gloine, the project enabled Dr David Lawrence, a specialist in stained glass history and conservation, to photograph, as far as was practicable, all of the stained glass in the Church of Ireland.

The project was completed in 2017 and this resource may now be enjoyed by all in a free-to-view online catalogue.[5] A total of 3,198 windows in 657 churches have been surveyed and the database will hold some 45,000 factual items of data.

4 General Synod, 'Environmental charter' (2015), www.ireland.anglican.org/cmsfiles/pdf/Resources/ParishResources/PeopleCommunity/Environmental-Charter.pdf, accessed 17 June 2019.
5 www.gloine.ie.

The resource provided extensive illustrations in the recent publications *The Church of Ireland: an illustrated history*[6] and *A commentary on the constitution of the Church of Ireland.*

See house project

A truly significant project over the last quarter-century has been the review of all see houses (episcopal residences). The RCB Property Committee commenced the review in 1994 conscious of its trustee responsibilities and to exercise due care in the management of all resources, including real property. The committee considered the essential function of a see house and brought forward plans for the reform of the stock of see houses in order to meet the requirements of the modern era and a more economic vision of the future.

See houses that were no longer fit for purpose in the dioceses of Armagh, Clogher, Connor, Kilmore, Meath, Ossory, Killaloe, Limerick and Tuam were sold and replaced with houses that were more energy efficient and fit for modern family living.

The volunteers most engaged in this project on behalf of the RB were the successive chairpersons of the Property Committee during the period 1993–2018: Canon Graham Richards, Mr Richard McConnell, Mr Sydney Gamble, Mr Robert Kay and Mr Keith Roberts. The church was also greatly indebted to Mr Trevor Stacey, the recently retired head of property and trusts, who managed the complexities of twenty-five years of renovation and new-build projects with a small team based in Church of Ireland House.

A tribute to volunteers

The scale of activities under the direction of the church's trustee body is impressive, and all the more so when the voluntary nature of RB members is recalled. A member of the RB executive will not only attend meetings of the executive and full RB ten or eleven times a year, but will also sit on at least one of the RB's subcommittees, often acting as chair of that body and overseeing projects of significant scale.

Volunteers bring a wealth of professional experience to the aid of the RB, and the length of service of many members is a testament to the huge sense of commitment felt by many to the church. The RB itself puts huge emphasis on acknowledging the contribution of volunteers and facilitating them to play an active and dynamic role in decision-making through its committee structure. Professional staff support this activity and there have been many very able people recruited to maintain the capacity to advise and implement decisions over the decades. The membership of the trustee body reflects properly the changes in society since 1870 but the spirit

6 Brian Walker and Claude Costecalde (eds), *The Church of Ireland: an illustrated history* (Shankill, Co. Dublin, 2013).

of freely given time and professional skill remains unaltered. Their efforts have allowed us to inherit intact an institution that has at its heart the purpose of supporting the church and its mission, and it is with confidence bred of success down the years that this resilient organization faces the future.

A NOTE ON THE RB LIBRARY

The RCB Library was founded in 1931, based on the gift of 5,000 books from the Irish Guild of Witness, founded by Rosamund Stephen, and on books from her father's library. It was housed in the RB premises, then in St Stephen's Green.

In 1969, separate premises were found in Churchtown for the increasing numbers of volumes and in 1981 the library adopted an archival role for the church, whereby parochial and other records and artefacts could be held securely in purpose-built accommodation.

This facility, funded from RB general funds and diocesan and individual gifts, is a resource for theological students and academics, for general historical research and for genealogical archaeology and, while fast outgrowing its premises, the RCB Library is a significant part of the church and a significant national archive.[7]

---

7 The RCB Library's contribution to the life of the Church of Ireland and to Irish academic life is treated in more detail in Raymond Refaussé's essay in this volume.

15

Architectural changes and the arts in the life of the Church of Ireland

Paul Harron

Since 1969 the Church of Ireland has not required many entirely new church buildings; rather, over the past fifty years, the focus in both parishes and cathedrals across the island has tended to be on gradual adaptation to changing needs in response to evolving patterns of attendance and styles of corporate worship. In their chapter 'Buildings and faith: church building from medieval to modern' in *The laity and the Church of Ireland, 1000–2000*, McBride and Larmour provided accounts of several of the new church buildings of the 1960s, especially the ones that were more overtly modern in appearance and wrote:

> [T]he scope for new building steadily diminished as the twentieth century drew to a close. At the dawn of a new age [in 2000], Church of Ireland architecture seems likely to confront new challenges ... [which] will undoubtedly place new demands on architectural ingenuity and also raise crucial questions about the future of the existing church building heritage of the Church of Ireland.[1]

This short overview of the period 1969–2019 will attempt to recount the more major and striking developments of how and where architects and artists have shown ingenuity in meeting the contemporary design and artistic needs of Church of Ireland people. In terms of buildings, it cannot be a comprehensive account or catalogue of all those projects that have provided innovative responses within local contexts. It is also not the place for recounting the ways in which churches have been deconsecrated and put to alternative uses across Ireland in the last half-century where congregations have declined or even disappeared altogether. For those interested in case studies relating to the conversion and reuse of churches (of various denominations but including many from the Church of Ireland), these are well covered in *New life for churches in Ireland: good practice in conversion and reuse* (2012).[2]

---

1 Paul Larmour and Stephen McBride, 'Buildings and faith: church building from medieval to modern' in Raymond Gillespie and W.G. Neely (eds), *The laity and the Church of Ireland, 1000–2000* (Dublin, 2002), p. 331   2 Paul Harron (ed.), *New life for churches in Ireland: good practice in conversion and reuse* (Belfast, 2012).

With regard to the Church of Ireland's responses to both the joy and 'burden' of owning so much 'built heritage' and also seeking to use it for present-day worship and activities (the challenges posed by McBride and Larmour), a variety of approaches have been taken. At a central level, a relatively significant degree of concern at the potential for some parishes to go too far down unconventional lines or, equally, to opt for very bland or 'off the peg' (as it were) design solutions, must have been sufficiently felt and feared one decade into the new century for the Liturgical Advisory Committee of the General Synod to present a report and publish it as a booklet in 2010, entitled *Liturgical space and church reordering: issues of good practice*. The authors stated:

> Because the Church of Ireland has such an abundance of old buildings, it is inevitable that the adaptation of liturgical space to meet today's requirements for worship will, in most cases, have to be done in centuries-old churches – the atmosphere and style of which demand respect. However, we are anxious to show how such buildings can meet the unfolding needs of our time, if the work carried out is of suitable quality and sensitivity, and we feel it is important that parishes are encouraged not simply to baulk at the concept. We also feel strongly that, as in past generations, the churches in which we worship need to receive the artistic imprint of our generation not least so that future worshippers will be able to reflect on the art that inspired and challenged us.[3]

THE COMPLETION OF BELFAST CATHEDRAL

First, however, to the completion of Belfast Cathedral: the building of the cathedral – dedicated to St Anne, as was the parish church on which site it was built, and commonly (rather affectionately) just referred to as St Anne's – was a highly protracted process. Begun in 1899 to the designs of Sir Thomas Drew in a simplified Hiberno-Romanesque style, it was erected in distinct stages as money became available (with several architects succeeding Drew). While the apse and ambulatory were completed in 1959, it was only in 1974 that the south transept was finished (containing the Chapel of Unity and the cathedral organ), and the north transept was built as late as 1981 – both to the designs of John McGeagh (although the north transept was completed under the eye of Robert McKinstry following McGeagh's death). The exterior of the south transept includes some very pared-back decorative Romanesque elements as well as a low-relief sculptural saltire; the junctions between the 'old' and 'new' parts of the building are starkly obvious, not least in the change from the honey-coloured stone of the nave to the newer whiter stone available in the later twentieth century. The north transept is characterized by a hugely emphatic structural-sculptural stone Celtic cross ('the largest

3 *Liturgical space and church reordering: issues of good practice* (Dublin, 2010), pp 6–7.

in Ireland'[4]), while the quite shallow interior contains the Chapel of the Royal Irish Regiment and many regimental artefacts (the space having been reordered in 2015). It is notable that, aside from any discussion about their appearance, both these transepts were brave 'carry on as normal' projects in themselves, completed as they were while Belfast city centre was being routinely torn apart in the Troubles (rather in the same indefatigable spirit shown by the cathedral's successive deans and musicians by continuing to serve and make music there during this turbulent period). As Galloway noted, money-raising efforts were hampered by the view that industrialists could be financing 'a possible bomb target'; between 1974 and 1980, the girders of the unfinished transept 'resembled a dark skeleton against the sky'.[5] (Those with longer memories, or who have seen the stark archival photographs, will recall how very narrowly St Anne's survived the Luftwaffe bombs during the Belfast Blitz in 1941 – the surrounding area was almost entirely obliterated.)

A former dean of Christ Church Cathedral, Dublin, John Paterson, mused in an essay in 1997 entitled 'Irish cathedrals – burden or bonus?' on the importance of the arts in the list of priorities when renovation work to cathedrals (and churches generally) is carried out. He wrote: 'A blending of the contemporary with the old can actually demonstrate the continuity of the Christian centuries' and singled out the 'new interior plate-glass west doors in Belfast Cathedral' as 'possibly the finest recent example of such a blending in any Irish cathedral'.[6] These tall doors, erected in memory of Bishop McCappin of Connor, do indeed impress – they not only incorporate depictions of the coats of arms of the two dioceses the building serves but also allow passers-by tantalizing views into the nave and right up to the twinkly lights of the choir and chancel from the street and square in front of the cathedral steps.

In 2007, a 52m-tall, needle-like, brushed stainless steel 'Spire of Hope' was lowered into place, suspended over the crossing, the brainchild of Dean Houston McKelvey. At last, the cathedral had a culminating roofline feature, albeit one which was very different from that originally envisaged by Drew and from McKinstry's subsequent design for a tall fleche; however, the sleechy subsoil on which the cathedral is built could not sustain a heavy tower or spire. The stainless steel spire, designed as a result of an architectural competition of 2004 (funded by the regeneration body Laganside) by Box Architects (Colin Conn) and fabricated in Switzerland, is arguably rather derivative of Dublin's Spire ('Monument of Light') in O'Connell Street of 2003 by Ian Ritchie Architects, and it sits somewhat strangely with the rest of the building's exterior, yet it is an indisputably optimistic commission and internally is highly dramatic and effective, extending its sharp point down into the choir and bathing the space below in natural light via a large

---

4 Very Revd Houston McKelvey, 'Cathedral quarters', *Lion & Lamb*, 44 (2008), p. 17.   5 Peter Galloway, *The cathedrals of Ireland* (Belfast, 1992), p. 30.   6 John Paterson, 'Irish cathedrals – burden or bonus?', *Search: A Church of Ireland Journal*, 20:2 (1997), p. 98. Paterson argued that cathedrals are, 'if seized in an imaginative way … always a bonus'!

square of glass through which the point penetrates. Rather wittily, especially in the Ulster context and in that very Irish way of nicknaming public art, the Spire of Hope was dubbed 'the Prod' by local wags (among other gems). McKelvey said of it:

> The design was chosen because it is of our day and generation. It is quite a feat of engineering to put up a spire that height which is not in contact with the ground ... Timing is everything and we sold our shares at the time when the market was good and managed to even out-distance the rising price of steel. I like to think that it was quite literally a God-given opportunity and if we didn't take this opportunity it would never be done. It is an expression of hope in God; it is also an expression of faithfulness. It is a public statement that we are here, we have our values, we have our beliefs and we want to share them.[7]

CATHEDRAL RESTORATIONS AND REORDERINGS

As responsible custodians, inevitably there have been a number of major restoration projects in historic Irish cathedrals during the period. Space does not permit recounting these in any great detail; however, among them have been the following.

St Mary's Cathedral, Limerick – which marked its 850th anniversary in 2018 – was restored from the early 1990s onwards in various phases. In 1991, the interior walls were completely stripped of plaster (rather like Killarney Roman Catholic Cathedral but also the Church of Ireland cathedrals at Kilkenny and Kildare). The result certainly makes the cathedral feel atmospherically ancient. St Mary's Cathedral, Tuam was rescued and revived (aided by EU structural funds) from 1988 to 1997, and the Synod Hall portion, formerly the chancel, is used for community functions and concerts as well as diocesan synods. The sixteenth-century Lady Chapel in St Laserian's Cathedral, Leighlin – 'a delightful and unspoiled treat' of a cathedral[8] – was restored, refurbished and reopened in 2014 through a 'cocktail' of public, private and church funding, making it suitable and accessible for hospitality for the wider community as well as for worship and prayer.

St Patrick's Cathedral, Armagh, was restored in various phases from the 1980s onwards, with extensive repair to the interior plaster and stone work, the stained glass and the robing room. Under Dean Patrick Rooke (later bishop of Tuam, Killala and Achonry), the crypt was opened up for visitors and 5 Vicars' Hill – the former diocesan registry – was imaginatively restored and revamped as a public museum in 2011 (and other houses in Vicars' Hill were also refurbished and put to innovative cathedral-related and business purposes).

The board and chapter of the great national cathedral of St Patrick in Dublin undertook a major project to restore its thirteenth-century Lady Chapel in 2012–13,

7 McKelvey, 'Cathedral quarters', op. cit.   8 Galloway, *The cathedrals of Ireland*, p. 154.

including the cleaning of its jewel-like windows. The official cathedral guidebook states that it costs €5,500 per day to run and that charging visitors allows for essential repair and conservation works, which between 2004 and 2014 amounted to over €6m.

Christ Church Cathedral, Dublin – which, along with St Patrick's, is a major historical Dublin tourist attraction and also asks visitors to pay for entry outside service times – has been looked after exceptionally well during the past fifty years. In 1982 a new organ was housed in the north transept, and in 1999 a doorway between the nave and the south transept was inserted to give access to the medieval crypt, wherein the extraordinary treasury is now housed. The magnificent Music Room above the Chapter Room at Christ Church, with a wooden wagon roof and a large Neo-Gothic fireplace, was restored and refurbished in 2014 and is used for events and lectures as well as by the cathedral's choir. However practical and necessary it may have been, a major architectural 'loss' to the Church of Ireland during the period (if not a symbolic one) was the cessation in the 1980s of using the old Synod Hall, which is attached to the cathedral by a delightful 'bridge of sighs'. The former Gothic-style hall now houses Dublinia, an interpretive centre on viking and medieval Dublin.

St Columb's Cathedral, Londonderry, has also been extensively refurbished in recent years, inside and out (works completed in 2011), and is currently in a resplendent state, fitting for its status as the first Anglican cathedral built in the British Isles after the Reformation.

By and large these projects have not involved any substantial reorderings of the internal configurations, although sometimes seating arrangements have been made more flexible and lighting and sound facilities greatly upgraded. However, two rather more radical reorderings of cathedral churches are worth highlighting: Down Cathedral and Lisburn Cathedral.

At Down Cathedral a very long-running series of works on the fabric of the building took place from the mid-1980s right up to 2015. The discovery of extensive dry rot required the complete replacement of the interior plaster walls and vaulting, initially with the cathedral (which is without a parish) being closed between 1985 and 1987; the exterior was also sandblasted. However, post-Good Friday Agreement and in the light of increased optimism about the tourist potential of historic locations across Northern Ireland, during the early 2000s Downpatrick's links with the story of St Patrick brought the availability of grants to open up the cathedral further to the wider community and visitors. With funding from the NI Tourist Board (and others) the cathedral's narthex was re-imagined with the relocation of the ancient granite baptismal font (thought to have been a water trough although possibly the base of a high cross) to the centre of the space, a refurbished gift shop situated behind glass in the former chapter room and a series of interpretive panels on the theme of 'I was a stranger and you welcomed me' (Matthew 25:35), added to the inclusion of practical facilities such as accessible toilets and new lighting. The architectural work was carried out sensitively by Consarc

architects and the graphic design and artistic scheme – including the commissioning of a slate sculpture in the porch drawing the eye upwards – by Alison Gault
(G2 Design). On the completion of the narthex phase of the refurbishment in
2011, Dean Henry Hull remarked,

> For a long time we have been speaking of the Cathedral as a place of pil-
> grimage and prayer, even a house of prayer for all nations. Our Benedictine
> heritage also reminds us of the need to be hospitable in welcoming people as
> we would welcome Jesus. These ideas have been woven into the interpretive
> panels [and the project itself].[9]

A few years later, the cathedral's sanctuary was completely redesigned, with the
aim of making the cathedral more versatile for larger services, the work completed in 2015. A new polished limestone floor brought everything in the body of
the church onto one level, replacing a cramped raised sanctuary. Extraordinary
new seats for clergy with high backs forming the illusion of a reredos, an
oval Communion table and a new lectern (a gift from Holy Cross Monastery,
Rostrevor) were created, all made from stained American oak with brass and
stainless steel crafted in Cookstown. At the two locations on the aisle where the
Scripture is read or preached, a circular mosaic has been placed in the floor; each
has a motif from the Book of Kells and words from the Gospels. A new sound
system was also installed and the cathedral's interior was completely repainted;
once again the architectural work was carried out under the supervision of
Consarc, with the architect Brian Quinn responsible for the sanctuary and furniture design. Some may find the changes surprising; they are certainly very
contemporary in appearance and contrast with the collegiate-style bow-fronted
pews that distinguish the nave. However, boldness may well be a virtue here in
a space which is already full of architectural conceits, quirks and contrasts (to
say nothing of whether or not the gravestone outside it actually marks the location of the remains of Ireland's patron saint). Heritage is vitally important and
must be respected, yet it is also living and, as is often said, does not require the
curtailment of creativity.

Lisburn Cathedral – a lively parish church and the cathedral church of Connor
diocese (although the bishop of Connor is the ordinary of Belfast Cathedral also)
– has also been significantly reordered internally, in a process contemporaneous
with the latter phase of transformation at Down Cathedral. The work, completed
in 2015 and carried out by Des Cairns Architecture, arguably reflects well changes
of thinking in how architects sympathetic to the mission of churches can best serve
them. In 2008, the architect Michael Whitely wrote:

9 Diocese of Down and Dromore, 'Renovated narthex celebrated at Down Cathedral', 14 Oct. 2011,
www.downanddromore.org/news/2011/10/Renovated-narthex-celebrated-at-Down-Cathedral#.
XDD4d1z7Tcs, accessed 5 Jan. 2019.

The primary questions should be 'What type of building do we need to support our vision, mission and ministries?' rather than 'How can we use this building we have inherited?' Poor design will hinder the expression and development of ministry rather than encourage it. Many church leaders have recognised that the building should serve its purpose rather than dictate it, and thus most new church buildings reflect much more honestly their mission and opportunities for community engagement.[10]

The cathedral now – in addition to innovative new state-of-the-art lighting and AV provision, comfortable seating (chairs rather than pews, which had been replacement pews dating from the 1970s), carpeting and general redecoration – contains a cafe area in a transitional space situated through the porch (which is at the base of the tower) and the body of the church, underneath the gallery and separated from the nave by a planar glass screen; during worship times, the area acts as a vestibule and a welcome/parents' zone. The cathedral's chancel had been opened up during alterations carried out in the 1990s, enabling it to be used flexibly for performances as well as liturgical purposes – the style of worship and music at the cathedral during recent decades having moved to reflect the contemporary as well as the traditional. The refashioning of the building has been in many ways very effective and in providing a cafe area is demonstrably community-facing.[11]

PARISH CHURCH REFURBISHMENTS AND REORDERINGS

Much in the same spirit as at Lisburn Cathedral and in line with Whitely's musings above, a number of parish churches have made similar internal adaptations to meet contemporary worship needs and styles and to connect more with their communities. Willowfield Parish Church in East Belfast – a quite dramatic High Victorian polychromatic building designed by John Lanyon in 1872 – was overhauled by Tate Stevenson Architects in the past decade, with a rich-red and cream paint scheme, new lighting, new fabric-covered seats – replacing pews in both the nave and choir (the pews from the latter removed to a new prayer room created near to the porch) – and a sweeping reordering of the chancel, opening it up on a raised dais. Rather extraordinarily for a Church of Ireland setting, a large new Communion table is adapted to also act as a font for baptism by immersion if required. The overall impression of the scheme is, as well as highly practical, flexible and inviting, rather effective in enabling the viewer to appreciate the quality and beauty of the original Victorian roof structure, stained glass windows and pretty mosaic work. The church is also now connected to an adjoining heavily used community centre/suite of halls (the Micah Centre).

10 Michael Whitely, 'The architecture of faith', *Lion & Lamb*, 44 (2008), p. 9.   11 For further details on the scheme, see Paul Harron, 'Cathedral for the community', *Perspective*, 24:2 (Mar./Apr., 2015), pp 28–32.

While less dramatic, a similar type of reordering scheme can be seen in a somewhat similar type of urban Dublin parish: Holy Trinity, Rathmines, where – among other interventions – the chancel area has been morphed into a wide dais, allowing for more informal preaching/presentations/activities and space for a band to lead contemporary-style worship.

Tate Stevenson Architects also carried out the recent redevelopment and provision of discreet accommodation linking to community facilities at Calry Parish Church, Sligo (a Gothic building of 1823 by Joseph Welland) in a modern but sensitive idiom. Meanwhile, within the building of St George and St Thomas' Church in Cathal Brugha Street, Dublin, a low-budget but inventive and subtle insulated wooden space to provide storage and a children's room was introduced at the entrance of the building to the designs of Clancy Moore Architects, winning a prestigious RIAI award in 2009; the assessors described it as 'delicate yet bold'.[12]

There have been many fine reorderings and refurbishments to churches across the island in recent years, bringing old and cherished buildings to life again. Some, such as those at St Matthew's, Shankill, Belfast; St Mary's, Comber; Donaghadee Parish Church; St Mark's, Newtownards; St Colman's, Derrykeighan (Dervock); and St Werburgh's, Dublin,[13] to name only a few, have retained their fabric and furniture largely as was. Others have been sensitively refurbished yet with a rather more interventionist approach, such as Magheralin Parish Church; St George's, Carrick-on-Shannon (which also doubles as a visitor and heritage centre);[14] Ballyholme Parish Church; and Bangor Parish Church (following a fire in 2012). Often, these interventions have involved the introduction of separate quiet spaces for prayer or other ancillary uses (almost twenty-first-century side chapels) – behind glass in the case of Magheralin, for example (completed 2018, Des Cairns Architects).

Special mention should be made in this context of St Thomas' Church, Lisburn Road, Belfast. By the same architect as Willowfield Parish – John Lanyon – and dating from 1870, it is one of Belfast's High Victorian ecclesiastical architectural gems. Once an extremely busy parish, marked changes in demographics and church attendance in this part of the city meant that by 2006 the congregation had much more space than it needed. Between 2006 and 2008 – and in this instance availing of Heritage Lottery Funding to complement other funding sources – Consarc Conservation carried out a range of interventions including the removal of two-thirds of the existing pews from the nave and the introduction of a crèche, a kitchen and a meeting room in the side aisles. The transformation was described in a case study in the RSUA journal *Perspective* by David Evans in highly

---

12 RIAI, 'St George and St Thomas Church', www.irisharchitectureawards.ie/annual-awards/2009, accessed 19 Oct. 2018. The church building sadly closed in 2017, although it may perhaps find a new purpose within the diocesan life of Dublin and Glendalough.   13 For an account of recent developments at St Werburgh's, see Paul Harron (ed.), *New life for churches in Ireland* (Belfast, 2012), pp 131–3.   14 Ibid., pp 42–8.

complimentary terms: 'These spaces, each occupying two bays, are enclosed by glazed screens and such is the finesse in the detailing of the timber frames that their impact on the spatial unity of the interior is negligible ... This project has given new lustre to the interior of a memorable church.'[15] It is indeed a very fine job, so much so that indoor bowls can be played in the space at the rear of the nave from where the pews were removed without it seeming terribly odd.

NEW CHURCH BUILDINGS

As stated at the outset, the Church of Ireland has not required the building of many completely new churches since 1969. In short, it has had no equivalent of Liam McCormick with his delightful portfolio of Co. Donegal Catholic Church buildings in the 1960s and '70s. Those that have been built have taken a largely functional, simple design approach rather than seeking out high architectural ambition – for example, as at St Colman's, Kilroot (1981) or Holy Trinity, Woodburn (1992), both in the vicinity of Carrickfergus. Slightly less utilitarian in appearance is the recent church of St Saviour's, Dollingstown within Magheralin Parish, with a curving façade featuring a large stained-glass window in the gable above the main entrance, although internally it is a Spartan, galleried auditorium. For all of that, these churches meet the present needs of congregations and are perhaps the logical outworking of Whitely's statement above in terms of new builds.

Additionally, church services have often found homes in multifunctional new spaces, which in practical ways are often laudably innovative in terms of serving wider community needs – as at the Jethro Centre in Lurgan (part of Shankill Parish) or St Columba's, Whiterock in north Belfast, which opened in 2011 with an adjacent nursing home.

In Co. Kerry, St Mary's Church, Killorglin was built to replace St James' Church, which had fallen into disrepair. Consecrated in 1997, it was designed in an unusual 'Celtic cruciform' style by Peter O'Farrelly, using ragstone and featuring a high, conical, partially glazed roof and an octagonal worship area, screened off from the rest of the building, which functions as a community centre.

In Northern Ireland, the Troubles and societal unease have necessitated occasional rebuilding or re-siting of church buildings. In the case of the former, Belvoir Parish Church (Church of the Transfiguration) on the southern outskirts of Belfast (strikingly sited on the outer ring road, with a needle-like spire atop a dramatically pitched roof) of 1964 (architects: Ostick and Williams) had to be entirely rebuilt in 1993 following a huge IRA bomb nearby in 1992. As for societal conflict, St Saviour's Church, Craigavon, consecrated in 1972, was abandoned in the mid-1980s and relocated to another part of the area; the new building (by G.P. and P.H. Bell) of 1986 has suffered repeated vandalism and fire damage since – in 1982, 1992 and 2005 – although admirably it has been restored after each attack.

15 David Evans, 'New light, old chancel', *Perspective*, 17:5 (Sept./Oct. 2008), pp 66–70.

CHURCH HALLS

Space does not permit any extensive examination of church halls, and indeed, these, too, are generally highly functional, practical spaces. They are also now often used in addition to (and sometimes as alternatives to) older parish church buildings for 'family friendly', special or community-based services and events. Halls too numerous to recount, of various sizes, have been built up, down and across the island in the past fifty years. Some are even very well designed. By way of interesting and high-quality recent case studies, two may be usefully (if briefly) mentioned.

Seagoe Parish Hall, near Portadown, of 2010, designed by Knox and Markwell Architects, is directly connected to the listed church by way of a glazed link into a fine circular, much-glazed rotunda welcome/coffee bar space with a 'secret' circular prayer room at its core, as well as on into a suite of meeting rooms and a large hall. Careful attention has been paid to materials: a mix of stone, glass, render and zinc. It is a building of great practicality and surprising grace, and – situated as it is just off the M1 motorway – its use is in high demand.[16]

St Elizabeth's Church, Dundonald has built a fine pavilion-like hall on a podium attached to the front of its 1960s church building, designed by Hall Black Douglas in 2015. Such is the success of the thoughtful design that the addition provides a great deal more than extra accommodation for use before and after services and throughout the week, making the entire church complex a much more legible and welcoming building at the heart of a busy community.[17]

WORSHIP SPACES IN SCHOOLS

Within the Church of Ireland educational context, a quite recent pleasing development worth noting (if only briefly) has been the introduction of reflective worship areas/chapels in some secondary schools, as at Kilkenny College, which moved to a new campus in the mid-1980s; at Bandon Grammar School, opened in 2014, housed in a former headmaster's room; at Ashton School in Cork (2016); and at Dundalk Grammar School, opened in 2017, housed in a converted barn.

SEE HOUSES

While space does not afford comment on new rectories of the period (and while many are doubtless admirably designed few are likely to be one of the outstanding houses of their locale in contrast to how it may have been the case

16 For further details on the scheme, see Paul Harron, 'Spiritual, social and surprising', *Perspective*, 19:5 (Sept./Oct. 2010), pp 64–70.   17 For further details on the scheme, see Paul Harron, 'Pavilion of welcome', *Perspective*, 24:3 (May/June 2015), pp 48–52.

pre-disestablishment), very brief mention may be usefully made of new see houses commissioned since 1969.

Interestingly, Armagh has had two 'bites of the cherry' in constructing a new primatial see house in the time frame. Having sold the grand Georgian Palace (in its own large demesne) to the local council for its headquarters, Armagh diocese instructed Edwin Leighton, its diocesan architect, to design a new two-storey, modernist brick villa on the north side of the Cathedral Hill next to the Armagh diocesan office in 1975. The superb dignified and stately gate pillars from the former Palace (by Thomas Cooley) were relocated to the new site, as was a stained-glass panel with the primatial coats of arms for incorporation into the house. C.E.B. Brett actually found enough to admire in the modest building to include it in his *Buildings of County Armagh* volume, remarking that it was 'not, for its period, half bad; and does considerable credit to its architect ... [F]or a private house of this date, it has an exceptionally spacious feeling.'[18] However, it was never a house that enabled much entertaining and people were generally not overly fond of it as a home for the most senior bishop, so following Archbishop Eames' retirement, his successor Archbishop Harper lived temporarily in a house on the mall while a replacement see house, designed by the diocesan architect, this time Stephen Leighton (Leighton Johnston Associates), was built – it was completed in 2012, five years after Archbishop Harper took up office. This is a generously proportioned, nicely detailed and well appointed villa in a – safe, some might say pastiche – neo-Edwardian style;[19] it also incorporates the stained glass panel with the primatial coats of arms in its galleried hallway and it includes a private chapel overlooking the mall and with views across to the observatory and Armagh Royal School (both primatial foundations).

In 2003, An Bord Pleanála finally allowed the former Georgian Bishop's Palace in Kilkenny a change of use to become the Heritage Council's new headquarters; in turn, the diocese of Cashel, Ferns and Ossory erected a new, somewhat more modest Bishop's House in the gardens in 2005.

Kilmore diocese also sold its Georgian pile of a Bishop's Palace and replaced it with a contemporary dwelling to the rear of Kilmore Cathedral, completed in 2013. Once again generously proportioned and nicely detailed with ample space for a bishop's entertaining, the choice of style by Foster Associates of Navan was safe – pastiche Georgian.[20] The RCB has responsibility for providing episcopal residences and clearly rarely seeks out a cutting-edge design role for itself; that aside, these dwellings indicate that these bishops' housing needs have been very well provided for in recent years.

18 C.E.B. Brett, *Buildings of County Armagh* (Belfast, 1999), p. 138.   19 Church of Ireland, 'The archbishop of Armagh receives the keys of the new see house', 4 Feb. 2012, www.ireland.anglican. org/news/3932/the-archbishop-of-armagh-receives, accessed 10 Jan. 2019.   20 Church of Ireland, 'Keys to new Kilmore see house handed over', 14 June 2013, www.ireland.anglican.org/news/4632/ keys-to-new-kilmore-see, accessed 10 Jan. 2019.

ART COMMISSIONING

As for art commissioning, McBride and Larmour rightly noted in their 2000 summation of buildings that 'In general ... the Church of Ireland ... was united in its suspicion of ritual and its caution toward the introduction of furnishings and fittings alien to its generally "low church" attitudes [was] a situation that is only slowly changing today.'[21] There are, of course, exceptions, and there is in 2019 a wider diversity of churchmanship, which has sometimes led to the commissioning of new integrated artwork and craftsmanship in furniture; however, there has been no avalanche of artistic patronage during the period. Tellingly, the pages of the Church of Ireland journal *Search* contain scant focus on the visual arts or crafts in the life of the church in the past thirty or so years, save for a philosophical/reflective historical piece by Hilary Pyle on the creative artist and Christian worship in 1981 (which actually valued the puritan absence of visual art depending on the artist's mindset – a point which has its merit).[22]

Unlike the Methodist Church of Great Britain, for example, which decided to build up a collection of contemporary artworks over the past fifty years,[23] the acquisition and/or commissioning of new visual art within the Church of Ireland has been on an ad hoc basis (and hard to capture), and with the limited need for new church buildings during the past half-century there have been fewer commissioning opportunities per se. However, one area of continuing ecclesiastical patronage of the arts is that of episcopal portraiture. Various dioceses continue to commission portraits of their bishops, not infrequently by notable Irish artists.

The diocese of Armagh's collection for the Armagh Synod Hall includes two oil portraits by the renowned Ulster artist Basil Blackshaw (1932–2016). The first is of Archbishop George Otto Simms, painted in 1969, as he took up his position, and the second is of Archbishop John Ward Armstrong, painted in 1983, halfway through his tenure as primate (1980–6); both are works of considerable presence. Upon Archbishop Alan Harper's retirement in 2011, an enigmatic three-quarter-length portrait of him by noted Northern Irish artist Mark Shields was commissioned.

In 2018, Clogher diocese commissioned the Belfast-based emergent talent Stephen Johnston to capture the likeness of Bishop John McDowell for Clogher Cathedral's collection (an almost continuous run of episcopal portraits since the Reformation), which also includes portraits by Derek Hill (1916–2000) of bishops Hannon, McMullan and Heavener, among others.[24] Johnston's remarkable photorealistic depiction of Bishop McDowell incorporates a nod to historical portraiture

21 Larmour and McBride, op. cit., p. 350. 22 Hilary Pyle, '"Eternity's hostage to time": the creative artist and Christian worship', *Search: A Church of Ireland Journal*, 4:2 (Winter 1981), pp 20–8. 23 The 'Faith and the artist' exhibition of works from the Methodist Church Collection of Modern Art was shown at the Royal Hibernian Academy, Dublin in Nov./Dec. 2018 24 The Clogher portraits up to and including that of Bishop Michael Jackson, by English artist Andrew Festing, are included in J.B. Leslie et al., *Clergy of Clogher* (Belfast, 2006), pp 249–55.

with the inclusion of the Clogher diocesan coat of arms and the arms of Portora Royal School (of which the bishops of Clogher were chairmen until the school's closure and re-formation as Enniskillen Royal School in 2016) in each of the top corners of the large-scale unframed canvas.

The special qualities of cathedral spaces (noted by Paterson above) have allowed opportunities for the creation and commissioning of unique artworks, both permanent and temporary. A widely admired work at Christ Church Cathedral, Dublin, is German-Irish sculptor Imogen Stuart's deceptively simple, lovely 46cm-high bronze *Madonna and child* of 1991 in the Lady Chapel. Stuart (b. 1927) has been described as 'one of the foremost of the all-too-few serious artists actively involved in the creation of religious art in Ireland',[25] and it has been noted that her work 'can be found in almost every religious institution in the country, its Christian basis acceptable to both Protestant and Catholic'.[26]

In 2009, Dean Dermot Dunne of Christ Church Cathedral, Dublin commissioned the Trinity Icon for one of the side chapels. Written by Georgetta Simion – a prolific icon writer of the Romanian school – in the style of the famous Russian iconographer Andrei Rublev, it is now considered to be among the cathedral's aesthetic treasures but also, intrinsically, is part of the spiritual life and outreach of the cathedral. Dunne says that icons and iconography have now become 'an integral part of cathedral life and worship in the cathedral'.[27] Building on a collection of icons presented to Dean Paterson in 2004 by the Romanian iconographer Michael Cucu, the cathedral acquired four more icons written by the accomplished iconographer Adrienne Lord of Dalkey, Co. Dublin. These acquisitions are icons of the Ascension, St George and the Archangel Michael with an icon of the crucifixion in the Latin style. With the return of the stolen relic of the heart of St Laurence O'Toole to the cathedral in 2018,[28] Adrienne Lord was commissioned to write three further icons: one of St Laurence and the other two are of St John and St Mary to accompany the Latin crucifixion. These icons are situated in the north transept, where the heart of St Laurence is now placed in a specially crafted display case designed by the Cork sculptor Owen Turner who also crafted an ambry (cabinet) that houses the holy oils used for blessing the sick and for use at baptisms. Furthermore, in January 2019 Revd Olive Donoghoe – a student of

25 Peter Harbinson, *The Crucifixion in Irish art* (Dublin, 2000), p. 96.   **26** Kate Robinson, 'Imogen Stuart: sculptor, church designer', *Studies*, 91:363 (Autumn 2002), p. 219.   **27** Interview with Dean Dermot Dunne and the author, Jan. 2019.   **28** Following Laurence's canonization in 1225, some relics of his were returned to Dublin where they lay in the considerable relic collection which the cathedral had until the Reformation. Although there is of course no practice of the veneration of a relic in the Church of Ireland, a metal heart-shaped case was for many years put on display in the cathedral's Chapel of St Laud and has traditionally been associated with St Laurence O'Toole – devotees often left Wicklow heather beneath it, symbolizing his link with Glendalough. The heart casket was stolen from the cathedral in March 2012. Following a long-running investigation, the heart was recovered, undamaged, by An Garda Síochána after a six-year absence. It was officially handed over by Assistant Commissioner Pat Leahy to the archbishop of Dublin at a service of choral evensong on the 26 April 2018.

Cucu – presented to the cathedral seven icons representing the seven archangels which she wrote over seven years while on retreat; these are on display on the walls of the south ambulatory.

Staying at Christ Church, major contemporary landscaping works in the grounds of the cathedral were undertaken in 2018 as part of a major tourist project supported by Dublin City Council and Fáilte Ireland (developing sites as part of the Dubline Capital Investment Scheme). While the works addressed drainage issues on the western part of the grounds, a stone labyrinth – or 'garth' – along with the opening of the south carriage gates, the installation of a viewing platform, a steel rendering of the cathedral's timeline and bedding of new shrubbery all form part of a dynamic landscape-art approach to breathing new life into the space at the side and east end of the cathedral. The labyrinth element also invites modern-day pilgrims to undertake a prayerful spiritual 'journey' within the cathedral's precincts.[29]

A similar contemplative labyrinth landscape-art commission was also introduced at St Fin Barre's Cathedral, Cork, in 2015, although there it was composed of grass and gravel beneath a grove of trees.[30] St Fin Barre's, completed in 1870 just as the Church of Ireland was disestablished, is the near-perfect French Gothic Revival architectural creation of William Burges, variously rightly described as 'one of the most remarkable sights in Ireland' and 'the most richly decorated and, of its kind, the most beautiful cathedral of the Church of Ireland',[31] so it is no discredit on its current stewards that artistic commissioning has focused on adding to its precincts rather than to its set-piece fabric.

St Patrick's Cathedral, Dublin took an innovative approach to remembrance, and marking the centenary of the First World War in particular, with its artistic installation in 2014 of a stark, 18ft distressed-steel 'tree of remembrance' in the north transept, symbolically surrounded by barbed wire; over the centenary period of 2014–18 messages of hope were attached to the monument.[32] The concept was that of cathedral staff member Andrew Smith, working with Bisgood Bagnall ironworks of Tallaght. Following its success as an interactive and engaging piece, a poignant temporary artwork of 36,000 handwritten, glistening paper leaves – representing each of the lives lost in the war – was suspended over the cathedral's nave by artist Ciara Ní Cheallacháin in November 2018.[33]

29 Liberties Business Area Improvement District, 'Contemporary landscaping revitalises Christ Church Cathedral', 19 Nov. 2018, www.libertiesdublin.ie/contemporary-landscaping-revitalises-christ-church-cathedral, accessed 20 Feb. 2019. 30 Church of Ireland, 'New labyrinth to be dedicated at Saint Fin Barre's Cathedral, Cork', 15 Oct. 2015, www.churchofirelandcork.com/2015/10/15/new-labyrinth-to-be-dedicated-at-saint-fin-barres-cathedral-cork, accessed 20 Feb. 2019. 31 Galloway, *The cathedrals of Ireland*, pp 61–2. 32 St Patrick's Cathedral, 'The tree of remembrance', 26 May 2016, www.stpatrickscathedral.ie/the-tree-of-rembrance, accessed 10 Jan. 2019. 33 'Cathedral art to honour Irish First World War victims', *Belfast Telegraph*, 31 Oct. 2018, www.belfasttelegraph.co.uk/news/republic-of-ireland/cathedral-art-to-honour-irish-first-world-war-victims-37479239.html, accessed 10 Jan. 2019.

A final cathedral artwork worthy of mention – this time in what we might call applied art – takes us full circle to St Anne's Cathedral, Belfast, with the 2012 commission of *The Titanic pall* made by Helen O'Hare and Wilma Kirkpatrick, textile artists at the University of Ulster. The 12ft by 8ft pall, made of merino felt, backed with Irish linen and dyed an indigo blue, evoking an image of the midnight sea in which the *Titanic* sank, is a memorial to those who died in April 1912, and was a gift of the Friends of St Anne's Cathedral. A large central cross is fashioned from numerous tiny crosses and hundreds more crosses (and a number of Stars of David), in different sizes and shapes, each individually stitched in silk, rayon, metallic and cotton threads, fall away towards the velvet-rimmed edges of the pall, symbolic of lost lives sinking into the dark ocean.

The vision behind the new pall (which the cathedral did not have and required) came from the then dean of Belfast, John Mann, who said at the time that the theme of the lost lives was inspired by Ulster composer Philip Hammond's *Requiem for the lost souls of the Titanic*, which was performed for the first time in the cathedral on the centenary of the sinking. When not used as a pall, the artefact is displayed on the wall of the nave, adjacent to Sir Edward Carson's tomb.[34]

Also in the field of textiles, Belfast Cathedral contains an impressive collection of colourful needlework kneelers depicting a great variety of subjects. Usually undertaken by highly talented but unsung heroes (more often than not, heroines), kneelers and cushions such as these – the beautiful work of grateful hands – grace churches and cathedrals right across the church estate and readers will likely know of many close to their own locales.

Finally, the commissioning of new stained glass has probably proved the most fertile visually artistic territory of all in the past fifty years, although the quality has inevitably been somewhat variable. The art form is beyond my area of expertise but the Church of Ireland has been very fortunate to have been able to avail of the huge knowledge of the stained glass consultant Dr David Lawrence[35] over an extended period of time from the mid-1990s onwards, and the RCB is to be commended on delivering the Gloine stained-glass online research inventory, which provides a great bank of visual and written information: www.gloine.ie. A cursory search of the years 1969–2016 reveals that over twenty studios and a wide range of artists have been involved in creating over 450 new windows. Of the range of names, David Esler is the most prolific and, interestingly, very many of the new windows have been designed in Northern Ireland.

As a concluding, optimistic example of a parish that during our whole period of consideration in the 1970s, '80s, '90s and 2000s consistently sought to commission new glass as part of its ongoing vision to glorify God in the built fabric of its

34 Church of Ireland, 'Lost lives of *Titanic* commemorated in cathedral funeral pall', 20 Mar. 2012, www.ireland.anglican.org/news/4007/lost-lives-of-titanic-commemorated, accessed 26 Oct. 2018.   35 See also David Lawrence, 'Stained glass in the Church of Ireland', *Search: A Church of Ireland Journal*, 19:1 (Spring 1996), pp 5–13.

church building, the parish of Ballyholme, Co. Down is a beacon. In 2018, a new window (by CWS Studio of Lisburn) of St Bronagh completed a unique gallery of Irish saints.[36]

36 Diocese of Down and Dromore, 'New stained glass windows in Ballyholme complete a gallery of Irish saints', 18 Sept. 2018, www.downanddromore.org/news/2018/09/New-stained-glass-windows-in-Ballyholme-complete-a-gallery-of-Irish-saints#.XDe2SVz7Tcs, accessed 10 Jan. 2019.

16

The Church of Ireland and the Irish language

Aonghus Dwane

As it marked the centenary of its disestablishment in 1969, the Church of Ireland contemplated an island that seemed set on significant transformation, both North and South. In Northern Ireland, the relative absence of violence (masking an uneasy status quo) that had existed since partition of the island in the 1920s seemed to be evaporating. The desire to maintain the Union against the backdrop of latent resentment among the nationalist-Catholic minority led to a certain attitude among large sections of the Protestant community, expressed both politically and cultur-ally. This was accentuated with the onset of an armed insurrectionary campaign from the 1970s until the late 1990s, when a transition to a more peaceful environ-ment gradually took place. In the South, meanwhile, notwithstanding economic travails, the Republic in 1969 seemed set fair for a more tolerant atmosphere, as the post-Vatican II era witnessed an increase in ecumenical contacts among Christian churches and communities. In 1969 the Irish language faced differing contexts North and South. In the North it had been systematically neglected under the unionist Stormont administration, and traditional Gaeltacht communities in the Glens of Antrim, Rathlin and other areas had disappeared over time. In the South, the language was embedded in the education curriculum, and there were official expressions of support – often, however, leading to little progress in the develop-ment of the language on the ground, as the influence of English, accentuated by the pervasiveness of radio, television and Anglo-American popular culture, con-tinued to encroach upon surviving Gaeltacht communities. Against these differing backdrops, the Church of Ireland remained an all-island church straddling the two jurisdictions. It also had to bear in mind its long and complex history in regard to the Irish language and the production of Irish-language worship materials. Much of this antecedent history is documented elsewhere, and this essay aims to set out the key developments in the fortunes of the Irish language in the Church of Ireland and, to a lesser extent, the wider Protestant community, both North and South, in the period since 1969.

In 1970, Cosslett Quin's translation of the New Testament, *An Tiomna Nua*, was published, one of the most significant events in making the scriptures available in Irish since Bishop William Bedell's Bible, published posthumously in 1685. It was around the same time, and partly as a response to events in the North, that an ecumenical service in Irish was instituted in Dublin's Christ Church Cathedral during the week of prayer for Christian unity, something that became an annual event. The service, organized jointly by Cumann Gaelach na hEaglaise (the Irish Guild of the Church of Ireland) and the Roman Catholic group Pobal an Aifrinn (the People of the Mass), was for many years presided over jointly by a Church of Ireland bishop (Donald Caird until 2010) and a Roman Catholic bishop, and it has traditionally featured a choir of primary schoolchildren from Gaelscoil na Cille in Ashbourne, Co. Meath. Since 2011, a consort from Christ Church Cathedral choir has also participated in this service. There are hymns, readings and a sermon in Irish, the latter delivered in alternate years by a preacher from the reformed tradition and a Roman Catholic preacher. A reception is held in the cathedral crypt and the service continues to attract a large, mainly Roman Catholic, congregation, having become an established fixture in both the ecumenical and Irish-language calendars in Dublin.

As archbishop of Dublin and subsequently archbishop of Armagh in the 1960s and 1970s, George Otto Simms was noted as an authority on the Book of Kells and Celtic spirituality, as well as for his abiding interest in the Irish language. During a brief period, from 1977 to 1980, it so happened that the three most senior bishops in the Church of Ireland were well-known Irish speakers: George Otto Simms in Armagh, Henry McAdoo as archbishop of Dublin and Donald Caird as bishop of Meath and Kildare. This led Lil Nic Dhonnchadh of Cumann Gaelach na hEaglaise to remark: '*Má tá fonn ar bhuachaill óg dul chun cinn a dhéanamh in Eaglais na hÉireann, ba chóir dó an Ghaeilge a fhoghlaim!*' ('If a young man wishes to progress in the Church of Ireland, he should learn Irish!')

For much of the period since marking the centenary of disestablishment in 1969, the Church of Ireland was exceptionally fortunate in the sterling leadership in Irish-language matters given by Donald Caird. A native Dubliner, Caird had developed a deep love of the language as a result of periods spent in the west Kerry Gaeltachtaí of Dún Chaoin and the Blasket Islands as a student in the 1940s. He became a member of Cumann Gaelach na hEaglaise in this period, and maintained an interest in Irish during periods spent in Northern Ireland as a curate and chaplain, in Wales as a lecturer and in Rathmichael Parish in Co. Dublin in the 1960s as rector. In 1970, Caird assumed episcopal office on his election as bishop of Limerick, Ardfert and Aghadoe, his diocese encompassing the Kerry Gaeltacht areas in Dún Chaoin, the Blaskets, as well as on the Iveragh Peninsula. Around 1970, occasional Irish-language services were being held in the church of Cill Mhaoilchéadair in Dún Chaoin, with the renowned Irish composer Seán Ó Riada and his famous Cór Chúil Aodha choir having participated. In 1975, Caird was appointed by Tom O'Donnell TD, minister for the Gaeltacht, as a member of the first statutory body for the promotion of Irish, Bord na Gaeilge, under the chairmanship of Dr T.K. Whitaker. He went on to become bishop of Meath and Kildare (1976–85) and archbishop of Dublin (1985–96), and was widely recognized nationally as an authority on the Protestant tradition in Irish-language and cultural matters. Caird was in demand as a speaker, delivering addresses at many

Irish-language events over the years, such as the poetry festival *Éigse na Máighe* in Co. Limerick, a service for the centenary *ard fheis* (annual conference) of Conradh na Gaeilge (the Gaelic League) in 1993 and the *Éigse Thomás Bháin* cultural festival in Inis Meáin in 1996, among others. He wrote and lectured on Douglas Hyde (1860–1949), the son of a rector, founder of the Gaelic League and first president of Ireland. Like his hero, Caird encouraged the depoliticization of the Irish language and sought to present it as offering possibilities for mutual understanding rather than division, pointing on numerous occasions to the Church of Ireland's history of engagement with Irish. He noted that Hyde had lamented the coming of politics into the Gaelic League in 1915, whereas prior to this, there had been much revivalist interest among Ulster Protestants, one Richard O'Kane notably signing the minutes of his local Orange Lodge Ristéard Ó Catháin. Leading an ecumenical act of thanksgiving and intercession during a Solemn Pontifical Mass held to mark the silver jubilee of the Gael Linn organization in October 1978, Donald said

> [T]here is at present a real hope that, within the future, everyone who calls himself or herself Irish, whatever part of the country they come from, will feel free to learn and speak Irish without reference to job, religion, politics or personal ideology.

Men and women all over Ireland could speak Irish without any disloyalty to their particular heritage or without the implication of uniformity or 'orthodoxy' in matters of political or religious beliefs, or historical traditions.

When the Irish-language association of Roman Catholic priests, An Sagart, published a translation of the Bible, *An Bíobla Naofa*, in 1981 (containing the first substantial translation into Irish of the Old Testament since Bedell's Bible), Caird was presented with a copy at its launch by his friend Fr Pádraig Ó Fiannachta, who had been central in the translation from Hebrew and Greek into Irish. The Church of Ireland, in its Irish-language services, began to make frequent use of this translation, particularly in view of the fact that no other modern translation of the Old Testament was available. In 1992, Caird was invited to speak at the launch of a reprint of *An Bíobla Naofa*.

Dáithí Ó Maolchoille, who had first joined the *cumann* as a young accountant, steered the work of Cumann Gaelach na hEaglaise over a number of decades, organizing, publicizing and maintaining the regular services in Irish as well as providing assistance in keeping with the Church of Ireland tradition of producing worship material in the language. Accompanying him in this work was *cumann* secretary Leaslaoi Ó Briain, a librarian at Trinity College. With the constant encouragement and support in the House of Bishops of Bishop Caird, it was thus ensured that the Church of Ireland continued to accord recognition to the importance of keeping worship material in Irish up to date. A small sum was also provided each year from central church funds towards services in Irish. An Irish language translation of the 1984 *Alternative Prayer Book* was produced. In 1994, in addition to a supplement to the aforementioned publication, Cumann Gaelach na hEaglaise produced a book of hymns, *Ceol Diaga do Chóracha*. The *Church Hymnal* also featured a number of hymns in Irish, such as a modern translation of the traditional hymn '*Bí, a Íosa, im' chroí-se*' and Seán Ó Riada's '*Ag Críost an Síol*', their inclusion being widely welcomed in the church community. In the fifth edition of the hymnal, published in 2003, the following modern translations are accredited to Donald Caird and the Revd Gary Hastings: '*A Aonmhic na hÓighe*', '*A Rí an Domhnaigh*', '*Síormholadh is glóir duit, a Athair shíoraí*', '*Don Oíche úd i mBeithil*', '*Fáilte Romhat a Rí na nAingeal*', '*Gurab tú mo Bheatha*', and '*Deus meus, adiuva me*'.

The 1990s saw the passing from the Irish scene of a unique experiment in Protestant Irish-language education. Coláiste Moibhí, the only Irish-medium secondary school under Protestant management, was one of the last survivors of the preparatory-college system established in the early years of the Irish state to ensure students intending to train as teachers in primary schools (where the language was and remains compulsory) had a sufficient command of Irish. In its latter years, it shared a campus in Rathmines, south Dublin, with the College of Education (to which it acted as juniorate), and it constituted a living Irish-language community of pupils in the fifth and sixth years of the Leaving Certificate programme. The school survived for some decades longer than its Roman Catholic counterparts, but by the mid-1990s a view was taken at official level that it had outlived its purpose on both educational and financial grounds. By then, most of the students training to be primary teachers for Protestant schools were coming from other secondary schools and only a minority from Coláiste Moibhí. Donald Caird, archbishop of Dublin and chair of its board of management, expressed the hope in 1995 that the closure of Coláiste Moibhí would not mark a point of decline in the Protestant community's interest in the Irish language. Agreement was reached between the College of Education and the Department of Education that the college would establish an extra post of lecturer in Irish and develop an Irish-language enrichment programme. To general regret, Coláiste Moibhí closed. However, something of a remnant of its legacy survived up to 2012 in the monthly Irish-language service of Holy Communion held in the College of Education chapel on the Rathmines campus. The story of Coláiste Moibhí and the preparatory colleges was documented in a book by the late Valerie Jones, *A Gaelic experiment*, published in 2006.

Since the 1980s, the Dublin diocesan magazine *Church Review* featured a regular Irish-language column, '*Scéala na nGael*', written by Risteard Seathrún MacÉin, with details of upcoming services and including regular competitions. In 2005, the *Church of Ireland Gazette* under the editorship of Canon Ian Ellis instituted an occasional column in Irish, which was a significant departure at the time.

The national cathedral in Dublin, St Patrick's, has for many years hosted a celebration of Holy Communion in Irish on St Patrick's Day. Close by, the diocese's Christ Church Cathedral had for many years been home to a regular pattern of services in Irish, including a monthly celebration of Holy Communion, *An Chomaoineach Naofa*, in the Lady Chapel on Sunday evenings and, in the 1980s and early 1990s, a monthly choral service involving secondary schools.

Since the beginning of the 1970s, years of violent conflict in Northern Ireland had seen increasing polarization between the communities, with the Irish language being one of the casualties. This greatly compounded its deliberate marginalization under the Stormont administration since the 1920s. Successive efforts to address the political alienation of the nationalist minority, and stem an enduring level of support on the part of a section of that community for republican paramilitary activity, bore little fruit until the signing of the Anglo-Irish Agreement in 1985 in the face of overwhelming unionist opposition. Measures were envisaged to address the position of the Irish language, which was in a parlous state. Identified increasingly by some as a cultural signifier of militant nationalism and republicanism, it attracted little interest on the part of most of the Protestant population. Valiant efforts were made by Irish-language enthusiasts, overwhelmingly drawn from the nationalist community, to promote Irish. An Irish-speaking mini-Gaeltacht district had been established by a number of families on the Shaw Road in the late 1960s. An Irish-medium primary school, Bunscoil Phobal Feirste, was established in 1971, and for thirteen years survived without state assistance, receiving official recognition only in 1984. An Irish-medium secondary school was established in Belfast in 1987 and given formal recognition in 1991. A daily newspaper, *Lá*, was launched in 1984, and a cultural centre, An Cultúrlann, was established on the Falls Road. However, much of this activity attracted at best limited support from official circles in Northern Ireland and, against a backdrop of ongoing conflict, featured little involvement or support from Protestants there. Efforts at a political level to establish an end to the conflict gathered pace in the early 1990s and a ceasefire was declared by the IRA in 1994. This created space for a revival of interest in Irish among some in the Protestant community. A new agency, An tIontaobhas Ultach (later renamed the ULTACH Trust), was established in 1990 to promote Irish on a cross-community basis. It set out to develop positive attitudes towards Irish through a programme of community engagement across various sectors of society and provided support for a range of voluntary groups, investing in projects aimed at the development of networks of active Irish speakers. It also provided some support for Irish-medium schools and engaged in advocacy work on provision for Irish in broadcasting. The signing of the Good Friday Agreement in 1998 ushered in a new era of power-sharing and dialogue in Northern Ireland, and formal commitments were made in relation to the language by the British government. In the Presbyterian community, in 1997, the worship group An Tor ar Lasadh (the Burning Bush) was established, holding monthly services featuring music and readings in Irish, with Revd Bill Boyd at Fitzroy Presbyterian Church, Belfast. The group remains active.

On 18 September 2004, a translation in Irish of the new *Book of Common Prayer – Leabhar na hUrnaí Coitinne* – was published by Cumann Gaelach na hEaglaise and launched at a conference on Celtic worship in Down Cathedral, organized jointly by An tIontaobhas Ultach, Iomairt Cholm Cille (the Irish-Scottish Gaelic cultural agency, later renamed Colmcille) and Cumann Gaelach na hEaglaise. The book had been translated by Canon Gary Hastings, then rector of Westport, a northerner and accomplished traditional Irish flute player. The Downpatrick event featured talks on various aspects of the history of the Irish language in Protestant churches, a service and contributions from Scottish and Irish Gaelic singers. *Leabhar na hUrnaí Coitinne* had an initial print run of approximately 1,000 hardback copies and its publication was supported by Bord na Leabhar Gaeilge and the General Synod's Literature Committee.

In the west of Ireland, meanwhile, an Irish-language component was introduced to the main Sunday service at St Nicholas' Collegiate Church in Galway city, under choir director Mark Duley and rector Patrick Towers, with several responses being sung in Irish. In 2006, St Nicholas' held a bilingual Eucharist with singers from the Aran Islands and Scotland.

Christ Church Cathedral in Dublin became an increasing focus of Irish-language activities in the first decade of the new millennium. New settings in Irish of the canticles '*Magnificat*' and '*Nunc Dimittis*' were composed by choir member Caitríona Ní Dhubhghaill, and were followed by compositions by other choir members. In 2006, Áras Éanna, an arts centre on the Aran Islands, partnered with the cathedral to host a joint bilingual summer school on the Celtic cultural revival of the late nineteenth and early twentieth centuries, featuring lectures, tours and performances in Irish and English, held in the cathedral in Dublin and on the islands of Inis Oírr and Inis Meáin. As part of this initiative, which was encouraged and supported by then Dean Desmond Harman (who attended the entire programme in Dublin and on the islands), the cathedral choir under director Judy Martin and organ scholar Tristan Russcher prepared a service of evensong in Irish. In 2007, in collaboration with the cultural agency Colmcille, a major symposium on St Columba took place in the cathedral, featuring lectures on the saint, evensong and a concert with Irish Gaeltacht-based artists and Scottish Gaelic psalm-singers. An art exhibition inspired by '*Amra Cholm Cille*', the oldest poem in Irish, was held in the crypt. With the advent of Dean Dermot Dunne and new choir director Ian Keatley, choir members such as Felicity McElroy and Simon McHale embarked on further compositions of choral settings for evensong in Irish. In Trinity College Dublin, meanwhile, under chaplain Revd Darren McCallig and in cooperation with the college's Irish language office and the student body An Cumann Gaelach, the college chapel hosted bilingual services of evensong sung by the chapel choir to coincide with the annual *Éigse na Tríonóide* festival in Trinity.

A number of works have been published recording various aspects of the history of the Irish language in the Church of Ireland. Important examples are Nicholas Williams' *I bprionta i leabhar: na Protastúin agus prós na Gaeilge, 1567–1724* (1986) and several works by the Methodist lay preacher and notable Irish-language writer and teacher Risteard Ó Glaisne, including his biographies of Cosslett Quin and

Douglas Hyde. He also wrote *Gaeilge i gColáiste na Trionóide, 1592–1992* (1992), *Coláiste Moibhí* (2002) and *De Bhunadh Protastúnach* (2003). Ó Glaisne was a recipient of the prestigious Gradam an Phiarsaigh, being presented with the Irish-language award in 1988 by then President Patrick Hillery, who said, '*I measc na ngaiscíoch sin a bhfuilimid go léir faoi mhórchomaoin acu, tá Risteárd Ó Glaisne, bail ó Dhia air. Duine umhal, duine crúóghach, duine geanúil, gealgáireach nach santaíonn glóir ná buala bos é Risteárd.*' ('Among those heroes to whom we are grateful is Risteárd Ó Glaisne, God bless him. Risteárd is a humble person, an industrious person, a warm and joyful person who does not seek glorification or applause.')

In 1989, President Hillery was presented at Áras an Uachtaráin with a new history of the Irish language in the Church of Ireland, *An Ghaeilge in Eaglais na hÉireann*, where he was joined by Dáithí Ó Maolchoille and Leaslaoi Ó Briain of Cumann Gaelach na hEaglaise, and author Risteárd Giltrap, principal of Coláiste Moibhí. This work set out, for the general reader, a chronology of the church's contribution to Irish in three successive stages since the seventeenth century: evangelical, antiquarian and revivalist. Giltrap in his foreword expressed appreciation for Donald Caird having steered him towards valuable sources of information, and observed of Caird's leadership in relation to the language that 'a good example was better than goodwill'. In 2003, the Irish language station TG4 broadcast a substantial documentary on the history of Protestants and Irish entitled *No rootless colonists: na Gaeil-Phrotastúnaigh*.

Donald Caird maintained his long-standing passion for Irish after his retirement as archbishop in 1996. As well as giving talks and attending cultural events, he celebrated Holy Communion on a regular basis for the *cumann*, and appeared in a number of television programmes on the Irish channel TG4. In 2010, at the annual Irish-language service for church unity at Christ Church Cathedral, he dedicated a new altar frontal in memory of the late Cumann Gaelach na hEaglaise secretary Leaslaoi Ó Briain. In the same year, at a special dinner in the headquarters of Comhaltas Ceoltóirí Éireann in Monkstown, Co. Dublin, the Gradam an Phiarsaigh award for services to the Irish language was presented by Pat Carey TD, minister for the Gaeltacht, to Donald Caird, with his wife Nancy accepting the award on his behalf. Caird died in June 2017.

In late 2008/early 2009, a delegation from the Church of Ireland's Church in Society Committee met with representatives from the Ulster Unionist Party and Democratic Unionist Party in Northern Ireland to put forward the church's view on the Irish language. In particular, the view was advanced that an interest in the language could be entirely compatible with a unionist political outlook, and a document was presented to the parties, and in May 2009, to General Synod.

Following the death of Leaslaoi Ó Briain in 2007, Church of Ireland historiographer Dr Kenneth Milne and this writer joined Dáithí Ó Maolchoille on the *coiste* (committee) of Cumann Gaelach na hEaglaise, and options were considered in relation to securing the work of the *cumann* for the future. Arising out of this, regular general and committee meetings were put in place, and services and occasional events publicized. It was nonetheless clear that reliance on voluntary effort and occasional keynote events alone was unlikely to ensure a consistent and sustainable development of the language in the longer term, in the Church of Ireland community. In 2010, the cross-border agency for the promotion of Irish (and successor to Bord na Gaeilge) Foras na Gaeilge invited expressions of interest from community organizations seeking to employ Irish-language development officers. Looking ahead to the marking in 2014 of the centenary of its foundation, Cumann Gaelach na hEaglaise submitted an application and was successful in securing funding to employ an officer and undertake a programme of activities. Caroline Nolan was appointed as full-time Irish-language development officer of Cumann Gaelach na hEaglaise in 2011 and the *coiste* was expanded to include some additional members, including Canon George Salter and former primary school principal Máire Roycroft, both from Cork, and well-known for their interest in Irish and its promotion over several decades.

The *cumann* embarked on a new era of expansion and development, hosting its own stand at the 'marketplace' at General Synod and producing a prayer card in Irish. The *cumann* also established a presence at the annual Irish-language festival Oireachtas na Gaeilge, holding a service of reflection and thus adding an important ecumenical dimension to the gathering. An annual competition was organized for secondary schools, and a trophy, Corn Bedell, presented to the school making the greatest effort in the promotion of Irish each year. The centenary of the foundation of Cumann Gaelach na hEaglaise was duly marked in April 2014 with a special service in St Ann's Church in Dublin's Dawson Street (where the parish rooms had hosted its initial meetings in 1914). A mobile panel exhibition detailing the history of the language in the Church of Ireland and of the *Cumann* itself was produced. In June 2014, members of the *cumann* were hosted by President Michael D. Higgins at a reception in Áras an Uachtaráin, where the bishop of Cashel and Ossory, Michael Burrows (patron of the *cumann*), gave an address and presented a set of the *cumann*'s publications to the president; and in August the present author's biography of Donald Caird was launched.

On her state visit to Ireland in 2011, Queen Elizabeth II used some words of Irish when addressing those assembled at the state banquet in Dublin Castle. This gesture had an influence in relaxing some traditional suspicion of the language among Protestants and unionists in Northern Ireland. A new group, Turas, pioneered by Linda Ervine, sister-in-law of the late loyalist leader David Ervine, and funded by Foras na Gaeilge, was established at the East Belfast Mission in traditionally loyalist east Belfast, and it continues to run courses in the Irish language there. A bus tour of Gaelic east Belfast has been pioneered by Gordon McCoy of Turas.

Cumann Gaelach na hEaglaise established links with a group holding regular Irish-language services at St George's Church in Belfast, and the *cumann*'s Irish-language development officer Caroline Nolan was invited to an event there, at which Charles, prince of Wales, and Camilla, duchess of Cornwall, visited a stand hosted by the *cumann* and expressed interest in its work. *Leabhar na hUrnaí Coitinne* (2004) of course contains prayers in Irish for the queen and the president of Ireland, as appropriate. The *cumann* also established a website and social media presence, ensuring its work could reach a new audience. The use of the Irish language in services continued to be supported by the *cumann*, with developments including a regular service of Holy Communion at St Fin Barre's Cathedral in Cork, services at St James' Church in Dingle, at St Canice's Cathedral in Kilkenny, at Christ Church Cathedral in Waterford, as well as a new monthly service at St Patrick's Cathedral in Dublin, with the encouragement of its dean, William Morton.

The output of published material produced or supported by the *cumann* also increased. In 2013, at the suggestion of Bishop Michael Burrows and reflecting on experiences in Wales, a new service book in bilingual format, *Holy Communion and other services*, was produced, the book being launched at a symposium in Christ Church Cathedral with guests from the church in Wales in attendance. In St Canice's Cathedral in Kilkenny, a new hymn book, *Ardaigí Bhur gCroí*, with an accompanying CD, was launched in 2015. A special order of service for the 1916 centenary commemoration was produced in bilingual format by the church's Liturgical Advisory Committee. In 2017, the *Church of Ireland Directory* began featuring a bilingual list of parish names, together with an explanation of their meaning. Risteard Giltrap's book was reissued in bilingual format, with *An Ghaeilge in Eaglais na hÉireann / The Irish language and the Church of Ireland* being launched at Christ Church Cathedral in January 2019 by Bibi Baskin, a former editor of the Irish language newspaper *Anois*, television personality and member of the Church of Ireland.

In 2016, Dáithí Ó Maolchoille, the long-serving *cathaoirleach* and treasurer of Cumann Gaelach na hEaglaise, and a key figure in maintaining the tradition of Irish-language preservation and promotion in the Church of Ireland throughout the period of time covered by this retrospective, was succeeded in the role by Trevor Sargent, former Green Party leader and TD, who was ordained to the priesthood in 2018.

In 2019, the position of the Irish language in the Church of Ireland and wider Protestant community generally seems healthier, and its future more secure than in 1969. Perhaps the wish expressed by Donald Caird forty-one years earlier, 'that men and women all over Ireland could speak Irish without any disloyalty to their particular heritage or without the implication of uniformity or "orthodoxy" in matters of political or religious beliefs, or historical traditions', is slowly being realized.

17

Church of Ireland archives and publishing

Raymond Refaussé

In 1969 the state of the archives of Church of Ireland was thus. Some church records had been transferred to the Public Record Office of Ireland after 1922, although, of course, all those records which had been in the PROI in 1922 had been destroyed; a few collections had been deposited in the Public Record Office of Northern Ireland; and a small number were in the Representative Church Body Library in Dublin. However, the vast majority of the church's records remained in the custody of the bodies that had created them: the parishes, dioceses, cathedrals and the two central church administrative bodies – the General Synod and the Representative Church Body. And, for the most part, everyone seemed happy with this arrangement.

However, things were beginning to change both in the Irish archival world and in the Church of Ireland. The opening of a new Department of Manuscripts in Trinity College Dublin in 1971 and a new Public Record Office in Belfast in 1972 had introduced archivists and researchers to higher standards for the care and custody of records. In the church, the 1970s witnessed diocesan re-organizations, the amalgamations of rural parishes and the closure of some prominent Dublin churches, with a consequent emergence of concern about how the care of church records was to be effectively managed. In 1971 the report of the Library and Ecclesiastical Committee of the General Synod warned that the 'Church of Ireland should not be too complacent about the care of its records',[1] and indeed there was little to be complacent about. The new RCB Library, opened in 1969, had little provision for church records, with only a small strong room, while the new Church of Ireland House in Dublin, the place of custody of the records of the General Synod and the Representative Church Body, had been similarly equipped with very rudimentary records storage. Elsewhere, parish records were frequently crammed into damp wall safes, while diocesan records accumulated in offices and cathedral records were exiled to unsuitable towers and crypts. There were, of course, some exceptions. Bishop Richard Hanson, newly arrived from England, where archival standards in both church and state were light years ahead of Ireland, created an archives room in Clogher cathedral; Maurice Talbot, the

1 *Journal of the General Synod … of the Church of Ireland* (hereinafter *General Synod Journal*). Report of the Library & Ecclesiastical Records Committee, 1971.

energetic dean of Limerick, upgraded the cathedral strong room to provide for the records, not just of St Mary's cathedral but also of the city parishes; and a number of parishes abandoned wall safes in favour of large stand-alone safes. However, the prevalent archival culture of the Church of Ireland was one of disinterested neglect.

The first significant incidence of neglect had emerged in 1970 with the discovery that the muniments of Christ Church Cathedral, Dublin, had been consigned to the crypt, where they had been damaged by damp. A report from the distinguished keeper of manuscripts in Trinity College, William O'Sullivan, noted that the manuscripts were 'sopping wet', the bindings covered in fungus, and that some had begun to crumble. The damaged material was gradually dried out and, for the most part, salvaged, but recommendations about the significance of the collection and how it should be restored were largely ignored.[2] Surprisingly, this disaster attracted little attention. There was no mention of it in the reports of the Library and Ecclesiastical Records Committee (although the 1971 reference to complacency may have been a veiled reference) and it does not seem to have been discussed by the Representative Church Body, or if so the discussion was not minuted.

However, worse was to follow, for in 1974 it emerged that the records of the united dioceses of Dublin and Glendalough had been seriously damaged by damp, many beyond repair, having been abandoned in the basement of the Synod Hall. On this occasion the disaster could not be quietly dealt with as it had come to the attention of the Irish Manuscripts Commission, which was the official advisor to the government on archival matters. A memo from the chief officer of the RCB revealed that the condition of the Dublin Registry had prompted the IMC to express its concern about the conservation of Church of Ireland records throughout the country, to emphasize their importance for historical research and to offer assistance. The chief officer's memo recommended that the Finance Committee, in effect the executive of the RCB, should be consulted with a view to urgent action being initiated for 'information from various sources indicates that valuable records have already been lost, sold, stolen, and have been allowed to rot'. The conclusion of the memo was very clear: 'The Church of Ireland is open to accusations of carelessness and neglect. The ideal solution seems to be a central repository with a qualified custodian.'[3] However, while the Finance Committee noted the problem and expressed its anxiety that something should be done and practical help sought, it concluded that 'finance is not available for a Church of Ireland central repository'.[4] A subsequent 'full and frank' discussion between representatives of the RCB and representatives of the IMC emphasized the seriousness of the situation and the need for action, and this, together with increased demands on the RCB Library to take custody of parish records, was sufficient to prompt

2 Muniments of Christ Church Cathedral, Dublin, Representative Church Body Library, (hereinafter RCBL) ʿ6/5/8/1. 3 Minute book of the Representative Church Body, RCBL, RB/1/34–5. 4 Minute book of RCB Finance Committee, RCBL RB/3/61.

a request to the RCB to advise the 1977 General Synod on the establishment of a central repository for Church of Ireland records. This task was delegated to the Library and Ecclesiastical Records Committee, which reported that 'a central archive repository for Church of Ireland records is an urgent necessity, the most likely site for such a development being the Library/Divinity Hostel complex at Braemor Park'.[5] Concerns about the wisdom of having all the records in one location, the absence of accurate information on the extent of local holdings, the availability of appropriate staffing, and of course finance, delayed what to many was the appropriate course of action, and it was not until June 1980 that the RCB agreed that a central repository should be established in the RCB Library and that an archivist should be recruited. The archivist, Raymond Refaussé, who had been a member of staff in the Department of Manuscripts in Trinity College Dublin, began work in January 1980, with the principal tasks of surveying the parish and diocesan records and preparing an estimate of the amount of space that would be required for an archive centre.[6]

Meanwhile the Public Record Office of Ireland had resumed the microfilming of parish registers in 1971, with a survey of records in the diocese of Meath, which revealed that some 18 per cent of records were missing.[7] This and subsequent surveys served to emphasize the extent of the Church's archival problem. The experience of the PROI survey was replicated in the responses to the archivist's survey of parish records, as the returns to questionnaires sent to parish clergy revealed, at least in the first instance, that significant quantities of records could not be located. Equally worrying was the attitude of clergy. Many dutifully returned the questionnaire, some even expressing enthusiasm for the project, but a significant number simply did not respond, and a number chose to be outraged by what they considered an unnecessary additional administrative burden.

But worse was to follow, for in 1982 the RCB decided that, for financial reasons, it could not continue to employ the archivist beyond his initial three-year contract.[8] The Library and Ecclesiastical Records Committee urged that this decision be reconsidered, but the Finance Committee responded that difficult decisions had to be made. The issue was raised at the General Synod, was discussed in the pages of the *Church of Ireland Gazette*, and was a matter of some concern in the wider archival community. The problem was resolved by the retirement of the RCB librarian and the amalgamation of the librarian and archivist posts. From the beginning of 1984 the RCB Library would be both a library for the Church of Ireland Theological College and the wider church, and the official repository for the archives of the Church of Ireland, with two members of staff – a librarian and archivist and a library assistant.

---

5 Minute book of the Library & Archives Committee, RCBL, RB/15/3.   6 Minute book of the RCB, RCBL, RB/1/36.   7 Public Record Office of Ireland. Inventories of the parochial records of the Diocese of Meath (Church of Ireland).   8 *General Synod Journal*. Report of the Library & Ecclesiastical Records Committee for 1982.

The final piece of the new archival strategy was the provision of storage accommodation for archives at Braemor Park, the estimates for which had been identified as a priority for the archivist. The initial estimates were rejected and the development was scaled down to meet financial targets. Furthermore, the new accommodation, an extension to the RCB Library, was to be shared with the Theological College, which would have teaching facilities on the first floor, and the ground floor would be a purpose-built archives strong room. The new facility was completed in 1984 and opened by Archbishop John Armstrong

If the road to apparent archival respectability for the Church of Ireland had been long and somewhat troubled, nonetheless it had been achieved by meeting the recommendations of the Library and Archives Committee. The church had accepted that it had a responsibility to care for its archives, an archivist had been appointed, and archival storage had been provided at the RCB Library. Building on this foundation the archival dimension of the church developed significantly in the 1980s and 1990s. There was a steady flow of parish records from local custody to the RCB Library, due in no small measure to an initiative of the principal of the Theological College, Canon Jim Hartin, who invited the librarian and archivist to give an annual seminar to the ordinands on the care and custody of church records. As well, large collections of cathedral and diocesan collections, such as those of the two Dublin cathedrals and the diocesan records of Meath and Kilmore, Elphin and Ardagh were transferred to Braemor Park. These archival collections were augmented by the deposit of records of church-related organizations such as the Sunday School Society for Ireland, the Association for the Promotion of Christian Knowledge and the Church Education Society. In their heyday these bodies had offices and staff but as the church contracted so the scale of their activities was reduced and they were largely run by volunteers. They were glad to find a home for their records and the RCB Library was equally glad to take them in as they so obviously complemented the official archives of the church.[9]

While the growing body of records in the library was a gratifying vindication of the need for an archival facility it became quickly apparent that the policy was becoming a victim of its own success. By 1989 some 80 per cent of the storage accommodation had been filled and a considerable backlog of cataloguing had built up. The introduction of computerization in 1990, and, specifically, the commissioning of a specially designed database to catalogue parish records, eased the pressure somewhat. However, the large diocesan, cathedral and manuscripts collections, which were not susceptible to computerization, remained a problem and one which could only be solved by additional professional staff, but it was not until 1998 that Susan Hood, an archives graduate of London University, was appointed as assistant librarian and archivist.[10]

Meanwhile, the archival responsibilities continued to mount. In 1991 the church plate inventory was transferred from Church of Ireland House, and in the

9 *General Synod Journal.* Reports of the Library & Archives Committee.   10 Ibid.

following year Mary Furlong was appointed to develop and manage, in the library, a church plate database. Many of the chalices, patens and flagons had been presented and, as they often had inscriptions, they significantly complemented the church's written records. A similar complement to the written records was the establishment of an oral archives in 1996, which aimed to record the reminiscences of prominent members of the church, beginning with the veteran Dublin churchman Archdeacon Raymond Jenkins. Furthermore, in 2000 it was agreed that the episcopal portrait collections, which were scattered in see houses, deaneries and cathedrals, should be regarded as archives since in many instances they included the only known images of Church of Ireland bishops. This required the development and management of another database in the library and, inevitably, the subsequent transfer of portraits that could not be hung locally.[11]

As the quantity of archival material in the library continued to grow the Library and Archives Committee became increasingly concerned about the need for additional accommodation for storage, staff and researchers. In 1994, a strategy paper developed by Desmond Linton, a member of the committee and a prominent figure in Irish library circles, suggested that the solution for the short to medium term was that the Theological College should vacate the library and that the resultant space should be redeveloped.[12] The building of an extension to the Theological College made this strategy possible and in 1998 the reordering of the library was completed. A new archives-storage area was created from a former television studio and boiler house and the teaching area on the first floor was converted into reading rooms.

The official opening of the reordered library by David Ford, Regius Professor of Theology in Cambridge, ushered in a new phase of the church's archival life. In 1999 the records of the General Synod and the Representative Church Body, and the collection of redundant church plate were transferred to the library as Church of Ireland House was being refurbished. However, following the completion of the refurbishment, these collections did not return to Church of Ireland House but remained in the library, and while they were a welcome addition to the archival holdings in Braemor Park, they occupied a significant part of the new storage accommodation. While these accessions had been unexpected, a further tranche of accessions was the result of a deliberate policy decision by the RCB. Acting on the advice of the Library and Archives Committee, it recommended that parishes should mark the millennium by closing registers of baptisms and burials in the year 2000, opening new registers and transferring the closed registers to the archives. This recommendation was in essence a response to the realization that a significant number of parishes were still using registers that were over a hundred years old, and in some instances substantially older, and that such records were at risk through continued use and poor storage. The response from the parishes largely mirrored that to the parish records survey, with many readily responding

11 Ibid.   12 Minutes book of the Library & Archives Committee, RCBL, RB/15/3.

and others reluctant to purchase new registers while the current ones still had empty pages. Nonetheless the initiative significantly added to the collections in the library. Many of the registers that were transferred in the years after 2000 were in poor physical condition and so a significant increase in the otherwise small budget for conservation, a consequence of the Celtic Tiger years, was welcome.[13]

With the increased collections came an increased use of them, principally by historians and genealogists, and the related responsibility of making lists and indexes of the collections as widely available as possible. With cooperation of the IT staff in Church of Ireland House, more and more of the handlists of collections, which previously had been available only in the library, were made available online through special library pages on the Church of Ireland website. In 2012 the introduction of an 'Archive of the Month' feature, initiated by the assistant librarian and archivist, was successful in highlighting to the wider world important aspects of the collections. However, the most important online cataloguing initiative, begun in 2011, was a project to photograph and catalogue the library's extensive holdings of architectural drawings of church buildings. This work was carried out by the architectural historian Michael O'Neill, and was the first time such an ambitious project had been attempted for any collection of Irish drawings.[14]

Throughout the first decade of the twenty-first century there was a steady stream of archives and manuscript collections into the library and by 2010 the Library and Archives Committee was warning of the need for more storage. In the short term this was met by transferring uncatalogued and closed collections to the basement of the refurbished Church of Ireland House, which had been equipped with a large mobile shelving unit. But by 2013 the storage problems were deemed to be critical and a presentation was made to the Executive Committee of the RCB in the hope that the projected renovation of the Theological Institute could be accompanied by an extension to the RCB Library. However, while a significant investment in the refurbishment of the institute was approved no development of the library was sanctioned and reluctantly the librarian and archivist agreed to the only alternative – the use of commercial storage for closed, uncatalogued and little-used collections.[15]

While the development of a Church of Ireland archive in the RCB Library had been an undoubted success there was one aspect of the project that remained problematic, and that was the location. There was no significant local interest in Churchtown and no passing trade. Those who used the archives commuted to do so. And so the development of ancillary facilities that might have complemented and further developed interest in the archives did not take place – no exhibition facility, no public lectures, no seminars on sources for church history. But if people could not be brought to Braemor Park for such outreach then the outreach would have to be taken to them, and this was done through the medium of publication.

13 *General Synod Journal*. Reports of the Library & Archives Committee. 14 Ibid. 15 Ibid.

In 1994 a parish register series was initiated, followed in 2002 with a texts and calendars series, which aimed to publish important source materials such as vestry books, churchwardens' accounts and diocesan visitations. The parish register series had been originated and published by the RCB Library as, remarkably, the Church of Ireland did not have its own publishing facility.[16]

In 1969 the church's liturgical resources, the *Book of Common Prayer* and the *Church Hymnal* were published by Oxford University Press, while the administrative annuals, the *Journal of the General Synod* and the *Church of Ireland Directory* appeared under the imprint of the APCK and Irish Church Publishing, respectively. In addition, the church's newspaper, the *Church of Ireland Gazette*, and its theological journal, *New Divinity* (later *Search*), were independent productions. Not that there was anything new about this. The disestablished Church of Ireland had long been using outside agencies for publication purposes, especially the APCK, while the members of the Divinity School in Trinity College, who largely constituted the church's theological dimension, tended to make their own publishing arrangements. The church had established a Publications Committee in 1951 and this had been restructured in 1961 to encourage the writing of historical and doctrinal works, to recommend to the Standing Committee grants to facilitate publication, and to transact business with the APCK and others to complete publication.[17] This was essentially the situation in 1969 and seemed, in the absence of any significant comment to the contrary, to be serving the church's needs.

With the centenary of disestablishment looming, 1969 presented a golden opportunity for Church of Ireland publishing, but as in the past, much was left to others, with the Publications Committee assuming a distinctly limited role. Of the two major publications, R.B. McDowell's *The Church of Ireland, 1869–1969* was published by Routledge, while *Irish Anglicanism, 1869–1969*, edited by Fr Michael Hurley, was published by Allen Figgis. The McDowell book had been discussed by the committee, which had concluded that it 'had no function in this matter', and there was no mention at all of the Hurley book in their minutes. Much of their concentration was on what were described as the 'centenary essays', which were published by APCK as *Directions: theology in a changing world*, edited by Hugh Woodhouse, Jim Hartin and Kenneth Milne, and they also recommended for publication a short study by Hugh Shearman, *How the Church of Ireland was disestablished*. Other disestablishment publications appeared, which owed nothing to the Publications Committee or the APCK, such as the proceedings of a Belfast conference, booklets by clergy such as Robin Eames, Stephen Cave and Michael Kennedy and an excellent catalogue of an exhibition in the National Gallery curated by Hilary Pyle.[18]

Following the disestablishment celebrations, the Publications Committee turned its attention to more prosaic matters. A list of subjects discussed in 1973 for

16 Ibid.   17 Minute book of the General Synod Publications Committee, RCBL, GS/2/29/1/1.   18 Ibid.

possible publications gives a flavour of this. Among the topics were belief in God, Christian marriage, belief in the future life and RE material for schools. Almost, although not quite, absent from the list was the type of controversial literature that had been so much a part of Church of Ireland publishing in the late nineteenth and early twentieth century – writings that sought fervently to define the Church of Ireland not by what it was but by what it was not, that is, Roman Catholic. However, while such a shift in emphasis suggested a growing maturity and confidence in the church, the old failings remained. These topics were discussed at length in the Publications Committee but few of them saw the light of published day.[19]

By the mid-1970s concern had emerged that the committee was no longer fit for purpose. After consultations with the Communications Committee, it was agreed that while there was a continuing need for a Publications Committee a new constitution was needed. In 1974 the committee was reconstituted, the principal effect of which was to reinforce the place of the APCK in Church of Ireland publishing. Of the thirteen members of the committee, five were to be APCK nominees. The Publications Committee could appoint readers for manuscripts, but it was the APCK Committee of Management that would have the final decision as to whether or not a manuscript would be published, and, in addition, the Publications Committee would report annually to both the Standing Committee and the APCK.[20] This new arrangement provoked a characteristically trenchant response from Revd Desmond Harman, who suggested that the Publications Committee was irrelevant, should be dissolved and that the APCK should be invited to fulfil the duties of the Committee.[21]

The committee continued as before, but in its report to the 1978 General Synod expressed concern about the lack of funds for the publication of new literature. The APCK's book stock had been destroyed in a fire in its Dublin book shop in 1976 and there was a shortage of appropriate literature for schools, teachers, students, confirmation candidates, lay readers and 'the many who ask for information about the Church of Ireland'. The committee noted that a revised edition of Kenneth Milne's church history and an updated edition of J.L.B. Deane's church handbook would require a considerable subsidy if they were to be published at a reasonable price. Tellingly, the committee noted that 'Neither the APCK nor the Central Funds of the Church are able to provide such a subsidy'. The agreed solution was a public appeal, which by January 1979 had realized £1,450, leading the committee to the obvious conclusion that 'It is obvious that a much greater sum will be needed before the publication of much needed Christian literature can be undertaken.'[22] By 1980 the Publication Fund had risen to £1,982 and allocations were made to support W.G. Wilson's *Faith*

---

19 Ibid. 20 Ibid. 21 Papers of the General Synod Publications Committee, RCBL, GS/2/29/2. 22 Minute book of the General Synod Publications Committee, RCBL, GS/2/29/1/3.

of an Anglican, published by Collins, and the Milne and Deane booklets, which were published by APCK. In 1980 the new and energetic bishop of Cork, Samuel Poyntz, had been elected chairman and he was one of the first authors in a series of booklets entitled *Our church* initiated by the House of Bishops. The first two booklets by Poyntz and James Mehaffey, bishop of Derry and Raphoe, appeared in 1983 while a third, by Noel Willoughby, bishop of Cashel and Ossory, was published in 1984. They appeared under the APCK imprint and were financially supported by the publications committee. Disappointingly, no further titles in this series appeared.

Although the public appeal appeared to have been sufficient to allow publication to continue, the issues of promotion, distribution and sales were problematic. The APCK had closed most of its shops in 1978 and so the network on which Church of Ireland publications depended had all but vanished. Some of the outlets subsequently re-opened and the Sunday School Society also provided an outlet in Dublin. But this proved to be a false dawn, with the last APCK outlet in Dublin (at St Ann's) closing in 1995 and the Sunday School Society's Resources Centre closing in 2012. The volume of sales being generated by Church of Ireland publications was insufficient to maintain these outlets and there was no appetite to subsidize them from central church funds despite repeated pleas that such a course of action was not only appropriate but essential.

Furthermore reform was again on the agenda and in a form that would further diminish the involvement of APCK. In 1984 the General Synod agreed to a new communications structure, which would come into effect in 1985. This would see the Publications Committee replaced by a Literature Committee, which would be a subcommittee of a new Central Communications Board, and for the first time a committee in which there would be no specific place for the APCK. The terms of reference were, at best woolly, with much emphasis on advising, encouraging and consulting rather than on being given authority and resources to develop a new publications apparatus. However, with Bishop Poyntz in the chair, Revd Richard Clarke as honorary secretary, and a committee beefed up with professional support from Harold Clarke, chairman of Easons, and Fr Bernard Treacy from Dominican Publications, there were at least some grounds for hope that there might be more action than words. The new committee was diligent and dutiful. There were discussions with the board of the APCK about marketing, a seminar on religious publishing was organized in 1988, proposals for a logo to identify Church of Ireland publications were formulated and the need for a Church of Ireland publishing house was reiterated. Financial support was provided for an adult education handbook, a video on vocation, a supplement to the *Church Hymnal* and *Sing and pray*, and a leaflet intended principally for visitors to cathedrals and historic churches, written by the bishop of Cork and Revd David Hewlett, was produced in large numbers in the summer of 1990.[23]

23 *General Synod Journal*. Reports of the Literature Committee.

This work was made possible, not alone because of the enthusiasm of the new committee, but also because of a new source of financial support, the *Alternative Prayer Book*. One of the continuities in church publishing had been the printing of revised services that had been devised by the Liturgical Advisory Committee. These were essentially exercises in printing rather than publishing, with little in the way of bibliographical data and were basic booklets intended largely for distribution to parishes at nominal prices. Beginning with a revised Holy Communion service in 1967, followed in 1969, with a baptismal service, the issue of these booklets became more frequent in the 1970s and culminated in the publication, by Collins, of the *Alternative Prayer Book* in 1984. The *APB* was significant in several respects. Firstly, it was an important physical representation of the ongoing work of liturgical revision; secondly it broke the link with OUP as the church's liturgical publisher of first choice; and thirdly, its sales produced a revenue stream that was set aside to support future publications. In 1989 the Literature Committee considered 'an imaginative stewardship of the APB Royalties Fund to be one of its primary functions'.[24]

However, the APB Royalties Fund was also not without problems, neatly summed up by the Literature Committee in its report to the 1991 General Synod:

> If the Literature Committee is to fulfil its brief … the current publishing anarchy within the Church – whereby contact is seemingly made with the Committee only when there is the hope of obtaining assistance from the APB Royalties Fund, or when the use of the Church of Ireland logo is desired – should cease.

The committee intensified its discussions with different publishing groups, stressing the need for coordination in publishing and marketing, identified as 'imperative' a unified marketing procedure and continued to make grants for publications such as a new series of leaflets, devised by the APCK, on aspects of the church's teaching; a report of the 1996 Young Adults Forum in Dublin; and a booklet of essays to commemorate the Great Famine. However, there was a sense of growing frustration, for while useful work continued to be done, the modus operandi had not significantly changed since the days of the old Publications Committee. Most publication was still undertaken by commercial publishers with resort to the advice of the Literature Committee only when financial support was required. The committee continued to assert the necessity for a publishing house and made this the centrepiece of its submission to CHL Consultants, who had been engaged by the General Synod in 1998 to consider the church's publication strategy. The consultant's report, unsurprisingly, recommended the appointment of a publications officer, but equally unsurprising was the refusal of the Representative Church Body to finance this recommendation. The Literature Committee was 'acutely disappointed'.[25]

---

24 *General Synod Journal.* Report of the Literature Committee, 1989. 25 *General Synod Journal.* Reports of the Literature Committee.

However, there seemed little alternative, at least in the short term, but to continue with the prevailing system, and as circumstances allowed, to renew the Literature Committee. Bishop Poyntz had left the committee in 1995, and was followed in succeeding years by Harold Clarke and by Richard Clarke, who, during ten years as honorary secretary, had constantly been to the fore in seeking to professionalize the church's publications strategy. Sean O'Boyle of Columba Press joined the committee, Raymond Refaussé succeeded Richard Clarke and in 2003 Kenneth Milne succeeded Bishop Michael Mayes as chairman. The appointment of a director of communications in 2001 had offered some hope of more professional input but the amalgamation of the post with that of assistant secretary of the General Synod significantly diluted the potential of this initiative. Grants continued to be made for new publications such as *A time to build*, a book of essays to celebrate the millennium. Co-published by APCK and Columba Press, this was a significant publication in that it marked the end of APCK as a book publisher for the Church of Ireland and introduced Columba Press as a serious alternative. The printing of revised services continued and this work of liturgical revision was brought to splendid conclusion by the publication of the *Book of Common Prayer* (2004), published by Columba Press and managed with extraordinary diligence and professionalism by Canon Brian Mayne of the Liturgical Advisory Committee and Seán O'Boyle of Columba Press. As with the publication of the *APB*, the sales of the new *BCP*, together with those of the revised *Church Hymnal*, which had been published by OUP, produced a strong and sustained revenue stream for the renamed General Synod Royalties Fund. A new challenge was how to effectively spend these funds.[26]

An obvious way to use these new funds was for the Church of Ireland to begin to build a structure that would allow it to publish on its own behalf. After extensive consultations the Literature Committee recommended the establishment of a new publishing imprint, Church of Ireland Publishing (CIP), and in 2004 this was approved by the Standing Committee. CIP was registered as a publisher, ISBNs were allocated and a website was commissioned. Susan Hood, in addition to her role as assistant librarian and archivist, was appointed as publications officer, with a brief to support the work of the Literature Committee, to liaise with those groups and individuals who presented material for publication, to oversee the production of publications, and to create and maintain a distribution network. CIP joined CLÉ, the Irish publishers' association, and the publications officer was trained through it, and related programmes, as well as working alongside the celebrated Irish designer Bill Bolger. All of this was funded by the General Synod Royalties Fund, grants from which continued to be recommended, in the first instance, by the Literature Committee.[27]

Most of CIP's early publications were in the form of short booklets which were the work of church committees. And so, for example, there were booklets on social

26 Ibid.   27 Ibid.

issues from the Church and Society Committee; on relations with the Methodist Church from the Covenant Council; and guidelines for interfaith dialogue from the Commission for Church Unity. More substantial were *The authority of Scripture*, from the Bishops' Advisory Council on Doctrine and Malcolm Macourt's statistical analysis of the Church of Ireland, *Counting the people of God?*

Of course applications still arrived seeking support from the General Synod Royalties Fund. The first decade of the twenty-first century was particularly rich in the publication of works on Irish church history and the Literature Committee recommended grants to subvent the publication, among others, of books of essays on the clergy and on the laity of the Church of Ireland, and histories of the two Dublin cathedrals, all of which were published by Four Courts Press, which had emerged as the dominant force in Irish history publishing. However, theological publishing was more challenging. *Search*, which had succeeded *New Divinity* as the church's only theological journal, had been published regularly since 1978 but otherwise, apart from a post-retirement efflorescence from Archbishop Henry McAdoo and the work of Dean Stephen White, little of substance was being produced.

In response to this lacuna, and to encourage a new generation, the Literature Committee suggested to the staff on the Church of Ireland Theological Institute that the best dissertation by a final-year student in CITI should be published by CIP. The Braemor Studies series, as it was to be called, began in 2013 and has appeared annually since, with all the costs being met from the General Synod Royalties Fund.[28] It was never expected that this series would be profitable or even break even, although some titles have sold surprisingly well. More challenging has been the wider theological dimension. A Lent book, to be published by Columba Press, was commissioned for 2014 and although it made an impact in a crowded market the exercise suggested that a repeat would be difficult.[29] This was borne out by the events of 2017. The publication by CIP of a book of reflection by Canon Cecil Hyland,[30] which covered its costs due largely to sustained promotion by the author, contrasted with the experience of a book of essays on preaching that struggled to make an impact. Both were high-quality works that emphasized an eternal publishing verity – it is relatively easy to produce a book but much harder to sell it. In 2015 CIP had developed an online purchasing facility through the Church of Ireland website, which in the absence of Church of Ireland bookshops and the closure of Columba Press provided a much needed focus for promotion. But even with this, sales were difficult, suggesting that Church of Ireland publishing was always likely to be more an act of faith than an economic investment.

So how stands Church of Ireland archives and publishing in 2019? Raymond Refaussé retired in June 2016 and was succeeded as librarian and archivist by Susan Hood. She has inherited the challenge of providing appropriate storage for the growing body of archives which are being transferred to the RCB Library,

28 Ibid. 29 Ibid. 30 Ibid.

especially in the wake of the introduction of GDPR, as well as managing a large government funded project to digitize parish registers. Unsurprisingly, these new responsibilities have significantly reduced the time she can devote to being publications officer and so the Literature Committee faces considerable challenges to maintain CIP and secure it on a professional basis.

It is evident that the road to archival respectability for the Church of Ireland has been long, and at times arduous, but ultimately successful. Yet challenges remain, especially the provision of adequate storage accommodation and the need for a policy on electronic records. In publishing, the challenges are more profound for, if the Church of Ireland is to continue to regard the written word as a vital part of its mission, then significant investment will be required. The external agencies that for long supported Church of Ireland publishing are either gone or are no longer fit for purpose. Electronic publishing may fill part of this gap, but the necessity for hard-copy publishing will remain, as will the church's responsibility to provide it.

18

Theological training in the Church of Ireland

Áine Hyland

The fifty-year period from 1969 to 2019 was one of radical change in Irish society. During that time, a conservative and insular society became more outward-focused and globally engaged. The introduction of free second-level education in the Republic of Ireland in 1967 contributed to this change. Whereas in the mid-1960s more than 50 per cent of young people left school by the age of 15 with no post-primary qualification, by 2018 the young population of Ireland was among the best educated in the Western world. From the point of view of religion, in the 1960s the vast majority of the population, North and South, belonged to Christian churches, and religious observance and church attendance were high. By 2016, church attendance had fallen off significantly, and the Church of Ireland popula-tion in the Republic of Ireland had fallen from 3.3 per cent of the population in 1971 to 2.8 per cent in 2016. That year, the Church of Ireland population in the South was 126,400 and in Northern Ireland it was 260,000. Another major change that occurred during this period was the decision of the Church of Ireland in 1990 to accept women for ordination. The first women were ordained to the priesthood in June 1990 and the first female member of the episcopate was consecrated in 2013.

It was not surprising that during this period there was considerable soul-searching within the Christian churches about their role in society, and particularly about the role of ordained ministry. In the case of the Church of Ireland, those applying for ordination were no longer predominantly young male school-leavers. A growing number of applicants were mature men and women who were already university graduates and who had been in the (secular) workforce for a number of years. The period was also one in which other professional bodies – medical, teach-ing, engineering – were reviewing their training models to ensure that the needs of an increasingly complex and demanding world would be met.

Prior to 1969, the preparation of candidates for ordained ministry in the Church of Ireland took place in the Divinity School of Trinity College Dublin, with students living in the Divinity Hostel in Mountjoy Square until 1964, when a new hostel was built in Braemor Park, Rathgar, Dublin 6. Initially, the programme for ordinands was at diploma level; it was later extended to ordinary (pass) and subsequently honours degree level. The B.Th. at ordinary level was for many years the normative qualification for ordained ministry in the Church of Ireland.

The Church of Ireland Theological College at Braemor Park was established in 1979. With the transformation of the Braemor Park hostel into the college, a new era of training began. While the college continued to have strong links with Trinity College, the focus of training moved from Trinity College to Braemor Park. By the early 2000s, all training for Church of Ireland ministry for both stipendiary and non-stipendiary candidates was centred there. The training for stipendiary ministry culminated in the award of a B.Th. by the University of Dublin – teaching for which was split more or less evenly between the Theological College and Trinity College. Being the only theological college in the Church of Ireland, it has always drawn ordinands from the whole of Ireland, North and South.

From the 1980s onwards, the course for those training for non-stipendiary ministry was also located in the Theological College in Braemor Park. Non-stipendiary ordinands pursued a course for the certificate of Christian Studies from St John's College, Nottingham over three years, with liturgy and the history of the Church of Ireland as additional subjects. As well as spending at least six residential weekends in the college in Braemor Park, students were supported by diocesan tutors, and were required to write four essays per unit (two units per annum), which were submitted for outside assessment. At the turn of the millennium, there was growing criticism within the church of the approach to ministry training. This criticism could not be aired at the General Synod because the college was the responsibility of the bishops alone. Robert McCarthy, dean of St Patrick's Cathedral, wrote in a *Catalyst* pamphlet in 2002 that

> the college has been subjected to open criticism by members of Reform (Ireland), an extreme 'evangelical' some would say fundamentalist group … It has (also) lost (or never had) the confidence of many of those selected for training for the ministry … [T]he old system of an examination by the Bishop's examining chaplains has been abandoned as hopelessly old-fashioned, but nothing has been put in its place … [O]f those ordained between 1991 and 2001, some 36% have left the ministry of the Church of Ireland.

Partly to counteract this criticism, the bishops set up a Theological College Council in 1999. The college management committee and the academic committee were answerable to the council, which was chaired initially by the bishop of Meath, Richard Clarke. In the *Church of Ireland Gazette* in December 2000, Bishop Clarke wrote:

> In conjunction with the college staff, the Council and its Academic Committee anticipates a major review of the current curriculum and the development of new models of ministry to meet the changing demands on the Church for the 21st century.

In December 2002, the Academic Committee, chaired by Bishop Michael Jackson, then bishop of Clogher, met for two days to consider aspects of future training in the Church of Ireland. Arising out of these discussions, a number of recommendations were made that led to a decision by the House of Bishops to undertake a formal review of the Church of Ireland Theological College. The review team was to consist of the Venerable Bob Langley, archdeacon of Lindisfarne (chair of the team); Revd Canon Alan Abernethy, then parish priest of Ballyholme, Co. Down and subsequently appointed as bishop of Connor; Per Hansson, professor of education, Uppsala University; Alan Hibbert, professor of mathematics, Queen's University Belfast and this author, who was then professor of education and vice president of University College Cork. This review, which was based on the approach to inspection set out by the Church of England House of Bishops' Committee for Ministry Formation, commenced in June 2004 with a visit by the chair of the team to the Theological College in Braemor Park. Some months later, in November 2004, the review team met to plan their approach to the review.

During the following months, there was widespread consultation with various stakeholders including the principal and staff; the Theological College Council; the student body; and the House of Bishops. A one-week visit by the review team to the college (from 28 February to 5 March 2005) was a central plank of the review. During this visit, the review team slept and lived in Braemor Park, immersing themselves in the residential life there, attending prayers and worship with the staff and students as well as lectures and classes both at Braemor Park and in Trinity College. At the time of the visit, there were 29 students (21 men and 8 women) for stipendiary ministry at the college with 26 students (18 men and 8 women) on the auxiliary ministry course. Of the 29 residential students, 24 were following the B.Th. course in Trinity College, while the remaining 5 were pursuing various further degrees (M.Phil., Ph.D., etc.). The auxiliary ministry students followed a specially designed course, broadly based on the certificate in Christian studies at St John's College, Nottingham. The residential course and the auxiliary ministry course operated independently of each other and there was little or no interaction between the staff or students of the two courses.

The report of the review team was completed by summer 2005 and sent to the House of Bishops. The main messages of the report were:

- an affirmation of the commitment of staff and students, and the achievements of recent years;
- the need for greater clarity of the aims and objectives of the institution, where they are owned and how they are to be delivered;
- a shift in focus in the way the task of theological education is perceived from content to formation and the integration of theology and experience;
- a creative use of previous experience, not least of the different strands of Christian tradition;

- a commitment to lifelong learning;
- a shared approach to and responsibility for the life of the college, including the auxiliary ministry course, by the House of Bishops, College Council, staff and students; and
- the modelling in a variety of ways of a common exploration of discipleship, within the life of the college and the course, and between the training institutions and the wider church.

Perhaps the most crucial area identified by the review team was that of the need for clarity about the aims and objectives of the college in serving the mission of the Church of Ireland. The review team pointed out that from those aims and objectives, everything else would flow, including not only the teaching and learning programme but the structures of governance, the broader issue of training for stipendiary ministry, the auxiliary ministry course and continuing ministerial education.

The report of the review team was considered by the House of Bishops at its meeting in November 2005. It was agreed that a Ministry Formation Team would be set up, but first the bishops had to formulate a 'Mission of the Church', which would underpin all the subsequent planning by the formation team. Following consultation and reflection, the mission was formulated as follows:

> The Church of Ireland, as an authentic part of the universal church of God, is called to develop growing communities of faith, in and through which the Kingdom of God is made known, and in which the whole people serve together as followers of Jesus Christ for the good of the world, to the glory of God.

The Ministry Formation Team consisted of Bishop Ken Clarke of Kilmore, Bishop Michael Jackson of Clogher, Bishop Richard Clarke of Meath, Canon Alan Abernethy and a layman – Andrew McNeile. Andrew McNeile's considerable experience as a leader and expert on change management in the business world was to prove invaluable during the subsequent deliberations and work of the Ministry Formation Team. During the following year, the team met regularly and drafted and re-drafted its plan, in regular consultation with the House of Bishops. By the end of 2006 the broad outline of the plan had been agreed and since its implementation would involve a wide range of stakeholders and partners, engagement with these partners was under way.

The broad 'statement of purpose or intent' of the project plan was

> To equip fully all members of the church, ordained and lay, to fulfil effectively the church's mission in the 21st century and to ensure that the methods used to train people will throughout, effectively connect learning and practice.

The plan aimed to ensure that theology would not be learned in isolation but would be connected and applied to real ministry situations.

The plan took as its starting point the overall aspirations of the House of Bishops for those being trained for ministry. These aspirations were to:

- connect learning and practice: ensure that theology is not learnt in isolation but connected and applied to real ministry situations; enable students in subsequent ministry positions to be able to apply their learning to the challenges they face and to connect culture and theology;
- nurture gifting for ministry and mission in an entirely new and ever-changing social context;
- to deepen spiritual self-awareness and theological wisdom;
- to develop holiness and integrity of character;
- to initiate a process of lifelong learning and deepening vocation; and
- to enable those who are trained to be open theologically to fresh challenges in a lifetime of ministry.

The plan set out the characteristics of the ordained ministry under eleven headings:

- spirituality;
- theological reflection;
- pastoral care;
- vision;
- leadership;
- worship and preaching;
- worship and liturgy;
- communicating the faith;
- management and change;
- administration; and
- vocation.

Each of these characteristics would be identified, developed and nurtured at three stages – selection, initial training and continuing ministerial education (CME). The ministry-formation plan was comprehensive and coherent and provided the guiding principles under which the new approach to training would be developed and implemented.

The implementation schedule provided guidelines on curriculum development; the appointment of a new director; new facility construction; role of the diocesan director of ordination (DDO); key implementation changes; and a staffing outline. The plan also proposed solutions to issues that had arisen during consultation, e.g. issues relating to logistics and selection; managing change; legal issues; college

---

1 ECTS: European Credit Transfer System.

and plant; and finance. It was a carefully crafted plan that left nothing to chance. The plan was presented at the House of Bishops' meeting on 22 November 2006, and a fuller version was discussed and approved at the bishops' residential meeting in February 2007. This document, which had the full support of the House of Bishops, was to be the guide and checklist for all aspects of ministry formation in the coming months and years.

The new plan envisaged a radical change in ministry training. While there would continue to be two pathways towards ordination, the traditional separation of stipendiary and non-stipendiary candidates and the distinction between their academic qualifications would no longer exist. From now on, all candidates, whether for stipendiary or non-stipendiary ministry, would follow the same academic course – they could choose a full-time residential route or a part-time route with a more limited residential requirement. It was hoped that in this way, candidates who had family responsibilities (e.g. married candidates – male or female – with young children or other caring responsibilities) would be facilitated, albeit on a part-time programme that would take longer to complete than a full-time programme. Prior to selection, all candidates would be required to complete a one-year foundation course and if they successfully completed this course, they would then follow a three-year, 120 ECTS credit,[1] level 9 degree course leading to the master's in theology (M.Th.).

The proposed changes in ministry training mirrored similar changes in training for other professions. For example, at around the same time as the decision was taken to extend Church of Ireland ministry training to master's degree level, Engineers Ireland had extended its requirements for registration as an engineer to master's level, and the graduate programme for secondary teachers in Ireland would shortly be extended to master's degree level (the professional master's degree in education). In the case of Church of Ireland ministry formation, by the beginning of the millennium almost all candidates for training were mature men and women who were already university graduates or equivalent and many had been actively engaged in lay ministry for a number of years. It was likely therefore that they would have the level of skills, competencies and understanding appropriate to academic study at postgraduate level.

The ministry-formation plan envisaged that the Church of Ireland Theological College would be phased out and replaced by a new Theological Institute, with a new director and staff. It also envisaged that a new facility would be built that would include family accommodation and improved library facilities, possibly sharing a campus with the Church of Ireland College of Education in Rathmines. In the event, this never happened, as the collapse of the banking sector and the severe world economic downturn between 2008 and 2014 militated against any major capital investment. Moreover, in 2016, as part of a national programme for re-organizing initial teacher education, the Church of Ireland College of Education became associated with Dublin City University's Institute of Education and was relocated on the St Patrick's campus of the institute in Drumcondra on the north side of the city. Instead, the existing residential accommodation in Braemor Park was refurbished and modernized and made more suitable for the incoming candidates for ministry training.

The task of convincing Trinity College to validate the proposed ministry-formation programme and to collaborate in its delivery was more challenging than initially envisaged. From September 2007 until April 2008 a working party (of which this author was a member) collaborated with a small team from the Aspirant School of Religions in TCD to flesh out the curriculum, ensuring that it was in line with the bishops' plan and also that it fitted the TCD structures. While in other professional degree programmes in the university sector it was accepted that integration of theory and practice would be the norm, and opportunities were provided in a practice setting for students to become reflective practitioners in their profession, it was not easy to convince some of the TCD academic staff that such an approach was appropriate in the training of clergy. But the bishops' plan was unambiguous and the initial course outline submitted to Trinity College stated that the programme would

> combine a strong academic emphasis which focuses on the foundation sources of Christian belief, namely scripture and the theological disciplines, with a practice-based model of learning. The aspect of personal formation is paramount in the programme as is the integration of belief with ministerial practice.

The academic aspirations for the course included the following:

- full integration between theory and practice;
- universally recognizable levels of academic accreditation;
- different learning styles and approaches;
- active participation in the learning process;
- respecting different academic and theological viewpoints;
- principles of lifelong learning;
- engaging all age groups; and
- distinguishing and linking intellectual enquiry and faith focused information.

Negotiations were not helped by the fact that within Trinity College, a major administrative reorganization was underway. Separate independent departments were being rationalized into a structure of schools – and an Aspirant School of Religions had been set up to take overall responsibility for the Department of Religions and Theology (which had previously provided the B.Th.) and the Irish School of Ecumenics. Negotiations had also begun with the Jesuit-run Milltown Institute about the transfer of that institute to Trinity College. In 2011, that transfer was completed and the institute was relocated to the Trinity College campus and renamed the Loyola Institute.

Following protracted negotiations and discussion, and some compromises, agreement was reached between CITI and TCD – and the new M.Th. was approved by TCD in October 2008. The M.Th. would be a three-year programme consisting of 120 ECTS – 40 in each year. In years one and two, 30 per cent of the modules would be delivered on the Trinity campus by Trinity staff and the remainder of the programme would be delivered by CITI staff on the Braemor Park campus. The third year would be devoted to parish training, during which candidates would reflect on and document their experience in a ministry portfolio. During the third year candidates would also write a dissertation (worth 30 ECTS credits), which would integrate the three strands of biblical, pastoral and theological studies. The assessment of the dissertation would include a thirty-minute *viva voce* examination, which would provide an opportunity for candidates to further discuss their thesis and to showcase their research and findings in verbal form.

MEMORANDUM OF UNDERSTANDING WITH TRINITY COLLEGE

Parallel with these academic and programme-based discussions, a formal memorandum of understanding was being discussed between the bishops and the provost of Trinity College. Initial discussions took place in June 2006 and eventually in September 2008, the TCD board agreed the memorandum of understanding. Under the terms of this memorandum, it was agreed that all involved would be clear that the M.Th. would be a professional course to prepare candidates for ordination and that 30 per cent of the teaching of this course would be undertaken by TCD. The memorandum, which covered the period 2008 to 2018, set out details on access, governance and staff appointments, as well as how a balance would be achieved in terms of oversight, admissions, management and governance. It was also agreed that the academic goals in the bishops' plan would form the basis of a course review at the end of five years.

SETTING UP OF THE CHURCH OF IRELAND THEOLOGICAL INSTITUTE

The Church of Ireland Theological Institute came into existence on 1 September 2008 with a new director, Revd Dr Maurice Elliott. Dr Elliott had studied languages in St Andrews and theology in both Dublin and Belfast. He holds a doctoral degree from Queen's University Belfast. His academic interests include Anglican Reformation ecclesiology and the theory and practice of contemporary Christian leadership. Prior to taking up the post of director of CITI, he had spent fifteen years in parochial ministry in Northern Ireland. In every way, he was the ideal candidate for the post.

The first cycle of the foundation course started in April 2008 and in autumn 2009, the first cycle of the M.Th. course began. To be accepted onto the M.Th.

course, candidates would be required to successfully complete the foundation course. Candidates would also be required to have either: 1) an honours degree in theology or another discipline; 2) an appropriate qualification and at least three years ministerial experience or equivalent professional experience; or 3) otherwise satisfy the Course Admissions Committee that they have the ability to complete and benefit from the course.

REVIEW OF THE M.TH. (2015)

Two significant reviews of the M.Th. were carried out in 2014/15 – one by the House of Bishops and one by a review team set up by Trinity College, in accordance with a statutory requirement that all university programmes must undergo quality-review on a regular basis.

The reviews commented very favourably on the progress that had been achieved since the setting up of the M.Th. The joint CITI/Trinity College review found the programme to be 'a successful partnership' that was delivering on the aims and objectives of the M.Th. The reviewers gave 'strong approval and commendation' of what was being achieved each year. The academics on the review team commended 'the high academic quality attested by dissertation and degree results' and commended the 'clear provision of integrated learning and formation' as well as the evident pastoral support and the development of a broad range of subject-specific and transferable skills. The review found that the facilities – including the library, IT, accommodation and catering – were of a high standard, with a strongly committed support staff. They also found that the commitment, input and quality of the academic staff to be 'of the highest standard'.

Student participation, achievement and satisfaction rates were found to be high, particularly by comparison with the previous B.Th. degree, with students being equipped both academically and professionally to a higher standard than was the case prior to 2008. The review praised the combination of professional training and academic education offered by CITI and Trinity as a model 'which compares favourably with best practices in the sector', noting that 'this partnership of church and academy appears to be one of the more successful, by comparison with other forms of ministerial training in the UK and Europe'.

The reviewers made a number of constructive recommendations, including a restructuring of the M.Th. that would allow part-time students to complete the course in four rather than six years. They also recommended the provision of further teaching in biblical studies as well as an additional module in doctrine.

RESTRUCTURING OF THE M.TH. PROGRAMME (2017)

As a result of these recommendations, the M.Th. programme was restructured in order to allow for more extensive teaching in biblical studies and doctrine, and the part-time programme was reduced in length from six years to four years. The restructured programme took effect from autumn 2017. Both the full-time and the part-time programmes stress the role of the minister as a reflective practitioner who can articulate Christian belief within contemporary culture and who understands the challenges and opportunities this presents. Within this framework the practice of ministry is explored in ways that enable an effective and creative response to the world in which we live. The course is ecumenical in its scope, is adaptable to the needs of other Christian denominations and to forms of ministry other than the ordained.

As of autumn 2018, there are a total of thirty candidates registered on the M.Th. programme, studying either on a full-time or part-time basis. Nine of these are women. Eleven are deacon interns (in their final year); 4 are second-year full-time students; 5 are part-time in years one to three; and 10 are full-time first-year candidates. (In contrast, it is interesting to note that the number of men who entered the Roman Catholic Seminary in Maynooth in 2017 was 6.) As regards staff, by 2018, there were four full-time staff in the Theological Institute: Revd Dr Maurice Elliott; Dr Katie Heffelfinger; Revd Dr Patrick McGlinchey; and Dr Bridget Nichols. It is clear that there continues to be a robust and healthy interest in ministry training in the Church of Ireland.

ORDAINED LOCAL MINISTRY

In 2018, following a decision of the General Synod in 2016, a new route to ministry was introduced – ordained local ministry. An ordained local minister will not be an incumbent of a parish but will be someone who can exercise some leadership role within a local congregation. The nature of their deployment is likely to vary from diocese to diocese.

The route to ordained local ministry will be via an open-learning course, the underlying philosophy of which is that it will be integrated so that the development of learning and understanding takes place beside the honing of practical ministerial skills and continuing spiritual formation. There will be a blended form of learning with the use of lectures, tutorials, workshops, online learning and self-study. It will be a flexible open-learning certificate course provided through Queen's University Belfast. Five modules may be undertaken in years one and two with a further two modules in year three. The modules provided in September 2018 are biblical studies, theological reflection, worship and preaching, introduction to pastoral skills and church history. Staff from both CITI and Edgehill Theological College were involved in the module preparation. (Edgehill Theological College is the institution for training for the ministry of the Methodist Church in Ireland.)

In September 2018, 26 candidates registered for the ordained local ministry course. They come from 8 different dioceses and 10 of them are women. At the time of writing, the ordained local ministry course had only just begun and it is too soon to make any judgment about the effectiveness or otherwise of the course.

LAY READER TRAINING AND TRAINING
FOR CHILDREN'S MINISTRY

CITI also provides training for lay readers and other lay men and women who support the church in various ways. The office of a lay reader is one of a number of lay ministries within the Church of Ireland that is authorized and voluntary. There are currently over 300 readers in Ireland, North and South. The training course for lay readers is offered jointly by CITI and St John's College, Nottingham and leads to either the award of a graduate certificate in ministry validated through the University of Durham or a fully equivalent self-accredited version of the same course as a foundation programme in theology and ministry. The course is run over two years and consists of one residential weekend and six study days at the institute. Study areas include theological perspectives, Christian ministry, homiletics, liturgy, church history and spirituality. The modules are introduced by lecturers from St John's College, Nottingham with additional input from the academic staff at the institute.

The institute also provides training for children's ministry. The children's ministry certificate was originally coordinated between CITI, Church of Ireland Children's Ministry Network, Building Blocks and the Consultative Group on Ministry among Children. The training course is run over seven Saturdays from October to May and has taken place in regional centres such as Dublin, Lisburn, Moira and Cork. The training is based on core skills for children's work.

CONCLUSION

There have been significant developments in theological training in the Church of Ireland during the past fifty years. In 1969, preparation for ordination was at Diploma level, whereas today, candidates are required to complete a master's degree in theology, the final year of which is parish-based. There is greater flexibility in the routes to ordination than there was in the past. It is now possible for candidates to study either on a full-time or a part-time basis and the new ordained local ministry route is clearly very popular, although it is too early to make any judgment about its long-term success or viability.

The numbers registering for the M.Th. continue to be high – there are currently 30 students registered (part-time and full-time) for it. In 2018, 14 candidates were ordained to the priesthood; in 2017, 16 were ordained; and in 2015, 14 were ordained. The future of ministry training in the Church of Ireland looks good and is in good hands in CITI.

19

The Church of Ireland's role in education in the Republic of Ireland[1]

Susan M. Parkes

PROTESTANT IDENTITY

In 1922, with the political partition of Ireland, the Church of Ireland found itself a religious minority in the new Irish Free State. In 1911 the Church of Ireland population of all Ireland was 13.1 per cent. However, in the census of 1926, the Church of Ireland population of the Free State had declined from 249,535 to 164,215 and by 1961 to 104,016 out of a population 2,818,341. Determined to keep its identity and ensure that its youth were educated and socialized together, the church supported the existing denominational structure of education and strove to maintain the Protestant voluntary secondary schools and the parish national schools. Under the *Ne Temere* decree of the Catholic Church (1908) the children of a mixed marriage were required to be brought up in the Catholic faith, so the Protestant youth were encouraged to attend a school under Protestant management and to socialize with their co-religionists.

In the Free State after 1922 there was no major change until the 1960s in the structure of the Irish education system as inherited from the nineteenth century, except for the introduction of compulsory Irish language, history and geography into the school curriculum. For most of the nineteenth century the Church of Ireland had remained outside the national school system (established in 1831) because of the rule that religious instruction was to be taught separately from secular and moral instruction. The Church Education Society, founded 1839, had supported parish schools through voluntary subscriptions. However, following the disestablishment of the Church of Ireland in 1869, most parish schools joined the national school system in order to receive state finance for maintenance and salaries. By that date the national system, while remaining de jure nondenominational, had become de facto denominational, with each church managing its own schools.

After 1922 the Church of Ireland overcame the compulsory Irish-language requirements by having its own all-Irish preparatory college for teachers, Coláiste Moibhí (1926), and its own Church of Ireland Training College for national school

1 I wish to acknowledge the advice of Dr Kenneth Milne and of Dr Ken Fennelly, secretary of the Church of Ireland Board of Education, when researching this article.

teachers. The aim was a policy of integration rather than assimilation, and the church recognized the major role of the education system in maintaining its identity, and the value of state support. The General Synod Board of Education was responsible for the education policy of the church and from the mid-1960s the remit of this board, which previously had been concerned only with religious education, was extended to include both primary and secondary secular education, and a new appointment of a full-time Board of Education secretary was made in 1963. The board continues to present an annual report to the General Synod and under the current service-level agreement with the Department of Education and Skills (2016) fulfils four major functions for schools under Church of Ireland management, namely, support and advice to school management on a day-to-day to basis; representation of the management interests in discussions or correspondence with the Department of Education; liaison with the schools and representation of the management interests of schools at national level; and, finally, promotion of a consistency of approach in relation to school management and governance across the Church of Ireland member schools, so as to support compliance with statuary obligations, Department circulars and rules.

The last fifty years, 1969–2019, have witnessed a remarkable growth in Irish education. The introduction of free secondary education in 1967 led to the rapid expansion of both post-primary and vocational schools and the introduction of new comprehensive and community schools. The abolition of fees in third-level education in 1995 further increased the numbers staying on in second level in order to obtain the Leaving Certificate qualification for competitive third-level entry. In 1964 there were 4,800 primary national schools in Ireland, of which one-tenth were under Church of Ireland management and there were 740 single-teacher national schools for the ages 4–14, of which one-half were Church of Ireland. At secondary level there were 42 Protestant schools located across the country, including boarding schools serving rural communities.

GROWTH OF SECOND-LEVEL SCHOOLING, 1967

The prospect of the introduction of free secondary education was already well recognized in Ireland by the early 1960s. In Northern Ireland free secondary education had been introduced in 1947 following the Butler Education Act in Britain in 1944. This system was based on local education authorities with selection at 11+ by a qualifying examination for entry to either an academic grammar school or a new type of a more practical intermediate secondary school. However, by the 1960s, there was growing criticism of the system of selection and the Labour Party in Britain strongly favoured a comprehensive secondary-schooling model with no pupil selection at 11+. In Ireland the comprehensive model became the chosen one and in 1963 the minister for education, Mr Patrick Hillery, announced the opening of a number of new state-funded comprehensive schools, to be built in areas where there was shortage of post-primary school places. In addition, the local authority vocational schools henceforth would be allowed to offer a three-year Intermediate Certificate course and free school transport would be made available. This was the first indication that the state was to adopt an interventionist policy in education rather than just providing financial capitation support for second-level voluntary schools.

The OECD report *Investment in education* (1965) had a major influence on government education policy by stressing the key role education plays in national economic growth, and that greater access to second- and third-level education was vital for national development. In 1966, George Colley, the minister for education, announced that the secondary and vocational sectors would be brought together and that the government planned to build three new types of comprehensive school in the west at Cootehill, Carraroe and Shannon. In September 1966, the minister for education, Donogh O'Malley, unexpectedly announced that free secondary education would be introduced from September 1967. He deplored the failure of the education system to provide equality of opportunity, and regarded 'as a dark stain on the national conscience' the fact that that 1,700 pupils in the country had completed their formal education at primary level only. The secondary sector was taken by surprise by the O'Malley announcement and concern was expressed as to how the system would cope with such an influx of pupils. However, most of the secondary schools agreed to 'enter the free scheme' and opened their doors to greater numbers and began to offer a comprehensive curriculum.[2]

CHURCH OF IRELAND EDUCATION POLICY, 1960S

The church recognized that under the influence of the *Investment in education* report there would be major changes in education and that the church should be prepared to take advantage of them. Therefore, under the wise and far-sighted leadership of Most Reverend George Simms, archbishop of Dublin, the General Synod of the Church of Ireland in 1962 set up two advisory committees, one on primary and the other on secondary education in the Republic of Ireland. The Secondary Committee was chaired by the Rt. Reverend Gordon Perdue, bishop of Cork, Cloyne and Ross and consisted of fifteen members, both clerical and lay. The secretary was Dr Kenneth Milne, the newly appointed secretary of the Church of Ireland Board of Education. The advisory report on primary education, which was chaired by Most Reverend George Simms, was presented at the same time and these two reports became the basis of the Church of Ireland's education policy of reform for the future. The Board of Education report for 1965 stated that the vocation of the church in education was twofold – to 'put before our young people the idea of true citizenship' and 'to enable them in terms of trainings of mind and hand to play that part. Education is a means to an end.'

---

2 In the period 1966–82, the number of primary-school pupils increased from 505,000 to 574,000, while at secondary level, with introduction of 'free education', the number increased from 143,000 to 325,000. At third-level, for the same period, attendance rose from 13,000 to 24,000.

CHURCH OF IRELAND PRIMARY SCHOOLS,
1960S AND 1970S

The 1965 report on primary education, which was included as part of the annual report of the Board of Education for that year, emphasized the need for the amalgamation of small schools into large and better-equipped central institutions and that education should be recognized as a 'potent factor' in the social life and welfare of the state. Education needed to be expanded to equip the young for the opportunities now offered by a developing economy, and it was important that the Church of Ireland primary schools should not be allowed to become substandard. Therefore, the church began to support the government policy of the closure of small schools and the creation of larger central schools, to which pupils would travel daily by the school bus.[3] Over the next few years, consultation took place between the Board of Education, the Church of Ireland bishops and the Department of Education, and the provision of Church of Ireland primary schools in each diocese was examined. The leadership of the bishops and the advice of the Department of Education proved crucial and, though some local churches regretted the loss of their parish school, a central school could offer larger senior classes and improved facilities. These factors were essential if the Church of Ireland community was to continue to support its own rural schools. However, one loss was that whereas in some remote areas Protestant children had walked to the nearest local Catholic national school, the creation of centralized Protestant schools resulted in the pupils travelling daily long distances and a denominational divide in schooling was reinforced. The department and the church together had been already providing school-travelling costs for a number years and this policy was continued. In 1975 boards of management of national schools were established, with elected representatives of teachers and parents, and this increased involvement in the running of the local school and strengthened the parochial base.

In addition, the church maintained its own denominational Church of Ireland College of Education (CICE) for national school teachers, which was located in Rathmines, where it had moved from Kildare Place in 1969. It accepted applications from students of the other reformed churches. It was essential to maintain an adequate supply of qualified national teachers to support the church's primary school system and the Department of Education sanctioned an agreed number of entrants required to maintain the Protestant schools. The college played an important role in the national implementation of the new primary curriculum of 1971, in particular through the pioneering work of an advocate of the new methodology, Ms Millicent Fitzsimons, the college vice principal, and of her successor, Mrs Margaret Farrar. In 1975 the bachelor in education degree was established with the University of Dublin and Church of Ireland College of Education students attended lectures in education in Trinity College one day a week; the bachelor in

3 In 2019, the number of single-teacher schools overall in the Republic had been reduced to 24, only 6 of which were under Church of Ireland patronage.

education was a three-year pass degree with a fourth year for honours, thus creating a graduate primary teaching profession. The university had had a longstanding agreement with CICE dating from 1922 by which its students had attended undergraduate arts and education lectures in TCD and could complete a BA pass degree in two more years. The new TCD bachelor in education fourth honours year qualified CICE students to undertake postgraduate degrees. Two other colleges of education, Froebel College, Sion Hill, Blackrock and Coláiste Mhuire, Marino, also became associated colleges in the TCD bachelor in education degree.

CICE maintained close links with the Church of Ireland parish schools, where its students undertook mandatory teaching practice and its graduates were recruited to the schools' staff. The Protestant preparatory college for teachers, Coláiste Moibhí, founded 1926, which had been located in Rathmines since 1969, offered a two-year course for Leaving Certificate students through the medium of Irish. However, in 1995, it was closed by Department of Education despite the efforts of Archbishop Donald Caird of Dublin, a strong Irish linguist, to retain it. CICE acquired an extra lecturer in Irish and first-year students were offered more time in the Gaeltacht to maintain the required standard of Irish.

In the 1990s, the College of Education, under the leadership of the principal, Mr Sydney Blain, became a centre for special education, offering a national in-service programme of remedial education for both primary and post-primary teachers, which added a vibrant group of staff and students to the college. Student exchange with Stranmillis College in Belfast and a summer placement in Africa were organized. The historic links of the college to the nineteenth-century Kildare Place Society resulted in the campus becoming a centre for the history of Irish education. Under the initiative of Dr Kenneth Milne, the first lay principal, the archives of the KPS were listed and made available to researchers. A number of CICE publications included *Kildare Place: the history of the Church of Ireland Training College, 1811–1969,*[4] and *Irish educational documents.*[5] The Plunket Museum of Irish Education was opened in the old stable yard, designed to facilitate school visits, and it collected historic school effects including furniture, textbooks and teaching aids. Some of these were displayed in an exhibition in the National Museum in Collins Barracks in 2012. The college was particularly proud when one of its past students was appointed chief inspector in the Department of Education and Science in 2010.

In 1992 a government green paper, 'Education for a changing world', proposed that in the future primary teacher education should change to a consecutive model whereby a student would study first for a degree and then undertake a one-year postgraduate teacher-training course. The colleges of education, including CICE,

4 Susan M. Parkes, *Kildare Place* (Dublin, 1984; 2nd ed. 2011). 5 K. Milne, Áine Hyland, Gordon Byrne and John Dallat (eds), *Irish educational documents*, 3 vols (Dublin, 1987, 1992, 1995). Other CICE publications included Valerie Jones, *A Gaelic experiment: the preparatory system and Coláiste Moibhí, 1926–1961* (Dublin, 2006); Valerie Coghlan, *The bicentenary book: from Kildare Place to the Church of Ireland College of Education, 1911–2011* (Dublin, 2011).

reacted immediately to reject this proposal as their very existence depended on the three-/four-year consecutive course. It was vigorously argued that a one-year graduate course was too short to encompass the essential needs of initial training. CICE presented a strong submission to the Department of Education defending the consecutive model as did the TCD School of Education, The proposal for teacher consecutive education did not develop further but it was a warning that the future of mono-technic colleges of education would be under question. In 2016 the Church of Ireland college merged into Dublin City University Institute of Education and relocated to Drumcondra, where the Church of Ireland Centre on the All Hallows' Campus provides religious education and supervised teaching practice for students in Protestant national schools.

CHURCH OF IRELAND ADVISORY REPORT ON SECONDARY EDUCATION, 1965

An insightful, radical report, presented to the General Synod in 1965 recommended that the Protestant secondary schools should be encouraged to amalgamate and form larger and more effective units with updated facilities. The forty-two secondary schools under Protestant management were visited by members of the committee, as well three important Protestant second-level schools in the North and three Roman Catholic secondary schools in the Republic. The report strongly stated, 'We have been greatly impressed by what our schools have achieved with inadequate buildings, inadequate finance, and inadequate initial salaries for our teachers. Despite this we are convinced that unless radical steps are taken immediately, the present schools will not be able to provide our children with an education equal to that available to the rest of the nation, or up to European standards.'

The 1965 committee were aware that most Protestant schools were governed by voluntary boards and that the General Synod itself had little control over individual schools. The report therefore recommended the setting up of

> a joint committee with the Presbyterian and Methodist churches and the Religious Society of Friends to formulate a common policy for Protestant secondary education and to enter into discussions with Minister for Education and the governing bodies of Protestant schools for the purpose of implementing such as policy.

The 1965 report also emphasized the need for improved conditions for secondary teachers so that young Protestants would be encouraged to enter the teaching profession. It was essential for the survival of Protestant schools that there was a supply of graduate Protestant teachers. The negative issues were low teacher salary scales, the 'deplorable' living conditions for staff in some boarding schools, and the extra-curricular duties such as games supervision required of junior staff. In an article in the Jesuit journal *Studies* in 1968, in which Seán O'Connor, assistant secretary at the Department of Education presented an analysis of the O'Malley scheme, Dr Milne welcomed the changes but commented on the difficulties which the Protestant schools would have with their scattered population and with increased numbers of lay teachers required to offer a comprehensive range of subjects.[6] He emphasized the value of the vocational sector in the rural areas but explained that the church would prefer Protestant children to have their free second-level education in a school under Protestant management.

The 1965 Church of Ireland Advisory Committee concluded its report with a dire warning:

> We would end as we began, by stressing the dangers of the present critical situation, which is likely to get worse before it gets better. To arrest the downward trend in Protestant secondary education is not going to be easy, to reverse the trend is a truly formidable task. All concerned – the Churches, the Government, the governors of schools, the teachers, and above all the parents, will have to take secondary education much more seriously in the future if Irish standards are not to fall far behind those obtaining elsewhere in Europe … We must be willing to be ruthless and radical when so much is at stake … Time is short, and the sands are running out.

1970S COMPREHENSIVE AND COMMUNITY SCHOOLS

The outcome of the 1965 report was that in the coming decade the church encouraged the Protestant secondary schools, despite historic vested interests, to make difficult decisions. The schools in Dublin began to negotiate with each other, to sell up school premises in the city and move to spacious sites in the suburbs, and an innovative group of government-funded Protestant comprehensive schools was established. Capital building grants became available from the department and new sites could be acquired.

Therefore, by the 1980s, a thriving system of twenty-one second-level schools under Protestant management had been formed. Co-educational partnerships were forged and smaller schools were merged into larger ones. For example, the High School, Dublin joined with Diocesan School for Girls (1969) in Rathgar, Mercer's and Morgan's schools merged with the King's Hospital at Palmerstown (1971) and the Incorporated Society Schools, Kilkenny College for boys and Celbridge Collegiate School for Girls, were combined on a new site in Kilkenny (1973) . Thus a strong base for growth was created. Alexandra College move to Milltown (1971), Wesley College moved to Ballinteer (1969), St Andrew's College, under Presbyterian management, became co-educational and moved to Booterstown

6 Seán O'Connor, 'Post-primary edication: now and in the future', *Studies*, 57 (Autumn 1968), pp 233–50 at p. 227; Kenneth Milne, *A church of Ireland bibliography* (Dublin, 2005), pp 261–9.

(1973), while Rathdown School (an amalgamation of three girls' schools – Park House, the Hall School, and Hillcourt) formed a viable school for girls in Glenageary (1973). Two non-denominational schools, Sandford Park in Ranelagh and Sutton Park in Howth, expanded in numbers.

In other parts of the country the older schools strove to improve their facilities and offer a broader curriculum. The Incorporated Society for Protestant Schools, as patron, supported the growth of its schools, Bandon Grammar, Sligo Grammar, Dundalk Grammar and Kilkenny College. Midleton College was to serve east Cork, Villiers School the Limerick region and Wilson's Hospital in Multyfarnham (joined with Preston schools in Navan and Abbeyleix) the midlands. In Waterford, Bishop Foy's School joined with the Quaker Newtown School; in the north-east, Monaghan Collegiate and the Royal School, Cavan increased their numbers; and St Columba's College continued as a co-educational boarding school in Rathfarnham. Most of the rural schools offered boarding accommodation, which was essential given the scattered Protestant population, and grants to cover these costs were forthcoming from the government.

In addition, with the support of the Department of Education and extra funding from the World Bank, four new comprehensive schools under Protestant management were opened, which offered free education. The first such comprehensive school, the Royal and Prior, was opened in Raphoe, Co. Donegal in 1967. In Cork, Rochelle School, the Cork High School and Cork Grammar School joined together to form the new comprehensive co-educational Ashton School (1975) and in north Dublin, Mountjoy, Hibernian Marine and Bertrand and Rutland schools united to form Mount Temple (1972), on the Mountjoy site in Clontarf. The south Dublin-based Newpark Comprehensive School (1972), which was formed by merger of Avoca and Kingstown grammar schools, opened in Blackrock. This group of four Protestant comprehensive worked together to liaise with the Department of Education. Other schools since have entered 'the Free Scheme', namely Kilkenny College, Wilson's Hospital and St Patrick's Cathedral Grammar School, while the new comprehensive East Glendalough school opened in Wicklow town (1987), along with Temple Carrig, Greystones (2016), a new voluntary secondary school under the patronage of the Church of Ireland archbishop of Dublin.

At first there was strong opposition from some members of the Church of Ireland to this new type of school, as it was feared that the fee-paying voluntary schools would lose pupils. It was argued that state funding would be diverted from the mainstream schools[7] and that a divisive class system could be introduced, whereby better-off Protestants retained their middle-class schools while the less well-off attended the comprehensives. However, the new comprehensive schools proved strong and were in a position to offer free education and an innovative curriculum. At the outset they had no fees, no school uniform, a cooperative discipline and were led by young, enthusiastic staff. The concept of a 'transition year'

<hr>

7 See Robbie Roulston, 'The Church of Ireland and the Irish state, 1950–1972' (PhD, UCD, 2013).

for fourth-year pupils in which there were no formal examinations and which followed an open, pupil-centred curriculum, was first pioneered in one of the comprehensives.

SECONDARY EDUCATION COMMITTEE, 1967

Nevertheless, the advent of free secondary education in 1967 was a major challenge to the Protestant schools and the newly formed Secondary Education Committee consisting of representatives of the four churches was faced with the difficult task of finding a method of funding Protestant secondary schools. The government capitation grant that was to be paid to schools in lieu of fees was less than the fees already charged in Protestant schools, and since the majority of the school staff were salaried lay teachers rather than religious, the running costs were higher than in Catholic schools. Therefore, the government paid a 'block grant' for Protestant schools, which was to be administered by the newly formed Secondary Education Committee and to be distributed on a means-test basis. The Protestant secondary schools therefore would be able to continue to charge modest fees for parents who could to afford them, while less well-off parents could apply to the SEC for a grant. The SEC grant was to play an important role in providing access to the fee-paying schools and the government eventually, after lengthy negotiations, agreed to pay a 'boarding grant' for pupils who lived at distance from a Protestant-managed school. This arrangement ensured the continued existence of the fee-paying Protestant schools as a central core of Church of Ireland secondary education, both day and boarding. The 1967 block grant scheme has continued to work well for forty years and, under a memorandum of understanding between the Department of Education, the SEC and the school management boards, the SEC receives its funding in a four-year cycle.

COMMUNITY SCHOOLS OF THE 1970S

In the 1970s the government launched another plan to increase the provision of second-level education – this was the building of new community schools, which would bring secondary and vocational schools closer together in non-selective, co-educational, comprehensive schools, which also would cater for adult and further education. The concept of a new, large single school, which would combine the secondary and vocational schools in an area, had been suggested first by Seán O'Connor, assistant secretary of the Department of Education, in his seminal article in the journal *Studies* in 1968. The community schools were to be under a management committee representative of the secondary-school managers, the local VEC and the church authorities. The Church of Ireland was 'gravely disturbed' by this proposal as there was little place for Protestant representatives to have influence in the management of these schools. The General Synod Board of Education and the Presbyterian General Assembly Synod made a formal protest regarding the plan. It was a difficult time for the Church of Ireland to decide whether it should support the concept of integrated community schools which would cater for the widest possible range of needs, or to seek to maintain its own discrete number of schools, both boarding and day, to preserve its identity.

The debate on the ownership and control of the community schools was to continue throughout the 1970s and the final deeds of trust were not signed until 1981. Under these it was agreed that there was to be a ten-member board of management – three representatives of the VEC, three of the religious, two of parents and two of teachers, with the principal as a non-voting member. The Catholic Church retained a strong position by obtaining the right to reserve teaching places in the schools for teachers of religion, safeguards for religion and paid Catholic chaplains. The community schools proved to be a successful venture and have become important centres of education in local areas, often replacing two or more smaller existing schools. By 1991 there were fifty-two community schools in operation. A number of VECs introduced community colleges modelled on the community schools, with a ten-member management board, with a clause that 'minority religious representatives on the board will be considered for membership by the VEC if so requested'. The local Church of Ireland clergy retained the right of access to teach religious education to Church of Ireland pupils attending these schools.

While some Protestant parents began to send their children to the local community schools, where proximity was an important factor and up-to-date buildings were on offer, overall, the Protestant boarding schools retained their position by upgrading their facilities and moving to a pattern of five-day boarding, which reduced boarding costs. This pattern also allowed pupils to retain a strong link with home and their parish each weekend. By maintaining a network of schools across the country, the option of children attending a school under Protestant management remained available to the majority of Protestant parents. However, as the secondary school fees were now subsidized by the block grant system, some secondary schools were able to charge substantial fees, despite efforts to keep them as low as possible.

ADVISORY COMMITTEE ON RELIGIOUS EDUCATION IN THE 1970S

An important area where the Church of Ireland was active from the 1970s was in the field of religious education. Traditionally, second-level schools had entered their pupils for the annual General Synod Examinations, for which book prizes were awarded, but this system ceased in 1965 except on a voluntary basis. As religious education was not a subject for the state examinations, it tended to be overlooked in the school curriculum. In 1969 the General Synod Board of Education established an Advisory Committee on Religious Education (ACRE) which 'was authorized to survey the present trends in religious education in both Ireland and elsewhere' and 'to collect evidence from teachers regarding the present state of religious education in schools with Church of Ireland pupils'. The ACRE report, which was presented to the General Synod in 1972, was chaired by the primate, the Most Revd G. Simms and the secretary was Dr K. Milne of the Board of Education. The committee consisted of both clerical and teacher members and the outcome was a far-sighted report that demanded improved teacher training for religion teachers, the provision of up-to-date teaching resources and a new RE syllabus for all levels. Two other recommendations were, firstly, the proposed introduction of a formal state examination in religious knowledge which would raise the status of the subject, and, secondly, the importance of retaining school assemblies as an important part of the religious education of the pupils. If the denominational education structure was to be maintained, it was essential that religious education should be of a high standard.

As a result, *Guidelines for an experimental curriculum in religious education for secondary schools* was published in 1976 by the Board of Education, based on a series of working parties of teachers of religion, both clerical and lay. Discussions began between the churches and the National Council for Curriculum and Assessment regarding an agreed syllabus for a state examination in religious education, and Dr Milne was to chair the NCCA religious-education course committee for a number of years. The task of creating a syllabus proved difficult and lengthy so it was not until the 1990s that the first public examinations in religious education could be offered in the Junior Certificate cycle in schools and eventually also in the Leaving Certificate. The academic status of the subject increased and religious education gained a stronger place in the curriculum and the Board of Education is represented on the NCCA religious-education development group by Ken Fennelly. However, by 2018, while the overall number of candidates taking the RE exam in Junior Certificate was over 25,000 out of a total cohort of 65,000, the take-up at Leaving Certificate level has proved much lower, and in 2018 the number of candidates for Leaving Certificate RE was just over 1,200. The Church has now lost some degree of control over the RE syllabus since it became part of the state examination system, and there is an opening for the church to offer a formal certificate for second-level religious education teachers.

Religious education became an integrated part of new primary curriculum of 1971, which was closely related to the needs of the child. A programme, *Themes in religious education for primary school children,* published by the Religious Education Council in the North, was adopted first as an example of this approach. In 1986 a Religious Education Committee was set by the General Synod to define the aims and objectives in religious education and was issued in 1990. However, this programme was under-resourced and by 1997 needed to be revised.

In 1997 the governors of CICE funded a survey study of religious education in schools under Protestant management, the results of which indicated strong support for the inclusion of RE in the primary curriculum. In January 1999 an RE Curriculum Committee was set up under the chairmanship of the Most Reverend Dr Richard Clarke, bishop of Meath, which included representatives of the Methodist and Presbyterian churches' Boards of Education, along with parents and teachers. Ms Jacqui Wilkinson, who had undertaken postgraduate research in religious education, was appointed editor and coordinator of the new programme. One source of ideas was the *Alive–O* programme published by Veritas for the Episcopal Commission for Catechetics, and it was agreed that ideas in this programme could be adapted for the Protestant RE programme, including the provision of pupils' and teachers' workbooks

In 2001 the Board of Education published its own syllabus, entitled *Follow me*. This RE programme, which became a part of the new 1998 primary curriculum, consisted of a series of lively illustrated graded textbooks along with workbooks, and it has been adopted successfully by most of the Church of Ireland primary schools. The programme has four aims – firstly, to develop a knowledge and understanding of beliefs, worship and witness of the Christian faith and in particular of the Church of Ireland and other reformed traditions; secondly, to explore the biblical witness to God as Father, Son and Holy Spirit; thirdly to develop children's own religious beliefs, values and practices through a process of personal search and discovery; and, fourthly, to develop an awareness of and a sensitivity towards those of other faiths and none. Under the leadership of Ms Jacqui Wilkinson, lecturer in religious education at the Church of Ireland Centre at DCU, the Church of Ireland offers a formal certificate in religious education undertaken by student trainee teachers and in addition there are in-service certificate courses for already qualified teachers in Protestant national schools.

MANAGEMENT AND GOVERNANCE OF SCHOOLS, 1970s–90s

Primary schools

The major issue for the Church of Ireland in the 1970s–90s related to the governance and management of schools at both primary and secondary level. In 1969, at primary level, the patronage of national schools lay in the hands of the bishop of the diocese and the rector was manager of the school. Neither teachers nor parents were included. The Catholic Church authorities were reluctant to surrender control to the laity and the main concern was that a majority of the religious trustees on the board of management must be maintained. However a popular demand for more democratic control was growing. An influential case that involved the Church of Ireland was the Dalkey School project of 1974. The Church of Ireland parish school in Dalkey had a high reputation and was oversubscribed, as non-Church of Ireland parents wished their children to attend. However, while some parents wanted to expand the school, the rector and vestry decided that it was already adequate for the needs of the parish children. The issue therefore arose as to whether a state-funded parish national school could restrict its pupil numbers in this way. A group of influential parents was formed to argue the case and eventually it decided to set up its own multi-denominational national school in Dalkey, which opened in 1978. The Department of Education eventually was persuaded that this organization could be the patron body of a new type of national school, which would be 'equality based, co-educational, child-centred and democratically run'. The organization, Educate Together, was formed in 1984 and by 2018 it managed 82 primary schools and 9 second-level schools, particularly in areas where there is a growing population. The position of parish national schools continues to concern the church as they are considered vital for the survival of the local Protestant community and have been a major factor in the strength of a parish. The boards of management for national schools which were established in 1975 included both elected teachers and parental members along with the principal teacher and nominees of the patron. These management boards lessened clerical control and allowed for broader democratic decision-making, in particular encouraging parents to become involved in their local school.

The Equal Status Act 2000 enabled denominational schools to use religion as a criterion for determining the priority of student admissions. This gave rise to reports that parents were baptizing their children for the purpose of obtaining a school place. The commencement of section 11 of the Education (Admissions to Schools) Act 2018 amended the Equal Status Act 2000, and religion is now prohibited as a selection criterion for primary-school admissions. However, the 2018 act contained provisions to enable students who are members of a minority religion to access a school that provides a religious-instruction or religious-education programme that is of the same or similar religious ethos to their own.

POST-PRIMARY EDUCATION

At secondary level, in the 1990s a major debate took place regarding the future structure and organization of the entire school system. Historically, Irish secondary schools have had a direct link to the state Department of Education with no other levels of decision-making, except for local-authority vocational schools. However, with the increasing numbers of pupils attending second-level schools, the need for a different partnership was foreseen. In November 1985 the Fine Gael minister for education, Gemma Hussey, published a green paper entitled 'Partners in education', which proposed the introduction of local and regional structures for the provision of education – these were to be thirteen new local education councils (LECs) consisting of representatives of the local authority, the voluntary secondary schools, the vocational, community and comprehensive schools, parents, post-primary teachers and primary-school representatives. The Church of Ireland was very concerned about these proposals as a Protestant school could be the only such school in a local region and voice of the Protestant schools as a group would be lost. Also it objected to the suggestion that LEC representatives would sit on the boards of management of all schools. A newly formed Protestant Secondary School Council of Governors wrote to the minister to express strongly their objections.

Gemma Hussey, who as a consultative-style minister had already established an Interim Curriculum and Examinations Board (1984) and the National Parents Council (1985), was moved from office in a cabinet reshuffle,[8] and the regional plan went no further, but the concept of a middle tier of management continued.

GREEN PAPER: 'EDUCATION FOR
CHANGING WORLD, 1992'

In June 1992 the Fianna Fáil minister for education, Séamus Brennan, issued a green paper called 'Education for a changing world'. It was a radical document and widely discussed. It proposed major changes to the structure of school-management boards, reducing the churches' control by allowing a minority position only for the patron on the board. Brennan stressed the economic function of education and its importance in growth of the economy, and suggested that technological education should become compulsory in schools. The tone of the green paper was not well received by educationalists and resulted in criticism of its lack of a coherent philosophy of education and its under-valuation of the role of the arts in personal development.

The Church of Ireland's detailed submission to this green paper was presented to the minister for education in November 1992, emphasizing the need for diversity of structures and the maintenance of the majority control of the patrons of the schools:

> The Church of Ireland Board of Education therefore insists that the structure proposed for the Board of Management for primary schools must be amended to incorporate the position of the Patron and to allow for the Patron to nominate a majority of members to each board.

NATIONAL EDUCATION CONVENTION, 1993

A general election was held in November 1992 and the chairperson of the Labour Party, Niamh Bhreathnach, was appointed minister for education in the coalition government. In October 1993, the minister set up a National Education Convention, which was held over ten days at Dublin Castle and was the first major democratic event in Irish education. The secretary general was the leading educationalist Professor John Coolahan of Maynooth University. The Church of Ireland delegation was led by the Venerable Gordon Linney and Mr David Meredith, secretary to the Board of Education, along with Mr Brian Duffy of the SEC. The Church of Ireland submissions emphasized that the chief areas for concern of the church were the composition of boards of management of schools, the proposed

---

8 In 1984, Minister Hussey also issued the discussion paper 'The ages of learning', which laid down a plan for a six-year cycle at secondary level, with a transition-year programme in the fourth year.

regional boards of education, the future structure of teacher education and the need for a Teaching Council to oversee the profession.

In September 1993, prior to the establishment of the National Convention, a conference was organized by the SEC at the King's Hospital to which were invited representatives of all the vested interests in Protestant education, including the Secondary School Council of Governors, the Irish School Heads' Association and Protestant secondary-school parents. The purpose was to brief the interested parties and to rally support for their submissions to the convention. The convention report summed up the Church of Ireland submission:

> The situation of the Protestant minority is quite different with a very scattered and low density, with less clear bonds to local parish communities at primary level and almost no connection at post-primary level. In addition a substantial proportion of children attending their schools are not Protestant. In such a situation they feel strongly that the Patron's right to nominate the majority on Boards of Management is essential to maintain the Protestant ethos of the school.

EDUCATION BILL, 1998

Based on the discussions at the National Convention, a white paper entitled 'Charting our education future' was published in 1995, but strong opposition to these proposals remained. In 1994 a government position paper on the proposed regional education councils was circulated and round-table talks were held, but no agreed solution emerged. In September 1994 there had been another set of round-table talks on the government's position paper on the proposed governance of schools, to which the Church of Ireland Board of Education presented a critical paper strongly defending the church's position:

> We have recognised the increased desire for participation and partnership in the running of schools, on the part of parents and teachers. We have never been convinced, not do we accept, that this desire should lead to an equality of representation for parents and teachers.[9]

However, in 1997, when the education bill was eventually published, the patrons' minority rights were still reduced. The Church of Ireland objected again to the composition of proposed boards of management and a protest meeting was organized by the church in March 1997. The government was aware that if an attempt was made to impose the education reforms on the Protestant community it could be seen by their Northern co-religionists as restricting Protestant freedom in the

9 John Walshe, *A new partnership for education* (Dublin, 1999), p. 109, quoting from Church of Ireland Board of Education, 'Presentation to Round Table Discussions', Dublin Castle, 12 Sept. 1994.

Republic of Ireland. The Venerable Gordon Linney, archdeacon of Dublin, in a speech at the meeting stated that:

> The Education Bill before the Dáil at present undermines substantially the ability of patrons, trustees, owners of the schools to effectively maintain the ethos and traditions of the schools which they hold in trust … It severely restricts the power and the rights of the Patron who will be required to hand over the executive responsibility for running the school to a Board of Management which is subject to the Minister.

In June 1997 there was a change of government and Micheál Martin became minister for education. The plan for regional councils was dropped and the patrons' rights were restored and given statutory recognition. When the amended 1998 Education Act became law, the majority on the boards of management was restored to the patron/trustee owners and these boards, including both teacher and parent representatives, were to be accountable to the patron for upholding the characteristic ethos of the school.

After the 1998 act, the Protestant secondary schools had to adjust to greater governance accountability and increased teacher and parental participation. The inspectorate of the Department of Education introduced a policy of 'whole-school evaluation', resulting in formal reports of all school activities. More emphasis was placed on the quality of education offered. The self-elected boards of governors remained as the school patron/trustees, with a separate board of management for the school, which included governors and elected teacher and parent representatives. The 1998 act was the first education act since the Vocational Education Act 1930, and it created a statutory structure for development in areas such as adult education, disadvantaged schools and reform of the school inspectorate. It also gave legal authority to the composition of the boards of management and to the appointment of teachers and parents.

SECOND-LEVEL DEVELOPMENTS

In 2009 the Protestant secondary schools faced another management issue – this was the change in the government policy of treating these secondary schools as 'fee-paying schools' rather than being part of the 'free scheme'. There had been widespread public criticism of fee-paying private schools being in receipt of teachers' salaries and capital grants from the state, and it was suggested that such schools were 'elitist'. The church argued that the Protestant schools were part of the 1967 'free-education scheme' and thus received their share of state funding through the block grant distributed by the SEC. However, the department decided to move the schools into the 'fee-paying' category despite strong objections. In 2009 the Protestant secondary schools lost their ancillary grants for caretaking, secretarial support, libraries, etc. In addition, the pupil-teacher ratio for the schools was increased by two units from 18:1 to 20:1, whereas for schools in the free-education scheme it was to be 19:1. A conference of the Protestant schools was organized in October 2009 by the Committee on Management for Protestant Secondary Schools. The former archdeacon of Dublin, Revd Gordon Linney, addressed the meeting, defending the 1968 free-education scheme,

> which conferred on Protestant children some equivalence with Roman Catholic children who had access for free secondary education in Catholic schools, [which] is being eroded without warning or consultation, a scheme which had the support of every Government until now for over 40 years.

CONCLUSION

The primary schools remain based on the parochial system, albeit with democratic boards of management, while the secondary schools maintain their individual identity with self-elected board of governors. Capitation grants, teachers' salaries and maintenance costs continue to be paid by the state and the 1968 'free-education' block-grant scheme, which has been operated by the SEC for forty years, has allowed the Protestant secondary schools to charge affordable fees and to offer a comprehensive entry. The provision of boarding schools for the scattered rural community has enabled pupils to have access to quality education and yet maintain their roots in the home locality. The Protestant comprehensive schools continue to offer a choice to parents who are seek free post-primary education in their own religious tradition. A policy of integration rather assimilation has been maintained.

However, one major social change since 1970s has been in Protestant third-level education, where Trinity College, once a predominantly Protestant college, has become a multi-denominational university, increased in size and serving the whole Irish community. Following the reforms of the Second Vatican Council (1962–5) and the lifting in 1970 of the Catholic Church's ecclesiastical 'ban' on attendance at TCD, the religious barriers among young people began to break down and Protestant students now socialize widely and have become integrated into the third-level-education sector regardless of their religious affiliation.

Undoubtedly, the advocacy of faith schools by the majority Catholic Church has provided strong support for the Church of Ireland's position to educate its children in their own religious tradition. The Church of Ireland leaders were fortunate – because of the openness of the voluntary education sector, they have had direct access to the minister for education when requested, and the specific concerns of the Protestant-managed schools have been readily considered by the Department of Education.

However, by 2010, there was an increasing public demand for a primary-school system that was not under church patronage. In 2011 the minister for education,

Ruairi Quinn, set up a Forum on Patronage and Pluralism to consider the key issues. At that time 96 per cent of primary schools were under church patronage, the great majority of which were managed by the Catholic Church. Some change has occurred to date, and in 2013 the sixteen new Education and Training Boards, restructured from thirty-three Vocational Education Committees, were given the remit to provide new non-denominational primary schools, and a policy of pre-consultation of parental choice of patronage has become important. Yet the parochial system of national schools has proved robust, well managed and satisfying to a majority of parents, both Catholic and Protestant, while the strength and quality of the Protestant-managed post-primary schools has been upheld.

In this remarkable fifty-year period of growth of Irish education, 1969–2019, the Church of Ireland has responded to change and has maintained its influence on the education of its members. As a result the Protestant community as whole continues to support its own denominational schools and the majority of Church of Ireland children receive their education in schools under Protestant management in the Republic. The General Synod Board of Education is responsible for the church's policy in education and, given the scale and complexity of twenty-first-century education, there is a demand for a professional and quality education system with a committed vision. In a time of change, therefore, planning for the future at both primary and secondary level will require insightful leadership, increased resources, consultation with parental choice, cooperation with the Department of Education and, most importantly, the support of the church as a whole.

20

The Church of Ireland's role in
education in Northern Ireland

Rosalind M.O. Pritchard

'TRANSFERRING' SCHOOLS: THE HISTORICAL CONTEXT

Educational politics in Northern Ireland are permeated by religious and political controversy. This has been so from the very beginning. Historically, the issue of transfer of schools from church to state control became one of the most divisive denominational issues in Northern Ireland and still resonates today. The divided system had its origins in the years immediately after the foundation of the Northern state in 1921. The minister for education, Lord Londonderry, was commissioned by Sir James Craig to reform education in Northern Ireland. The minister was a convinced supporter of integrated education and an opponent of sectarian education. The latter, he believed, had become characteristic of many national schools in the South; he wanted to do things differently in the North. The Government of Ireland Act 1920 laid down that the devolved Northern Ireland parliament was not permitted to endow any religious body with state funds; if schools wanted funding they ought not to be denominationally controlled. Lord Londonderry asked Robert Lynn to work out a plan for educational reform, and a committee bearing Lynn's name was established.

However, Catholic clerics declined to serve on it, and refused to give evidence when formally invited to do so. By this abstentionism, they lost a valuable opportunity to make their influence felt in Northern Ireland, but to have done so would have been to acknowledge the legitimacy of Northern Ireland. Fleming states: 'From this refusal all subsequent problems can be traced; justification remains a matter of debate amongst historians. ...[T]he Catholic Church wounded itself by boycotting the reform process.'[1] Abstentionism went so far that pupils in NI Catholic secondary schools continued to sit for the examinations of the Dublin-based Intermediate Education Board. Similarly, their teachers at first refused to accept their salaries from the Northern government, and called upon the Free State to finance Catholic education in NI.[2] However, in October 1922 Catholic

1 N. Fleming, 'Lord Londonderry and educational reform in 1920s Northern Ireland', *History Ireland*, 9:1 (2001), www.historyireland.com/troubles-in-ni/ni-1920-present/lord-londonderry-education-reform-in-1920s-northern-ireland, accessed on 7 Nov. 2018.   2 D. Kennedy, *Catholic education in Northern Ireland, 1921–1970.* (Belfast, 1971), p. 30.

schools lost financial backing from Dublin and reluctantly accepted the ministry's authority in Northern Ireland in order to receive government funding.

The Lynn Committee made a genuine attempt to resolve these and other problems in a non-sectarian manner, and its work culminated in a parliamentary act of 1923. It wanted local government control to be in direct proportion to the total amount of government funding that the school received.[3] It was willing to give some finance, even to managers who did not accept the principle of local control. For a start, all salaries were to be paid by the ministry of education. However, managers would not receive *full* funding unless they transferred their schools; the Church of Ireland had problems in doing so, most notably because there was a prohibition against giving religious instruction. It was not until the Education Act (Northern Ireland) 1930 was passed that they cooperated fully. That act made provision for the representation on local education committees of managers who transferred their schools, and also provided for Bible instruction by the teachers in the schools. These concessions enabled the Church of Ireland to transfer its schools in increasing numbers. By contrast, Daniel Mageean, Roman Catholic bishop of Down and Connor, asserted:

> We cannot transfer our schools. We cannot accept simple Bible teaching. I wish to emphasize this point. Simple Bible teaching is based on the fundamental principle of Protestantism, the interpretation of sacred scriptures by private judgement.'[4]

Such was the genesis of a divided school system in Northern Ireland; and herein lie the roots of the Transferor Representatives' Council (of which more below). Kelly states that the Church of Ireland 'made a serious effort to get a joint scheme of education adapted for the whole of Ireland by the two new governments'.[5] However, the 1930 act is stated by Hyland et al. to have 'constituted a major reversal of the non-denominational principles which the 1923 Act had advocated'.[6]

As a kind of consolation prize, the Ministry of Education was permitted to give Catholic voluntary schools government funding of up to 50 per cent of capital expenditure, and the local authorities were empowered to pay 50 per cent of the cost of lighting, heating and cleaning the schools. Some Protestants felt that the increased funding to voluntary schools amounted to 'the endowment of Roman Catholicism to the extent of £2 million' (a figure firmly denied by the Ministry of Education).[7] Some Catholics believed that the transferred schools were in essence Protestant, and so were as denominational in ethos and identity as their Catholic

---

3 D.H. Akenson, *Education and enmity: the control of schooling in Northern Ireland, 1920–50* (Newton Abbot, 1973), p. 53.   4 Ibid., pp 113–14.   5 T.F. Kelly, 'Education' in M. Hurley, *Irish anglicanism* (Dublin, 1970), p. 56.   6 A. Hyland, K. Milne, G. Byrne and J. Dallat (eds), *Irish educational documents* (Dublin, 1995), iii, pp 57–8.   7 N. Atkinson, *Irish education* (Dublin, 1969), pp 186–7.

counterparts for which funding was inferior.[8] No denomination was satisfied. Sectarian pressures had created a system of religious segregation that was 'separate *and* unequal'.[9] Since 1993, however, Catholic schools in Northern Ireland have received 100 per cent of their costs from the NI government. Notwithstanding this financial arrangement, the Catholic Church has been permitted to retain legal ownership of school premises and property; it has not been required to transfer the schools to state control and the revised funding arrangements are intended to leave intact the ethos of its schools.

GOVERNANCE AND RELIGIOUS AFFILIATION

Northern Ireland has a complex, segregated educational system that reflects its religious divisions. In the 2011 census, 41 per cent of people described themselves as Catholic, 19 per cent Presbyterian, 14 per cent Church of Ireland, 3 per cent Methodist, 6 per cent other Christian, 1 per cent other religion and 17 per cent no religion or none stated. Most Catholic schools are designated 'maintained' and are managed by the Council for Catholic Maintained Schools (CCMS).[10] The CCMS is now a powerful and influential body that was established under the 1989 Education Reform (Northern Ireland) Order. It held its first statutory meeting in 1990 and has therefore existed for almost three decades. It is the employing authority of teachers in its sector. Its functions are to promote effective management of Catholic maintained schools, to oversee quality assurance, to maintain school estates and to give advice to government. It presides over 466 schools; these are attended by 121,733 pupils, which is about 37 per cent of the total.

The remaining schools fall into the categories of 'controlled' (the largest sector), voluntary, integrated, Irish-medium or 'other maintained'. The antecedents of most Controlled schools were Protestant; and as we have seen above, control of them was gradually transferred to the state in the first half of the twentieth century. Three denominations – Presbyterian, Church of Ireland and Methodist – now comprise the Transferor Representatives' Council (TRC), which has the right to nominate representatives to boards of governors.[11] Controlled schools are not necessarily denominational schools: they represent a variety of faiths and they host pupils who have no religion at all. However, they do have a concept of education that is directly informed by Christian teaching and values. The Transferor Governor Handbook states that they understand the world and humanity within the context of belief in God and the Christian faith. They encourage the inclusion of core values based upon the Bible and shared Christian understanding; they place great value on high-quality religious education and collective worship, as specified

8 Hyland et al. (eds), *Irish educational documents*, iii, pp 57–8.   9 Akenson, *Education and enmity*, p. 195.   10 Catholic voluntary grammar schools also exist, and are under the control of either Catholic diocesan or religious trustees. CCMS has no control in these schools.   11 The TRC was the vision of Canon Dr Houston McKelvey in the 1980s, along with his Presbyterian and Methodist counterparts.

in the 1986 Education and Libraries (Northern Ireland) Order. Applicants being interviewed for principalships may be asked what they would do, if appointed, to promote spiritual and moral values, religious education and a Christian ethos.[12] However, the General Synod of the Church of Ireland report from 2015 states that 'a key component of the religious aspect of the ethos of a Controlled school is its unique *un-denominational approach to Religious Education and collective worship*' (author's italics).

Controlled schools are governed by the Education Authority (EA), which assumed its functions in 2015 and has been called 'the most significant change in administration of education in forty years'.[13] The reformed churches were anguished about their future representation on the proposed authority, whose predecessor, the Education and Skills Authority, was first proposed in 2007 but became mired in controversy.[14] Transferors were to have rights only over the schools that had been transferred, but no rights over *new* controlled schools. Historically, by virtue of the Education Act of 1968, transferors had been given rights of nomination to *all* controlled schools, i.e. both new schools built by the local authorities and those schools they had already transferred. Through custom and practice, transferors had governance rights over some schools that they had never owned, managed or originally transferred. Now they were to lose these, ostensibly on the grounds of 'equality legislation'. The transferors' disadvantageous situation contrasted with the comfortable, powerful situation of the Catholics, who would still have rights over all maintained schools *including new ones*. In 2006, the General Synod of the Church of Ireland wrote:

> The status of transferors has never been adequately recognized by government and compared with the statutory nature of the CCMS, the TRC is vastly under-resourced and does not have the capacity to adequately represent the views of the Controlled sector to which it is organically linked. This is a huge inequality which the Churches have consistently raised with successive ministers.

The TRC lobbied with a 2007 document in which they sought comparable arrangements that would 'make reasonable and equitable alternative provision for

---

12 This is a suggestion from transferors in their handbook, and in an actual interview situation, all governors would have to agree to put it as a question.   13 General Synod of the Church of Ireland, report from 2014, p. 286.   14 The creation of ESA was favoured by Education Minister John O'Dowd, from Sinn Féin, but was opposed by the Democratic Unionist Party (DUP). The Hansard Report of 2009 (see paras 29 and 54) gives a flavour of the debate at the time, reporting some committee members' concern that the controlled sector and the community it served, largely the Protestant/unionist community, were being disadvantaged by the arrangements envisaged in the education bill and the second education bill. Fears that the transferors would lose their influence under the ESA (despite the fact CCMS were originally to be absorbed into it) ultimately led to the failure of ESA and the establishment of the less ambitious Education Authority.

the Protestant churches to continue to carry out the role they have always played in education'.[15] It deplored the attempt to 'remove the Christian ethos as of right from the Controlled sector of education'. It sought 'parity of protection for the Christian ethos in schools attended generally by Protestant children' – the same as that 'currently enjoyed in the Catholic Maintained sector of education'. It concluded that

> The effect of the proposed new reforms will be that, while a broad Christian ethos will be retained in Catholic schools, it will no longer be reflected in schools which pupils from the Protestant tradition will attend. Catholic schools will continue as of legal right to have faith representatives on Boards of Governors; however, schools attended mainly by Protestant pupils will be prohibited by law from having any official Church representation.

The TRC threatened submission of a petition of concern to the Northern Ireland Assembly to prevent passage of any legislation that would destroy parity of treatment with the Catholic Church by removing the Christian ethos from controlled schools. The reformed churches won their case. The education bill presented to the NI Assembly in 2009 refrained from proposing change to existing transferors' rights. There are now over 1,800 transferor governors, of which more than 600 are from the Church of Ireland. This confers on it the 'opportunity to manifest and develop leadership effectiveness and school ethos'[16] – in other words the chance to make heard the voice of the Christian faith in Northern Ireland. The Minister and Department of Education remain responsible for setting policy, but as a stakeholder in education, the TRC retains an important Christian advocacy role. It has a direct influence over all schools and not just controlled schools when it comes to the implementation of policy.

There remained another inequity: the disparity between the fragmented administration of the controlled schools and the effectiveness of the CCMS. The Church of Ireland noted with deep concern 'the continued disadvantaged position of Controlled schools throughout Northern Ireland due to a lack of a dedicated advocacy and support body' and called upon the Department of Education 'to take steps to resolve that injustice and ensure equality of treatment for all schools'.[17] The churches were able to argue successfully for a new body, the Controlled Schools Support Council (CSSC) which was established in 2016. By 2018, 94 per cent of controlled schools had opted to register as members. The Church of Ireland welcomed the CSSC as a body which for the first time ensured that the controlled sector would have a representative voice on an equal footing along with

15 Transferor Representatives' Council Briefing Document, 'Review of public administration in education proposals in respect of school governance and accountability', 27 Nov. 2007, www.ireland.anglican.org/cmsfiles/pdf/Information/Submissions/TRC/trc_aec_271107.pdf, accessed on 22 Sept. 2018.   16 General Synod of the Church of Ireland, reports for 2017.   17 General Synod of the Church of Ireland, reports for 2014, p. xcii.

other sectors.[18] The CSSC now represents 558 schools comprising 48 per cent of the total number. These are staffed by over 8,500 teachers and attended by over 140,000 pupils. It is evident that in certain respects, the reformed churches have had to struggle to maintain and develop their role in education, but when they act resolutely and in a unified manner, they can clearly achieve their objectives.

ATTEMPTS TO OVERCOME DIVISION

The members of the respective associated communities do not cross the controlled and maintained school sectors to any notable extent – they tend to stay within their own cultural groups, thereby reflecting existing divisions in Northern Ireland's post-conflict society; 70 per cent of pupils attending controlled schools are of Protestant denomination and 96 per cent of pupils attending Catholic maintained schools are of Catholic denomination. Notably, less than 1 per cent of pupils attending Catholic maintained schools are Protestant and only 7 per cent of pupils attending controlled schools are Catholic.[19] To help overcome divisions, the controlled and maintained sectors are complemented by a small sector for integrated education. This has a statutory basis in Article 64 of the 1989 Education Reform (NI) Order, which defines integrated education as 'the education together at school of Protestant and Roman Catholic pupils' and lays upon the Department of Education the formal duty of encouraging and facilitating the development of such schools. There are currently 65 integrated schools in Northern Ireland attended in 2015–16 by 20,000 children – just 7 per cent of all pupils; 45/65 are primary schools and 20/65 are post-primary schools.

The development of this sector has made slow progress since Lagan College, the first integrated school, was founded in 1981 with 28 pupils. Integrated schools are supposed to meet certain quotas for the denominational composition of the school population; the guideline is that Catholic and Protestant components should eventually each reach 30 per cent of the overall school population. However, Topping and Cavanagh, who constituted a panel reviewing the functioning of integrated education, found that opinions about the composition of such schools were changing and were no longer so narrowly construed as before.[20] Quite a sizable minority (22 per cent) of their respondents did not necessarily agree that the defining feature of integrated schools should be about educating Protestant and Catholic pupils together; they wanted the schools to include pupils from a wide range of social, cultural and racial backgrounds and included other criteria such as quality. The panel recommended that, in view of NI's changing demography and increasing diversity, the existing legal definition of 'integrated' education should be revised to make it appropriate for the twenty-first century. Likewise, Gallagher judged

---

18 The CSSC is ultimately responsible to the Department of Education, not to the TRC.   19 M. Topping and C. Cavanagh, *Integrating education in Northern Ireland: celebrating inclusiveness and fostering innovation in our schools* (Bangor, 2016), p. 15.   20 Ibid.

that the goal of reconciliation was not adequate by itself as an ethos for integrated schools; and that it needed to be strengthened by achievements in school improvement and in the provision of facilities.[21] Borooah and Knox speculated that many parents were reluctant to send their children to integrated schools because such institutions blurred traditional boundaries and might cause a sectarian backlash within the family, community or faith group.[22] To date, no Catholic school has been transformed into an integrated school. Since 2015, the possibility of jointly managed schools has existed, but there has been no take-up on this either.[23]

The concept of 'shared education' has now become more prevalent than that of 'integration' though both approaches are intended to contribute to the development of a more tolerant society. A Shared Education (Northern Ireland) Act was passed in 2016; it defines 'sharing' as 'the education together of: (a) those of different religious belief, including reasonable numbers of both Protestant and Roman Catholic children or young persons; (b) those who are experiencing socio-economic deprivation and those who are not'. This is to be 'secured by the working together and cooperation of two or more relevant providers'. A single educational establishment demonstrating a mix of religious belief and a wide range of socio-economic status will *not* satisfy the legal definition of shared education. Schools in general have a duty to encourage, facilitate and promote sharing, and this is in keeping with church principles. The Church of Ireland in its draft equality report states: 'Shared education and jointly managed schools not only flow from the Christian duty of reconciliation but also offer practical benefits for children as well as a strong moral example.'[24]

Shared education works through school partnerships, teacher professional learning and networks for school improvement. It is underpinned by contact theory. Teachers and pupils visit each other's schools for cross-campus teaching and for the use of facilities. Resources such as equipment, transport, computers, teaching plans and materials, assembly halls, sports grounds, science laboratories and music/drama facilities are being shared across schools which are gradually developing a self-supporting network. One source of finance is from the European Union Peace IV CASE Project. The EU and the Republic of Ireland both contribute funding, and their work extends beyond NI to some of the border counties of Ireland, targeting schools with little prior experience of delivering shared education.

21 T. Gallagher, 'Shared education in Northern Ireland: school collaboration in divided societies', *Oxford Review of Education*, 42:3 (2016), p. 367.   22 V. Borooah and C. Knox, *The economics of schooling in a divided society: the case for shared education* (London, 2015).   23 See www.education-ni. gov.uk/sites/default/files/publiations/de/2015-15-jointly-managed-schools.pdf.; also R. Meredith, 'Faith school: Desertmartin PS and Knocknagin PS to make NI history', 16 June 2016, www.bbc. co.uk/news/uk-northern-ireland-36547453, accessed on 30 Nov. 2018.   24 General Synod of the Church of Ireland, reports for 2017, p. 263. One of the most successful ecumenical educational achievements in the early 1990s was the RC church and TRC working together with DE in producing the Religious Education Core Syllabus – a common core of RE taught in all schools in NI. This was a notable achievement in its day and was subsequently revised about ten years later.

Evaluation is ongoing. The school inspectors integrate 'sharing' into their inspection process, and information about compliance is collected every six months; lessons learned are fed back into the system with the firm intention of embedding them into schools' self-evaluation and strategic plans. In May 2018, the first report, 'Advancing shared education', was presented to the Northern Ireland Assembly in conformity with the 2016 act's requirement for a formal report every two years.[25] Not all schools are yet involved – some are unable or unwilling to engage in the sharing process, though it is gaining momentum. The position in May 2016 (when the 2016 act came into force) was that there were 313 schools and early years settings involved in 136 shared education partnerships, accounting for 16,969 pupils. By 31 March 2018 this had increased to 583 schools/early years settings, accounting for 59,049 pupils involved in 254 partnerships.

Queen's University has a Centre for Shared Education directed by Professor Joanne Hughes. It develops, supports and evaluates the sharing process and has served as an inspiration for other countries, such as Macedonia and Israel, which also struggle with community conflict. Loader and Hughes,[26] in a review of the sharing project, report that on the positive side reconciliation is becoming a core activity rather than an add-on. Schools are trying to avoid the short-term, low-impact activities that were sometimes a feature of past endeavours to promote mutual understanding. Pupils in shared education do demonstrate more favourable attitudes than pupils at non-participating schools; furthermore, there is a ripple effect within the wider community, even among those who are not directly involved – joint events for parents and inter-school collaboration act as a model of positive, cooperative relations. A great advantage is that no change in school structure or governance is needed for sharing to take place, so there is no need to renounce distinctive identity and ethos. Sharing can develop at a pace appropriate to local circumstances. On the negative side, there is an endemic tension between the desire to protect in-group culture and the need to promote social cohesion. Over time, the reconciliation objectives may become de-emphasized, routine and superficial; they may fail to address, in depth, issues of identity, conflict and injustice:

> The concern is … that, rather than taking the opportunity to challenge narratives and structures that perpetuate inequality, shared education will serve only to facilitate contact within the existing framework of intergroup relations.[27]

Hughes et al. highlight an additional tension: the neoliberal framing of education, in particular the focus on performativity and league tables, may stymie the

25 Department of Education Northern Ireland, 'Advancing shared education: report to the Northern Ireland Assembly' (Bangor, 2018).   26 R. Loader and J. Hughes, 'Balancing cultural diversity and social cohesion in education: the potential of shared education in divided contexts', *British Journal of Educational Studies*, 65:1 (2017), pp 3–25.   27 Ibid., p. 18.

potential for shared education.[28] Their argument is that the education system deprioritizes initiatives aimed at social good on the basis that they detract from more 'important' priorities such as exam success rates.

OUTCOMES OF EDUCATION IN NI SCHOOLS

Rankings and selection

The Department of Education Northern Ireland (DE) does not produce GCSE or A-level rankings, and does not endorse them. However, the *Belfast Telegraph* routinely compiles league tables for public examinations, using material obtained from DE under the Freedom of Information Act. Grammar schools took the top 54 places for GCSE results in 2016/17. The top six schools at GCSE level were Catholic, except for Down High School. At A-level, the top ten schools were also Catholic.[29] In England, Catholic schools do well too. There, the Department for Education notes that they typically outperform the national average by 5–6 per cent in GCSE.[30] Similarly, the number of Catholic schools rated good or outstanding by Ofsted (the inspecting body) is consistently 9–10 per cent above schools nationally.

Northern Ireland has been the subject of criticism for its retention of grammar schools, which were attended by 45 per cent of pupils in the year 2017/18. Pupils at grammar schools do better than pupils in most other school types, though the academic gap between the grammar and other post-primary sectors is narrowing. In 2008/9 the sectoral difference in achievement of three or more A-levels at grades A*–C was 34 per cent; but in 2016/17, that gap had narrowed to 23 per cent.[31] In 2016/17, 69 per cent of pupils in the final year of an A-level, or equivalent course, achieved three or more A-levels at grades A*–C. This had risen from 66 per cent in 2015/16 and 65 per cent in 2014/15; so the educational performance of NI pupils is on an upward trajectory.

Martin McGuinness, Sinn Féin (SF) minister of education in Stormont 1999–2002, began the process of scrapping the 11-plus exam, which he had failed as a child; and Caitríona Ruane, SF minister of education 2007–11, declared an end to the 11-plus for entry to grammar schools. She denounced it as an outdated and unequal education system for allocating pupils to different school types, despite

28 J. Hughes, C. Donnelly, R. Leitch and S. Burns, 'Caught in the conundrum: neoliberalism and education in post-conflict Ireland – exploring shared education', *Policy Futures in Education*, 14: 8 (2016), pp 1091–1100.   29 All figures from R. Black, 'Catholic schools clinch top 10 places in A-level league tables in Northern Ireland', *Belfast Telegraph*, 14 Mar. 2018, www.belfasttelegraph.co.uk/news/education/league-tables/revealed-alevel-league-table-for-northern-ireland-schools-2018-36703884.html, accessed on 26 Oct. 2018.   30 Department for Education, 'Memorandum of understanding between the Catholic Church and the Department for Education', Crown Copyright DFE-00120-2016.   31 Black, 'Catholic schools clinch top 10 places in A-level league tables in Northern Ireland', *Belfast Telegraph*, 14 Mar. 2018.

the fact that they were all obliged to follow the same curriculum. Many grammar schools, however, continued to run their own selection procedures; some using the Post-Primary Transfer Consortium (PPTC) and some using the Association of Quality Education (AQE) examination bodies. If children wanted to maximize their choices they sat *both* the PPTC and the AQE tests, which resulted in their having to take five examinations on five successive Saturdays. It has recently been decided to set one examination for all pupils wishing to undergo the selection procedure for grammar-school entry, but it will be some years before a new system is fully in place. The intention is still to have these examinations administered by the grammar schools rather than by the state.

The issue of selection is divisive both within and between the denominations. The Catholic bishops announced a phased move away from academic selection, whereas the Church of Ireland took the view that the ending of selection did not offer a panacea for overcoming either educational or social divisions. They adopted an analytical approach, and appointed a working group (WG) in 2015 to consider a discussion paper drafted by Canon Dr Ian Ellis. There had been a long and tangled debate following the Burns Report in 2001,[32] and the paper was intended to help the church to find some clarity in its position. A significant number of parents were obviously willing to submit their children to the ordeal of taking entrance examinations for grammar schools. Members of the WG inferred that the ending of selection might be openly resisted by some parents who would perceive it as putting the needs of one group of children over those of another group. The WG members upheld the primary principles that all children of God were of equal value, and that it was vital to support the socially disadvantaged. Perhaps their most important conclusion was that

> Removing a selection test will do little to enhance the transformative effect of education for a working class child if his/her parents place little value on education and provide a culturally poor home environment, showing little interest in the child's progress and doing nothing to encourage or consolidate that progress.

The most essential factor for a child's development was not the income or education level of the parents, but the attitude of those parents to the value of education and what it can produce. The WG believed that selection was not inherently unjust, and indeed Peter Weir of the Democratic Unionist Party, who was minister of education in 2016, also supported the right of schools to select on the basis of academic ability. It was, incidentally, the first time since 1999 that a non-Sinn Féin politician had held the education portfolio.

---

32 Burns Report: *Education for the 21st century: report by the Post-Primary Review Body* (Belfast, 2001).

Under-achievement of Protestant boys

The issue of selection at 11 has now been overtaken by concern about inequality. There is more poverty among Catholics than among Protestants. Entitlement to free school meals (FSMs) is a proxy indicator of poverty based on parents' eligibility for certain social-benefit payments. The 2015/16 annual NI school census gives the breakdown of pupils entitled to a free school meal as 26 per cent Protestant and 34 per cent Catholic, with some in 'other' categories. These figures contrast with England where overall eligibility for FSM stands at about 14 per cent. Though Catholic pupils are poorer, their educational outcomes are better. This has changed from the mid-1980s, when those leaving Catholic schools were doing worse academically than those in other school types. In 2015, a report on educational inequalities noted,[33] with concern, that the achievement of Protestants was lower than that of Catholics at post-primary level; and that this gap had widened over the period of their study. Under-achievement was compounded by gender and was particularly characteristic of males; in the 16–17 age group, 68 per cent of girls, but only 51 per cent of boys, were studying A levels or the equivalent. For younger pupils, the pattern was the same. In 2016/17 36.6 per cent of Protestant boys entitled to FSM gained five GCSEs at grades A*–C (including English and maths) compared to 45 per cent of Catholic boys so entitled.[34] These data show that boys in general, and Protestant boys in particular, are not building a secure future for themselves.

Various scholars have suggested reasons for Protestant boys' underachievement. Brewer et al. argue that relationships have been *over*-emphasized during attempts to manage the NI conflict and that structures have been *under*-emphasized. As a result, they say, 'The disadvantaged structural position of working class Loyalists … went by neglect.'[35] Smith, in an empirical study of alienation within the Protestant working class, shows that its members perceived the peace process and the Good Friday Agreement as inequitable – to the benefit of Catholics rather than of Protestants.[36] They believed that Catholics were better at using their social capital and local leadership to apply for peace and reconciliation funding. Protestant churches seemed to be not even 'of the community', especially as there was competition between them to maintain their congregations. By comparison, the Catholic Church was a force for social cohesion. Division and individualism seemed to Smith's interviewees to be a source of powerlessness. Furthermore 'The [previous community] reliance on immediate access to employment had resulted in a devaluation of education … leaving a legacy of a culture not geared to education.'[37]

33 S. Burns, R. Leitch and H. Hughes, *Educational inequalities in Northern Ireland: summary report* (Belfast, 2015).   34 A.M. Gray, J. Hamilton, G. Kelly, B. Lynn, M. Melaugh and G. Robinson, *Northern Ireland peace monitoring report number 5 from the Community Relations Council* (Belfast, 2018), p. 163.   35 J.D. Brewer, G.I. Higgins and F. Teeney, *Religion, civil society, and peace in Northern Ireland* (Oxford, 2011), p. 185.   36 C.A. Smith, 'Protestants and policy in Northern Ireland: a case of Protestant working-class alienation' (PhD, Ulster University, 2003).   37 Ibid., p. 339.

Some figures seem to lend credence to this assertion about employment; 24 per cent of Protestant youths are unemployed, whereas this is the case for only 17 per cent of Catholics. Yet NI has the highest rate of working–age economic inactivity in the UK at 28 per cent (compared with Scotland and England at 22 per cent). This makes it difficult for some pupils to benefit from role models of discipline and hard work because the parents are not employed. The traditional labour market for Protestants no longer exists: shipbuilding for example has been replaced by services, construction work and the public sector. This is destructive of community culture and of economic well-being. Agriculture now represents only 2 per cent of NI's economic output, whereas services account for 70 per cent of economic activity and 78 per cent of employment. The role of the families is vital. The Social Mobility Commission in England stated that parental expectations and encouragement, support with homework and investment in private tuition all play an important role in explaining the attainment of some ethnic groups.[38] As detailed above, the Church of Ireland made a similar point when analysing selection.

AUSTERITY AND EDUCATION IN NORTHERN IRELAND

Divided educational systems usually cost more money than integrated ones due to factors such as duplication of provision, inefficient utilization of space and reduced capacity to make economics of scale. Northern Ireland has a high proportion of small schools, but this is not due to the rural nature of the region. The population density is double that of the Republic of Ireland. Topping and Cavanagh attribute the proliferation of small schools to the multi-sector school system, single-sex schools and the selective system of education.[39]

The education system is currently in crisis, and money is being wasted not just at school level, but at tertiary and political level too. Schools are subject to great financial stringency. Numbers are rising, and funding is falling. The amount of money available for each pupil is being cut year on year, for both primary and post-primary pupils. In June 2018, 200 principals, from across all area learning communities, sent an open letter to the authorities, highlighting the problems that they were facing. Between 2015 and 2018, 692 teachers and 738 support staff lost their jobs. The principals complained that they were 'being required to make excellent teachers redundant during a time of ongoing and increasing industrial action' and highlighted the negative impact that this would have on the quality of education and leadership'.[40] The Education Authority is also in deficit; the Northern Ireland Audit Office criticized it for over-spending its budget by £19 million in 2016/17.

38 Social Mobility Commission, 'Asian Muslims and Black people do better in school, worse in work, 28 Dec. 2016, www.gov.uk/government/news/asian-muslims-and-black-people-do-better-in-school-worse-in-work, accessed on 8 Nov. 2018. 39 Topping and Cavanagh, *Integrating education* , p. 17. 40 R. Meredith, 'NI post-primary principals say education facing "crisis"', BBC News, www. bbc.co.uk/news/uk-northern-ireland-44540086, accessed on 8 Nov. 2018.

One obvious area in which economies could be made is in the sector of teacher education. Here, denominational issues link to financial issues. Teachers are trained at Northern Ireland's two universities, Queen's and Ulster; at Stranmillis University College (state-controlled, about 1,475 students in 2016/17) and at St Mary's (Catholic, about 990 students in 2016/17). The two colleges have their own estates and buildings, with concomitant outgoings, whereas at the universities teachers are educated within component chools or departments. The cost of Northern Ireland's teacher-education provision was so high, and seemed to vary so much according to institution that Dr Stephen Farry, the minister for employment and learning, commissioned a formal enquiry into the teacher-education infrastructure. This revealed that in 2011/12 the cost of training a cohort of teachers was as follows: QUB £852,000; UU £692,000; Stranmillis £3,818,000; St Mary's £3,784,000. For the colleges, the basic unit of funding used in England was enhanced in NI by several premia, bringing funding to a level that would sustain them in view of their small size and diseconomies of scale. In other words, the government was helping the colleges to survive but at great expense: they cost 35 per cent more than their English equivalents. As part of the enquiry, an international report was produced to address both the quality and the cost of teacher education in NI.[41] The panel members were asked to examine whether the available funds could be more effectively deployed by the institutions 'if they were prepared to move to a more shared or integrated system'.[42] The panel suggested various options for structural change: enhanced collaboration; two centres; a federation; or a unitary structure. The status quo was said *not* to be an option.

The heads of all the teacher education institutions were called to give evidence to the Northern Ireland Assembly.[43] The response of St Mary's was particularly robust. The principal, Professor Peter Finn, wished his college

> to continue as an autonomous, values-based, higher education institution in the Catholic tradition; ... to continue to promote and to develop [its] distinctive ethos and identity in the higher education sector; to be located on the Falls Road in Belfast.

'We seek', he proclaimed, 'an accommodation of faith-based teacher education, not its integration or merger into what is a secular system'. In the event, St Mary's carried the day; little changed. Stranmillis, also, was also able to fight off a merger with Queen's, though this did not have the same religious resonance as at St Mary's.

41 P. Sahlberg, P. Broadfoot, J. Coolahan, J. Furlong and G. Kirk, *Aspiring to excellence: final report of the international review panel on the structure of initial teacher education in Northern Ireland* (Belfast, 2014). 42 Ibid., p. 3. 43 Northern Ireland Assembly Committee for Employment and Learning Official Report (Hansard), *Review of initial teacher education infrastructure St Mary's College* (Stormont, 2014).

The reasons for the prevalence of the status quo are complex. The spirited defence of faith-based HE no doubt played a part, but the minister commented that

> part of the difficulty was the governance around St Mary's ... While it was almost 100 per cent funded by public money, it was not an Arms Length Body of Government and had its [own] governance and appointments arrangements. The Office of National Statistics was exploring the reclassification of St Mary's. I did try to remove the premia payments to Stranmillis and St Mary's of ca. £2m per year which were paid for their small size but were not value for money. I was overruled by the NI Executive on this decision in February 2015.[44]

Divisions are thus endemic to education in Northern Ireland, from primary to tertiary level. Borooah and Knox judge these harshly.[45] They claim that grammar schools remain cocooned in complacency, and that they are failing the community by restricting admission in terms of the economic circumstances of their pupils: 'In effect, the tax payer pays grammar schools to transmit deprivation through generations.' The General Synod of the Church of Ireland has no doubt that fragmentation caused by sectoral interests fosters inequality and leads to waste.[46] Peter Robinson, former first minister, also speaks of the need to create a single educational system in the belief that educating children separately 'is fundamentally damaging to our society'.[47] However, the Church of Ireland remarks: '[T]he structure of our divided school system is a product of our history and not easily changed.'[48] The fact that the Catholic Church fights hard for its version of faith-based education ensures that the reformed churches have their own sector, by default, thereby entrenching segregated education. Improving contact and sharing education may be necessary, but are not sufficient, if the disadvantages of segregation are to be fully overcome. We shall leave the last word to Fr Denis Faul,[49] who said that maximizing the coming together of people would 'not necessarily solve the problems unless at the same time you had some mechanism whereby you dissolved the power of the various organisations that split people apart'.

44 Personal communication to author; written permission was given to quote it.   45 Borooah and Knox, *The economics of schooling in a divided society*, p. 82.   46 General Synod of the Church of Ireland, report for 2017, p. 263.   47 General Synod report for 2011.   48 Ibid., p. 330.   49 Brewer et al., *Religion, civil society, and peace in Northern Ireland*, p. 188.

Contributors

Michael Burrows is the bishop of Cashel, Ferns and Ossory, and chairman of the Commission on Ministry.

Richard Clarke has served as the archbishop of Armagh and primate of all Ireland since 2012, and was previously the bishop of Meath and Kildare from 1996 onwards.

Adrian Clements is the former chief officer and secretary general of the Representative Church Body, the central trustee body for the Church of Ireland.

Paul Colton is the bishop of Cork, Cloyne and Ross and is an honorary research fellow in the School of Law and Politics at Cardiff University, where he completed his PhD in 2013 in the field of canon law.

Hazel Corrigan is the lay honorary secretary of the General Synod for the Southern Province.

George Davison is the clerical honorary secretary of the General Synod for the Northern Province, rector of St Nicholas, Carrickfergus, and archdeacon of Belfast.

Aonghus Dwane has worked for many years in the Irish-language sector and has organized various cultural events at Christ Church Cathedral, Dublin. He is a lawyer-linguist with the European Parliament in Brussels, and a writer. His biography of former archbishop of Dublin, Donald Caird, was published in 2014.

Ian Morton Ellis is rector of Newcastle, a canon of St Patrick's Cathedral, Dublin, and a former editor of the *Church of Ireland Gazette*.

Ken Gibson is the lay honorary secretary of the General Synod for the Northern Province.

Lynn Glanville trained as a journalist and has been communications officer for the united dioceses of Dublin and Glendalough since 2011. Prior to which she had extensive experience in print and broadcast journalism.

Paul Harron was formerly Church of Ireland Press Officer (2008–18). He works professionally as a senior communications manager but is also an architectural and art historian. His PhD (QUB, History) was on the architectural practice of Young & Mackenzie of Belfast. He edited *New life for churches in Ireland* (Belfast, 2012).

Kerry Houston is head of the Department of Academic Studies, TU Dublin Conservatory of Music and Drama; director of the Research Foundation for Music in Ireland; chairman of RILM Ireland; director of chapel music, Trinity College Dublin; and assistant keeper of music, St Patrick's Cathedral, Dublin.

Áine Hyland is emeritus professor of education and former vice president of University College Cork, and a member of the Royal Irish Academy. She was a member of the team that reviewed the Church of Ireland Theological College in 2002 and a member of the first governing board of the Church of Ireland Theological Institute.

Michael Jackson is the archbishop of Dublin, bishop of Glendalough and primate of Ireland. He was previously bishop of Clogher and currently chairs the management group of the Anglican Communion's Network for Inter Faith Concerns (NIFCON).

Kenneth Kearon has been bishop of Limerick and Killaloe since 2015. Prior to that he was secretary general of the Anglican Communion from 2005 to 2014.

Ginnie Kennerley was one of the first women ordained in the Church of Ireland, in 1988. A former journalist, she has ministered in Bray, Narraghmore and Castledermot, and is editor of *Search: A Church of Ireland Journal*.

John McDowell is the bishop of Clogher and a former president of the Irish Council of Churches.

Harold Miller is the bishop of Down and Dromore and chairman of the Liturgical Advisory Committee.

Kenneth Milne is the Church of Ireland historiographer and was formerly the principal of the Church of Ireland College of Education, Dublin. He is honorary keeper of the archives at Christ Church Cathedral, Dublin.

Daniel Nuzum is the Church of Ireland chaplain at the Cork City Hospitals and adjunct lecturer in the College of Medicine and Health, University College Cork.

Fergus O'Ferrall was the lay leader of the Methodist Church in Ireland (2016–18) and he is an accredited local preacher and author of a number of works on Irish history.

Susan Parkes is an emeritus fellow of Trinity College Dublin. She was a governor of the Church of Ireland College of Education and author of *Kildare Place: the history of the Church of Ireland Training College and College of Education, 1811–2010* and editor of *A danger to the men? A history of women in Trinity College Dublin, 1904–2004*.

Rosalind M.O. Pritchard is emeritus professor of education at the University of Ulster, Coleraine, a member of the Royal Irish Academy and secretary of the European Association for Institutional Research.

Raymond Refaussé is a former librarian and archivist at the Representative Church Body Library, Dublin, the central repository and reference library for the Church of Ireland.

Patricia Storey is the bishop of Meath and Kildare, president of the Church of Ireland Youth Department, and a former youth worker.

Gillian Wharton is the clerical honorary secretary of the General Synod for the Southern Province, rector of Booterstown, and a canon of St Patrick's Cathedral, Dublin.

Robin Bantry White is a former clerical honorary secretary of the General Synod for the Southern Province, and also previously served as archdeacon of Cork, Cloyne and Ross.

Index

Numbers in **bold** refer to plates.

see house project 201
sustentation fund 196
volunteers 201–2
Republic of Ireland
   Anglo-Irish culture 24
   church closures 76–7
   Church of Ireland (confident minority) 98
   commemoration of independence 157–8
   cultures in 24
   disestablishment centenary 21, 26, 98
   educational system, changes in 25
   EEC membership 98
   English culture 24
   Gaelic culture 24
   liberalism 193
   parochial reorganization 76–7
   referendums 100–1
   religion 90
   secularism 128, 160
   state-church liaison 27
   Ulster Protestant culture 24
Revised common lectionary, The (1992) 38, 40, 41
Rhodes, Pam 9
Ripon Affair 96
Ritchie, David 197
Robinson, Gene, bishop 146
Robinson, John 57
Robinson, Joseph 57
Robinson, Mary 99
Robinson, Peter 283
Roe, Henry 189
Role of the Church Committee (ROCC) 93–4,
   95, 96, 189, 191–2
Rolston, Jack, canon 78
Roman Catholic Church
   clerical sexual abuse of children 101, 128
   Consilium Conferentiarum Episcoporum
      Europae (CCEE) 117
   Eucharist and 120
   Faith and Order Commission 114
   faith schools 268
   Healthcare Chaplaincy Board 79
   ICCTRA and 105
   Irish constitution and 24, 98
   lectionary 41
   liturgical changes 30, 56
   Ne Temere decree 252
   in Northern Ireland 25, 92, 271–2, 280
   texts used by 40
   see also Vatican II
Roman Catholic hierarchy
   CCBI observer status 120
   One bread, one body 120

Roman Catholics, 'ban', TCD and 99
Rooke, Patrick, dean 206
Roseingrave, R. 57
Royal School of Church Music (RSCM) 49,
   49n14, 50
Roycroft, Máire 226
Ruddock, Bruce, canon 143
Rufli, Joan (*later* Russell) 62
Runcie, Robert, archbishop of Canterbury 4,
   118
Russcher, Tristan 224
Ryan, Dermot, archbishop of Dublin 1
Ryan, Maureen, canon 70

Safeguarding Trust 19, 78, 180
Safeguarding Trust Board 192
Sagart, An 221
Said, Revd Yazid 159
St Anne's Cathedral, Belfast 33, 47–8, 54
   BBC broadcasts 48
   Black Santa 11
   Chapel of the Royal Irish Regiment 205
   Chapel of Unity 204
   choir 47–8
   completion of 204–6
   ecumenical cross-community choir 48
   Information Centre 96
   Kegworth remembrance service **19–20**
   needlework kneelers 217
   ordination of woman priest 97
   organists 47–8
   'Spire of Hope' 205–6
   Titanic pall, The **47**, 217
St Ann's Church, Dawson Street, Dublin **14**,
   226
St Augustine's, Derry 72
St Bartholomew's Church, Dublin 51
St Canice's Cathedral, Kilkenny 227
St Colman's Church, Derrykeighan 210
St Colman's Church, Kilroot 211
St Columba's, Whiterock, Belfast 211
St Columb's Cathedral, Londonderry 48, 51,
   207
St Elizabeth's Church, Dundonald **43–4**, 212
St Fin Barre's Cathedral, Cork 48
   diocesan music outreach project 48
   Irish-language services 227
   labyrinth landscape-art 216
   organ restoration 51
   organists 48
   Steering Committee 155
St Fintan's Church, Durrow, County Laoise
   51n19

social theology 102
Societas Liturgica 39
Society for Promoting Christian Knowledge
    (SPCK) 137
Society for the Propagation of the Gospel (SPG)
    137
Spanish Reformed Church 142
Spiecker, Eberhard 123
sport, Sunday worship and 84
Standing Committee 92, 93, 94, 95, 97, 186,
    192, 197
    8th amendment and 103
    Anglican Covenant Working Group 149
    Book of Reports (1972) 106
    committees overseen by 192
    News and Information Service 104
    'Newstime' 105
Stanford, Charles Villiers 43, 43n2, 53, 57
Steed, Revd Helene 118
Stephen, Rosamund 202
Stevenson, J. 57
Stevenson, Nora 62
Stewart, Sir Robert Prescott 56, 57
Stobart, Peter 48
Storey, Patricia, bishop of Meath and Kildare 7,
    70, 72, 73, 110
Stranmillis University College, Belfast 54, 256,
    282
Stuart, Imogen 215
Studies (journal) 258, 260
Summer Madness festivals 17–18, 85, 86, 90
Sunday School Society for Ireland 231, 236
Swanwick Declaration (1987) 119–20
Sweeney, Peter 47

Talbot, Maurice, dean 228–9
Tate, Nahum 52, 52n23
Tate Stevenson Architects 209, 210
Taylor, Anne 68
Templeton, Revd Irene (née McCutcheon) 6, 67
TG4, *No rootless colonists: na Gaeil-
    Phrotastúnaigh* 225
Thatcher, Margaret 20
Theological College Council 242, 243
theological training 241–51
    Academic Committee and 242–3
    auxiliary ministry students 243
    Bachelor of Theology 241, 242
    children's ministry 251
    criticism of 242
    lay reader training 251
    master's in theology 246, 249–50
    ministry-formation plan 244–6

non-stipendiary ordinands 242
ordained local ministry 250
stipendiary ordinands 242
see also Church of Ireland Theological
    College; Church of Ireland Theological
    Institute; Edgehill Theological College
Theology 22, 26
Thompson, Revd Peter 11, 38, 39, 55, 57
Toner, Tom, monsignor 23
Topping, M. and Cavanagh, C. 275, 281
Towers, Revd Patrick 224
Tractarianism 28, 138
Transition Pathway Initiative 200
Trinity College, Dublin
    Aspirant School of Religions 247
    Bachelor of Education 255
    Bachelor of Theology 241, 242, 247
    'ban', Roman Catholics and 99, 268
    bilingual evensong services 224
    Divinity School 241
    Éigse na Tríonóide 224
    library 53
    Manuscripts Department 228, 229, 230
    master's in theology 248, 249–50
    memorandum of understanding with 248
    Milltown Institute, transfer of 247
    ministry-formation negotiations 247–8
    multi-denominational 268
    School of Education 257
Tripartite Consultation 122, 126
Turner, Edgar, canon 27
Turner, Owen 215

Ulster Church Music Centre 50
Ulster Tower 24
United Church of England and Ireland 21, 35
United Reformed Church 127
United Reformed Church in England 37
University of Cambridge 161

Vatican I 141
Vatican II 24, 98, 113, 121
    bilateral dialogues 114–16, 126
    Church of England observer 96
    ecumenism and 143
    liturgy, revision of 30, 56
    Lumen Gentium (1965) 115
    Nostra Aetate (1960) 162, 163
    reforms 268
    Unitatis Redintegratio (1964) 115
Vicars' Hill, Armagh 206
Violence in Ireland: a report to the churches (1976)
    123